Living in Silverado

Living in Silverado
Secret Jews in the Silver Mining Towns
of Colonial Mexico

David M. Gitlitz

University of New Mexico Press
Albuquerque

© 2019 by the University of New Mexico Press
All rights reserved. Published 2019
Printed in the United States of America

First paperback edition, 2022
Paperback ISBN: 978-0-8263-6442-5

Library of Congress Cataloging-in-Publication Data
Names: Gitlitz, David M. (David Martin), author.
Title: Living in Silverado: secret Jews in the silver mining towns of colonial Mexico / David M. Gitlitz.
Description: Albuquerque: University of New Mexico Press, [2019] | Includes bibliographical references and index. |
Identifiers: LCCN 2019005817 (print) | LCCN 2019009636 (e-book) | ISBN 9780826360809 (e-book) | ISBN 9780826360793 (printed case : alk. paper)
Subjects: LCSH: Crypto-Jews—Mexico—History—16th century. | Jews—Mexico—History—16th century. | Silver miners—Mexico—History—16th century. | Silver mines and mining—Mexico—History—16th century.
Classification: LCC F1392.J4 (e-book) | LCC F1392.J4 G49 2019 (print) | DDC 972/.02—dc23
LC record available at https://lccn.loc.gov/2019005817

Cover illustration: from Agricola, *De re metallica*, 1621. Used with permission of the Biblioteca Francisco de Burgoa, Centro Cultural Santo Domingo, Oaxaca.
Designed by Felicia Cedillos
Composed in Minion Pro 10.25/14.25

To the memory of my mentors: Raimundo Lida, who urged me to learn to doubt and hounded me into studying Hebrew; Francisco Márquez, who led me to appreciate the yin and yang of breadth and depth, and showed me how artificial were the boundaries between disciplines; Stephen Gilman, whose timely kick in the butt a half century ago launched me on this fascinating journey; and the countless others whose influence is woven into the fabric of this book.

One time the scale was swaying as he was weighing some silver, and his servant Francisco Váez said: "This scale is really dancing!" And Manuel de Lucena replied: "If only God could dance like that."
—REPORTED BY GÓMEZ PERTIERRA, DECEMBER 2, 1594

CONTENTS

LIST OF ILLUSTRATIONS   ix
ACKNOWLEDGMENTS   xi

Introduction   1
Chapter 1.   Beginnings in the Raya de Portugal   9
Chapter 2.   Going to Mexico   13
Chapter 3.   The Castellanos's Jewish Life in Mexico City in the 1530s and 1540s   25
Chapter 4.   Tomás's First Mine: Ayoteco   33
Chapter 5.   Tomás de Fonseca's Pachuca Mine and the Mining Revolution   43
Chapter 6.   Tomás's Mine in Tlalpujahua   61
Chapter 7.   Tomás de Fonseca Reconnects   77
Chapter 8.   The Portuguese Come to America   85
Chapter 9.   From Solitary Worship to Community   103
Chapter 10.   The Taxco Miners   125
Chapter 11.   The Jewish Life of the Taxco Miners   153
Chapter 12.   Pachuca and Manuel de Lucena's General Store   185
Chapter 13.   Lucena's Judaizing Community in Mexico City and Pachuca   205

Chapter 14. Judaizing from Tlalpujahua   229

Chapter 15. Destruction and Survival   237

Chapter 16. Some Conclusions   287

APPENDIX 1. Origins and Arrivals   301

APPENDIX 2. Holiday Observances   310

APPENDIX 3. Enríquez-Lucena Holiday Attendees   325

NOTES   329

BIBLIOGRAPHY   387

INDEX   403

ILLUSTRATIONS

Figure 1.   Miner crushing ore   37
Figure 2.   Miner working a vein   39
Figure 3.   Train of pack mules   40
Figure 4.   Old Tlalpujahua mine entrance   63
Figure 5.   Mining tools   66
Figure 6.   Stamping mill   68
Figure 7.   Chorrillo arroyo cliffs, Taxco   126
Figure 8.   Chorrillo waterfall, Taxco   127
Figure 9.   Juliantla "synagogue crypt"   140
Figure 10.   Cantarranas aqueduct, Taxco   148
Figure 11.   Cantarranas amalgamation patio, Taxco   148
Figure 12.   Inquisitor signs for Catalina Enríquez   188
Figure 13.   Signature of Jorge de Almeida   239
Figure 14.   Signature of Antonio Díaz de Cáceres   249
Figure 15.   Signature of Héctor de Fonseca   275
Figure 16.   Signature of old Tomás de Fonseca   279
Figure 17.   Signatures on a petition   284

ACKNOWLEDGMENTS

I owe much to the many people who at various stages of this journey inspired and assisted me:

To the late Dr. Josefina Ramos de Cox, archaeologist at the Pontificia Universidad Católica de Lima, who over a year of fieldwork on the Tablada de Lurín some fifty years ago nourished me in the appreciation of geological detail; and in more modern times, to geologists Fernando Palero, Pedro Rodríguez, and David Fastovsky for their advice and encouragement;

To the talented librarians and archivists at the University of Rhode Island, Lisbon's Torre do Tombo, the Consejo Superior de Investigaciones Científicas in Madrid, Cincinnati's Hebrew Union College, the Bancroft Library at the University of California–Berkeley, and the Biblioteca Francisco de Burgoa in Oaxaca; and especially to the efficient and client-friendly staff of the Archivo General de la Nación in Mexico City;

To Rodrigo Espino Hernández for his insights about Jorge de Almeida's hacienda in Taxco; and to Gustavo Bernal, painter, sculptor, and museum administrator extraordinaire, for his kindness in sharing his old maps of Tlalpujahua;

To my daughters, Abby and Deborah, for their encouragement and patience, and to Deborah for exploring old mines with me in the hills of Tlalpujahua.

But my greatest debt is to Linda Davidson, my late wife and frequent coauthor, superb detective, bibliographer of remarkable memory and prodigious attention to detail, and editor par excellence, who deserves much of the credit for bringing this book into being.

Introduction

> Let us consider the great cities that there are, and the rich mines, and that we will all be the lords of them, and prosperous, and rich.
> —HERNÁN CORTÉS, AS REPORTED BY
> BERNAL DÍAZ DEL CASTILLO, 1568[1]

JULY 31, 1492, was the last day on which Jews could remain in Spain legally. It was also Tisha b'Av, the Jewish fast that commemorates the destruction of the First and Second Temples in Jerusalem and the beginnings of the Jewish Diaspora. Two days later, Christopher Columbus set sail for Japan with six converted Jews among the ninety-six members of his crew. As the admiral's three small boats left the shelter of La Rábida's estuary, they likely sailed past other boats ferrying Jewish refugees to Morocco.

Expulsion, conversion, and discovery: three seismic events that contributed to shaping the unique lives of each of the people we will meet in the course of this book.

Living in Silverado tells three stories. The first is a story of migration: how in the sixteenth century, a considerable number of Portuguese-Spanish villagers came to New Spain, as Mexico was called in those days.[2] We will see where they came from, why they came, how they came, and the various experiences that shaped them in their journeys.

The second story is how a subset of newcomers to America made their living in the mining communities. We will see how some dug for silver, some refined silver, some bought and sold silver, and some managed the general stores that supplied the miners with credit and their material needs. All of them lived in and were shaped by the culture of silver during its rapid evolution over the course of the sixteenth century.

The grandparents and sometimes the parents of these people had been Jews. The third story, interspersed with the portrait of the professional world, is the religious life of these immigrants from newly Christian families: those who still thought of themselves as Jews, those who acknowledged their Jewish ancestry while they embraced Christianity, and those who struggled to figure out just what they must believe and do to ensure the salvation of their souls. Each of these stories is part and parcel of the others, so while this book will from time to time focus on one aspect or another of their lives and senses of identity, at other times the threads will weave together to create a textured fabric of secret Jewish life in the mining towns of colonial Mexico.

Three factors were common to the protagonists of *Living in Silverado*: they were Portuguese of Spanish descent, they were Christians of Jewish descent, and in Mexico they were engaged in some aspect of the silver mining industry. Although they will be treated as a group, it is important to remember that like you and me, the protagonists of *Living in Silverado* were from the moment of their birth unique individuals, with certain talents and proclivities of character. Each was molded over time by their families, their relationships, and the accumulated experiences of their individual lives. Juan Ignacio Pulido Serrano, in his review of the historiography of these New Christians, cautions us that because these people had multiple and simultaneous senses of self-identity, it is a mistake to assume simplistically that religion was necessarily "the main factor defining the individual's identity," or to assume that of the many overlapping communities in which he functioned, religion was necessarily the most important, or that "identity accrues to the individual on the strength of the religious community to which he belonged; and it is this religious identity which . . . is both all-embracing and exclusive."[3]

In thirty-five years of reading Inquisition dossiers dealing with crypto-Jews in Spain, Portugal, and Mexico, a number of patterns have caught my attention.[4] One that helped shape this book involves the demographic history of the *conversos* who came to Mexico in the second half of the sixteenth century and the fact that so many of them were born in Portugal to families of Spanish origin who then returned to Spain before jumping to the New World.[5] While most of these immigrants settled in Mexico City, where the men engaged in business ventures that ranged from street peddling to international import and export, some of them sought their fortunes in the burgeoning mining towns north and south of the Valley of Mexico. Their choice to live and work in the periphery of colonial New Spain rather than in its center affected both their economic and their religious lives.

It is true that these people all had Jewish ancestors, and that in Mexico some of them adhered to remnants or permutations of their families' ancestral Jewish beliefs and practices. But they were also citizens of their towns, partners of spouses or lovers, and participants in their professional communities. Most were enmeshed in networks of clients and creditors. Some were avid readers; others, illiterates. Some had wide pre-Mexico experience on the high seas, or in Italy or Turkey or West Africa, while others came directly from a Portuguese village through Sevilla to the New World. Some of the men gambled or made music with their friends; some of the women sewed or embroidered garments in the company of their own friends or neighbors. Some partook of the culture of the metropolis of Mexico City; others the culture of the mining camps. Their membership in each of these diverse and sometimes overlapping communities—geographical, professional, avocational, familial, religious—influenced their values, their habits of thought, and their priorities. At times the diverse components of their identity spoke to them in harmony. Other times, when their loyalty to the values and behavioral norms of one of these communities was incompatible with those of another, the dissonance forced them to agonize over making a decision—where to live, whom to partner with, how to educate their children—and later to regret whichever path they had chosen.

In the late Middle Ages, Christian Iberia's centuries-long war to retake southern Iberia from its Muslim rulers had honed Spanish techniques for conquering and catechizing. In the sixteenth century, European religious and territorial wars and Europe's American ventures created vast new opportunities for clerics, soldiers, and the bureaucrats who supported them. New markets blossomed, capitalism took root, and merchants and other entrepreneurs followed closely behind the soldiers and the friars. By the 1520s, the grandsons of Iberian peasants who had rarely ventured beyond the nearest large town now roamed and ruled much of the world.

This world now ran on money, money being the portable tangible objects, made precious by their scarcity, that by tacit agreement were accepted as a universal medium of exchange. The foremost of these was gold, followed closely by silver. Both could be struck into coins or valued according to weight and purity. Both had the honored validity of precedent, both had been in use since antiquity, and both—along with jewels—were cited as markers of wealth in the Jewish and Christian Bibles and the Qur'an. In the rapidly expanding economies of Renaissance Europe, the opulence-addicted monarchs, their hungry armies, and their wide-ranging merchants all depended on increasing the supply of money. Precious metals from America, thought Spain's Fernando and Isabel, Charles V, and the Hapsburg Philips, were their godsend.

The enthusiastic tone with which Charles V in 1526 encouraged New World prospectors of every class and station is not surprising:

> It is our desire that all our vassals, be they of whatever status, class, eminence, or dignity, Spaniards or Indians, shall be permitted to extract gold, silver, mercury, and other metals, they themselves or their servants or their slaves, from whatever mines they may find, wherever they be located; and that they may mine them freely without impediment; and that mines of gold, silver, and other metals shall be accessible to all, wherever they may be located . . . so long as . . . all appropriate laws and regulations be observed.[6]

The soldiers from the conquering armies who had rendered distinguished service or were of noble birth were rewarded with grants of land and with *encomiendas*, communities of Indians whose care was "entrusted" (the literal meaning of the Spanish term *encomienda*) to the landowner. The *encomenderos* were obliged to husband the land and to provide the indigenous inhabitants instruction in Catholicism and in the Spanish language. In return, they were entitled to a portion of the labor of the entrusted Indians (*encomendados*). In practice, the Indians worked as virtual slaves. The encomenderos, even before they settled into their new roles as cattle ranchers or farmers, pressed their Indian workers to show them their sources of gold. Almost invariably these were the beds of streams that had washed dribbles of the metal down from the mountains. Within a few years, these placer deposits had been largely panned out. Finding new sources of gold was difficult. The prospectors soon learned that gold was a shy temptress, rarely exposing herself on the surface of the ground.

Silver, on the other hand, was much less demure. In Mexico, most silver is found in the chain of mountains that extends from the present day

Arizona–New Mexico border south to the Isthmus of Tehuantepec, with the strongest concentration between Zacatecas and Taxco. As the magma that formed these mountains cooled, the silver within the magma generally compounded with a number of other minerals. When these silver compounds were exposed to weather over long periods of time, they oxidized, forming relatively soft reddish minerals that the Spanish miners called *colorados* or *pacos*. Deeper veins, lying below the water table, are harder and have a darker color. The miners called them *negrillos*. The earliest colonial miners quite naturally concentrated on the colorados.[7]

How did these soldier-farmer-prospectors learn to recognize the telltale signs of silver? In Mexico in the 1520s, there were no written guides to identifying minerals. Indian informants could lead prospectors to the rare outcroppings of the metallic mineral in its pure form, but they had no experience with the much more common silver-bearing compounds. Although Columbus in his later voyages had brought a number of skilled diggers and panners, there appear to be no records of how or even whether these technicians diffused into the American mainland. Nor are there records of anyone's concerted effort to teach mining techniques. Presumably, the unidentified handful of professional miners from Spain who made it to Mexico in the 1520s and 1530s passed their knowledge to their colleagues in the field, and the circle of field-instructed prospectors expanded as new lodes were discovered and new searchers headed out into the mountains.[8]

The vast majority of the immigrants to the Iberian New World did not come from a sense of adventure or in search of some abstract value like freedom of religion. Most came for one of four reasons. Clergy came to save souls; soldiers and bureaucrats, to serve the king. A few were fleeing some intolerable living condition: a shrewish wife, an abusive master, or threat of arrest by civil authorities or the Inquisition. Almost everyone else came to get rich. And for that purpose, even while agriculture and commerce grew and flourished and offered the surest paths to modest wealth, for many newcomers the entrepreneurial passion was for mining. In their fervor they minimized the many significant risks: the vast distances, inhospitable landscapes, diseases, and frequently hostile indigenous peoples.

By law, the immigrants all had to be Christians descended from at least two generations of Christians.[9] Nonetheless, some of the immigrants were New Christians who had recently converted from Judaism, and an undeterminable number of these conversos continued to practice their version of Judaism clandestinely. A few of these crypto-Jews became miners, and many others sought to make their fortune in occupations that supported mining.

The earliest of these—Tomás de Fonseca and his father, Gabriel de Castellanos—arrived in 1534. Of all the secret Jews involved with the mining business in sixteenth-century Mexico whom we will meet in this book, the man with the thickest calluses on his hands will be Tomás de Fonseca, known variously as Tomás de Fonseca *el viejo* (the old man) or Tomás de Fonseca of Tlalpujahua. These nicknames will distinguish him from his younger nephew Tomás de Fonseca Castellanos, who will begin working in Taxco a quarter of a century later.

Introduced to mining as a teenager by his father, Tomás soon struck off prospecting on his own. Leaving his father's diggings in Ayoteco in southern Puebla, he wandered north, trying his luck for several years in Mazapil, Zacatecas, and Pachuca. Finally, in the high, rounded Michoacán hills of Tlalpujahua, old Tomás struck a modest lode. He lived most of the rest of his life there, leaving Tlalpujahua only sporadically to visit his relatives in Taxco and Mexico City, and twice when the Inquisition hauled him back to Mexico City.

Through old Tomás and his extended family, we will see how intensifying Inquisition activity in Iberia spurred many Portuguese crypto-Jews to come to Mexico. We will meet the crypto-Jewish businessmen who clustered around the investor-miners Jorge de Almeida and Antonio Díaz de Cáceres in Taxco, and the storekeeper Manuel de Lucena in Pachuca. We will explore the flourishing Judaizing communities of Taxco and Pachuca in the 1570s and 1580s, the minimal Judaizing community in Tlalpujahua during those years, and the destruction of these communities in the 1590s. We will look at the differences between the religious life of the large informal minyan of secret Jews in the metropolis of Mexico City and that of those in the periphery, who found other ways to sustain their Jewish identity.

We will also encounter the well-known family of Luis de Carvajal the younger, whose passion for proselytizing as he shuttled among the mining centers helped to weave together the Mexican secret Jewish communities of the 1580s and 1590s. Two of Luis's sisters became the wives of Jorge de Almeida and Antonio Díaz de Cáceres. The network of these people's family ties helped sustain the secretly Jewish entrepreneurs who lived in the scattered mining camps.

With regard to these people's religious culture, the book will ask several questions. What sort of Judaism did these Portuguese immigrants bring with them, and how did they acquire and sustain it? How did they create and maintain their social networks? How did they deal with the pressures to assimilate to the mainstream Catholic environment? And why did so few of them make any significant effort to transmit their crypto-Jewish heritage of beliefs and practices to their offspring?

Another of this book's goals is to open a window onto how life was lived in those pioneer mining towns. Much has been written about the colonial Mexican mining industry, but mostly at the macro level. Little attention has been given to the daily lives of the miners and the small town merchants who supplied them. What did the mining haciendas of the protagonists look like? How were they staffed, and how did they function? What sort of merchandise was stocked in the villages' general stores? What sorts of houses did the proprietors live in, and how were they furnished? What did they and their wives and mistresses wear? And eat? How did these miners and merchants and their families spend their work and leisure time? How did they travel when they came from Europe to Mexico? Or from their mining towns to Mexico City?

On the whole, the copious archival material about Mexico that survives from the sixteenth century is long on exports and imports, legal regulations, financial dealings, administrative and political affairs, and criminal and civil lawsuits, but it is short on personal data. The dossiers assembled by the Mexican Inquisition are one major exception. As the inquisitors delved into the beliefs and practices of the crypto-Jewish miners, they recorded enormous amounts of anecdotal data that shed light on other aspects of their lives. The inquisitors interviewed the accused person's family members, friends, servants, neighbors, and business associates. They sequestered and meticulously inventoried the prisoner's possessions. They required accused persons to detail their genealogy, to narrate the major events of their lives, and to respond in detail to the specific charges against them. At each interview, scribes took down the particulars of the questions and testimony, often nearly verbatim.[10] Occasionally, and principally in cases where the inquisitors believed that the accused persons were lying, holding back, or refusing to explain inconsistencies in their testimony, the interviews were relocated to the torture chamber. Some of these inquiries, called *procesos*, dragged on for a half decade or more while the accused person languished in the Inquisition's Secret Prison. The written record of some individual investigations filled a thousand pages.

Much of the liturgy of Judaism, from daily prayer to the annual cycle of festivals, features the ritual retelling of seminal events in Jewish history: the wanderings of Abraham, of the sons of Jacob, of Moses; the story of Esther's defense of the Jewish Diaspora in Persia; of the Maccabees' briefly successful resistance against the Greeks. Prime among the unifying themes in these stories are the migrations of a tribal religious community, its efforts to find a safe haven (that always proves ephemeral) and to maintain cohesiveness as observant Jews in the face of persecution and pressure to assimilate to the culture of the majority. The story of the secret Jews in the mining towns of colonial Mexico that begins in 1534 with Tomás de Fonseca bears retelling both as a chapter in Mexican Jewish history and as a reflection of one of the archetypal myths of Judaism. The Fonsecas, Almeida, Díaz de Cáceres, and Lucena, together with their wives and children, recall the saga of other Jews across the vast landscapes and timescapes of the Diaspora: members of a tribal minority searching for a home, striving to make a living, and struggling with very mixed success to resist the pressures—both coercive and seductive—to assimilate to the dominant religious culture.

'Ovdim hayyinu . . . We were toilers in the silver mining towns of Mexico.

Chapter 1
Beginnings in the Raya de Portugal

> Tomás de Fonseca, native of Freixo de Espada-à-Cinta,
> Raya de Portugal, resident of the mines of Tlalpujahua.
> —PROCESO OF TOMÁS DE FONSECA, 1596[1]

AMONG THE THOUSANDS of Jews streaming toward the Portuguese border in the summer of 1492 were Lorenzo de Castellanos and his wife, Blanca Lorenza, Tomás de Fonseca's paternal grandparents.[2] Lorenzo had been born in A Coruña, an Atlantic port city in Galicia in the northwest corner of Spain.[3] The city, which prospered in the late fifteenth century from fishing and from shipping wool to Britain, France, and the Low Countries, had one of the largest Jewish districts in the region.[4] Blanca, too, was Galician. The documents do not mention what had propelled Lorenzo to leave his native town with his young wife to serve Francisco Enríquez in Alcañices, a village in the province of Zamora, just south of the Galician mountains, less than an hour's walk from the Portuguese border. Nor do they indicate what sort of service he proffered the nobleman. It is likely that Enríquez, a member of a minor Castilian noble family that exercised sovereignty over five small Zamoran towns (Tábara, Valver, Villavellid, Cabreros, and Alcañices), was just beginning his rise to prominence and was in need of able secretarial help in administering his estates.[5]

When news of the royal order of expulsion reached Alcañices, Lorenzo de Castellanos decided to take his wife to Portugal rather than convert.[6] It is quite possible that Enríquez helped him to secure a position of some sort with the Portuguese king, Manoel I, who was not averse to employing talented Jewish newcomers in the burgeoning bureaucracy of his kingdom.[7]

Lorenzo de Castellanos, like so many Jews and conversos in the Raya de Portugal, as the strip of land on both sides of the Spanish–Portuguese border was commonly called, undoubtedly had relatives and friends on both sides. The majority of Jews in the region were small merchants dealing in textiles, which were the most important manufacture in the mountainous border country of Galicia, Zamora, Trás-os-Montes, and the Beiras, landscapes difficult for grain farming but ideal for pasturing sheep and for cultivating silkworms. The rough landscape of the region—deep river gorges and steep boulder-strewn ridges—meant that the border between the two countries was porous. The towns on both sides were brisk trading centers for goods, both legal and smuggled, and Lorenzo may well have flitted back and forth between the two countries like so many of the small businessmen who were his neighbors.[8]

We do not know where in Portugal Lorenzo and Blanca settled initially. Their son Gabriel de Castellanos was born in Freixo de Espada-à-Cinta,[9] a small fortress town high above the Douro River gorge that slices through the rough terrain three kilometers east of the town. In the late fifteenth century, Freixo had undergone a minor boom resulting from expansion of the silk industry centered in Bragança, a city not far to the northwest. As in other towns in the region, Freixo's sizable fifteenth-century Jewish community had grown after the 1492 Spanish expulsion. In the early 1500s, Freixo's newly prosperous villagers were gussying up their houses with ornate stone window frames carved in the innovative Manueline style, so many of them that today these windows are Freixo's pride and the touchstone of its modest tourist industry.[10]

When King Manoel I, under pressure from the Spanish monarchs, in 1497 ordered that all Jews in Portugal either become Christian or leave the country without taking their children, baby Gabriel was converted, together with his parents and most of the rest of Portugal's Jews.[11] Although his family undoubtedly spoke Galician or Castilian at home, when Gabriel was five or six years old, he learned his first letters in Portuguese. In many villages it was the parish priest who taught local children their ABCs, and he may have instructed Gabriel in Latin as well. What is clear is that Gabriel acquired sufficient skill so that years later in Mexico he was able to support his family as a schoolteacher. In his youth Gabriel acquired some knowledge of Hebrew as well, either from his father or from one of the teachers who formerly had prepared children to read Hebrew texts and often carried on the same work even after the forced conversions had turned them and their client families into Judaizing New Christians.[12] Gabriel knew many of the daily prayers by rote well enough to recite them decades later in Mexico.[13]

When Gabriel was in his early twenties, he married the conversa Felipa de Fonseca, who was from either Porto or Viseu, two large Portuguese commercial cities that had supported prosperous Jewish populations in the late fifteenth century.[14] After their marriage, Gabriel took Felipa to Freixo. They undoubtedly occupied a house just below the castle in the former *judiaria*, which by then had become the converso neighborhood.[15] There too lived Lorenzo Álvarez de Castellanos, the only one of Tomás de Fonseca's many uncles and aunts whose name he could recall in 1590 when he was interrogated. Lorenzo Álvarez had children named Pelayo Álvarez Castellanos and Blanca Lorenzo. Pelayo was also a second cousin to Jorge de Almeida, another of the miners we will meet later in this book, with whom he lived for a time in Ferrara. Pelayo's sister Blanca Lorenzo ran an inn in Sevilla, where many of the conversos profiled in this book lodged before sailing to America. In Mexico, Pelayo traveled widely among the mining centers and had a store for a while in Taxco. In 1590 Tomás could not recall where Pelayo was then living.[16]

Gabriel and Felipa had four children. Guiomar, Lope, and Isabel were born prior to 1520; Felipa gave birth to Tomás in Freixo de Espada-à-Cinta around 1520, and she died only a few months later.[17] Not long after Felipa's death, Gabriel fell for a married woman in Porto named (María) Blanca Rodríguez. Gabriel stole her away from her husband and spirited her across the border into Spain to Jarandilla, a city near Plasencia in the agriculturally rich Valle de la Vera in the province of Cáceres. Although the two could never formally marry, they lived together as man and wife until her death in Mexico four decades later.[18] Shortly after reaching Jarandilla, Blanca gave birth to a son, whom the couple named Julián de Castellanos, the surname intimating that Gabriel was the boy's father. However, until his dying day, Tomás de Fonseca insisted that Julián was no brother of his because Blanca had already been pregnant when Gabriel whisked her away from her husband's house.

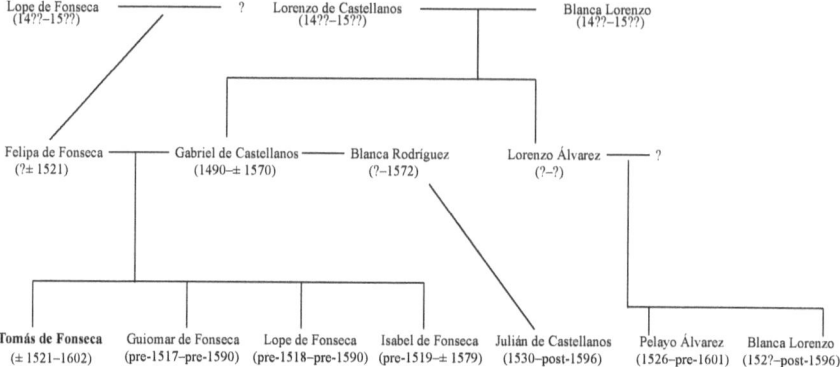

Julián told his inquisitors that he had been baptized in Jarandilla and that Antonio and Catalina Sánchez, who served in the household of the Count of Oropesa, had been his godparents.[19] Both Tomás and Julián learned their first letters from the parish sexton in Jarandilla, and Tomás even served as an altar boy.[20] The children's Jewish education took place privately, at home, with their father, Gabriel, as their principal teacher. In matters of religion, Blanca followed Gabriel's lead as best she was able, instructing Gabriel's daughters Isabel and Guiomar how to keep house in the Jewish way.

In due course, Isabel de Fonseca married twice and gave birth to old Tomás's nephew Tomás de Fonseca Castellanos, who became a miner and shopkeeper in Taxco. Old Tomás's sister Guiomar de Fonseca also married twice, once to an Old Christian and once to a New Christian who was an active Judaizer. Tomás's brother Lope Teodoro de Fonseca rejected the family's Jewish heritage and became a cleric. All three siblings eventually migrated to Mexico, although Lope later returned to Castilla, and all three predeceased Tomás.[21]

Chapter 2

Going to Mexico

> When we were sailing over, there was a Portuguese woman on our ship named Antonia Fernández, wife of somebody Oliveira who now runs a tavern in [Puebla de] los Ángeles, who always invoked the name of Jesus when the ship rolled or something happened. And Ana Váez and Isabel Rodríguez, Manuel Díaz's wife, laughed and poked fun at her ... for calling on Jesus. And Antonia Fernández said, don't you see that they are making fun of you? When we get to Mexico you'll see what happens to them, because they are Jews.
>
> —ISABEL LÓPEZ, 1594[1]

Setting out

Sixteenth-century Spain had many deep-sea ports but only one official gateway to America: Sevilla. The city's natural attributes are legion. It lies at the heart of Spain's richest agricultural area, on a bend of the navigable Guadalquivir River, eighty-nine kilometers inland from the coast, safe from marauding pirates and foreign navies. Favored by the Romans and Visigoths, it served as capital of the Muslim Almohad Empire in the thirteenth century. When King Fernando III conquered it for Christian Castilla in 1236 and moved his court into the Alcázar Palace, Sevilla became his southern capital. The city boasted the largest and most powerful Jewish community in Andalucía. As the economic powerhouse of southern Spain, it also attracted large numbers of Genoese and Flemish bankers and investors. Every Andalusian noble family had a residence, often a sumptuous palace, in Sevilla.

It did not take long for the Catholic Monarchs to realize that Columbus's discovery was vital to Spain's ascendency as a major European power and that systematic exploitation of the New World required effective control by the crown. Where better to exert that control than Sevilla? In 1503, just one decade after Columbus's return to Spain with his momentous news, Queen Isabel established the House of Trade (Casa de Contratación) in Sevilla. The institution's title made clear its purpose: to create wealth by fomenting commerce. Isabel gave the Casa de Contratación jurisdiction over all traffic with the Indies. Isabel's grandson, Emperor Carlos V, renamed it the Casa y Audiencia de las Indias, with a governing council called the Consejo de Indias, which he charged with oversight of all matters regarding navigation, exploration, trade, immigration, administration, and governance of the Indies. The Audiencia's tentacular reach encompassed power to grant licenses and permits; to establish regulations, restrictions, and exceptions; to collect taxes and tariffs; to record and organize data; and to employ an ever-expanding corps of officials. It may well have been modern government's first great administrative bureaucracy. It is a marvel both that it functioned as well as it did and that the records it so meticulously kept have largely survived.

There, in the Audiencia, on October 9, 1534, a stone's throw from the wharves, in the forerunner of the building that today houses the record of the event, Gabriel de Castellanos was granted permission to depart to the New World for himself; two of his children, Guiomar and Tomás de Fonseca; Blanca Rodríguez (the woman he was calling his wife); and her (or their) son Julián de Castellanos. Tomás de Fonseca, the boy we will come to know as old Tomás, was fourteen years old.

The document that records this event states that the Castellanos family was part of a group of thirty married couples that the bishop of Mexico, Fray Juan de Zumárraga, had requested come help settle the new land.[2] The bishop's concern, quite simply, was that almost all the immigrants who streamed into New Spain in the decades immediately following the Spanish conquest of Tenochtitlán were men. Extant immigration records for the period from 1520 to 1539 account for 13,262 European immigrants by name; only 836 (6.3 percent) of them were women. Of these, 30 percent were wives traveling with their husbands, 10 percent were wives traveling to meet their husbands, 6 percent were widows, and 54 percent were female children or unmarried women, many of these possibly house servants accompanying immigrant families.[3] It is easy to understand why the sexual partners of the conquistadors and the first wave of settlers (the *primeros pobladores*) were almost invariably Indian women and why the first generation of *criollos* (which in the lexicon of the times meant people of European descent born in the New World) were preponderantly mestizos, people of mixed race. Although the mestizo nature of the population of many Spanish American countries is generally viewed today, from the perspective of social science, as a strength, it was of great concern to a segment of the early colonial power elite. The church focused less on the nature of the mixture than on the legal and moral status of its participants; for the clergy, the men who cohabited with Native women in America were at best fornicators. A substantial number of the Spanish male immigrants had left wives at home, promising to send for them once they had settled in the New World. Few of them did. Those who legalized marriage with their Native partners were very likely committing bigamy, a serious crime against both civil and canon law. Encouraging immigration by entire families during this early period was a logical and, in the eyes of the church, laudable strategy.

The document that records passage of the Castellanos family to Mexico also speaks to their genealogy and their civil status:

> Gabriel Álvarez Castellanos, son of Lorenzo Álvarez and Blanca Lorenza, resident of Jarandilla, and Blanca Rodríguez, his wife, and Tomás, Julián, and Guiomar, his children, to sail on the *nao* of Blas Gallego in the Bishop of Mexico's group of thirty married people. Alonso Gómez, resident of Jarandilla, which is near Salamanca, their neighbor, is familiar with them and knows that they are married and joined as man and wife, and that they are not among the prohibited class.

Simple, straightforward, and perjurious. Alonso Gómez was either mistaken or lying in two key areas, either of which should have precluded granting the family permission to travel to America. Blanca and Gabriel were not married, at least not to each other. And Gabriel was very definitely a member of the prohibited class of people because his immediate ancestors included Jews.

Attesting to "purity of blood" (*limpeza de sangre*)—that is, a genealogy unsullied by any Jewish or Muslim ancestors—was becoming a standard entry credential for any sort of position of influence in Spain, even though, as with much restrictive legislation, in practice the requirement was often ignored or circumvented through evasion or corruption.[4] The American evangelization enterprise complicated matters. Both the church and the monarchy felt strongly that Spain's obligation to bring the vast Native populations of America to Christianity made it especially crucial to avoid any contamination of the missionary effort. In 1501, the Catholic Monarchs' instructions to the incoming third governor of Hispaniola, Captain-General Nicolás de Ovando, made clear the rationale for their concerns:

> Since we must work actively to convert the Indians to our holy Catholic faith, we must see to it that no persons are employed in the missionary work whose faith is under suspicion. This would only be a handicap. Therefore you are not to consent to, or make possible the immigration of Moors and Jewish heretics or penitents, as well as recent converts to our holy faith.

The prohibition seems to have been only thinly enforced, for in answer to a request by officials of the island of Hispaniola in 1508, King Fernando strengthened the enforcement procedure:

> Because the words and relations of such persons can bring great harm to the service of our Lord and to the conversion of the natives of these lands, and because our main task should be to exert ourselves in behalf of the good doctrine, . . . I decree that under no circumstances should you permit now or in the future the sons and the grandsons . . . of Jews, of Moors and penitents to enter and to conduct business there. I am also sending an order to the officials of the Casa de la Contratación in Sevilla to make sure that they do not send such people to the island.

A formal royal edict in 1511 reiterated the ban. In 1534, the year Gabriel de Castellanos applied for his immigration visa in Sevilla, Emperor Carlos V reinstructed the Casa y Audiencia de las Indias in a tone that made clear that this time the monarchy really meant what it said:

> You know that according to the regulations of that Casa, entry to our Indies is forbidden to penitents and to recent converts of Jewish and

Moorish origin. And so that no one will have any excuse now or later, I command you to announce this on the balustrade of that city [Sevilla] and warn those who emigrate to our Indies, regardless of what part, that they will lose and by this [decree] we declare that they have lost, the property they acquired and possess in our Indies. And we consign it to our exchequer and treasury. Acknowledgement of the announcement is to be recorded on the left side of this edict, leaving a copy of everything in the books of the Casa, so that it may be sent to the members of our Council in the Indies.[5]

Despite the fierce tone of the edict and the consequential penalties for disobeying, this section of the immigration regulations consistently proved difficult to enforce. In Castellanos's evasion of the law, we do not know whether Gabriel had sufficiently covered his family's tracks when he moved from Portugal to Jarandilla to deceive locals like the Casa y Audiencia's expediting official; whether the official had colluded in the deception out of sympathy for the New Christians, who found themselves hemmed in by the purity of blood laws; whether he had been bribed to perjure himself; or whether Gabriel had bribed some other official of the Casa de Contratación to issue him his bona fides.[6] Fifty-six years later, in Mexico City, Blanca Rodríguez's son Julián de Castellanos alleged to the Inquisition that the Portuguese king had intervened on Gabriel's behalf to have him included among the "thirty married couples," but that seems less credible than any of the common subterfuges that Gabriel may have used to secure permission to sail.[7]

The Journey

The ship that carried Gabriel de Castellanos and his family from Spain to the coast of Mexico was a *nao*, the merchantman workhorse of the "passage to the Indies" (*carrera de Indias*), as the great Spanish enterprise of moving people and goods back and forth to the Americas soon came to be known. Built for cargo rather than for speed, the round-bottomed naos displaced between eighty and one hundred tons.[8] With a modest load, they were capable of navigating the winding, slow-moving Guadalquivir from the Arenal docks in Sevilla to the river's mouth at Sanlúcar de Barrameda, despite the sandbars spaced along the river's course at intervals of eight to twelve kilometers. These impediments slowed even the lighter boats, which at each hazard had to wait for high tide and a following wind to be able to cross the shallows. The trip from city to sea commonly required a week or more, even with a knowledgeable pilot and favorable conditions. Boats of medium draft sometimes loaded their cargo at Las Horjadas, halfway to the coast, where the river begins to deepen. Heavier boats, which became the norm for the transatlantic crossing by the end of the sixteenth century, anchored at Sanlúcar or Puerto de Santa María, requiring passengers and freight to cover the distance from Sevilla to the coast in river-worthy packet boats or by land in carts or on horseback.

It was late October 1534, and a swift departure was needed to make the crossing before winter storms magnified both the risk and the discomfort of passage.[9]

At Sanlúcar, the Castellanos family crowded onto the deck with their fellow passengers, settled the meager belongings they were permitted to take with them, and watched as Audiencia officials inventoried the cargo and checked the papers of the crew members and passengers a final time. When the tide and wind were right, the nao weighed anchor, picked its way through the tricky sandbars at the mouth of the Guadalquivir, and sailed west toward the Canary Islands, a journey of a week to ten days. There the ship made minor repairs and replenished its supply of food, water, and firewood. Sailing due west, propelled by the trade winds that blow from Africa to America along the twentieth parallel, they reached the Lesser Antilles in about a month. After resupplying at Dominica or Guadeloupe, and then again in Puerto Rico, they ended their voyage on the coast of New Spain a month after that.[10]

The Atlantic passage was uncomfortable at best. In the 1530s naos tended to measure some eighteen meters from stem to stern and five from side to side (about half the surface area of a singles tennis court); the average depth of the hold, measured from the lowest deck to keel, was about two and a half meters. They were powered by sails suspended from three masts. From the mainmast to the after rail, a superstructure with wooden sides and a flat planked or canvas roof—known as the castle, the bridge, or sometimes merely the awning (*tolda*)—offered shelter to the crew and passengers. Inside it, wooden partitions carved out a tiny private space for the ship's officers. From the foremast to the bowsprit, a more modest superstructure, known as the forecastle, offered additional shelter.

The nao's main officers were the pilot, who was responsible for all matters pertaining to navigation, and the master, the chief financial and administrative officer, who was responsible for everything the ship carried (crew, passengers, provisions, and cargo), as well as for complying with the myriad government regulations regarding permissible cargo and taxation. Some ships also carried a captain, a military officer who was responsible for the ship's defense.

Sixty years after the voyage, as he recounted the outlines of his life to inquisitors in Mexico City, old Tomás de Fonseca recalled that the pilot on the nao that brought the Castellanos family to Mexico was named Blas Gallego.[11] Gallego, like many pilots of his era, was also a merchant; among the cargo in the nao's hold were goods that he owned and planned to sell upon landing, and other goods that he carried on consignment from Sevilla-based businessmen.[12] The ship's master was surnamed García, although old Tomás could not recall whether his given name was Andrés or Juan.[13] However, he did recall vividly that one night during the voyage, García fell overboard and drowned.[14]

Although these ships were tiny by today's standards, it served the owners' interests to cram them with as much as they could carry, both above and below deck. Ordinances promulgated by the Audiencia in 1534, the year of Gabriel's sailing, tried to stem the dangerous overcrowding by limiting a hundred-ton vessel to a maximum of sixty passengers,[15] which suggests that most ships must have been even more densely packed. A sixty-five-ton vessel sailing to Hispaniola in 1507, for example, transported, in addition to its crew of fifteen or so, eighty-three passengers, eighteen mares, twelve head of cattle, and an untallied number of live chickens and pigs to supplement the barrels of hard tack, salt fish, salt pork, chickpeas and beans, water, and wine to be consumed during the voyage.[16] The five members of Gabriel's family would have counted themselves fortunate to squeeze out as much as one and a half square meters each of space in which to eat, sleep, and pass the time during the voyage. Privacy, even for the most routine bodily functions, which custom relegated to a small platform built out over the water, was impossible. Seasickness, all but ubiquitous as the tiny nao bobbed in the waves like a cork, had to be suffered in public. To add to the passengers' misery, humans and domestic livestock were far outnumbered by uninvited travelers: the rats and mice and worms that infested the ship's provisions, and the fleas and body lice that feasted directly on their human hosts. The ration of a liter of water per day was barely sufficient to stave off dehydration, with none left for washing, had that been the custom.

Once a day there was ship's prayer, a communal service that the master was obliged to provide and the ship's crew and passengers were required to attend. Everyone gathered on deck before a statue or painting of the Virgin Mary or some protecting saint or saints. Led by the master if there was no priest aboard, everyone recited in unison the Pater Noster, Ave Maria, Apostles' Creed, Salve Regina, and Act of Contrition and chanted some special prayer tailor-made for one of the nao's patron saints: "Saint Nicholas, protect our keel, our tiller, our bridge, our rigging, the outside and the inside of our ship, bring us fortune on this journey and many others, with a calm sea, a strong following wind, a good voyage and a safe arrival."[17]

Communal prayer was not the only diversion. Tomás could have watched some crew member attempt to snag a fish or search the sky for hints of inclement weather. He could have sung to the accompaniment of a penny whistle or a *vihuela*, forerunner of the modern guitar. He could have eavesdropped on the other passengers' conversations, watched men gambling with cards or dice, or listened to a literate crew member or passenger read aloud from the ship's small store of books. The most popular books, judging from the frequency with which they appear in inventories of ships' cargos, were religious tracts: books of hours to guide the daily cycles of prayers, compendia of the lives of saints, and collections of philosophical meditations. One imagines that even more popular with the passengers were romances of chivalry—tales of knights and ladies, fanciful kingdoms, and bizarre creatures—adventures laced with violence and hinting at sex.[18]

The chivalric romances *Amadís de Gaula*, *Palmerín de Inglaterra*, *Oliveros de Castilla*, and *Caballero del Febo* all appear in sixteenth-century ships' libraries. Represented too, although in somewhat lesser quantity, were contemporary histories that related the exploits of Columbus and the conquests of Mexico and Peru, adventurous tales that must have been just as entertaining as the chivalric fantasies. Ariosto's *Orlando furioso* was a favorite too, as were Virgil, *The Odyssey*, and Castiglione's *Book of the*

Courtier. Libraries might have contained pastoral romances that were likewise in vogue during those years, such as Montemayor's *Diana*; these Arcadian fantasies in verse and prose endlessly dissected the emotional triangles (and sometimes polyhedrons) of love-besotted shepherds and their idealized shepherdess paramours. Most ships carried six or seven books, almost always a mix of religious texts and secular stories of one sort or another. One imagines that crews swapped them with one another other when ships coincided in port. Both religious tracts and romances were in essence escapist literature. In the words of Pablo Pérez-Mallaína, they "had in common a certain denial of the here and now, of the routine that bound their lives and made them yearn for the celestial paradise promised by religion and the fantastic worlds of poetic and novelistic imagination."[19]

In addition to providing a respite from the monotonously intrusive sway and stench of the westbound nao, the stories in these books, especially the romances, offered Gabriel, Blanca, and the children glimpses of immense, strange, marvel-filled worlds, where a person might see and be something new.

In 1534 New Spain's principal port of entry was the small island of San Juan de Ulúa, which protected the harbor of Veracruz. Only sixteen years had passed since the explorer Juan de Grijalva had first put ashore there, noting the island's pyramid to the Aztec god Tezcatlipoca. The sickle-shaped island, some five kilometers in circumference, was mostly coral rock, low lying, and bare of vegetation. The island's lee side offered the only decent protection along the whole central coast against violent Gulf of Mexico storms. Both the north and south entrance to its harbor twisted through shoals that could be difficult to navigate, though the harbor itself was decent enough, with anchorage of seven to nine fathoms and the beginnings of a rock jetty.[20]

The passengers, despite their delight at finally reaching New Spain safe and relatively sound and being able to escape the prison of the nao after two crowded months at sea, must have felt a twinge of apprehension and disappointment at what now lay before their eyes. Around a small plaza were a handful of one-story wooden buildings roofed with straw, among them offices for government officials, warehouses, and the beginnings of a church. The highest bit of ground, not far from the harbor, was being leveled for the foundations of a fort.[21]

Although today San Juan de Ulúa is connected to the mainland city of

Veracruz by a causeway, in the sixteenth century the island lay separate from the shore, conveniently allowing cargos to be registered and taxes to be collected before goods could be spirited away toward the interior. Insularity suited the shipowners as well. Ship crews were generally gathered from among the rough men in Sevilla's Triana district, adjacent to the river, and their credentials were vetted cursorily, if at all, in contrast with passengers, who had to secure formal permission to sail. The result was that men who could not meet the Audiencia's stringent criteria for immigration sometimes signed on as sailors with the intent of slipping away once their ship landed. As a preventive measure, sailors were routinely quarantined to San Juan de Ulúa and required to sleep on board their ships as the passengers and cargo were ferried to the mainland on barges.

The nascent Villa de Veracruz was not much larger than the cluster of port facilities on the island. Facing the beach were two inns whose proprietors, Juan Bautista Machorro and Juan Bautista Buitrón, offered a bed under a roof for new arrivals who could afford to pay two *tomines* for the lodgings.[22] Veracruz had originally been situated on scrubby, sandy terrain, whose highest dune was barely fifteen meters above sea level. But after disastrous floods in 1533, officials had repositioned the village to higher ground, where a handful of new straw-roofed buildings bordered a plaza. The road leading away from the beach toward the distant mountains in the west was flanked by warehouses and rough corrals for horses and mules, with their hostlers' huts close by. There were a few four-wheeled wagons and two-wheeled carts as well, but they were primarily for use on the coastal plain and foothills. For the long haul to Mexico City, the rough roads and the steep ascents made it more practical to transport goods by pack train than by cart. Juan López de Velasco noted a few years after this that Veracruz "is always growing, it is all merchants and dealers in merchandise, warehouses, buildings to house people, wagons, and goods; nobody around here works the land."[23]

The Native peoples of Mesoamerica had well-developed networks of roads that connected their major population centers, but they did not have wheeled vehicles or animals they could ride. Porters, called *tamames*, carried burdens, and these strong, nimble men could climb nearly vertical slopes, wade through waist-deep rivers, and squeeze through narrow canyon openings. Preconquest roads were paths that connected farming villages with regional market and religious centers. They also were the means by which tribute—the Aztec equivalent of taxes—flowed from the subjected peoples to the capital city of Tenochtitlán. The Spanish criteria favored the shortest distance from the coast to Mexico City, over the route with the lowest net change of altitude and the fewest precipitous ups and downs that would be difficult for beasts and carts. By the time the three-year war to conquer Tenochtitlán was over, Spanish armies had become familiar with all the Native routes from the central valleys to the coast. By the mid-1520s, they had chosen the northernmost of these as the most suitable.

As the Castellanos family set out on this route for Mexico City, they faced a long and arduous trip. The road angled north and west across steamy lowlands before leading into more temperate jungle-clad foothills. From there it ascended along a string of steep narrow river valleys to Jalapa. The strangeness of the landscape must have fascinated the travelers. There were brilliantly colored birds and butterflies, trees taller than any they had ever seen in Europe, dense drapery of vines and epiphytes, bromeliads and orchids. The road led through Indian villages of thatched huts, where people slept in hammocks, wore strange, colorful clothes, and spoke languages that were peculiar to the ear. The new arrivals traveled in groups led by the hostlers, whose animals were familiar with the roads. The hostlers were able to navigate the dangerous segments; they knew the sources of water and where it was safe to camp. At Jalapa, a hundred kilometers from Veracruz and eleven hundred meters above the coast, the exhausted travelers at last found an inn, and for the first time since leaving the beaches three to five days earlier, they were able to sleep indoors.

The conquistadors, and the settlers and merchants who followed hard on their heels, were well aware that the prosperity and security of New Spain depended on an efficient system of roads. Governing bodies supported the building and maintenance of roads and considered the licensing of services along high-volume routes a source of income. Hernán Cortés himself, in March 1524, issued the first set of statutes governing the licensing, administration, and taxing of roadway inns, basing his Laws Governing Inns (*Ordenanzas sobre ventas*) on long-standing Spanish models.[24] The rules established maximum prices for both food and lodging; required that beds be equipped with certain amenities, such as mattresses, pillows, and clean sheets; required that weights and measures be government approved; limited stays to three nights; and tried to encourage a decorous and moral environment by banning whores, pimps, and suspicious persons. Municipal governments—in the case of this road, Mexico City and Veracruz—retained the right to license inns; Jalapa's was licensed by the Veracruz municipal council in 1524 or 1525. The government owned the land and leased it to the innkeeper for a renewable fixed period, requiring him to finish construction within a certain time and to maintain the premises in good repair. Although no plan or description has survived for the Jalapa inn, others from the same period all resemble their counterparts in early sixteenth-century Spain. A stone or picket wall with a gate facing the road enclosed a large rectangular area. Half to two-thirds of the area was reserved for animals and the storage of goods. In the other third, a rectangular, one-story building with stone and/or adobe walls and a thatched roof housed travelers in small individual rooms that opened off a corridor or a central patio. Beds were of wood, mattresses of straw, sheets and with luck blankets of some coarsely woven cloth. This roller-coaster road was the main artery linking Mexico City and the coast, and over the next three years, a half dozen additional inns were licensed.

Leaving Jalapa, the Castellanos family faced a two-day ascent to the twenty-one-hundred-meter pass at Perote on the north flank of a volcano of the same name. They would have stopped partway up at the Venta de Aguilar and then, at the far side of the pass, at the Venta de Perote. From this inn the road descended another couple of hundred meters to a grassy plain, its horizon punctuated by snowcapped volcanoes and craggy chains of mountains. This vast basin, broken by the occasional clump of hills or river gorge, stretched some 120 kilometers west from Perote to the outskirts of Tlaxcala, the great rival city of Aztec Tenochtitlán, where again the Castellanos were able to sleep indoors. From Tlaxcala, the road rose once again to skirt the great volcano Ixtaccíhuatl along its northern flank. After a slow sixty-kilometer climb, the family rested at the inn at Calpulalpan before beginning their descent into the central Valley of Mexico, where their last stop was the lakeside town of Texcoco. In the morning the Castellanos left the Texcoco inn and were ferried across the lake to Mexico City. From the Veracruz beach to the new Spanish capital, the journey took them some twenty days.[25]

Chapter 3

The Castellanos's Jewish life in Mexico City in the 1530s and 1540s

> My brother [Tomás de Fonseca] was keeping the Law of Moses ... the way the aforesaid Gabriel de Castellanos his father had taught him in this city to which he had come with his father from Spain when he was fifteen years old. I observed him fasting the fasts of that law which he said his father had taught him, and praying the Psalms.
>
> —JULIÁN DE CASTELLANOS, 1590[1]

ALTHOUGH BARELY A decade and a half had passed since the Spanish had taken control of the island city of Tenochtitlán, the former Aztec capital was beginning to resemble the European cities its conquerors were striving to emulate. As Gabriel and his family walked through the emerging city, they encountered a rectangular grid of streets, broad avenues, half-finished stately stone buildings with impressive early Renaissance facades, plazas framed by churches, and colonnaded government buildings. Their ears rang with the pinging of hammers against stone. It was clear that the new monasteries that were to be the administrative centers of the missionary orders—Franciscans, Dominicans, Augustinians—were competing with each other in projecting splendor and influence. Extending west from the Main Church (Iglesia Mayor), as the new cathedral-in-progress was called, Calle Tacuba was establishing itself as the prestige residential avenue and the major commercial thoroughfare of the city.[2]

Gabriel de Castellanos, Blanca, and the three children needed a place to live, and Gabriel needed a job. Newcomers to Mexico City—those who did not come for a specific position in the church or government administration—sought work where they could find it. Recently arrived artisans—shoemakers, weavers, seamstresses, tailors, carpenters, tinkers—once they had secured a source of raw materials, could support themselves by way of the crafts they had practiced back in Spain, even though many found themselves in competition with cheaper and in some ways more skilled Native labor. Merchants who had brought capital with them could set up a store to sell imported European goods or could run a string of peddlers, who hawked those same goods in the city streets or in nearby towns. The emporium for foodstuffs and locally produced goods was the huge open-air Indian market (*tianguis*) that had begun long before the arrival of the Europeans and still thrives today in Lagunilla and la Merced. Immigrants who arrived without either capital or a useful trade were reduced to peddling or offering themselves in the market of physical labor. Those newcomers who hungered to get rich quickly, and were not averse to risk, hardship, or trying something totally outside their European experience, set off prospecting for precious minerals.

With his remaining cash, Gabriel rented rooms for his family of five in a house near the Hospital de Nuestra Señora on Calle Tacuba. The city's European population was growing. The first and second waves of immigrants were having criollo children, and new families like his own were arriving every day with their progeny in tow. Gabriel found that with the education he had acquired in Portugal and Spain, together with his talent for language, despite his lack of formal degrees he could make a reasonable living as a teacher. He set up a school on Calle Tacuba[3] and began teaching youngsters their ABCs. Julián, who was three years old when their nao landed in San Juan de Ulúa, was just beginning learning to read and write, and he probably attended his father's school.

Within six months, Gabriel had earned enough to buy an Indian slave from Jalisco for fifty *pesos de oro de minas*[4] and to pay his teenage son Tomás's tuition in the more prestigious grammar school of Dr. Blas de Bustamante in the Dominican monastery a few blocks north of the Iglesia Mayor. There Tomás studied both classic texts (the curriculum included Virgil, Juvenal, Terrence, and Cato) and canon law.[5] We know this because nearly a half century later, in an Inquisition audience chamber in the very same monastery, Tomás described this schooling to his Dominican inquisitors, apparently without any of them drawing attention to the irony of his sitting in the place he had once rehearsed his Latin declensions.

Tomás seems to have had a true facility for Latin as well as the ability to remember what he read, judging from the comments that some of his Judaizing colleagues, such as Manuel de Lucena, made to the inquisitors.[6] To his cellmate Thomas Day, in 1596, Fonseca quoted extensively from memory passages from the Jewish Bible and from *Mirror of Consolation*, Fray Juan de Dueñas's best-selling compendium of moral truths and aphorisms drawn from vivid and sometimes fancifully retold biblical stories.[7] On the whole, it appears that all through his life, old Tomás continued to read as widely as he was able in the frontier mining towns where he lived. The Inquisition's inventory of the contents of Tomás's house in Tlalpujahua, which was logged in Mexico City in 1605, included eleven books in Latin, among them an Old Testament, and six more books in Spanish.[8]

What we know about the Castellanos family's religious life during those early years in Mexico City comes mainly from Julián de Castellanos's testimony in 1590, more than a half century after the facts. Julián's Inquisition-assigned advocate, Gaspar de Valdés, urged him to confess fully to his inquisitors for the sake of his immortal soul. Julián seems to have taken this to heart, for two days after talking with Valdés, he requested an audience with the chief inquisitor, Francisco Santos García. He began to describe in great detail the Judaizing practices he had experienced in his youth in the company of his father and mother and his half sister Guiomar.[9] He rarely mentioned his older half brother Tomás, either because Tomás was largely absent from family gatherings or because he had developed such a hatred for Tomás that he could not bring himself even to speak his name.

Though Julián's testimony, which he later recanted, was shot through with inconsistencies and implausible claims, his basic descriptions of his family's religious life are consistent and are filled with details that seem impossible for him to have imagined or concocted from any source other than having lived them. What emerges is a tale of a well-educated, Jewishly observant, domineering Gabriel de Castellanos, who was scrupulous in instructing Guiomar, Julián, and undoubtedly Tomás as well in the fundamentals of Jewish practice and belief as he understood them. Julián described his own induction into Judaism this way:

When I was eleven or twelve my father Gabriel de Castellanos took me aside and in secret, in our house in Mexico City next to the Hospital de Nuestra Señora where I am living today, . . . [he] told me that what I must do in order to be saved was to love and serve the one true God, He who created the world and everything in it. And if I did that, I would be saved. And whenever I was in need, I should ask help only from Him, and not from some saint.[10]

Julián testified that a short time later, when he told his father, who had just returned from a business trip, that he had gone to church with some friends and had made confession to a priest, rather than directly to God and in private, Gabriel hit the roof, threatening that "if I ever did that again he would smother me between two pillows."[11] Some years later, when Julián admitted to his father that he still was not observing Jewish customs as scrupulously as his father had asked, and that he indeed sometimes flirted with Christian beliefs and practices, his father urged him once again to shape up: "Son, I have an obligation to tell you what is best for your soul, if you choose to do what I say. And if not, you'll see where you end up!"[12] Presumably Gabriel was just as strict with Tomás as he was with Julián.

The records do not indicate whether Blanca Rodríguez was an active Judaizer, or for that matter even a conversa, when she and Gabriel de Castellanos joined lives, but she seems to have grown up among Jewishly observant conversos. Gabriel supplemented her knowledge and monitored her practice.[13] Julián reported that his mother taught him many Jewish practices and explained to him some of the more unusual family customs, such as sweeping always toward the center of the room, which she claimed was a Jewish rite, commanded by Jewish law.[14] In Mexico City, Blanca baked the family's unleavened bread on Passover, emptied all the standing water in the house when someone died, and prepared the meals with which the family broke the Jewish fasts.[15]

In the Castellanos family's religious calendar, the Sabbath was the most important holy day. Late Friday afternoon, Blanca and Guiomar readied the house and prepared the family's meals. The family dressed in their best clothes and put clean linen on their table and on their beds. Of the many major and minor fast days in the Jewish liturgical calendar, the Castellanos observed four. Beginning the tenth day of the month of September, they fasted during daylight hours for ten days in a row. On the ninth day, they confessed their sins to God, privately, on bended knee, and that night they had to sleep fully dressed. The tenth day was the Día Grande, Yom Kippur, when, Gabriel told them, God judged human souls and determined their fates for the coming year. The family passed the Great Day itself with Gabriel reading aloud biblical stories found in *Mirror of Consolation*. Their second family fast was in honor of Queen Esther, who had fasted to gain the favor of King Ahasueros to save the Jewish people from Haman. The third was to honor Judith, who had cut off the head of Holofernes. And the fourth was in memory of the prophet Jonah.

The principal feast observed by the Castellanos family was Passover, which Julián recalled began on Palm Sunday.[16] Gabriel would buy a young lamb in the market. In an interior patio of their house, where no one would see, he slaughtered it by his own hand, muttering a Hebrew prayer as he cut its throat. He hung it from a rafter until all the blood had drained out. Then he cut it into pieces, and Blanca stewed it in a newly purchased pot with lettuce that substituted for the chard (*berzas*) that they had used back in the Raya de Portugal. Blanca prepared unleavened, unsalted bread for the meal, during which Gabriel recounted the story of Passover.

The dietary rules that the family followed were reduced to a simple four. They slaughtered fowl by cutting their throats, rather than strangling them like the Christians did. Blanca removed the sinew from a leg of lamb before cooking it. She soaked meat before cooking it to remove all traces of blood. And the family avoided pork in any of its forms: "We didn't put salt pork into our stews," Julián said, "or fry with lard, because in our house our father insisted that we do what the Law of Moses commanded."[17]

One of the most unusual rites practiced by the Castellanos family took place twice a year, on the eves of Christmas (December 24) and the Feast of Saint John (June 23). On those nights the family would not drink water but only watered wine, because on those nights, they believed, pure water would turn to blood.[18]

Gabriel was strict about the manner in which the family was to pray. They were not permitted to hold their hands together, as Christians do, but rather had to fold their arms. On important occasions, such as confessing their sins, they were to kneel. Their eyes should always be turned to heaven. Their repertoire of prayers consisted mainly of the seven penitential Psalms, the Ten

Commandments, and a few Hebrew prayers that Gabriel remembered. On rising from the table, he muttered a grace after meals in a language that Julián claimed he did not understand but presumed was Hebrew, explaining to his family that he was following a commandment that God had given to Moses.[19]

Equally important were the things the Castellanos family avoided doing. Unlike their neighbors, they did not display crucifixes or images of saints in their house, though sometimes they put them up to fool people who came to visit. They did not observe Sunday as a special day. They avoided pronouncing the names of Jesus or Mary, and they never ended their prayers with "Glory to the Father, the Son, and the Holy Spirit."

Tomás's sister Guiomar, like most young women in the working families of their time, likely did needlework at home to supplement family income. Not long after the family's arrival in Mexico, Gabriel had placed Guiomar, then in her early twenties and long past the age at which she should have been married, in the care of Dr. Pedro López, who agreed to find a suitable match for her.[20] The lucky suitor was Antonio Pérez Herrero, a man who had begun his career as a blacksmith before turning to business, in which he was so successful that he became known as Antonio Pérez *el Rico* (the rich man); as such he played an active role in in municipal life. Pérez Herrero was probably not of Jewish descent, though given Gabriel's strong sense of Jewish identity, it seems unlikely that he would have permitted his daughter to marry an Old Christian.[21] And Pérez was most certainly not a Judaizer; Guiomar's half brother Julián reported that Guiomar always came by herself to Gabriel and Blanca's house to celebrate the Jewish holidays because she was afraid to expose her Judaizing customs to her husband or their three children, whom they raised as Christians.[22]

Gabriel was especially strict about his household's need to keep their Jewish life secret.[23] Julián said that he always talked "with the strictest circumspection so that no one would be able to understand." "We would gather in secret because that is what my father wanted, so that no one would notice us." "We met at my father's house . . . because he was afraid that . . . [Guiomar's children] would be aware of what we were doing." "We ate the lamb secretly so we wouldn't be noticed."[24] Gabriel's heightened, truly obsessive sense of vigilance, even though it meant truncating a complete observance of the law, was not lost on his children. "That's what my father ordered, and he guided everything in our household. Lots of times we did not fully perform the rituals, so that we wouldn't be noticed or understood by the people who came to visit my father, for he was a very well-known man."[25]

Julián's description of his family's Judaizing focuses exclusively on what happened inside their home among members of his immediate family. Within those walls they practiced a wide repertoire of Jewish customs. In this they may have been atypical. As we will see in chapter 9, although many conversos settled in New Spain between the 1530s and the 1550s, the small amount of data about them that survives suggests that even among those who still maintained a vestige of Jewish identity, their level of Jewish religious observance was low. Likewise, they seem not to have engaged in any meaningful communal Jewish life, at least not enough to attract any paper-generating attention.[26] During their first decades in Mexico, the Castellanos family seems not to have participated in any sort of Jewish community, instead living their Jewish life in isolation. Outside their home, they projected themselves as respectable middle-class Christian citizens.[27]

To survive in the small, close-knit European community in Mexico City in the 1530s and 1540s, Gabriel de Castellanos had to develop the skills of a master chameleon: a Portuguese New Christian to his closest friends, a Spanish Old Christian to everyone else. "I knew Julián's parents," said Luis Alonso de Mercado, a bachelor longtime neighbor nominated by Julián to speak as a character witness in his proceso. "I knew they were Old Christians. They said that they came to this land when the Emperor [Carlos V] sent thirty married couples to help populate it, and in those days only clean people (*gente limpia*) were allowed to come. The old man had a strong character, and she was Portuguese."[28] The apothecary Hernán Gómez Rubio recalled that the old couple boasted of their lineage and of being honorable people. "I saw the old man every day in mass at the Hospital de Nuestra Señora.... I saw them confess and take communion, too."[29] Another witness, Melchor López Castellanos (no relation), confirmed this view: "Julián's parents were friends of my parents and were always at our house. I always heard it said that they were Portuguese Old Christians, and the father was a good man and a good Christian.... I often saw the old man in the Cathedral and the Church of San Agustín taking communion."[30] Juan de León, a friend of Gabriel and Blanca's for more than thirty years, echoed his neighbors when he stated, "I always held them to be of clean lineage. They all boasted of being nobles, *hidalgos*, and the people who knew them back over there thought so too.... The mother was a *bienaventurada* (a model of goodness); and the old man was a good Christian."[31]

The Castellanos's quiet family life in Mexico City changed when, after less than two years of teaching school, Gabriel became infected with a disease that was rampant in Mexico in those days and persisted for the next three centuries: silver fever.

Chapter 4
Tomás's First Mine
Ayoteco

> I went to the mines of Ayoteco in the province of Cuautla, 40 leagues from Mexico, where my father had a mine and had sent for me, and I worked there for 12 or 13 years . . . not continually, but off and on, coming and going.
> —TOMÁS DE FONSECA, JULY 11, 1590[1]

GABRIEL DE CASTELLANOS had not been teaching school in Mexico City very long before he began to hear people in the taverns, on the steps of the churches, and in the corners of the plazas saying that the quick money, there for the taking, was in silver. In popular imagination, to prospect was to find, and to find was to prosper: a shovel in the ground led invariably to silver in the pocket.

The conquistadors and first settlers had quickly learned that finding precious metals in the ground and prying them loose from the matrix of other minerals with which they had bonded was much more difficult than stripping personal adornments from the indigenous peoples. The first flush of pillage and extortion lasted barely a few years, and by the time Gabriel and his children arrived, thirteen years after the fall of Tenochtitlán, it was only a memory. When the conquerors pressed the Indians to take the Spaniards to their gold and silver mines, they were disappointed to learn that they were both few and unsophisticated. Gold, which the Mexicas called *coztic teocuicatl*, and silver, which they called *iztac teocuicatl* (excrement of the sun and of the moon, respectively), were so-called found metals, elements in a pure state that could be obtained by three relatively unsophisticated methods: picking up small nuggets lying on the surface of the ground; chipping off bits of native (that is, pure) metal from veins exposed on visible rocks; and placer mining, which is scooping sand and fine gravel from streambeds and swirling them in a pan to separate the stone from the heavier particles of gold that settle to the bottom.[2]

Metallic minerals other than gold and silver had been mined, refined, and extensively utilized in the central mountains of pre-Columbian Mesoamerica. Mining activity throughout the classic period (the first century BCE to the seventh century CE) was most intense among the Purhépechas, or Tarascans, centered in today's west Mexican state of Michoacán.[3] The Purhépechas dug mostly copper, which they found compounded with arsenic, sulfur, calcium, iron, and other minerals. To extract the copper from its compounds, they first ground the ore by hand to powder, using basalt or other volcanic grinding stones similar to those still used today in Mexico to grind corn. They refined the ore in small quantities by a sophisticated three-step process. In a small ceramic retort, from bottom to top they layered coal, powdered ore, and compounds of lead; they lit the coal and through a reed tube blew it to white heat until the liquified metals in the ore fused with the lead in the flux.[4] As imperfections rose to surface, the Indians skimmed them off with a green twig. The heavier fused mass settled to the bottom. The Indians separated the pure copper from the dross either by skimming when it was hot or by cracking the retort when it had cooled and chiseling apart the slag and mineral-rich compound.

Extracting compounded gold or silver required two additional steps. Once these metals had fused with the lead flux, the Indians heated the compound of mineral and lead over a bed of crushed animal bones and ash until the major part of the lead had oxidized or been absorbed by the ash and bone, which left a residue of much purer mineral. Then they heated the silver or gold a third time with salt, bat guano, and fusible sand that absorbed the remaining dross and left a button of relatively pure gold or silver.[5]

Though the early land grant holders had little luck finding existing gold or silver mines, by 1525 they had turned their attention to prospecting for the sources of the minerals and were beginning to develop mines in the states of Jalisco, Nayarit, Oaxaca, and Michoacán. As European settlement expanded outward from the core of the Aztec dominions, each new discovery brought more prospectors, soldiers, and missionary friars to the frontiers. In the early

1530s, prospectors had found silver in Zacualpan, Sultepec, and Zumpango, and by mid-decade in Tlalpujahua, Temascaltepec, Amatepec, and Taxco, where tin was also being mined.[6] Some of the prospectors mined the lodes they discovered; others sold their claims to people who preferred digging to wandering the hills.

In the 1530s, the areas around Cuautla, in the Mixteca Baja south and east of Mexico City, experienced a boom. Cortés had explored and conquered the region in the early 1520s, very soon after his destruction of Tenochtitlán, and it was then parceled out in encomiendas.[7] Before long, rumors about the mineral wealth of the region had begun circulating in Mexico City. It was not surprising, as old Tomás told inquisitors a half century later, that his father had caught wind of silver strikes in Ayoteco[8] and had bought a mine there in 1536.[9] In Mexico City, preparing to head south, Gabriel purchased a slave and the tools he thought he would need.

When Gabriel de Castellanos purchased an already-discovered mine rather than going out to scour the hills, he finessed what was probably the most difficult mining skill to acquire, the ability to recognize silver in the ground.

Silver is rarely found in its pure form in any great quantity. More often it is combined with arsenic, antimony, and sulfur in a bewildering number of different compounds. Dark threads of silver ore can be hosted in igneous, metamorphic, and sedimentary rocks, including andesites, slates, schists, and limestones. The veins of silver that in-fill these rocks have combined with pyrite, calcite, rhodonite, quartz, and numerous other minerals. Testing for silver today is a task for technicians. For prospectors in the 1530s, with no tools but their rock hammers to chip the stone, their eyes to probe its colors, their fingers to explore its texture, and their tongues to discern the flat taste of traces of metal, judging the quality of an outcropping was more art than science, and it frequently depended more on luck than on skill, as can be seen in an emblematic tale about some mule drivers on their way to Zacatecas who stopped near Cubillete and built a fire to heat their lunch. After they had eaten, they found puddles of fused silver next to the rocks from which they had built their fireplace. They began to dig, their finds attracted others, and the mining district of Guanajuato was born.

Two years after purchasing the mine, Gabriel wrote to his son Tomás, then about seventeen years old, to come join him, leaving the rest of the family to fend for themselves in Mexico City.[10] Tomás had a choice of two routes between Mexico City and Cuautla; both seem to have been in place by 1533. One route went east over the mountains toward Amecameca; the other south over the mountains toward Cuernavaca. Each route involved a strenuous climb of some 750 meters into the pine forests that covered the upper slopes of the Valley of Mexico and then a precipitous drop of 1,500 meters through parched, cactus- and scrub oak–dotted hills to the plains east of Cuernavaca. The two routes joined in Cuautla and then worked their way south through Ayoteco to Oaxaca.[11] By either of these routes, on horseback the trip from Blanca's house in Mexico City to Gabriel's mine in Ayoteco would take Tomás at least three days. By mule or donkey it would take two or three days longer; if Tomás had to walk, a week and a half.

Freed of the onus of prospecting, all Gabriel de Castellanos had to learn was how to dig out the ore, crush it, wash it to separate the lighter rock from the silver-bearing particles, and refine it to extract the silver from the minerals with which it had compounded. None of these operations required advanced technical knowledge, and he could achieve them with a few tools and minimal capital investment. An iron hammer, a pick, a pry bar and a shovel, a bucket, a metal pan, and some strong leather sacks, all of which he had likely purchased in Mexico City, comprised Gabriel's basic equipment. As for labor, he had brought a slave with him, and he could contract in Ayoteco for Indian workers as he needed them.[12]

Gabriel would have teased the metal out of the ore with the same methods used by the ancestors of his Indian workers, employing refining techniques that were likewise similar to those being used in much of Europe in the early 1500s. He and his workers crushed the ore with hammers and then ground it to powder by abrading it between stones. Gabriel smelted his ore in an iron crucible and fanned his fire to white heat with a bellows; pre-Columbian miners used stone retorts and blew oxygen to their fire through a reed tube. Gabriel separated the melted silver by pouring off the dross as slag. This relatively unsophisticated process recovered about 20 percent of the silver content of the ore, with the rest locked in the mine's tailings or the slag heap at the forge. The method was inefficient and profligate in its use of wood to fire the furnaces, so much so that by the mid-sixteenth century, miners had

Figure 1. Miner crushing ore. From Agricola, De re metallica, 1621. Used with permission of the Biblioteca Francisco de Burgoa, Centro Cultural Santo Domingo, Oaxaca.

denuded the areas around most of the Mexican mines, adding erosion to the problems with which they had to cope.[13]

Gabriel's mines would have been deep trenches or relatively shallow tunnels cut into one of the cactus- and brush-covered low hills of the Ayoteco mining district, which sprawls just north of the modern town of Chiautla.[14] Father and son would have spent their nights in a small shack that they had banged together from wood slats and chinked with straw-laced mud, situated near enough to their diggings for them to keep a watchful eye out for thieves. Other huts, at some distance from their shack, housed their workers. Near the mine entrance, a couple of Indian workers, perhaps augmented by

Gabriel's slave, crushed with iron hammers the ore that other Indian workers had hauled from the mine in leather sacks or wicker baskets, held against their backs by waist straps and by tumplines that braced against their foreheads. A nearby water source would have let his workers sluice the pellet-size gravel to separate out the heavier silver-containing ore. If Gabriel and Tomás had an oven in which to melt out the silver, one of their workers would have spent his days scouring the hills, competing with neighbors for firewood. Another would have searched out the lead oxide catalysts that they ground into beads (*greta*) or powder (*cendrada*); these were required to make the smelting process work. If Gabriel did not have an oven of his own, father and son would have had to freight the sacks of powdery silver-bearing ore on horse- or donkey-back to a refining station, a *hacienda de benificio* in the town of Ayoteco or at the mine of some wealthier neighbor. Periodically, perhaps once a week, they would have loaded their product into leather bags for the ride to the assay office of the *alcalde de minas* in Chiautla. Then, with a little money in hand, they may have stopped into one of the village's one-room stores for provisions or visited one of the eateries or brothels before heading back to their diggings.[15]

It was very hard work. For these journeymen miners in the 1530s and 1540s, the streets of America were very definitely not paved with precious metal. A tiny number of extraordinarily fortunate miners got rich; slightly more were able to wrest enough silver from the earth to make a decent living. Most miners, though, like most artists and writers today, had to find something other than silver to support their addiction to the pick and shovel. When opportunity knocked, men of modest means like Gabriel de Castellanos often answered.

One such opportunity presented itself in 1541. Viceroy Antonio de Mendoza called for men to help put down an Indian rebellion in Nueva Galicia (today the northwest states of Jalisco, Colima, and Nayarit, and part of Zacatecas). A decade earlier, Nuño de Guzmán had conquered that region in a brutal campaign that had slaughtered thousands of Indians in battle and tortured and murdered many others. Nuño de Guzmán was imprisoned, but throughout the 1530s, the reverberations of his campaign provoked scattered uprisings throughout the northern tribes that the Spaniards had designated with the collective term Chichimecas. The new lieutenant governor of Nueva Galicia, Cristóbal de Oñate, did what he could to suppress them but lacked

Figure 2. Miner working a vein. From Agricola, De re metallica, 1621. Used with permission of the Biblioteca Francisco de Burgoa, Centro Cultural Santo Domingo, Oaxaca.

sufficient forces to achieve definitive victory. When one of his captains put down a local revolt by arresting eighteen Chichimeca leaders and hanging half of them, the scattered tribes coalesced and threatened to seize control of the entire region. Pedro de Alvarado, an experienced warrior who had been one of Cortés's principal captains in the initial war of conquest, was sent to quash them, but he was killed in battle, crushed under a falling horse. With that, the viceroy decided to take personal command of the war, and he issued a general call for volunteers. Gabriel de Castellanos rose to the call, leaving Tomás in charge of the mine in Ayoteco.

A request for volunteers was the traditional way to raise an army. The late-medieval Spanish monarchies had no standing armies. When they needed troops, they conscripted soldiers or mustered volunteers, paid them a paltry wage, offered them rights of plunder, and held out the promise of bestowing greater reward for extraordinary valor or accomplishment upon presentation of claim after the fact. In southern Spain, many grants of land and title owed their origin to service during the war against Granada in the 1480s. Such a reward was an expectation of those who volunteered to serve in that war, and, barely one generation later, it was also expected by those who served in the campaigns to dominate the Native peoples of America. The 1541 war went

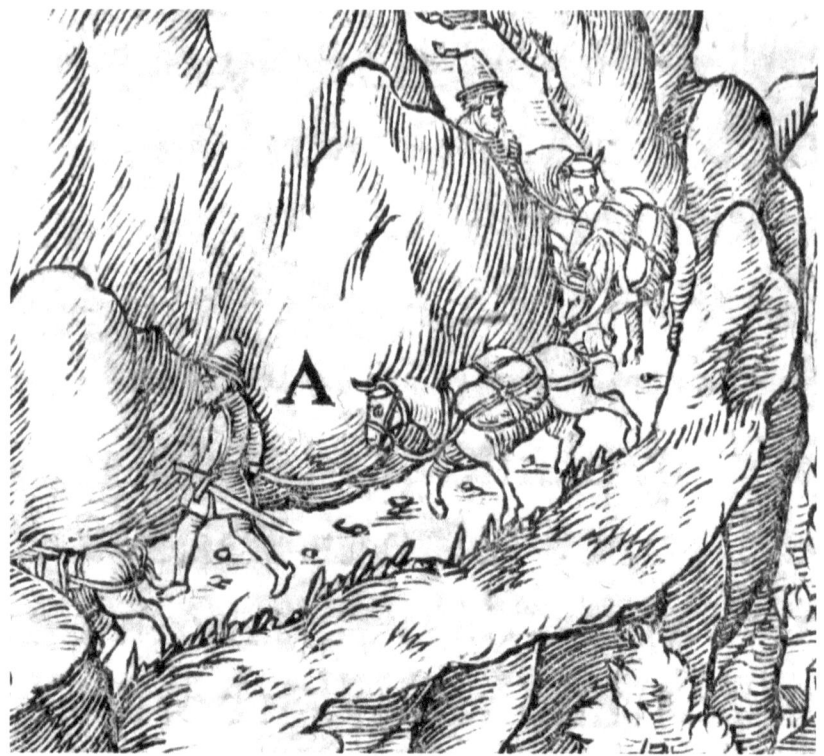

Figure 3. Train of pack mules. From Agricola, De re metallica, 1621. Used with permission of the Biblioteca Francisco de Burgoa, Centro Cultural Santo Domingo, Oaxaca.

well for the Spaniards, who clinched their victory at the craggy Chichimeca stronghold of the Peñol de Mixtón.[16] When the war ended, Gabriel went back to Ayoteco.

For some reason, Gabriel delayed lodging a claim, and not until 1549 did he petition the government to grant him an allotment (*repartimiento*) of Indians and monetary remuneration for his past services. His military service must have been unexemplary, for he chose to base his claim on having been an early settler (primer poblador) and resident in Mexico City. He stipulated that he had brought over his wife, Blanca Rodríguez, and his children, adding that for some of the children he had found spouses and that they in turn had given him grandchildren; that is, he had done his patriotic part to help populate the new land. In his petition Gabriel also claimed to be a hidalgo, a person of noble blood, none of whose ancestors had been Muslims or Jews. Surely, he argued, all those achievements merited the viceroyalty granting him an annual income.[17] There appears to be no record of his request ever being acted upon.

Some bits of testimony in the 1590s Inquisition trials provide two additional clues to Gabriel's and Tomás's lives in Ayoteco. One is that during those periods when their mine did not produce enough silver for them to live on, they loaded their donkeys with sacks of greta and cendrada lead oxide for the three-day trek to Taxco, where they sold the catalyst to miners more fortunate than they. Tomás and his father also made occasional forays into the Mixteca region southeast of Ayoteco to buy sacks of dried cochineal—the insects from whose bodies carmine dye is extracted—which on their sporadic trips to Mexico City they sold to wholesalers. The cochineal business sporadically provided Tomás with supplementary income during much of the rest of his life.[18]

The other datum is that in Ayoteco, Tomás took up with an Indian woman and around 1550 sired with her a son, Teodosio, who would grow up to help his father in the mines at Tlalpujahua. Nearly a half century later, when his inquisitors asked Tomás to give details about his family, the only thing Tomás chose to tell them about the boy's unnamed mother is that she had died.[19]

Chapter 5

Tomás de Fonseca's Pachuca Mine and the Mining Revolution

> I, Bartolomé de Medina, do declare that I learned in Spain through discussion with a German that silver can be extracted from ore without the necessity for smelting it, or refining it, or incurring any other considerable expense. With this information I resolved to come to New Spain ... to test it, knowing that if I were successful, I would render a great service to Our Lord, and to his Majesty and to all this realm.
>
> —BARTOLOMÉ DE MEDINA, DECEMBER 29, 1555[1]

THE PACHUCA LODES were discovered in late April 1552 on a hill called Tlaulilpa at the foot of the Sierra de Pachuca, ninety-five kilometers north of Mexico City. Shortly after that. silver was discovered high above Tlaulilpa at Real del Monte and Real de Arriba (today's Mineral del Monte and San Miguel del Cerezo). Together they became known as the Reales Minas de Pachuca. As word of the bonanza spread, the mountains at Pachuca began to draw miners like honey draws flies.

Tomás de Fonseca, then about thirty years old, was one of them. In Ayoteco he had learned enough about the various looks of silver in the ground to search the terrain for himself. Years later he bragged to inquisitors that he had been one of the first prospectors to work the Pachuca lodes and that he had mined there for six years until word of new strikes a hundred kilometers to the northwest drew him to Tlalpujahua.[2] Fonseca was present in Pachuca from 1552 to 1558, the very years in which technical innovations were developed in the Reales de Pachuca. These innovations very quickly changed the way silver was mined and refined in New Spain and the rest of the silver-producing world.³

In the mid-1550s, many men grew rich in the Reales de Pachuca, but Tomás de Fonseca was not one of them. The absence of any mention of him in the documentation having to do with Pachuca in those years, together with his decision in 1558 to try his hand elsewhere, suggests that he was one of the anonymous mass of also-dugs who swarmed the Sierra de Pachuca during those years. However, a wealth of contemporary sources tells us a great deal about Pachuca in those heady first days of the silver boom and the revolution in mining technology that Tomás must have witnessed taking place. Even if the technological leap did not benefit him immediately, it shaped Tomás's career as a miner for the rest of his life. And it had a direct bearing on all the people whose lives will be discussed in the rest of this book.

Growth of the *Reales de Minas*

By the mid-sixteenth century a few successful prospectors in Mexico were making a good living, but most were barely getting by, scratching out silver ore from surface trenches and shallow tunnels in dozens of scrubby mining districts like Ayoteco and a few more productive areas like Taxco, Sultepec, and Temascaltepec. The unsophisticated techniques in common use for both digging and refining silver ore made it very difficult to turn a profit. All this changed in the 1550s.

In 1546 Juan de Tolosa discovered the Valencia lode in the Cerro de la Bufa in Zacatecas. He and his colleagues opened the first major mines in Pachuca six years later, and shortly after that, Alonso Pérez de Zamora discovered the lodes at Real del Monte. By the 1570s, dozens of silver mines were flourishing in Mexico in three distinct areas. The central region, comprising parts of the modern states of Mexico, Morelos, Hidalgo, and Guerrero, included the mines around Taxco, Pachuca, and Tlalpujahua. The most important mining centers in Nueva Galicia, today comprising large parts of the states of Aguascalientes, Colima, Jalisco, Nayarit, and Zacatecas, were Fresnillo, Sombrerete, Chalchihuites, Mazapil, and the city of Zacatecas. In the far northern region of Nueva Vizcaya, including what is today Durango and the Mexican states bordering the United States, as well as Arizona and New Mexico, the most important mines were at Parral and the city of Chihuahua. In each of these areas, the material infrastructure required to support the influx of miners created a multifaceted economic interdependence that helped stabilize the expanding viceroyalty.[4]

These booming second-generation mining centers were known as *reales de minas*. The term *real* originally was used to designate a military encampment or a garrison post, and since these were almost always established to protect a mining operation, the *reales* and *minas* became linked in common parlance. *Real* eventually came to mean a mining district, with or without a contingent of soldiers, and also any village or city at its center. An individual mine was sometimes called merely a real. A formal designation as a real de minas meant that its control and exploitation had become the direct responsibility of the viceroy.[5]

By mid-century, the term *miner* had come to denote the owner of a mine, whether or not the person ever actually hefted a shovel. The men who actually worked the mines were known by a number of other names according to their particular jobs, the terms of their service obligation, or the way in which they were paid. The owner might own the property wholly or in partnership with one or more partners. The deeper the mine, the more capital was required to bring the ore to the surface, and this capital was often raised by selling shares in the mine. Large-scale farmers and ranchers, called *hacendados*, often bought shares in mines. So did businessmen, from the proprietors of small stores to the large-scale investors known as *tratantes*. So did many government officials. Women, too, sometimes bought shares in mines.[6] Each shareholder was, by definition, a miner, whether or not he or she ever participated actively in the mining or, for that matter, ever left the comfort of Mexico City.

Even people who did not own shares in mines were dependent on the mining-based economy. Almost everyone whose principal occupation was buying and selling, importing and exporting, and transporting and warehousing merchandise was in effect marketing to the mines. Almost everyone with any appreciable amount of capital leveraged it by lending some of it to miners in the form of cash, bonds posted to backstop contracts, or merchandise, to be repaid in silver at a rate more profitable than what could be bought on the open market. As Luisa Schell Hoberman noted, "Mining was the ideal enterprise for a merchant investor because it produced goods of high value per unit, was heavily capitalized, was located near Mexico City or on commonly used transport routes, and was easily subject to a monopolistic system of finance and distribution."[7]

The agricultural, commercial, governmental, and religious sectors explicitly acknowledged that it was mining that powered the colonial machine.[8] Nothing could be allowed to interrupt the flow of silver to the motherland. New Spain's viceroys were particularly sensitive to maintaining a legal environment conducive to orderly rapid growth. Viceroy Antonio de Mendoza in 1550 meticulously laid out the conditions of ownership (by discovery, purchase, or claim of abandonment), the rules regulating how to stake a claim, the radius around the mine entrance that could be included in a claim, and procedures governing the recording and disclosure of claims. Especially useful to the crown was the requirement that a claim be worked continuously, or else its ownership would transfer to the person who identified it as abandoned.[9]

The Mines Go Deep

By the mid-1550s, while the scramble to find new sources of silver continued unabated, the nature of the precious metal enterprise was changing. The easy diggings, where the silver lay close to the surface or could be reached by horizontally perforated adits a few dozen meters in length, had been mined out. The real wealth, as was increasingly becoming apparent, lay deeper underground. Mid-century miners followed the silver veins as far as they could, zigzagging or corkscrewing into the rock, but the deeper they went, the more problems they encountered. Longer tunnels required vent shafts. Deep shafts required illumination. Torches were cheap but smoky; wax candles were the most effective light source but also the most expensive.

Water seepage was a constant problem. Any perforation that descended below the level of the mine entrance accumulated water, which had to be removed continuously, either by pumps similar to those in ships or by carrying it to the surface by hand in buckets or leather bags. If the accumulated water could be reached by a vertical shaft, winches, powered either by hand or by horses turning a capstan, could be constructed. Some European mines were already using drainage shafts, drilled from below at a slight incline into the side of the mountain to allow gravity to remove the pooling water, but these were expensive to dig and required a sophisticated knowledge of geometry to target the point of intersection. These drainage adits came late to Mexico: the first, some 250 yards long, at a mine in San Luis Potosí, was not drilled until 1617.[10] All these factors limited the depth to which mid-century mines were able to penetrate. The more lucrative depths were not reachable until the 1570s.[11]

Long hauls of ore to the surface required an expanded labor force. Once the ore had been extracted, it had to be broken apart to remove the silver compounds from the useless and heavy surrounding matrix. The cost of this process increased with distance from the mine entrance; small dispersed stamping mills next to the shafts proved more profitable than large centralized mills. In addition, the long distances between the reales de minas and the coastal ports led to high transportation costs, both for the food, clothing, and mining supplies coming in and the processed silver going out.

To be successful then, deep-rock miners, in addition to time, energy, grit, and a high tolerance for risk, now required substantial capital. The fortunate few could draw from their personal resources: inherited money or profits siphoned from other mines or successful agricultural or commercial ventures. The church was another source of venture capital. Increasingly well-off from the exploitation of land holdings and bequests of the faithful, parish priests, bishops, and even inquisitors sometimes invested their surplus cash in mining.[12] Senior employees of the viceroyalty also participated, either through lending money or equipment to miners or by purchasing shares in mines. The authorities, fearing corruption of officials who were adjudicating claims, making decisions about water rights, distributing allotments of mercury, and managing the hundreds of other details at the intersection of industry and government, attempted to prohibit officials from participating in the mining industry, but with little success.

For mine owners, the principal labor expenses were the maintenance costs associated with feeding and housing the laborers and the Indian encomendados. During the second quarter of the sixteenth century, the encomiendas provided most of the mining labor, with encomenderos assigning Indian workers to mines within their own lands or leasing them to mines in neighboring areas. By mid-century, as the result of a number of fundamental changes, this system was no longer effective. For one thing, the 1542 New Laws of the Indies, which began to be enforced in 1549, prohibited many of the most flagrant abuses of the encomienda system, which its critics had likened to state-sponsored slavery. The encomienda was replaced by the repartimiento, under which each Indian community was required to provide a certain percentage of its population in rotation as wage laborers for short periods of time—six weeks was common. An *alcalde mayor* assigned these workers to employers according to the size of the employer's farm or mine operations.

Miners sometimes augmented their labor forces with one or two black slaves, often using them as overseers of the Indian laborers and supervisors of the refining process. However, blacks were never a major part of the workforce in mining, for owners soon learned that the cold climate at high altitudes and the damp, dust-choked ambience of underground work tended kill off black slaves at rates that did not justify the miners' investment.[13]

Another factor was the precipitous decline in the Native population by mid-century due to the ravages of European diseases—estimates run from a 50 to a 90 percent population loss—which reduced the amount of labor available and at the same time increased the value of individual workers.[14] Free workers, called *naboríos*, who supplemented or sometimes competed with the repartimiento workers, came to constitute some 70 percent of the labor force.[15] For both groups, employers were required to provide a salary, living quarters, and religious services.

The last major factor affecting the labor force was that most of the mines discovered in the third quarter of the sixteenth century lay in the far north, beyond the lands of the Mexicas, Purhépechas, Otomíes, Matlazincas, Tlaxtcaltecas, and other well-established, populous agricultural nations of Mexico's center. The north was sparsely populated with nomadic tribes of Chichimecas, who for most of the last half of the sixteenth century waged an intermittent guerrilla war against the European invaders from the south. Spanish military garrisons were sent north to guard the new mining centers and the trade routes that supplied them. The need for labor in mining centers like Zacatecas, Guanajuato, and Mazapil enticed whole communities of Indian workers, mostly naboríos, to relocate from the south, which squeezed the labor market of central Mexico.

Medina's Revolution

Refining silver involves two separate processes: separating the silver-bearing compounds from the matrix of rock in which they are found, and separating the silver from the compounds of which it is a part. The first process, while labor intensive, is conceptually simple. The ore must be crushed to the consistency of fine grain and then washed to remove the lighter, unwanted elements from the heavier, metal-bearing particles. Pre-Columbian miners and the earliest European miners in the New World crushed the lumps of ore with hammers; the European innovation was to replace stone hammers with those made of iron. As mining operations grew in size and capital became available, miners constructed stamping and grinding mills, of European design, to crush the ore. These mills were powered by horses or donkeys turning a wheel or, when circumstances permitted, the force of flowing water. The stamping mills used cams mounted on a shaft to raise and then drop heavy stone blocks onto the chunks of ore to crush them into pea-size particles. These were then ground to coarse powder between rotating stone wheels, much in the way wheat was ground to flour.

The second task, separating the silver from the other minerals with which it had bonded, involved complex physical and chemical processes that—until the advent of modern physics and chemistry—were not well understood by the people who used them. The techniques that eventually induced this separation to take place were developed by trial and error over at least a millennium and a half of experimentation. Although it is not conclusively supported by archaeological or textual evidence, some believe that Roman metallurgists had devised a way to separate gold from its matrix by mixing the crushed ore with mercury and water. Once the gold had bonded with the mercury, they squeezed the sludge through a finely woven cloth that trapped the impurities. They heated the residue to separate the gold from the mercury, which they could then reuse. The mines at Almadén, in the Spanish province of Ciudad Real, provided an ample supply of mercury-bearing cinnabar ore. Unfortunately, the Romans found, this process did not work so well with silver. Modern chemistry has learned that, unlike gold, silver rapidly oxidizes, and silver oxide erects a barrier between the silver and the mercury.[16]

This core problem—how to profitably separate gold and silver from its compounds—was a major focus of medieval Islamic and Christian experimentation, although it was often posed as the search for a method of transmuting base materials into precious ones, more in the province of alchemy (a term that, like *chemistry*, derives from the Arabic *al-kimia*) than in what we would call modern science. The so-called philosopher's stone that alchemists so eagerly sought was really a flux, or catalyst, that when added to the pulverized metallic compound would amalgamate with one element or another, permitting the precious metal to be pried apart from its mates.

By the early sixteenth century, (al)chemists were experimenting all over Europe in hope of finding an efficient method. Though they made significant progress, no method would refine a high enough percentage of the silver content of ore at a cost low enough to make the process practical on a large scale.[17] By then it was widely known that for sulfide ores, in which silver bonded with sulfur, large quantities of lead, either in its metallic form or as lead oxide called litharge (also called greta or cendrada, depending on the size of the pellets), when mixed with charcoal and heated in a furnace, would bond with silver. The bonded material was refined in a second furnace, where heat broke the bond and the lead could be skimmed off and reused. This method worked, up to a point, and was used in Mexico through the 1540s, but it was not very satisfactory. The yield was low, heating the lead released noxious fumes, and the corrosive litharge quickly destroyed the furnace.[18]

In the late 1540s, alchemistic experimentation was the hobby, and eventually the obsession, of a middle-aged textile merchant in Sevilla named Bartolomé de Medina. He was determined to perfect, and to make economically feasible, an amalgamation process that had been pioneered in Germany and was discussed in Vannoccio Biringucci's *De la pirotechnia*, published in 1540.[19] In Sevilla, Medina bought and sold African goatskins, French linens, British worsteds, and gold and silver jewelry. He diversified his business by importing from and exporting to New Spain, both on his own behalf and as the Spanish agent for various businessmen in Mexico City, including two of his brothers. He also invested in the maritime insurance industry and in some Mexican prospecting ventures. Raw material for Bartolomé's hobby was available nearby in small quantities from the Andalusian silver mines at Guadalcanal, Riotinto, and Tharsis, and at Almadén in Ciudad Real, which also furnished him with mercury. In the patio of his house in Sevilla, Medina mixed silver, lead, mercury, and a variety of other substances in a search for an efficient process of separating out the silver.

Both of Medina's Mexican siblings were involved by 1550 in extracting and processing ore. Eventually, frustrated by his inability to secure silver ore in Sevilla in sufficient quantities to satisfy his experimental needs, Bartolomé decided to join them. In 1553, at age fifty, he set off for Mexico City, where he quickly realized that his passion would be best served by his going directly to the mines. The recently discovered lodes in Pachuca were the closest. Near the Río de las Avenidas, he purchased a small hacienda with a flat stretch of ground that was to be his experimentation patio. For a year he fiddled with his mixtures, adding mercury and catalysts to silver ore, adjusting the percentages and the amount of time that the mixtures were left to stew, stirring some, letting others sit untouched, and carefully recording the results. He found that the most successful catalyst, or *magistral*, was copper or iron sulfate, sometimes called bluestone or greenstone.[20] By 1555 Medina was convinced that he had it right.[21]

Medina's process worked like this: Using hammers, miners rough-chunked the ore at the mine entrance and graded it according to size and eyeball estimates of the percentage of silver it contained. From there they transported it in wicker baskets, rawhide sacks, or large henequen cloths called *tilmas* to the processing plant, the *hacienda de beneficiar metales*, where they weighed it and credited it to the miner. At the hacienda, they crushed the ore to fine grains in a stamping mill or with water- or mule-powered grinding wheels (*tahonas*) and then reduced the grains to powder by *arrastre*, a process in which mules dragged large stones back and forth over the crushed ore. They then added water to bring the powder to the consistency of mud. On a large patio, they heaped this mud in mounds called *tortas*, to which they added salt and magistral. Mules trampled the tortas for up to six hours to homogenize the mixture in composition and texture. When it was ready, the patio master (*azoguero*) added mercury (*azogue*, from the Arabic *az-zawk*) in a quantity determined by his estimate of the richness of the ore. Workers stirred the azogue-enriched mud several times daily by treading it with their feet or by driving mules back and forth over it, until the mercury had dissolved the maximum amount of silver and amalgamated with it, forming small lumps called *pella*. This process could take from two weeks to several months, depending on the altitude, the temperature, the degree of humidity, and the silver content of the ore and the other minerals with which it had compounded. When the patio master deemed the amalgamation of the pella to be complete, workers washed the tortas in large vats to remove the mud and sand. Then they heated the pella in an oven to vaporize the mercury, which they recovered for reuse, leaving a silver residue that could be poured into flat ingots. The efficiency of the process depended on the skill of the patio master, who determined for each batch of ore how much mercury and how much of each of the catalysts had to be added, at what times and at what temperatures, and with what degree of stirring, as well as when the maximum results had been reached.[22]

Realizing that what he had developed was valuable intellectual property, Medina petitioned the viceroy, Luis de Velasco, to grant him an exclusive license for the process. He stated his case this way:

> I, Bartolomé de Medina, do declare that I learned in Spain through discussion with a German, that silver can be extracted from ore without the necessity for smelting it, or refining it, or incurring any other considerable expense. With this information I resolved to come to New Spain. Leaving my home, my wife and my children in Spain, I came to test it, knowing that if I were successful, I would render a great service to Our Lord, and to his Majesty and to all this realm. And having spent much time and money and suffered mental anguish, and seeing that I was not going to be able to make it work, I commended myself to Our Lady and I begged her to enlighten me and guide me, so that I might be successful, and I promised to donate to the poor in her name one quarter of all that I should gain . . . I request that for a period of six years no one be allowed to use this method without paying me a specified amount . . . December 29, 1555.[23]

The viceroy granted him the patent, good for six years anywhere within the Audiencia de México.[24] By 1561, 126 mines in the Audiencia had paid Medina his licensing fee.[25] There is no record that Tomás de Fonseca's mine in Pachuca was one of them, although it is clear from the copious evidence about his Tlalpujahua mines, two decades later, that Tomás, like most other Mexican silver miners of his time, had adopted the patio process without paying Medina for the privilege.

Medina's assessment of the importance of his discovery was, if anything, understated, for his patio process was so successful that it continued to be used worldwide, with only a few modifications and improvements,[26] for the next 350 years, until at the beginning of the twentieth century, cyanide was found to dissolve silver more efficiently than mercury.

Mercury

If silver was king in New Spain, mercury was queen. While all the other materials needed to process silver ore were found in Mexico in abundance, mercury had to be imported. As soon as Medina's patio process became known, and its implications appreciated by Spain's economic leadership, it became a matter of strategic importance for Spain to control the world's sources of mercury. On March 4, 1559, King Felipe II issued an edict prohibiting the export of mercury from all his dominions without specific license from the crown and making it a crime to purchase mercury from any source but the Spanish government. In 1588, as the nation readied its fleet for war against England, a second royal edict highlighted Spain's dependence on the metal: "One of the principal constituents of the wealth and prosperity of the Indies . . . is to ensure that sufficient mercury be mined and made available to the processing plants, . . . for they will produce only as much silver as there is mercury."[27] Fortunately for the monarchy, Hapsburg Spain controlled the world's three best sources of azogue.

The most important were the cinnabar mines at Almadén in the Spanish province of Ciudad Real. Pre-Roman peoples at Almadén had used red-tinged cinnabar as a colorant, as did the Romans. They also mixed it into medicinal unguents and experimented in using it in the refining of gold. During the Muslim period, the Almadén mines supported the scientific community's metallurgic and alchemical experimentations. In 1521 Spain's King Carlos V leased the Almadén mines to the German Fuggar banking family in return for their financing his successful bid to become Holy Roman emperor. The Fuggars managed the mines, under Spanish authority, until 1645. The widespread adoption of Medina's patio process increased demand for mercury exponentially in the second half of the sixteenth century, requiring Almadén administrators to demand additional workers. From 1566 until 1801, convicts and at times slaves were sent to augment the labor force. The

Almadén mines, in continuous operation for more than two thousand years, were the world's largest source of mercury, contributing over history more than 250,000 metric tons of the metal, approximately one-third of humanity's total production of the mineral.[28] The two-thousand-year run ended when the European Economic Community, sensitive to mercury's toxicity, closed the Almadén mines in November 2002; part of the stockpile of already mined ore was buried. A portion of the mines and several adjacent historic buildings have since been developed into a mining and mercury museum.

The Spanish Empire's second source of mercury was the Idrija mines in Bohemia (now the Czech Republic), which were discovered in 1497 and came under Spanish control with the ascension of the Hapsburg Carlos V to Spain's throne in 1520. A third major source of azogue was discovered in 1563 in Huancavelica, high in the mountains of Peru, and thus also under Spanish dominion.

The government strove to control the traffic in mercury from the time it was dug from the earth through the moment it was poured onto the tortas of silver ore on the patios of the haciendas de beneficio de metales in Mexico and Peru. Felipe II's reign is often decried for having engendered and nourished the octopus of modern government bureaucracy, and nowhere is this more apparent than with mercury, as M. F. Lang's classic study so devastatingly demonstrates. The crown regulated the production of azogue in Almadén, for example, even to the extent of specifying the precise number of convicts who would be sent there to crack the mercury-rich cinnabar ore with their hammers.[29] Under the supervision of middlemen hired by the crown-appointed administrator of Almadén, officials at the mines carefully measured and weighed the mineral as it was produced, and then again when it was sealed into leather sacks and loaded onto mules for the haul to shipyards in Sevilla. To transport it in carts would have been more efficient, but that was not feasible because the roads were in execrable condition and repairing them fell to another government department. Mercury is volatile, and officials expected a certain amount of degradation of the product in transport. But the azogue was of such high value that it was also liable to be bled off into the black market. The government approached this problem by not allowing the transporters to load the mercury until they had posted a bond by which they assumed financial responsibility for any unwarranted loss at track's end, where their cargo was again weighed and measured. The mule trains traveled all year long, but the transatlantic fleets sailed only at the one time of year when the winds were favorable, so the mercury had to be warehoused in Sevilla. There it was under the authority of the Casa de Contratación. Again the azogue was weighed and measured, both on its receipt and on its release. This impeded but did not stop a portion of the mercury from disappearing with the aid of corrupt officials.

From Sevilla the mercury was ferried by small launches to oceangoing galleons in Sanlúcar de Barrameda (Cadiz), with all the usual checks and inevitable losses. The crown-appointed consul of Cadiz was in charge now. A legion of underpaid guards, scribes, and notaries served as an access portal for unscrupulous black marketeers. At dockside, the consul oversaw the loading, and he also traveled with the once-a-year fleet to Veracruz, where he supervised the mercury's unloading. Like the muleteers in Almadén, he had to post a personal bond to ensure the integrity of the cargo, but his was a vastly larger sum of money, requiring him to borrow it or to secure guarantors who pledged to put up the cash should the mercury suffer any substantial losses in shipment. The crown also had to approve the character and solvency of each of the consul's guarantors.

In the harbor of Veracruz's port of San Juan de Ulúa, the cargo of mercury was off-loaded to packet boats that carried it to the wharves, where it was again warehoused until it could be loaded onto wagons or pack mules for transport to Mexico City. Teamsters were invited to bid for the privilege of carrying the azogue to Mexico City, where they would be paid for the amount they had loaded, less degradation and theft. In practice the government had to scramble to find sufficient freightage because the teamsters favored cargoes that involved less onerous paperwork and much less liability.

In Mexico City, the mercury was again warehoused. In the early years, the azogue's distribution to miners was somewhat haphazard, but by the end of the sixteenth century, the distribution was as obsessively regulated as the rest of the chain of production and transportation, with an excess of checks and a paucity of balances. Distribution was directed by a chief comptroller of mercury, who was charged with drawing up a plan for the mercury's distribution to regional disbursement centers based on each region's most recent records of silver production. The draft plan required approval at three levels: the viceroyalty's chief accountant for mercury, the viceroyalty's treasurer, and then the viceroy himself. Further complicating the distribution process was that each year's shipment arrived from Spain with new instructions regarding how the azogue was to be apportioned, how much was to be retained as a reserve, how it was to be priced, and under what terms of credit it was to be sold. The annual redesigning of the distribution process, in addition to being grossly inefficient, inevitably weakened public confidence in the system and increased the opportunities for cheating.

Once all these matters had been thrashed out and resolved, the chief accountant for mercury could release the mercury to the regional distribution centers, measuring it again at both ends of the journey. Toward the end of the century, the four distribution points were Mexico City for the central and southern region, Guadalajara for the west, Zacatecas for the near north, and Guadiana (now called Durango) for the far north. From these centers, the mercury was parceled out to the district offices, which were generally in a large town convenient to a group of mines, places such as Taxco and Pachuca in the central region, or Guanajuato and Sombrerete in the near north. Each district office was supervised by a viceroy-appointed alcalde de minas, a chief mining official. It was to these alcaldes that the miners (that is, mine owners) directed their petitions for their annual allotment, justified by how much silver they had produced in the preceding year and their most optimistic estimate of how much they expected to produce in the coming one.

Since there was never enough mercury to go around, negotiation was contentious at every level. And despite the elaborate safeguards and veneer of objective, quantitative criteria for decision making, the system was inevitably political and subject to the pressures of veniality. The weakest point was that the miners had to buy their mercury on credit, guaranteed by their coming year's production of silver, just like farmers who buy seed on credit and pay when their crop comes in. The alcaldes de minas had to assess the risks and exercise judgment. Was a particular miner trustworthy? Were his production estimates reliable or had they been inflated? Since the miners' petitions had to be submitted with affidavits from guarantors, who agreed to pay for the mercury should a miner default and to whom miners had promised a percentage when the silver was refined and sold), the alcaldes also had to assess the credibility of the guarantors. All this took time.

Despite its weaknesses, from beginning to end, the system was intended to move the mercury fairly, efficiently, and safely from its point of origin to the processing plants of the Mexican miners. The health of the Spanish Empire depended on the ability of the miners and the governing authorities to keep the silver flowing into the royal treasury back in Spain. Though the mercury distribution system's bureaucratic inefficiency and corruption worked counter to the purposes for which the system was designed, it still managed to function, after a fashion and with continuous tinkering in hope of improvement, for several hundred years.

Marketing the Silver

By law, and by ancient precedent in Spain, all subsoil resources belong to the crown.[30] The monarchy reserved the right to cede permission to a miner to exploit a particular silver deposit for a certain period of time in return for a percentage of the refined silver, which over time vacillated between a tenth (*diezmo*) and a fifth (*quinto*). In practice, of course, this meant that anyone was free to mine, so long as they paid the royal treasury office 10 to 20 percent of what they produced. Moreover, the product all had to be sold to the crown, and at the official approved rate; it was illegal for refined silver to be offered into the market without its first passing through the king's hands. As with mercury, the government attempted to control the marketing of silver at every step in the process, but it achieved only moderate success.

The law required miners to take any and all refined silver to the government assaying office to be assessed as to purity, then melted into ingots and taxed at the official rate, plus a small percentage for labor costs. The ingots were stamped with the royal seal, and from that point on they could be legally bought, sold, or traded. There were opportunities for malfeasance, and thus entrepreneurship, at every step. Silver could be mined, refined, and slipped into the black market by the Indian workforce without taxes being paid. Bernardino de Albornoz, the chief accountant of New Spain, perceived this problem in December 1525, at the very dawn of the colonial mining enterprise. Noting that "the Indians and even the slaves and the Christians have been accustomed to smelt [silver] each in his own house and even refine it, so that they evade paying duty to the king," he recommended that the government establish centralized smelting facilities, beginning with one in Michoacán.[31] This was done, but it did not stop the practice.

Miners generally paid their workers with room, board, supplies, and a wage so dismal that it invited the workers to pilfer chunks of ore. The mine owners, so long as the pilferage was not excessive, looked the other way to preserve their labor forces. By mid-century, so much silver was being diverted from the king's coffers by pilferage that a radical solution was proposed: to recognize the workers' routine venality by officially tolerating pilferage but to limit the amount that could be taken. The quota was set at about 10 percent.[32] Free-working naboríos were salaried for a certain number of hours of labor; if they worked extra hours, the law permitted them to keep half of the silver-bearing bits of ore (*pepenas*) that they found during that time, with the other half going to the mine owner.[33] Some naboríos smelted these pepenas themselves in small home ovens and used the refined untaxed silver as currency; others sold the pepenas to a merchant, who would refine them. Untaxed refined silver was known as *plata de rescate*—literally recovered, or ransomed, silver.[34] Buying it, selling it, and smuggling it was a part of the repertoire of business dealings of most miners and merchants in New Spain, including all those we will meet in upcoming chapters.[35]

More serious were the techniques for wholesale tax evasion and fraud. Assayers could be suborned. With a forged or stolen seal, such as the one owned by mine owner Jorge de Almeida, whom we will meet in chapter 10, unauthorized ingots could be stamped to indicate that the diezmo or quinto had been paid. With a little ingenuity and the purchased collaboration of customs officials, stevedores, and ship captains, major quantities of silver could be diverted into eager foreign markets, by far the greatest of which was Ming Dynasty China.[36] The mine owner Antonio Díaz de Cáceres, whom we will also meet in chapter 10, participated in this illegal trade. Estimates of the amount of American silver smuggled to China by the early seventeenth century run from one-third to one-half of all the silver produced.[37]

Not all the silver was shipped to Spain or to China. New Spain, too, needed coinage. Beginning in the 1530s, a portion of the legal silver collected by the Caja Real was minted into coins in Mexico's Casa de la Moneda,[38] and over the course of the sixteenth century, nearly half of the silver mined in New Spain remained there to fuel commerce.[39] From the very first, New Spain operated as a money economy, with very little direct exchange of goods. Importers sold their European cargoes to wholesalers for silver or extended them credit required to be redeemed in silver. Retail merchants bought their stock for cash or silver-based credit and sold it in their stores or via their strings of itinerant peddlers the same way.[40] In almost every transaction in New Spain, coins were counted or unminted silver was weighed on a scale to consummate the deal.

The mines of Mexico and Peru pumped silver and gold—the metals of money—into the arteries of Hapsburg Spain. From Veracruz, and to a lesser extent Tampico, the treasure ships made their way through the Caribbean and across the Atlantic, dodging reefs and storms and pirates, to unload their gleaming cargo on the wharves of Sevilla. During the 1520s, the decade of pillage that immediately followed the Spanish conquest, nearly 100 percent of the shipped metal was gold. But the percentage that was silver rose rapidly and steadily, until by the end of the sixteenth century, 92.8 percent of all the metal exported from Mexico was silver.[41]

Chapter 6

Tomás's Mine in Tlalpujahua

> In 1558 I went to the newly discovered mines of Tlalpujahua where for the last thirty-two years, more or less, I have lived as a miner.
> —TOMÁS DE FONSECA, JULY 11, 1590[1]

THE ROLLING OAK- and pine-covered summits of the Sierra de Tlalpujahua lie on the border of the states of Michoacán and México. The Tlalpujahua Valley, at 2,580 meters in altitude, sits about fifty kilometers north of mountains to which migrating monarch butterflies return each fall.

> Today's Tlalpujahua, a village of thirty-seven hundred, attracts visitors to its rugged surroundings, its narrow streets lined with stone and adobe houses capped with peaked tile roofs, its shops, and its mining museum. Its colonial economy was based on silver. From the late nineteenth century until 1937, it was a major producer of gold. In May of that year, a heavy rainstorm overwhelmed a large holding pond filled with the cyanide-laced residue of mineral processing. The mud slide killed two hundred to four hundred people and buried the lower sections of much of the original mining town under a nine-meter cap of mud. The old church tower, rising above a desolate meadow, stands as the victims' monument. Tlalpujahua is currently Mexico's largest producer of Christmas tree ornaments. There has been no mining since 1959. In 2005, because of its touristic interest, Tlalpujahua was named Mexico's twentieth Pueblo Mágico.

In the late fifteenth century, the area seethed in violent conflict, as the peaceful Mazahua farmers who lived in the region found themselves squeezed between two ascendant empires, the Purhépechas (also known as Tarascans) to the west and the Mexicas (Aztecs) to the east and south. To the north were the lands of nomadic warrior peoples whom the Spaniards fifty years later termed Chichimecas. The question of which of these peoples would succeed in dominating the high valley of the Mazahuas was rendered moot in 1522 when Spanish troops arrived.

The Spaniards' initial division of lands and peoples included Tlalpujahua in the vast Encomienda de Tarimeo, which was given to the conquistador Gaspar de Ávila as reward for his services in the conquest of the region. By mid-century it had passed to Gaspar's son, Pedro de Ávila Quiñónez.[2] The Spanish cattle and goat ranchers around Tlalpujahua were aware that the Native peoples had long been extracting small quantities of metal in the area, and Spanish prospectors had found bits and smatters of minerals but not enough to generate enthusiasm. Then, early in 1558, explorers struck major veins of silver, and overnight the hills echoed to the hammers of prospectors. The valley was designated the Real de Minas de Tlalpujahua.

When news of the silver strikes reached Pachuca, Tomás de Fonseca jumped at the opportunity to change his luck. He was thirty-eight years old. By February of that year, he was scouring the hillsides above the river that defined the Tlalpujahua Valley. Unlike Pachuca, which had been well picked over by the time Tomás arrived, Tlalpujahua was still relatively virgin territory. Early in March, Tomás found his lode, midway up a spur of a mountain on the northwest side of the river, and on March 9 he formally registered his claim for a

> silver mine in the district of Tlalpujahua in the vein that is called La Trinidad, not far from a small hut belonging to Juan Bautista Osorio, together with the land to build houses and mills and other things necessary to mining, near an arroyo that comes down from the hills between two Indian corrals, near the holdings of Juan Sarabia . . . I found them in virgin soil, and I have dug test pits and trenches.[3]

The witnesses who attested to his strike were Juan Rodríguez Tableros and Hernán Vázquez, who, with Juan de Zaragoza, worked a mine up an arroyo

Figure 4. Old Tlalpujahua mine entrance. Photograph by the author, 2011.

on the other side of the river. This time Tomás believed that the conditions were right to for him to prosper. Here was a workable vein of silver on land of gentle enough slope to permit building a house, with a nearby site flat enough to hold the processing patio and the mill, the *molino de moler metales*, that he would build when he had amassed enough capital to do so. Most importantly, his discovery was downhill from a constant water source.

At first there was no real town of Tlalpujahua. Prospectors built their shacks at the mouths of their diggings all through the hills that flanked the valley. In the first years there were probably two dozen or so such men. By the end of the century, the number of Spanish residents in the valley may have risen to as many as one hundred.[4] The Indian population of the region before the disastrous plague of 1576–1581 numbered only about one thousand, leading the mining community to petition the viceroy to authorize the importation of some three thousand slaves to augment the workforce.[5] Attending to these people's spiritual needs were a circuit-riding priest, Alonso de Espino, appointed by Michoacán's first bishop, Vasco de Quiroga, and two parish priests, Pedro Yáñez and Lorenzo Encinas, who traveled from Maravatío and Irimbo, respectively, each a good day's ride from Tlalpujahua. Despite Tlalpujahua's rapid designation as a real de minas, the government appointed an alcalde mayor de minas, Gaspar de Solís, only in 1570. A resident parish priest, Antonio de Morales, was assigned in 1575. A year later Solís formally laid out the town of Tlalpujahua, and building began on a church, a relatively modest building that took another twenty-five years to complete. By then Tlalpujahua's silver boom was nearly over. A 1619 episcopal visit recorded only forty Spanish residents and two hundred Otomí Indians in the village, with another thirty Otomíes and an equal number of black slaves working in the outlying mines.[6]

Tomás and His Mine

For nearly four decades, Tomás scratched at the earth in Tlalpujahua, shuttling from time to time to Mexico City to visit family members or leading his pack mules down into the Mixteca to buy cochineal and cacao to augment what, despite his initial enthusiasm, seem to have been meager pickings of silver.[7] In Tlalpujahua, Fonseca fought with his neighbors over water rights and competed with them for allotments of mercury.[8] It was in Tlalpujahua, in 1590 and again in 1596, that agents of the Inquisition arrested Tomás and took him to Mexico City for trial. He was the only resident of Tlalpujahua ever to be charged with Judaizing.

Tomás's initial workforce would undoubtedly have consisted mainly of himself and perhaps one or two free-labor naboríos. As soon as his mine began to produce ore, Tomás petitioned Tlalpujahua's alcalde de minas to assign him an allotment of Indians. Eventually Tomás's mine was allotted a repartimiento of six Indians. The six were legally considered a material good, and as such could be transferred to any new owner of the mine. If someday the mine should cease operating, they could be sold at auction.[9] In later years, Fonseca's workforce of Indians and slaves had increased enough to require him to build five shacks to house them.[10] Tomás's foreman, a post held in later years by Diego Hernández, probably shared his master's quarters, as did, eventually, Tomás's son Teodosio. For a brief period around 1564, Tomás's nephew young Tomás de Fonseca Castellanos lodged there too.

Upon filing his claim, Tomás was granted a *merced*, a formal permission to make use of the water source indicated in the claiming document and to build whatever machinery he needed to make his mining operation successful. We have no specific information about construction on Tomás's property in those early years, although a crude and probably symbolic drawing of his house appears on the 1575 Tlalpujaha map. The following year he expressed his intention to build his stamping mill adjacent to his house.[11]

Years later, following Tomás's second arrest, in March 1596, his property was inventoried in great detail. Given the estate's miserable condition and paltry contents at that time, its beginnings more than thirty years previous must have been humble indeed. The sequestration report describes Tomás's house as having adobe walls roofed over with jacal, a lattice of thin wooden stakes plastered with adobe. The five huts of Fonseca's workers' quarters must have been similarly constructed. Close by them was a structure that housed Fonseca's six mules, four donkeys, and packhorse. It is unclear whether this structure was a stable with formal stalls roofed with wattle and mud jacales or whether it was merely a corral; but it must have had some sort of covered storage area for Tomás's four bridles and leather saddles, a few brushes and combs, and iron tools used for shoeing the animals, all of which are listed on the inventory. The hacienda complex probably also included a shed for storing mercury and magistral.

Running through Tomás's property was a ditch (acequia) that tapped into the arroyo farther up the hill to bring water to wash the ore and to mix with the mercury and magistral on the amalgamation patio floor. A holding pond (*presa*) at the upper part of Fonseca's land ensured that he could work without interruption during the dry season. The hacienda's newest structure, built sometime after 1585,[12] was a water-powered stamping mill. Of the patio itself, the inventory makes no mention. It was, after all, merely a flat piece of ground ringed by a low wall, so it was not transportable, not auctionable, and thus of no value in and of itself, despite being the heart of Tomás's mining complex.

Tomás's mining equipment, like that of most other miners of his time, consisted mainly of iron tools of diverse shapes and sizes. The inventory lists pry bars: two large ones, one medium, and two small; a pick and two shovels; hammers for crushing, chipping, and cracking the stone; some awls and chisels; and what the inventory calls "other miscellaneous small tools."[13]

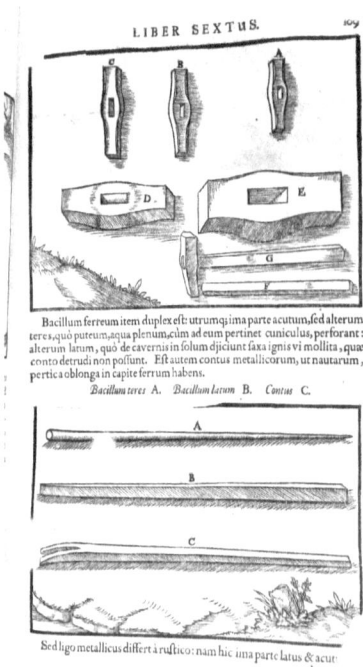

Figure 5. Mining tools. From Agricola, De re metallica, 1621. Used with permission of the Biblioteca Francisco de Burgoa, Centro Cultural Santo Domingo, Oaxaca.

For storing smaller items, Tomás had several wooden boxes, one noted in the inventory as very large. For carrying things, he had four wicker baskets of various sizes and twenty small leather bags. For washing the crushed ore, he owned two large basins; for smelting it, two small furnaces. For weighing his refined silver, he had two small sets of scales, with their weights stored in an old box. The loose sheaf of papers on which he recorded his accounts he kept in another small box.

Tomás's house was furnished as one might expect of a solitary miner of modest means. There were four chairs, a small and a large table, a large desk, three little painted chests, a small dilapidated portable writing desk, and one candelabrum. He had a wooden bed on which to unroll his mattress and a single pillow. Although no blankets appear in the inventory, presumably Tomás owned one or two—Tlalpujahua is so high in the mountains that it is cold every night of the year, and on winter mornings frost is common. Blankets do not appear on the inventory perhaps because he took them with him to prison as part of his personal effects, as was the custom. The only cooking or eating equipment mentioned in the inventory is a single spoon. Since men of Tomás's time rarely cooked for themselves, he probably took his meals with a woman who made her living providing hot meals for single men. Food was expensive, and it generally cost more in mining towns than elsewhere.[14]

Tomás's one extravagance was books. The inventory notes eleven books in Latin, including a copy of the Old Testament, and five unnamed books in Spanish, plus a copy of Antonio de Nebrija's 1492 Latin grammar and dictionary.[15] Testimonies before the Inquisition by some of old Tomás's Mexico City friends suggest that two of the five Spanish books were Fray Luis de Granada's *Symbol of Faith* (*Símbolo de la fe*) and Fray Juan de Dueñas's *Mirror of Consolation* (*Espejo de consolación*, of which more will be said later).[16]

Personal possessions aside, Tomás's most ambitious investment was his stamping mill. This was undoubtedly located near the mine shaft entrance, at the site where Fonseca's workers had previously used iron or stone hammers to crush the ore to powder. The stamping mill was an unsophisticated device in which water flowed under a wheel equipped with scoops, which turned a horizontal shaft mounted with cams. As the shaft rotated, the cams lifted heavy iron hammer blocks, called *mazos*, which, as they were released, fell and crushed the chunks of ore that had been shoveled under them. Fonseca's mill, which according to the inventory had eight cam-driven mazos, was a relatively large one for those days.[17]

Despite the centrality of a stamping mill to the economic success of any substantial mining operation, Fonseca struggled on his property without one for more than a quarter of a century before he succeeded in getting it built. The problem was that the mill required water to power it and therefore had to be located downhill from a constant untrammeled water source. The issuance of a building permit required official confirmation of this power source. In the arid Mexican hills, even where silver was sometimes plentiful, water generally was not, and conflicts over water were inevitable.[18] As the old saying goes, "Whiskey is for drinking, water is for fighting over."[19]

In March 1576, Tomás de Fonseca sued his uphill neighbors Cristóbal and Antonio Ramírez de Arellano for reneging on their agreement to build their mill first and do it in such a way that the runoff would go to Fonseca's land.[20] By 1576 the brothers' new *ingenio* was finished, but they claimed that the hydraulic system they had installed did not permit easy rechanneling of the water to Fonseca. Tomás requested permission to tap into their channel, as

Figure 6. Stamping mill. From Agricola, De re metallica, 1621. Used with permission of the Biblioteca Francisco de Burgoa, Centro Cultural Santo Domingo, Oaxaca.

was his right under the original merced, but the brothers rebuffed him and refused to reengineer their operation or permit him access to their land. Tomás sued, petitioning the court to order the Ramírez brothers to immediately cut him a channel, called an *herido de agua*.

On March 29, 1576, the court so ordered, adding the stipulation that Fonseca had to have his ingenio up and running within a year and that he had to work it for a minimum of four years before he could sell it or exchange his mine for another piece of property. Such a condition was a normal part of building permits for ingenios, for above all the crown wanted working miners, not land speculators, and therefore it devised regulations to ensure that there would be no gaps in the production of Mexican silver.

If only things were that easy. Twenty months later there was still no ditch, no water, and no ingenio. In November 1577, Tomás went back to the district court in Maravatío, the administrative center in eastern Michoacán with jurisdiction over Tlalpujahua, to lodge his complaint a second time with Martín Enríquez Viso, who, as councilman, governor, and captain-general, acted in the region with the authority of the viceroy. Enríquez Viso, after reviewing Fonseca's original petition and the facts of the case as presented, ruled a second time in Tomás's favor and ordered that the herido de agua be opened. In compliance with this ruling, the parties gathered at three o'clock on the afternoon of November 7, 1577, in front of Tomás de Fonseca's house at the entrance to his mine, where Fonseca formally presented the court's order to Agustín de Bustamante, Tlalpujahua's alcalde mayor.[21] The brothers Ramírez began to scream at the alcalde that Fonseca was lying about the water agreement that he claimed they had negotiated, that the facts he had stipulated in his petition were wrong, and that therefore the court order should not be executed, adding that if the alcalde would just follow them up the hill, he could see the truth for himself.

By the time the exasperated parties had all climbed to the spot where the channels were allegedly to have been divided, a third claimant to the water had appeared. He was Cristóbal Ramírez de Padrón, who was representing a miner farther down the mountain named Juan Martínez Carral. Ramírez de Padrón presented the alcalde with a document certifying that on September 13, 1577, the multititled Martín Enríquez Viso had granted Martínez Carral a mining claim, with the accompanying water rights, downstream from the Ramírez brothers' land. Martínez Carral was alleging that if half of the channel's flow was diverted to Fonseca, there would not be enough water left for him, causing irreparable economic damage to his own property, and that, given these complications, nothing should be done until all the parties could be gathered together to sort the matter out face to face. Under the circumstances, that seemed reasonable to the alcalde mayor, and he sent everyone home.

Four days later, old Tomás went back to court, this time with his friend and fellow miner Rodrigo de Quesada, to bear witness to the terms of the original agreement that he had made with the Ramírez brothers. The court scribe's transcription of Fonseca's testimony makes clear that the miner was just barely holding his frustration and anger in check.

> I've brought Rodrigo de Quesada here to testify—in order to avoid a lawsuit, for their resolution is often uncertain, and to bring peace between him [Cristóbal, one of the Ramírez de Arellano brothers] and me,—how we made an agreement, over eight years ago, both orally and

in writing, about how I would build a water-powered ingenio to process metal on the land that I have here in these mines, where I have built my buildings, and how the water would be channeled from his land onto mine..., and I began to dig the channel, and I made a holding pond, and his people saw me doing it, and it was an open and public thing.

To which Cristóbal Ramírez de Arellano replied that Fonseca had misconstrued the terms of the agreement, which he and his witnesses swore had been only oral and not written.[22]

After many further suits and countersuits, seven years and eleven months later, on August 23, 1584, Tomás de Fonseca and some of his neighbors again gathered on the hillside above the mines of the three squabbling parties, at a point on the stream just below the shack where long before a man named Ramírez de Quesada had formerly housed his slaves. This time Cristóbal Ramírez de Arellano was absent, though Juan Martínez Carral, the downstream neighbor, was there to make sure that sufficient water would continue to flow to the property he owned. The ceremony was brief. Fonseca formally requested that the new alcalde mayor de minas, Gaspar Pérez de Monterrey, allow him to access the water flow. Pérez de Monterrey took Fonseca by the hand and led him to the stream bank. Tomás picked up a short-handled hoe and with it opened the mouth of the channel. Then two of Tomás's Indian employees went to work with shovels to make sure the ditch was clear all the way downhill to where Fonseca was, at long last, building his stamping mill.

It was, unfortunately, a very long hill, and below the Ramírez de Arellano mine, below Fonseca's stamping mill, and below Martínez de Carral's ingenio lay the hacienda de beneficiar metales of Alonso de Palacios, who after a long silence now weighed in to the dispute with an objection to the decreased water flow to his land. In his lawsuit, submitted in January 1585, Palacios appealed not for justice but rather to the crown's economic interests:

> I've had a mill here for twenty-five years, processing silver and paying my fifth to the king. If I can't mill, then the Royal Treasury will suffer. I have a lot of silver to refine, a lot more than Tomás de Fonseca. Besides, I am a married man.[23] My ore has higher silver content than his. I will build two refining haciendas on my land in less time than it will take him with

his false claims and promises to build one. He's not doing this because he wants to be a settler here, but because he wants to do me injury. He's had ten years to build his stamping mill and he hasn't done it; so you can clearly see what malice he intends.

And with that, the work was stopped once again.[24] Surviving documents do not indicate when it finally went forward, but sequestration documents of 1596 attest that at some point the mill had indeed been built, and that it was now beginning to fall apart from neglect.[25]

The Miner Merchant

As a miner, Tomás de Fonseca seems to have been moderately successful. He never found a lode so large or so rich in silver content that it would make him wealthy, but then few miners did. A miner aspiring to a lucrative strike is like a young actor aspiring to a starring role: while they are working hard at their craft and waiting for a break, they have to find some other means of putting bread on the table. The veins of silver that Tomás's shafts pursued into the Tlalpujahua hills never grew so thin as to force him from the mining business, as so often happened to others. He extracted enough silver to make a living, to feed and pay a handful of workers, to stable a few donkeys and mules, and to contribute something to the support of his family. When his property was inventoried in 1596, the Inquisition found 300 *quintales* of amalgamated silver ore waiting to be smelted.[26]

This is not to say that Tomás's mining business always ran smoothly. In Ayoteco with his father, Gabriel, fallow periods had forced them to load their donkeys with bags of lead oxide to sell as a catalyst in Taxco to miners more fortunate than they. Tomás must have been experiencing a dry spell in Pachuca in the 1550s too, for when he learned of the Tlalpujahua strikes, he straight off packed his tools and went there. In the course of his 1590 and 1596 trials, Tomás testified that he had been living in Tlalpujahua off and on for thirty-eight years, mostly mining but also dealing in other commodities, such as cacao and cochineal. He bought these products in the Mixteca (today parts of the states of Puebla, Guerrero, and Oaxaca) and sold them in Mexico City.[27]

The cacao bean (*Theobroma cacao*) had been cultivated in the Mayan region of tropical Mesoamerica for at least three thousand years before the arrival of the Spaniards.[28] One favored preparation was to toast the cacao beans, grind them to a powder, mix them with corn flour and water, and then whip the mixture into a frothy drink that was presumed to have health-sustaining properties. The Mexica called the drink *xocoatl* (the *x* sound in the Aztec language being pronounced like the English *sh*), from which we get the word *chocolate*. Another way to prepare it was to make a porridge with the same ingredients, using less water and adding crushed dried chiles. The cacao beans had ritual uses too: the Mexicas of the central highlands offered the beans to the gods in sacred ceremonies. More tropical peoples, such as the Mayas, who in later times were subject to the Mexicas, paid part of their required annual tribute in cacao beans. In fact, the scarce, portable, durable beans were so prized that they became a medium of exchange, a form of currency that was used all over Mesoamerica, even by European settlers.[29]

Cacao first came to the notice of Europeans in 1502 when Columbus, finding it being drunk by Indians on the coast of Honduras, took some back to Spain, where it impressed the court of the Catholic Monarchs. In 1528 Cortés likewise impressed the court of Carlos V. By the early 1530s, when New World goods began to be exported to Spain in quantity, cacao soon became a favored product—small enough to be shipped with ease, slow to spoil, valuable enough to turn the merchant a tidy profit. Middlemen like Tomás de Fonseca scoured the southern villages for the beans. They aggregated their purchases in regional markets and sold them to major wholesalers in Puebla or Mexico City, who then freighted them to Veracruz to be shipped to Spain. When Tomás testified that he sometimes dealt in cacao and cochineal, he undoubtedly meant that during fallow periods he left one of his sons or a trusted employee to look after the mine while he roamed the Mixteca southland, buying cacao and cochineal for resale in the north.

Cochineal (*cochinilla; Dactylapius coccus costa*) is a parasitic scale insect that feeds on nutrients in moisture exuded by the prickly pear or nopal cactus (genus *Opuntia*; also known as the paddle cactus). Once their eggs are fertilized by the winged males, the females, who outnumber the males by some three hundred to one, lay their eggs, insert their proboscises into the cactus leaf pad, and begin to suck, eventually killing the pad. Over their three-month life span, the females produce carminic acid, which they store in sacs in their bodies and their eggs to deter other predator insects. When the insects are dried, this acid can be extracted and blended with salts of aluminum or calcium to make carmine dye, called *grana de cochinilla*, or simply *grana*.

Pre-Columbian peoples, particularly in the Mixteca region around Oaxaca but also in the plains of Puebla, farmed the insect by cutting off infected cactus pads, planting them, and then picking off the insects by hand, drying them, crushing them, and draining off the carminic acid. With it they prepared dyes that colored their cotton fabrics a brilliant scarlet, carmine, or purple. They also used grana as a cosmetic and to color artifacts of stone or wood. The insects were so tiny—twenty-five thousand of them in a kilo of fresh insects; seventy thousand when they were dried[30]—that gathering them was extremely labor intensive. So popular was the color, and so expensive to produce, that grana-dyed cloth and the dried cochinilla insects themselves traded at premium in pre-Columbian tianguis and were even used as a medium of exchange. In the late fifteenth century, the annual tribute paid to the emperor Moctezuma included forty bags of grana.[31]

Entrepreneurial traders of the generation following the conquest made a killing with cochineal, for the brilliant carmine dye was eagerly sought by European textile industries. Two mid-sixteenth-century historians, Francisco Cervantes de Salazar and Francisco López de Gómara, noted that it had become one of the most important Mexican exports to Spain.[32] Martín Enríquez, given the task in 1575 of assessing the extent of the Mexican cochineal trade for the king, informed Philip II that cochineal amounted to some seven thousand arrobas (each arroba equaling about twenty-five pounds) annually. The next year the amount doubled, and it remained near that level through the end of the century.[33]

Small traders like Tomás de Fonseca were an important part of the economic funnel that brought the sacks of cochineal from the Indian cactus farmers in Oaxaca and Puebla to the cloth dyers of Europe. The farmers sold dried cochineal from their homes or in their village markets to dealers, who then resold the insects to small wholesalers like Fonseca at regional tianguis in towns such as Oaxaca, Puebla, Tlaxcala, Tepeaca, Cholula, and Huejotzingo for transport to Mexico City or the Gulf Coast. The Atlantic export trade in cochineal in the late sixteenth century was controlled by fewer than a dozen major merchants based in Mexico City, entrepreneurs who operated either independently or as factors of Spanish importers located in Sevilla. It was to one of these major international traders in the capital that Tomás would have delivered the grana that he had bought in the Mixteca. His buyer may well have been Luis de Carvajal de la Cueva, the governor of the northern province of the Nuevo Reino de León, who is noted as having shipped thirty-eight arrobas of grana on a boat that landed in Vigo in 1580, or Simón Rodríguez, who is recorded as having shipped ten arrobas of grana on the same boat.[34]

Tomás dabbled in a third commodity as well: pigs. In 1562, a busy year for his lawsuits, Tomás stipulated to a local court that he had purchased twelve pigs from some Indians in Tepaxco, a village near Yuntitlán. The vicar of Yuntitlán, Alonso de Vargas, had agreed to keep the pigs for him. Now the vicar had refused repeated requests to give them up, and thus Fonseca respectfully requested that the court have the bailiff, Diego de Catemona, go to Yuntitlán and bring Fonseca his pigs. The court ruled for Tomás, with this succinct notation: "Have Diego de Catemona go get the pigs."[35] Attached to the proceedings is a letter in which Father Alonso Vargas pleads extenuating circumstances, argues that he meant no harm to anyone, and agrees to comply with the court order.

These twelve pigs were undoubtedly destined for the internal Mexican market. Prior to the 1550s, the reales de minas in central Mexico were supplied with the foodstuffs they required by local farmers. Spanish ranchers delivered goats, sheep, and cattle to the mining towns, either on the hoof or freshly slaughtered, and they were quickly retailed by local shopkeepers. Indians who tended small agricultural plots supplied vegetables and greens and sold them in the town's tianguis. After mid-century, as new mines were discovered in the semiarid and desert country to the north of the Bajío, in places such as Zacatecas, Guanajuato, San Luis Potosí, Chalchihuites,

Sombrerete, and Mazapil, supplying food to the miners and the boomtowns that grew up around the mines required the creation of systems to process, store, ship, and market food. The fertile flatlands of central Michoacán and the Bajío developed into food production centers. Hostlers with strings of pack mules and wagons—once the road system had improved enough to accommodate them[36]—freighted the grains and vegetables of the near-north agricultural belt to workers farther north. Fish from the coasts and from the lakes of Michoacán and the Valley of Mexico were dried and shipped to the mining camps. Meat, too, could be dried, although much of it continued to be driven on the hoof to the towns in which it was sold.

Was Tomás raising the pigs to feed his cuadrilla of workers or sell them to his neighbors to be turned into chops and stews and pork pies in the kitchens of Tlalpujahua? Was he going to smoke-cure them or dry them to jerky and then sell them to a shipper to cart to some meat-hungry town in the far north? All we can say for certain is that this sort of transaction—small-scale, local, somewhere between producer and consumer, and able to generate at most a few pesos of extra income for a struggling miner—was altogether common in Mexico in the third quarter of the sixteenth century.

Chapter 7

Tomás de Fonseca Reconnects

> My brother Tomás de Fonseca, during the times that he lived in Mexico [City] which he did from time to time coming and going from his father's house, kept the Law of Moses, because he told me so; he said that his father Gabriel de Castellanos had taught him . . . I saw him fasting the fasts of that Law.
> —JULIÁN DE CASTELLANOS, MAY 19, 1590[1]

IN 1552 GABRIEL de Fonseca left Ayoteco and returned to Blanca Rodríguez and his other two children, Guiomar and Julián, in Mexico City.[2] Perhaps Gabriel was lonely for family; perhaps his mine had played out; or perhaps he decided that if he could not make an adequate living by mining, his luck might improve in the metropolis. He seems to have found work as a magistrate, as Julián de Castellanos and Gabriel's grandson young Tomás de Fonseca speculated to inquisitors.[3] He also may have opened a shop retailing or wholesaling imported wine, given that he later helped both his son Julián and his nephew young Tomás de Fonseca Castellanos get started in the wine business.

In 1568, Gabriel, then in his mid-seventies, took sick with what would prove to be his last illness. He needed more care than Blanca, who was also getting on in years, could give him. By then Gabriel's many relatives in Mexico city, most of them living only a few minutes away from the home that he shared with Blanca, may have occasionally stopped by to visit him, but none of them came forth to help him in his time of need. So when Tomás became aware of Gabriel's illness, he went to Mexico City and for the next two years divided his time between Tlalujahua and the capital. In Mexico he reestablished contact with a number of his relatives, one of whom was the son of his lost younger sister Isabel, Tomás de Fonseca Castellanos.

When Gabriel de Castellanos had spirited the pregnant Blanca and his older children across the Spanish border to Jarandilla around 1526, he left his youngest daughter, Isabel, with some of her converso Fonseca cousins in the Portuguese city of Viseu. He did not send for her when he and the rest of his family sailed to Mexico late in 1534. Instead, Isabel grew up in Portugal in a community of Portuguese and Spanish relatives who shared an all but openly Jewish religious culture.

Headstrong even as a teenager, Isabel fell in love with her first cousin Álvaro de Fonseca, a practicing Christian,[4] even though both knew they would never be able to marry. She gave birth to their son, Tomás de Fonseca Castellanos, in about 1548. Years later, young Tomás narrated his family's soap opera to inquisitors in Mexico:

> My mother was raised by her grandmother, my great-grandmother, . . . who converted from Judaism to Christianity in Viseu, and as a Jew she taught Judaism to my mother. . . . I was not baptized, because being a Jew, as she was, she did not want me to be baptized. And they concealed my birth because she was not married to my father, who was her first cousin; they had not gotten a bull of dispensation so they could not even live together publicly as man and wife for fear of being punished for incest. In fact, when I was born, so that no one would know, she left Viseu for the village of Almeida, where we lived for a couple of years until my father died and we went back to Viseu."[5]

After Álvaro died, leaving Isabel pregnant with their daughter Francisca de Fonseca, Isabel's cousins in Viseu soon found a way to rid themselves of what was surely a family embarrassment. They arranged for Isabel to marry Tomás Méndez, a man of unsavory character who, since Isabel felt compelled to hide her Judaizing from him, was presumably an Old Christian.[6]

There is no doubt whatsoever that Isabel continued to be a fervent Judaizer despite her marriage to Méndez. In the fashion of most crypto-Jewish families with young children, she kept her religious beliefs and practices secret from the children, conscientiously raising them to be Catholic, reciting the Our Fathers and Hail Marys with them at bedtime, refraining from

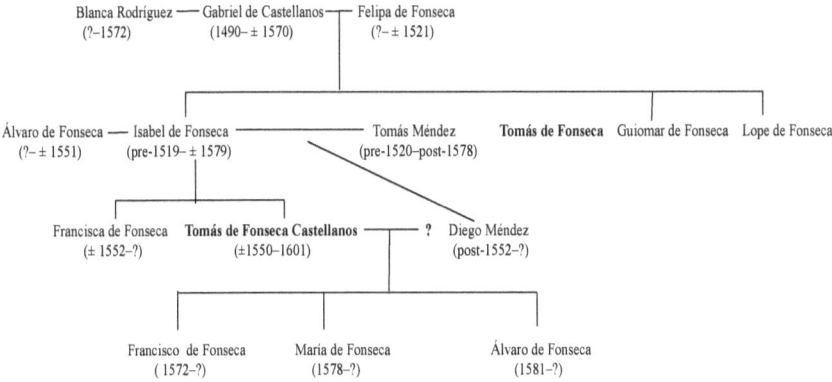

undermining their catechization by the village priest, and scrupulously hiding her own prayers and practices from the children's eyes and ears. But around 1562, when young Tomás reached puberty, which signaled the age of presumed discretion, in what may appear to us today an ironic precursor of the modern bar mitzvah ceremony, Isabel importuned her son to leave the law of Jesus Christ, in which his soul would not be saved, and instead "direct his heart to the one and only God, to observe the Law of Moses, . . . to await the Messiah, . . . and to keep this a secret and not tell anyone, especially not his stepfather Tomás Méndez, from whom he should guard himself as if he were the Devil."[7] From that time on, young Tomás considered himself a Jew.

Isabel had a son with Méndez, whom they named Diego Méndez de Fonseca. Before long his father, whether drawn by the New World's promise of riches or escaping an unhappy marriage, abandoned his wife and set sail for Mexico, taking young Diego with him. Fifteen-year-old Tomás left his mother's home and followed his stepfather to America in 1563.

On his arrival in Mexico City, young Tomás de Fonseca Castellanos sought out not Tomás Méndez but his grandfather Gabriel de Castellanos. Gabriel helped him get started by setting him up in a shop retailing wines.[8] But a sedentary life in Mexico City seems to have appealed to young Tomás about as much as it had to his grandfather Gabriel three decades previous, for after managing the wine store for a few months, young Tomás set out for Tlalpujahua to learn the mining business from his uncle, old Tomás de Fonseca.[9]

Young Tomás arrived in Tlalpujahua in 1564. Although young Tomás had never met his Tlalpujahuan uncle, and despite their disparity in age, the two family members quickly bonded. The sixteen-year-old boy must have been bursting to confide in old Tomás, and the relatively isolated, solitary life in the mines must have provided the two men ample opportunities for sharing confidences; among the inevitable topics was their shared Jewish heritage.

Old Tomás de Fonseca was a child of converts who had themselves been converted as children. He never had the experience of living in a community of openly practicing Jews. He spent his infancy and early youth among crypto-Jews in Spain, under the shadow of the Inquisition. For the most part, his knowledge of normative Judaism came to him from his books (which, except for the Old Testament, were framed in a Christian theological context) and from what he had learned about his Jewish grandfather's world thirdhand from his family members. His nephew had been raised in the 1550s among Portuguese crypto-Jews whose knowledge of Jewish traditions and commitment to their practice tended to be stronger than those of their coreligionists in Spain.

In Tlalpujahua in 1564, the two men observed together the Yom Kippur fast.[10] While there is no record of what they discussed, one can imagine that his nephew evoked in old Tomás memories of his own childhood experiences, his initiation in Jarandilla into the life of a crypto-Jew, and the moments of ritual he had shared as a young teenager in Spain with his father, Gabriel, and his sisters; and later in Mexico City, when Gabriel was initiating young Julián in the rudiments of Judaism.

Young Tomás remained with his uncle in Tlalpujahua for four years, helping him in the mines and learning the mining business. It seems likely that their conversations blew new life into the embers of Jewish identity that had been barely flickering in his uncle during the previous two decades. Then, in 1568, young Tomás took his leave, heading south to Taxco to forge his own life, much as his uncle had done when he had left his father, Gabriel, in Ayoteco so many years before.

By then young Tomás had put aside enough money to send for his mother in Portugal, so she could join him in Mexico and look for her husband and lost son. Isabel succeeded in locating her children, and she remained close to them until her death, sometime prior to 1578; but Isabel never found her missing husband, and she did not seem to have felt the need to make any connection with her father, Gabriel de Castellanos, who had essentially abandoned her so many years before.[11]

What of Old Tomás's Other Two Siblings, Guiomar and Julián?

After her marriage to Antonio Pérez Herrero, Guiomar had been in the habit of celebrating the Jewish holidays at her father's home with Blanca and her brother Julián without her husband and their three children, whom she feared might become aware of her Judaizing. When Gabriel took ill, Guiomar, probably because of the complexity of her own family situation, chose not to take on the responsibility of caring for him. Nevertheless, Guiomar was never far from Gabriel's mind. When her husband Pérez Herrero died sometime before 1570, leaving her relatively well-off,[12] Gabriel took steps to see that her widowhood would be short. He sent a letter to an old friend, Cosme Pereira, a lawyer and widower who was working for the Real Audiencia in Peru, a man he evidently knew to be a practicing crypto-Jew, informing him of his daughter's availability. Pereira came to Mexico in 1572, wed Guiomar, and quickly made his mark on the capital's growing community of Judaizers. Pereira's knowledge of Jewish culture rivaled that of Guiomar and Tomás's father, Gabriel, and he was enthusiastic about disseminating his knowledge.[13]

Julián de Castellanos was no help to his father either. He had been only two or three years old when Gabriel and Blanca Rodríguez brought him to Mexico in 1534. He lived with his parents until he was about eleven years old, learning his letters and absorbing—with some reticence—all that his father could teach him about Judaism. Around 1544 his father arranged for the boy to be apprenticed to Domingo de Orona, a silversmith who was making a name for himself in the colony for the quality of the processional crosses, chalices, ciboria, and monstrances he was fashioning for the cathedral and the religious orders.[14]

Julián worked for Orona for eight years, during most of which his father was mining in Ayoteco or fighting the Chichimecas in the north. When Gabriel came back to Mexico City, he set Julián up in a small shop selling silver items and wine, and there Julián worked for the next fifteen or sixteen years. Then, whether because the business failed or he had just grown restless, he left Mexico for the northern mining towns of Zacatecas, Sombrerete, Temascaltepec, and Sultepec, where he spent two years, probably as a peddler. He spent another year in the Soconusco (then called Guatemala but now coastal Chiapas). A head injury laid him up for another year. After these years of wandering, Julián returned to Mexico City, where his father helped him buy a small *obraje*. Working for Julián were a mulatto named Marianila, a number of Indians, and a few youngsters he described merely as *mozos*.[15]

> By the 1560s, obrajes were producing blankets and everyday clothing in substantial quantities all over Mexico. By all reports, and there are many, the obrajes functioned like modern-day sweatshops, paying minimal wages to workers, who were kept in near-slave conditions by the obraje owner, who obliged them to buy their tools and supplies from him at inflated prices on credit to lock them in perpetual debt.[16]

Obraje owners were expected to facilitate their workers' compliance with the requirements of the church, but Julián's behavior in this regard was unusual enough that it made an impression on his parents' friends, and his neighbors, for he cared enough for his Indian and European workers to take them regularly to mass.[17] Although some obraje owners grew rich, Julián eked out a miserable living at best.[18] During his years as an apprentice silversmith and obraje manager, Julián sired two children with a woman or women who are unnamed in the records. The boy, Florián de Castellanos, eventually followed his father into the obraje business and married a woman from the San Pablo neighborhood named Isabel Bernal. The girl, Juliana de Castellanos, widowed after a brief marriage to Pedro Díaz de Sotomayor, also lived in Mexico City.[19]

When his father took sick, Julián was living near the Hospital de Nuestra Señora in Mexico City with a friend, Luis Álvarez de Merón, an Old Christian hidalgo from Medina del Campo.[20] Because there was little love lost between Julián and his father, there was little chance that Julián would lend a hand in Gabriel's care. There was even less love lost between Julián and old Tomás, who obstinately refused to acknowledge Julián as legitimate kin.[21] Despite their disregard for each other, from time to time Julián and old Tomás did meet and talk. The older brother reminisced with the younger about how back in Jarandilla, Gabriel had instructed the two of them in the Jewish law and taught them to sing Psalms and to observe the Jewish fasts.

But their rapprochement was short-lived, and after the old man died in 1570, old antipathies surfaced. Julián later reported to the Inquisition that "after that time I never again saw or had any dealings with Tomás de Fonseca, not even to talk to him, because we have been at odds with each other."[22]

We have no record of what old Tomás and his father talked about during that difficult time, but Tomás, fresh from his four years of conversations with his nephew at the mine in Tlalpujahua, must have reminisced with the old man about their shared life in Jarandilla, their long journey from Extremadura to Mexico City, and their struggles and good times together at Gabriel's mine in Ayoteco.[23]

Gabriel was buried in the Hospital de Nuestra Señora.[24] Blanca followed him to the grave two years later.[25]

Tomás went back to Tlalpujahua, but the long visits to Mexico City during his father's illness had changed him. It was probably during one of those visits that old Tomás, then in his fifties, met a woman named Ana Jiménez. We know nothing about her, not even whether she was Spanish, mestiza, or Indian, although it seems likely that if she had been other than of Spanish origin, Tomás would have mentioned it, as he did with the Indian woman who had given birth to his son Teodosio back in Ayoteco so many years before. What we do know is that in the late 1560s and early 1570s, she and Tomás produced four children, all of whom took the surname Fonseca. In his 1590 trial, Tomás described Beatriz, their eldest child, as a robust, young, unmarried woman of twenty-plus years who was living with her mother, Ana, in Mexico City, as was her sister, Ana de Fonseca, born in 1573. The other two children were boys: Lope, born in 1571, and Gabriel, born in 1575.[26] They were helping their father at the mine at the time of his arrest in 1591. Ana and old Tomás never married, and they did not live together. Instead, Tomás commuted intermittently between Tlalpujahua and Mexico City, where she and the children shared the home of Juan de Chávez, Ana's brother-in-law, who had a business carting merchandise to Veracruz.[27] There are no suggestions in the Inquisition files that Ana ever met the other members of Tomás's family or any of his friends.

In 1577 Julián married Francisca Zarfate de Vergas, the daughter of a rich man whose sons had become lawyers. Over the next decade, Julián and Francisca had four children: Francisco (born in 1577), Graviel (1580), Gerónimo (1588), and Felipa (1589).[28] There is no record of old Tomás ever having had anything to do with any of them. And none of these grandchildren of Gabriel de Castellanos appear to have ever been accused of Judaizing.

Chapter 8

The Portuguese Come to America[1]

> Manuel de Lucena said: "You must be aware, I swear to God, that there are more Jews in Mexico than there are Christians, and they are richer, too." And I answered him: "They are Portuguese." And he said: "As God knows." I said: "Why does the Law of Moses adhere to these Portuguese more than to anyone else." And he answered: "That's why they are rich; God gives them more money and more property than he gives these butt-fucking Christian dogs."
> —LUIS DÍAZ, DECEMBER 7, 1594[2]

> Leaving Puebla I ran into a ... doctor of the Portuguese Nation named Fernán Juárez Tavares ... and with him was a young man ... named ... Jorge López, who in his country was called Antonio Something, a native of Torre de Moncorvo in the Kingdom of Portugal in the Raya de Castilla near the Duero River, towards Zamora. ... And since I knew the language that the Portuguese know, I drew near to Fernán Tavares in order to greet him.
> —GASPAR FONSECA, NOVEMBER 22, 1621[3]

THE GABRIEL DE Castellanos who set off to the New World in 1534 was an impetuous young Portuguese with deep roots in Spain, a taste for adventure, and someone else's wife. With him when he embarked were two of his three children and a son of hers who was possibly theirs. Gabriel was also an early harbinger of a migration of Portuguese-Spanish Judaizers that would blossom in the 1570s and continue through the 1640s.[4] The underlying reasons for this migration involved politics, religion, and economics, but the immediate causes of the surge were the intensifying activity of the Portuguese Inquisition and a precipitating catastrophic event in the summer of 1578.

The border between Spain and Portugal, despite restrictions imposed by the governments on both sides, had always been porous. Census data from the Spanish side of the border from the late 1490s, for example, indicate that many of the Jews who had fled Spain in 1492 and who had undoubtedly suffered the forced conversions in Portugal in 1497, had subsequently returned to live as New Christians in their former homes in Spain.[5] Other New Christians crossed the border frequently—monthly, even weekly—for reasons of trade. The people who lived in the villages on both sides of the border thought of their home territory as a single entity, the Raya de Portugal. They commonly spoke both languages, code-switching as circumstances warranted. It was altogether typical that when Tomás de Fonseca gave his particulars to inquisitors in Mexico City in 1590, he said he had been born in Freixo de Espada-à-Cinta (Portugal), and when they appeared unfamiliar with the place, he explained that it was near Zamora (Spain).[6]

> The family of the best-known Mexican crypto-Jew of the 1580s and 1590s, Luis de Carvajal the younger, is typical of this generation of conversos who had relatives in the Raya de Portugal, some of them Judaizers, some of them committed Christians. Luis's paternal grandfather, Gaspar de Carvajal, who spent much of his adult life in Portugal, had been born in the Spanish university city of Salamanca and owned property in Benavente, a market town a little farther north. Luis's parents had come from the Portuguese village of Mogadouro. His family included people surnamed Rodríguez (a name common in both countries) and Matos (a name clearly Portuguese in origin). Luis's five maternal great uncles, world-traveling members of the León family, were also connected on both sides of the border. Duarte de León, in Lisbon, was a member of the elite: he supervised trade with the Guineas for the Portuguese king. Álvaro de León was a wealthy merchant in Medina del Campo on the Spanish side. Francisco Jorge, who also served for a time in Guinea as captain-general, eventually migrated to Mexico and joined the Augustinian Order as a friar. Jorge de León de Andrada was a small merchant in Cortiços, a Portuguese village near Mogadouro along the border. Antonio de León was killed by French pirates as he was sailing back to Spain from India.[7]

In the Beira and Trás-os-Montes border villages the former Jews, all of whom were now at least nominally *cristãos-novos*, went on about their lives in relative tranquility for most of the early sixteenth century. The older generation had almost all been born in Castilla; their children and grandchildren were natives of Portugal. While a few of these *confesos*, as the Portuguese converts were called, assimilated into the prevailing Catholic culture of small-town Portugal, more of them lived as semi-clandestine Jews clinging to an ever-shrinking set of Jewish customs and beliefs. They had to be circumspect, but in at least the first three decades of the sixteenth century, the danger on the Portuguese side was minimal.

Impetus for Leaving

When the Portuguese Inquisition began in 1536, forty years after the forced conversions, it focused most of its energy on Judaizers in the large cities of Portugal's center and coastal regions. But by the mid-1570s it turned its attention to the small towns of the far northeast. The Inquisição sent investigative teams to the Beiras in 1575–1576, to Guarda and Viseu in 1578–1579, and to Trás-os-Montes in 1583, including the towns of Torre de Moncorvo, Freixo de Espada-á-Cinta, Mogadouro, Fundão, Covilhã, and São Vicente da Beira, the hometowns of so many of the New Christians who soon thereafter migrated to Mexico.[8]

The investigations shook the confeso communities. Elvira Azevedo's studies of the Portuguese trials from this period indicate that some Judaizing families in the northeast went voluntarily to the Inquisition to confess to minor infractions, seeking to head off more serious accusations. Others relocated to Portuguese towns in other parts of the country, hoping they might avoid denunciations by neighbors who had known their families since they had been Jews and might be hypersensitive to their residual practices. Others slipped back across the border to Spain.[9]

In Fundão, the villagers had been tipped off beforehand that the Holy Office was coming, and they met the visiting Inquisition team with violence. Estêvão Sampaio, the bailiff of Fundão's municipal council, stopped the Inquisition's officer at the church door.[10] This officer, Damião Mendes, reported that several men armed with harquebuses and swords knocked him down, broke his staff of office, seized his sword, roughed up his men, and set their horses loose. The Inquisition officials retreated, but they soon returned in force. After mass arrests and subsequent trials, an auto-de-fé was held in Fundão in April 1582. There a number of Judaizers in *sambenitos* were assigned penances ranging from the mildest—fines, brief imprisonment, public renunciation of their heresy—to the most severe. Several were executed.

Panic swept the region, most strongly in Fundão and its close neighbors Covilhã and São Vicente da Beira. Among those given penance in Fundão were relatives of people who would turn up in Mexico a few years later, where their Old World connection often facilitated their New World friendship. Duarte Rodríguez said that Francisco Rodríguez and his friends revealed their Judaism to him "because they knew some of his relatives in Fundão."[11]

Inquisição activity precipitated the exodus. Events of 1578 and 1580 influenced the patterns of relocation.

By the mid-1570s Portugal's dominance of the maritime trade with India and the Far East was fading into bitter memory. The fortified West African trading centers Portugal had established on the route to India found themselves under frequent attack by the navies of other European powers and the pirates they encouraged. Portugal's charismatic young king, Sebastião, dreamed of a great crusade against Morocco, and in June 1578, at age twenty-four, he led his army, which included a large portion of Portugal's noble class, into the Moroccan interior. At Ksar el-Kabir he encountered a Moroccan force that was superior in both numbers and tactics. After a few short hours of furious engagement, the Portuguese king and much of the ruling class lay dead. Two years later, Sebastião's Spanish uncle, King Felipe II, stepped into the power vacuum and annexed Portugal to Spain.

With the annexation, border restrictions between the two countries all but evaporated. Portugal's Judaizing New Christians were quick to take advantage.[12] In what David L. Graizbord has termed "a momentous shift in the geographic distribution of peninsular Judeoconversos," thousands of Portuguese-Spanish New Christians crossed the border into Spain.[13] Many of them were transients, merely passing through Castilla, Aragón, and Navarra on their way to European havens where they could practice Judaism more openly. Yet even though these destinations were well-known, some Portuguese crypto-Jews chose to remain in Spain or migrate to the Spanish colonies in the Americas. What must have seemed to them at the moment a wise decision eventually led to regret, for many of the Portuguese Judaizers did not fare well in Spain or its overseas dominions. In later years, the unchosen havens shimmered in the dreams that many of them related to their interrogators in both Spain and the Americas.[14]

Most of the rest of the conversos discussed in this book arrived in Mexico between 1580 and 1588, with the largest single party—many of them in family groups—disembarking in Tampico early in 1580 from the ship *Nuestra Señora de la Luz* in an expedition organized by Governor Luis de Carvajal y de la Cueva:

1580
    Governor Luis de Carvajal y de la Cueva[15]
    Felipe Núñez (governor's wife's brother)
    Francisca Núñez Viciosa (governor's wife's half sister)
    Alonso del Águila (Francisca Núñez Viciosa's husband)
    Francisca Rodríguez de Carvajal (governor's sister; wife of Francisco Rodríguez de Matos)
    Francisco Rodríguez de Matos (doña Francisca's husband)
    The Carvajals: eight of the couple's nine children: Isabel, Baltazar, Catalina, Luis, Mariana, Miguel, Leonor, Ana
    Gonzalo Pérez Ferro (governor's cousin)
    Catalina de León Carvajal (wife)
    Jorge de León (Catalina de León's brother)
    Ginebra Márquez de León (widow; Catalina de León's sister)
    Diego Márquez de Andrada (Catalina de León's brother)
    Manuel de Morales and his family
        Isabel López Pérez (wife)
        Andrés de Morales (brother)
        Bartolomé de Morales (brother)
        Three unnamed sisters
        Two unnamed children[16]
        Juan de Nava
        Juana de Muñoz, (wife of Juan de Nava)
        Catalina Enríquez
        Clara Enríquez[17]

1581
- Beatriz Enríquez la Paiba
- Paiba, Simón (return trip late 1580?)

1582
- Antonio Méndez

1582
- Antonio Álvarez (Manuel Álvarez's granddaughter)
- Manuel Álvarez
- Leonor Rodríguez (Manuel Álvarez's wife)

1583
- Domingo Rodríguez

1587
- Manuel Álvarez
- Manuel Díaz
- Antonio Fernández
- Diego López
- Isabel López
- Antonio Rodríguez (Manuel Álvarez's son-in-law)
- Francisco Rodríguez
- Isabel Rodríguez (Manuel Díaz's wife)

1588
- Gómez de Casteloblanco, Manuel

Mexican bishop Juan de Zumárraga had been granted inquisitorial powers in 1535, and over the next third of a century there had been sporadic prosecutions in New Spain for Judaizing. Institutional branches of the Spanish Inquisition were established in 1570 in Lima, 1571 in Mexico City (which also exercised jurisdiction over Spain's Asiatic colonies), and 1610 in Cartagena de Indias. In every corner of the worldwide Iberian Empire Judaizing conversos were being arrested and sometimes tortured; their assets were being seized;

some were being publicly burned, their exemplary punishment intended as a deterrent.

In Portugal the Judaizers' dilemma was similar to the one that had confronted Spanish Jews in the spring of 1492: whether to elect to be openly and for the most part safely Jewish somewhere outside of Iberia or risk being secretly and dangerously crypto-Jewish within their familiar Iberian world. Almost always it was the men who made the choices; social mores and the laws that embodied them made it very difficult for women to make such decisions independently. Men had to take stock of their religious values and assess the ranges of potential risks to their families. In the balance, if a Portuguese crypto-Jew cared more about being Jewish than anything else in his life, he was likely to flee the lands that were under Iberian control. If he cared more about economic opportunities, ties with Iberian family members, or the familiarity of known environments, he emigrated to Spain or even to America. Inaction, too, was a choice; some Portuguese Judaizers—like some Jews in Germany in the 1930s—dithered at home until it was too late.

Some confesos, such as the family of Manuel de Lucena, made an initial choice to leave the Iberian world but then had second thoughts. In 1570, when Manuel was six years old, his family took him from Portugal to the Italian duchy of Ferrara, which, thanks to the supportive policies of the ruling Este family in those years, may well have been the most welcoming place in Europe for Jews. In 1578, following an economic downturn in Ferrara, the Lucenas returned to Iberia. The following year, fourteen-year-old Manuel, without the others, sailed from Sevilla to Mexico, where eventually he opened a store in Pachuca. In September 1596, three months before he was burned at the stake in Mexico City at age thirty-two, he recounted to Inquisitors how his friends "used to take pleasure when they heard [me] tell that Jews in Turkey and Italy were very happy and suffered none of the restrictions that reign here."[18] Lucena was never recorded as having uttered the phrase "I wish now that my family had stayed in Italy," but he must surely have thought it.

We will probably never know precisely why Jews and Judaizers who were resident in Europe's safe havens turned so blind an eye to the risks inherent in their going back. The Lucena family's return from Ferrara to Iberia and then travel to the New World was not an isolated case.[19] The Portuguese confeso Ruy (Rodrigo) Díaz Nieto migrated first to the Low Countries and then to Ferrara, where he was known as Isaac Nieto. In 1551, when Ferrara expelled its New Christians, Díaz Nieto went back to Portugal. After a few years he returned to Ferrara, married, had a son, relocated to Venice, and returned to Spain; he sailed with his son to Mexico in 1594.[20] Juan Rodríguez de Silva, a Portuguese who had resided for a time in the Jewish quarter of the Greek-Ottoman port city of Salonica, returned to Madrid, and in 1590 he observed Yom Kippur in Mexico.[21] Another returnee was Jorge Jacinto Bazán, whose parents had migrated from Málaga to Marseilles and from there to Pisa, Livorno, and Salonica; Bazán was documented in Mexico in 1637.[22]

Judaizing conversos in New Spain almost never talked about why they had come to the New World. I have seen no evidence that they hoped to find a place in which they could practice their religion with more freedom than in the havens of Europe. The clues that surface in the documentation suggest quite a different motivation: the New World colonies offered to Judaizers willing to accept the risks associated with remaining in the Iberian ambit a chance to make a great deal of money in a relatively short time. Tropical woods, sugar, cacao, cochineal, slaves, and silver—the streets of the colonial world were not paved with precious metals, but to hear the talk in the taverns of Iberia, one might just believe they were. Going to America seems to have been mostly about economic opportunity. It may have been fear of the Inquisition that impelled New Christians to leave Portugal, but it was the dream of wealth that drew the ambitious and adventurous among them to the Indies.[23] Manuel de Lucena expressed this unambiguously in prison in Mexico in 1596 in a conversation with Fernán Rodríguez de Herrera:[24]

> Rodríguez de Herrera remarked that many Jews are going from Spain to France, some by land and some by sea, and when they get to Bordeaux they dress like Jews and they can go wherever they like. And I replied: "May God not take me until I can see my whole household in one of those places where they can see themselves free of the Christians' oppression of the Jews." And Fernán Rodríguez replied to me: "Well what do you think has brought me here to the Indies except that same reason and desire that you have spoken?" Meaning, I believe that he had come to the Indies to earn money to finance taking his family to those places.[25]

Sevilla

Almost without exception, to get to the Indies, immigrants had to pass through Spain's single authorized gateway to the New World, Sevilla.[26] Already Spain's biggest port when Gabriel de Castellanos and his family passed through in 1534, by the late sixteenth century Sevilla had become one of ten European megacities cities with populations numbering over one hundred thousand.[27] These economic powerhouses were creative engines of art, culture, and, above all, trade. On Sevilla's wharves, products destined for sale in the Americas jostled for space with raw materials and finished goods fashioned in the New World for European markets. When boats ferrying cargo from the deep-water American fleet tied up alongside the Torre de Oro, Sevilla's citizens could watch the oxcarts heaped with American silver hauling up from the wharves to the Casa de Contratación next to the cathedral. In Sevilla's air, the scent of money to be made was palpable. The city was an exciting, flamboyant magnet for talent, for adventurers, for entrepreneurial merchants and rapacious bankers, for people willing to accept the risks of investing in precarious ocean voyages.

There was money to be made on both sides of the ocean, for Sevilla the entrepôt was far more than just a transit point on the way to the Indies. A substantial number of the Portuguese Judaizers in Mexico in the 1580s and 1590s had lived and worked in Sevilla for years before relocating to America. For these men, Sevilla had become a second home, and as such the city contributed yet another stratum to their multitiered sense of identity. Manuel Gómez de Casteloblanco, for example, had been a jobber based in Sevilla who sold goods to small stores throughout Andalucía. His brother Gonzalo Rodríguez had a store on Calle de la Sierpe, both then and today Sevilla's main commercial thoroughfare and now known simply as Sierpes.[28] Diego López Regalón, born in São Vicente da Beira, owned a store on Calle de la Sierpe for twenty-eight years before migrating to Mexico in 1588 with his wife, Ana López, from Fundão.[29] Francisco Rodríguez's parents brought him to Sevilla from São Vicente da Beira when he was eleven. They apprenticed him to the Portuguese merchant Gabriel Herrera, who had a store on Calle de la Sierpe, where Francisco worked for eight years before crossing to the Indies.[30] Nine of the Portuguese Judaizers who ran afoul of the Inquisition in Mexico in the 1590s had owned stores on that one Sevillan street in the 1580s.[31]

Some Judaizers shuttled back and forth from Sevilla to Portugal quite regularly for business or to visit family, which were often one and the same reason. Manuel Álvarez, born in Fundão in 1540, was apprenticed by his parents when he was twelve to an uncle who was a tailor in Lisbon. At fourteen he was back in Fundão working for another uncle, freighting goods from Fundão to sell in Sevilla. After a couple of years of that, he struck out on his own, renting rooms in Sevilla for the next eight years while he peddled goods through the villages around Andalucía. At age twenty-four he went back to Fundão, married Leonor Rodríguez, and spent the next four years peddling linen cloth and thread in both Portugal and Andalucía. Once he had amassed sufficient capital, he opened a store on Calle de la Sierpe; he and his wife sailed to Mexico in 1588.[32]

Many international trading families of this period found it useful to keep one foot in Europe (which for purposes of trade meant Sevilla) and one foot in the Americas (the Caribbean islands, Veracruz, or Mexico City). Often one family member, such as Duarte Rodríguez, sank roots in Sevilla, where he could function as the eastern terminus of a shipping network, while another member would establish himself in America. In this family, Duarte's brother Simón Rodríguez supervised the sale of European imported goods and gathered raw materials or finished items to be shipped back to Spain.[33] Other Judaizers, after working for a few years in Mexico, went back to Europe to live. Simón Antúnez, after several seasons in Mexico City, returned and opened another store on Calle de la Sierpe.[34] Manuel de Morales, one of Mexico's most knowledgeable and enthusiastic Judaizers, returned to Sevilla in 1590. There he sheltered Luis de Carvajal's brothers Miguel and Baltazar when they managed to evade the Inquisition in Mexico.[35] Jorge de Almeida fled his Taxco silver hacienda in 1590 one step ahead of the Inquisition, to return to Spain.

In Sevilla these men did business together and socialized together. Within the limitations imposed by prudence, they shared with each other their knowledge of the Law of Moses. In groups constituted by extended family, business connections, and place of origin, they gathered to celebrate the major Jewish festivals or to share a Sabbath meal. The more learned among them, men such as Simón Antúnez and Manuel Álvarez and women such as

Inés Fernández and Leonor Rodríguez, took it on themselves to boost the level of knowledge and observance among the others.[36]

The *Confesos*

The family of Gabriel de Castellanos's son Tomás de Fonseca and grandson young Tomás de Fonseca Castellanos exemplify the amalgam of Spanish and Portuguese identity in this community. In crisscrossing the geographic border between Spain and Portugal and the religious and cultural borders between Judaism and Catholicism, the Fonseca-Castellanos family exhibits patterns of settlement and migration that were common among converso families in northwestern Spain and northeastern Portugal during the century and a half following the great expulsions.

Gabriel's journey to New Spain preceded by some four decades the migration of the first large cohort of Portuguese confesos, who arrived in the last quarter of the sixteenth century. Of the people whom the Mexican Inquisition accused of Judaizing between 1589 and 1604, 104 individuals are identified in the documents by country of birth.[37] Seventy-six of these (73 percent) were born in Portugal. Of the sixty-six Portuguese Judaizers who are also identified by the town in which they were born, fifty-four (82 percent) were born in the northeast, in towns belonging then principally to the bishopric of Guarda, in that part of the Raya de Portugal today called Trás-os-Montes and Beira Alta. This region had been an important magnet for Jews from the border region of Castilla.[38] Furthermore, thirty-four (52 percent) of these Portuguese-Mexican Judaizers came from a single cluster of three small towns lying close together on the east-facing slopes of the Serra da Gardunha: Fundão, Covilhã, and São Vicente da Beira.[39]

The twenty-eight Spanish-born Mexican Judaizers from this period were all born in Castilla. Twelve of them (43 percent) were from towns close to the border with Portugal. Another eight (29 percent) said they were born in Sevilla, a city whose role as gateway to the Indies meant that a substantial portion of its population was transient. The parents of six of those eight had been born in Fundão.[40]

MEXICAN JUDAIZERS 1580–1600 BORN IN PORTUGAL

Portuguese Birth Towns of Mexican Judaizers

Fundão	19
São Vicente da Beira	11
Covilhã	4
Total	34

Almeida	1
Castelobranco	2
Celorico	1
Escarigo	1
Freixo de Espada-à-Cinta	2
Guarda	1
Lamego	1
Mogadouro	1
Sarzeda	4
Seia	4
Vila Flor	1
Total	19

Other Portuguese Birth Cities and Towns of Mexican Judaizers

Alvalade	1
Braga	1
Lisboa	3
Porto	3
São João da Pesqueira	1
Santa Comba Dão	1
Viseu	3
Total	13

Portugal, Town Unspecified

Total	10

Total Portuguese birth towns of Mexican Judaizers = 76

MEXICAN JUDAIZERS 1580–1600 BORN IN SPAIN

Castilian Birth Towns from the Raya de Portugal
- Barrueco Pardo (Salamanca) — 1
- Benavente (Zamora) — 8
- Cáceres (Cáceres) — 1
- Jarandilla de la Vera (Cáceres) — 1
- San Martín de Trevejo (Cáceres) — 1
- Total — 12

Castilian Birth Towns from Other Provinces
- Cervera del Río Pisuerga (Palencia) — 1
- Medina del Campo (Valladolid) — 3
- Morón de la Frontera (Sevilla) — 1
- Sevilla (Sevilla) — 8
- Teba (Málaga) — 2
- Total — 15

Spain, Town Unspecified
- Total — 1

Total Spanish birth towns of Mexican Judaizers 28

Data compiled by Stanley Hordes indicate that the second great cohort of crypto-Jews, those who came to Mexico between the 1620s and 1640s and fell victim to the second great purge of Judaizers in the late 1640s, were born in the same array of Portuguese towns.[41] The data also suggest that the Inquisition in Mexico, fully cognizant of the substantial differences between the processes of conversion and assimilation of Jews in Spain and Portugal, in these two great purges focused more intensively on the Portuguese immigrant confeso community than on the New Christian conversos of exclusively Spanish descent.[42]

Sense of Identity

The Portuguese-Spanish crypto-Jews in Mexico in the late sixteenth century were a clearly identifiable group, both to outsiders and to themselves. Mexican Inquisition documents consistently labeled them "Portuguese," for want of a better term to indicate their fused identity.[43] Members of this Spanish-Portuguese community also routinely thought of themselves as a class apart. Witnesses testifying to the Inquisition made a point of indicating which people were Portuguese. Leonor Meléndez, serving as a character witness for Jorge Fernández in 1600, told inquisitors that although she knew him well when he served her family as an errand boy and squire, she had never known his name: "We usually just called him *el portugués*."[44] The storekeeper Manuel Álvarez and the street vendor Jorge Fernández each emphasized the distinction when they testified that they served both Portuguese and Castilian clients.[45]

For a New Christian, to be Portuguese, or even to associate with Portuguese people, incurred risk. Everyone knew that by the early 1580s, *portugués* had become a de facto synonym for crypto-Jew.[46] Antonio Méndez said that Jorge Álvarez had assumed he was a Jew "because I am Portuguese."[47] Almost everyone—members of the Portuguese Judaizing community and the Old Christian world at large—believed that New Christian families inevitably passed on their Judaizing habits. Antonio Gómez expressed it in a ditty: "Fillo es y pay serás / como fizeres asi, eo aurás" (You are a son, you'll be a father; as you do, so will they).[48]

No wonder, then, that when some members of the community were arrested, they attempted—always unsuccessfully—to distance themselves from the *portugueses*. Few put it quite as clearly as old Tomás de Fonseca when he recited his capsule biography to inquisitors in 1596: "I have had dealings with all of the principal people of this land, and I have always tried to avoid dealing with the Portuguese." When the inquisitor asked him why that was, he replied: "Because I find the Portuguese nation are rough in manner, different from Castilians; . . . the Castilians with whom I was raised and spent my life are all noble and straightforward people."[49] The inquisitors were well aware—because old Tomás had already told them—that he himself had been born in Portugal, in Freixo de Espada-à-Cinta, but they refrained from pointing out to him the irony of his remarks.

Membership in this hybrid community elicited mixed emotions: fear at being a likely target of inquisitorial scrutiny; pride in belonging to a cohesive group of people, a nation (*nação*), with a sense of its fervent commitment to its Jewish heritage; pride that sometimes expressed itself in annoyance when a fellow Portuguese was not observant enough. Manuel de Morales, who was born in the northern Portugal village of Seia and spent much of his youth in Venice, was heard to complain that "he didn't like dealing with the Portuguese people in Mexico City because they didn't keep the Sabbath as perfectly as the commandments of the Law of Moses required."[50]

The Portuguese language, too, contributed to this sense of group identity. Inquisition documents make clear that members of this community were by and large bilingual. Carlos Rodríguez, from Covilhã, spoke half in Spanish and half in Portuguese.[51] Gaspar de Mesa, who in the early 1590s called himself Juan Martín, had trouble being understood because "he spoke Portuguese with a heavy accent, and his Spanish was barely intelligible."[52] Sebastián Nieto, likewise, was never able to shake his Portuguese accent; his brother Antonio Nieto, on the other hand, spoke both languages perfectly. For many people, even a trace of a Portuguese accent was assumed to indicate converso origin.[53] Diego Díaz Nieto, born Ferrara to a Portuguese-Spanish father, with whom he came to Mexico in 1594, indiscriminately mixed Spanish and Portuguese versions of the Psalms in his prayers.[54] Manuel Tavares is another example. When the Inquisition arrested him in 1596 and he claimed to be a faithful Christian, they gave him the usual test, which was to recite the principal Christian prayers. The scribe noted that Tavares "gave his responses in Latin and crossed himself in Spanish; he said the Our Father, the Hail Mary, and the Apostles' Creed half in Spanish and half in Portuguese, and the Salve Regina in good Latin."[55]

Although Spanish was the street language of members of this community in Mexico, for intimate matters many felt more comfortable in Portuguese. Julián de Castellanos sought out the priest Antonio Fraile as his confessor because, he said, "he was a very old man, and very well known, and he was Portuguese, you could tell it by the way he talked."[56] For members of this community, salting their speech with the occasional Portuguese phrase was a kind of touchstone of identity, an assertion of membership in a special group of people. They were most likely to break into Portuguese when religion was the issue. One day, when Manuel Tavares and his friend Diego

Enríquez were dallying in setting off to mass, Diego's mother, Catalina Enríquez, jokingly urged them to get moving: "*Anda, anda, que muito ben lo has menester*" (Go on, go on; you need it, it's good for you).[57] When Luis de Carvajal remarked that the Bible relates how God promises to reward the people of Israel, Clara Enríquez chimed in: "*Pues nahó sab ho senhor mentir*" (God does not know how to lie).[58] Manuel Tavares, explaining to a cell mate why he had been praising the Law of Moses, exclaimed, mixing Spanish and Portuguese "*Dios me deje falar*" (May God let me speak).[59] One day an exasperated Cristóbal Gómez "sighed and raised his eyes to the sky and said: *O senhor mos lleve a tierra donde le podamos servir sin temer de nuestros enemigos*" (May God take us to a land where we can serve him without being afraid of our enemies). Francisco Rodríguez said that when he visited Beatriz Enríquez la Paiba in Mexico City in 1581, he said to her: "*Parécesme, señora, uma das judeas da nossa terra*" (It seems to me, Lady, you're one of the Jews of our land). Smiling at him, Beatriz replied: "*Oye, o senhor Francisco o qué me diz*" (Oh, tsk, the things this Senhor Francisco says to me!)[60] One time, when Rodrigo Tavares noticed a crucifix with a Christ figure hanging on a wall in a corner of Pedro Enríquez's store, he asked him in Spanish: "*¿Cómo tenéis éste aquí?*" (What's this guy doing up there?). Enríquez snapped back in Portuguese: "*He porque venda ben o vinho*" (It's because he's so good at selling wine). Tavares came right back in Spanish: "*Antes entiendo que se os ha de volver vinagre*" (More likely he'll turn it to vinegar).[61] The record of the second trial of Luis de Carvajal the younger is dotted with snippets of conversation in Portuguese like these.[62] Code-switching, slang, cursing, dirty jokes. Francisco Rodríguez said that as a practicing Jew, he believed that Christian sacraments such as baptism and confession, and the church's power to grant certificates of indulgence, were a joke. A witness reported that one day when Manuel Tavares told him he was on his way to church to pick up his jubilee indulgence, Rodríguez said to him in Portuguese: "*Ya vas ao meter no cu.*" For the inquisitor's benefit, the witness added, "*que quiere decir en castellano: Ya vais a meterlo en el culo*" (which means in Spanish: you'll shove it up your ass).[63]

Facility with the Portuguese language was a credential that gained a person entry to this community. Not knowing the language well could leave a person—even a person like Manuel de Lucena, who had been born in São Vicente da Beira—feeling excluded. Lucena often spent the Sabbath at the home of Manuel de Morales, who was born in Seia, in the Portuguese bishopric of Guarda in Trás-os-Montes. Morales would invite his guests to take turns reading aloud Bible stories that he kept locked in his writing desk. Lucena complained that when his turn came, "I couldn't read them because the papers were in the Portuguese language."[64] Antonio Méndez's daughter Isabel was similarly frustrated when she and her family interrupted their Passover celebration at Jorge Álvarez's house on the Calle Tacuba in Mexico City in 1592 to watch the Holy Thursday processions through the windows. Isabel reported that the Portuguese women were making fun of the marchers, but she could not tell exactly what they were saying because they were speaking Portuguese.[65] Probably these women were just making rude jokes in the language in which they were most comfortable. Other times, the use of Portuguese was clearly intended to exclude. Juan Pérez, who in 1597 shared a cell with Antonio Gómez and Rodrigo Tavares, complained that the two men not only sang songs in Portuguese but they spoke Portuguese when they didn't want him to understand.[66] Rodrigo's son Manuel shared his cell with Manuel Gómez Silveira and Jorge Fernández. When they wanted to exclude their fourth cell mate, the German Lutheran Simón de Santiago, they switched from Spanish to Portuguese.[67]

> Members of this Portuguese-Spanish Judaizing community considered themselves and comported themselves like what historian Américo Castro called a *casta*, a racially grounded term that assumes that the character and quality of an identifiable group of people are heavily influenced by their race, ethnic type, color, and sometimes birth country, religion, and language. Although the term *casta* in later years took on a very different meaning in Mexico, Castro used it to refer to a coherent group that is perceived as such by both members of the group and people external to the group.[68]

The Portuguese-Spanish Judaizing community to which old Tomás de Fonseca and his nephew Young Tomás adhered pegged its identity both to its members' residual Jewishness and to the very obvious Portuguese component of their identity. Either of these traits provided sufficient grounds to infer the other. Young Tomás knew that Duarte and Catalina Rodríguez were Jews because "they were of that *casta*, and were relatives of Justa Méndez."[69] When people did something Jewish, they were likely to say that they were doing it "a uso de Portugal" (in the Portuguese way).[70] Members of the group were proud to be Jews, and they were also proud to be Portuguese, members of a nação, a "nation" of families that during their frequent backing-and-forthing across the rugged border between Spain and Portugal over a period of 100 or 150 years had acquired a sense of Portuguese identity.[71] They tended to be familiar enough with the Portuguese language that they could use it as an identity-supporting device among themselves and as a secret language to keep their practices and opinions from the ears of the *castellanos* among whom they were immersed. They spoke of themselves as Portuguese, and they were labeled Portuguese both by their inquisitors and by the Castilian laypeople who turned them in. In almost every way, they formed a cohesive group. According to Julián de Castellanos, the priest Antonio Fraile was a good friend of Cosme Pereira "because they were both Portuguese, and all the members of this nation are good friends."[72] As Manuel Gómez Navarro put it in 1594, "they all deal familiarly with one another, and they do favors for each other, and they are all friends of the Carvajals, young Luis and his mother and his siblings."[73] Coreligionists by birth and by desire, they were neighbors in Portugal, neighbors in Sevilla, and neighbors in Mexico.

Chapter 9

From Solitary Worship to Community

> At Luis de Carvajal's house I often ate with Manuel de Lucena and other times with Tomás de Fonseca, the one from the mines of Taxco, and with Manuel Gómez Navarro, and with Cristóbal Gómez the Portuguese.
>
> —JUSTA MÉNDEZ, FEBRUARY 1595[1]

> About a year ago, traveling to Pachuca in the company of Manuel de Lucena and Sebastián Rodríguez, a little beyond the Carpio Inn, the two of them sang a song of the Law of Moses that begins "When we were captives we were walking by the rivers of Babylon," and so forth. When they finished singing, they talked about the Law of Moses.
>
> —MANUEL GÓMEZ NAVARRO, 1596.[2]

ALTHOUGH INDISPUTABLY MANY individuals of Jewish ancestry, and some of what they held to be Jewish beliefs and practices, made their way to the Indies during the first fifty years of colonization, evidence for any *community* of Judaizers during this period is thin. With the notable exception of Gabriel de Castellanos, evidence suggests that by and large the conversos who came to New Spain during the first half century of colonization were not very knowledgeable about Judaism or scrupulous in observing its customs. Most of the handful who were prosecuted for Judaizing were accused of expressing disrespect for Christian icons and ritual and for not fulfilling the routine obligations imposed by the church; only in rare instances were they said to follow specific precepts of the Jewish law. Hernando Alonso[3] and Gonzalo de

Morales,[4] who were burned in 1528 as the colony's first two alleged Judaizers, were accused respectively of staging a burlesque baptism and of urinating on a crucifix. Diego de Ocaña, a notary from Sevilla who was assigned penance in the same auto-de-fé, was said to have violated the church's prohibition against eating meat on Fridays, slaughtered fowl in the Jewish fashion, and avoided eating scaleless fish.[5] In 1536 Gonzalo Gómez, a farmer in Michoacán, was alleged to have avoided going to mass, denied the existence of hell and purgatory, mocked the sacraments, mistreated Christian icons, and encouraged fornication; in addition, he was alleged to have avoided working or traveling on the Sabbath.[6] The next man to be charged with Judaizing, Francisco Millán, from the Andalusian city of Utrera, in 1539 was also accused of having desecrated a Christian image.[7] Bishop Juan de Zumárraga, responding to rumors of widespread Judaizing in the colony, launched an investigation, but of the dozen or so people accused by informants, only one was brought to trial: Juan de Baeza, who in 1540 was accused of having circumcised some Indian children.[8] During these years. the single accusation of Judaizing against a woman, Beatriz Hernández, was not deemed serious enough to pursue.[9] Overlooked in these early inquiries of alleged Judaizers were Gabriel de Castellanos and his family, who had come to Mexico in 1534.

Scholars who have focused their attention on the demographic profile of colonizers in Mexico from the mid-1520s to the mid-1570s tend to echo Seymour Liebman's explanations of why it is so difficult to estimate the numbers of converso immigrants, the proportion of conversos in colonial society, or the proportion of Judaizers among the conversos. Liebman noted that because of regulations prohibiting people with Jewish or Muslim ancestors from entering the Indies, conversos (such as Gabriel de Castellanos in 1534) often deliberately obfuscated their genealogies. He pointed out the unreliability of the labels applied to individuals in many documents, how the Inquisition in the early years often characterized people who exhibited certain behaviors or beliefs as Lutherans (that is, Protestants) or Alumbrados,[10] and how by the last quarter of the century, the term *portugués* had become usually, but not always, synonymous with *converso*. He suspected a serious undercounting of conversos by missionaries, who were focused almost exclusively on indigenous communities, and by secular clergy, some of whom were themselves conversos and were uncomfortable drawing attention to matters of ancestry. Unfortunately Liebman, along with many other investigators, complicated these issues—and misled readers—by intermittently labeling all conversos as Jews, without distinguishing their ancestry from their current religious identity.[11]

Since the time of the Jerusalem Talmud, Judaism has required a quorum (minyan) of ten adult males for certain components of congregational worship. The minyan bolstered the natural inclination of like-minded and like-cultured people to associate with one another. It provided mechanisms for finding mates, acculturating children, and burying the dead. As in any closely knit community, the centripetal force generated by group membership fostered communality and discouraged deviance by members. Thus it constituted a defense against the seductive or coercive pressures to assimilate to the majority cultures among which Jews almost always found themselves living.

The concept of minyan—that is, of the requirement of a quorum for certain ritual observances—was not in the repertoire of beliefs or practices that conversos brought with them to the New World, at least not in any way that was formally noted. Moreover, if the converso men who came to Mexico during the first half century of Spanish dominion felt the need to come together to express their Jewishness, they did not act on those feelings in ways that would attract attention. For these years, we have no evidence of groups coming together to mark life-cycle events according to Jewish custom: no gatherings for funerals, ritual circumcisions, or weddings. Ensuring generational continuity was not high on their list of priorities, for the children fathered during these and subsequent years by old Tomás de Fonseca, Julián de Castellanos, young Tomás de Fonseca Castellanos, Álvaro de Carrión, and Héctor de Fonseca had indigenous or Old Christian mothers, and the men made no efforts to pass their religious traditions on to their progeny, or at least no efforts that were noticed and recorded.

In the first half century of New Spain, those converso immigrants who chose to nurture their Jewish identity tended to do so as individuals or within the narrow confines of family. Among the conversos we have been discussing, the only Judaizing activity in the Mexican mining reales prior to 1570 was reported in 1590 by Julián de Castellanos, who testified that he had heard that his half brother old Tomás de Fonseca and his nephew young Tomás de Fonseca Castellanos had observed one Yom Kippur fast together in the mid-1560s while they were working in Tlalpujahua.[12] In Mexico City, Gabriel de Castellanos, after he had returned from mining in Ayoteco, sometimes observed the Sabbath or Jewish festivals with his son Julián and with his daughter Guiomar and her second husband, Cosme de Pereira.

Prior to 1570 in the viceroyalty of Mexico there appear to have been no Jewish catalysts, no enthusiastic proselytizers of Judaism reaching out to other conversos to convene them to celebrate their Jewishness communally. The 1570s saw the arrival in Mexico of a number of other Judaizing conversos, nearly all of them born in Portugal, who brought with them some knowledge about Jewish rules of observance and some degree of commitment to living their Jewishness. However, if these men Judaized during the 1570s, for the most part it was in ones and twos.

This was especially true for men who sought their fortunes in the distant mining camps, such as Héctor de Fonseca. Very shortly after his arrival in Mexico in 1571, Héctor struck out for the northern silver fields. After brief, unsuccessful stints in Zacatecas, Mazapil, and Tlalpujahua, where he left no evidence of having Judaized, he settled in Taxco, where his cousin young Tomás de Fonseca was working at Gaspar de Enciso's silver-refining hacienda. Encisco's wife, Felipa, who was old Tomás de Fonseca's niece and Héctor's cousin, had been raised as a Christian by Guiomar and her first husband, Antonio Pérez Herrero. Despite the fact they were related and nearly neighbors, Héctor does not seem to have had much to do with his cousins. It was only after the arrival of two of his younger brothers, Jorge de Almeida and Miguel Hernández, and his proselytization by Luis Díaz in 1583, more than a decade later, that Héctor began to interact Jewishly with other conversos.

In the late 1570s, young Tomás de Fonseca was observed excising the sinew from a leg of lamb before roasting it; the same witness noted his avoidance of pork.[13] But no other allegations from that period surfaced in his trial. Diego López Regalón and his wife, Ana Arenas López, both from Fundão, brought their twelve-year-old musician son, Antonio López, to Puebla in 1573, but the first references to either of them Judaizing also come more than a decade later.[14] From 1572 on, Antonio Díaz de Cáceres was doing business in Mexico City. Sometime during the next five years, he must have made the acquaintance of old Tomás de Fonseca, for there is a reference to their having fallen out over a business deal.[15] But neither Antonio Díaz nor old Tomás reports a mutual friendship from that period, nor any shared Judaizing experience. Simón Paiba in the late 1570s was establishing his retail business in Mexico City. His active Judaizing is not documented until his family joined him in the early 1580s. If Judaizing individuals in Mexico during the 1570s felt the need to adhere to a community, they never expressed that hunger in such a way that it became part of the record.

It was in the early 1580s, when unsettled conditions in Portugal, the merger of that country with Spain, and intensified Inquisition activity in the border areas had loosed a stream of emigration, that conversos began to appear in the colonies in sufficient numbers to make possible, perhaps inevitable, communal Judaizing. Even so, during the decade from 1579 to 1588, the Mexican Holy Office opened procesos for Judaizing against only five individuals. As it turned out, only one of the five, Garci González y Bemerejo (or Bermeguero), had engaged in any overtly Jewish religious customs.[16]

The wave of conversos who arrived in the 1580s congregated in Mexico City, with some of the more adventurous fanning out to the mining communities.

Toward the end of that decade, the number of Judaizing conversos had risen to what authorities deemed to be intolerable proportions. The Inquisition's onslaught against the communities of secret Judaizers began in 1589 when Isabel de Carvajal, under questioning, began pouring out information about the Judaizing activities of her friends, acquaintances, and family members. In short order, the Inquisition opened procesos against ten Judaizers, eight of whom were members of the extended Carvajal family.[17]

The Mexican inquisitors—and through them, modern scholars—came to know more about Luis de Carvajal, his siblings, and his uncle Luis de Carvajal the governor than they did about any other Mexican Judaizers during the sixteenth century. Almost all procesos of alleged Judaizers in Mexico between 1589 and 1596 include testimony by or about young Luis de Carvajal and his family. The scandalous Jewishness of the Carvajal clan was so

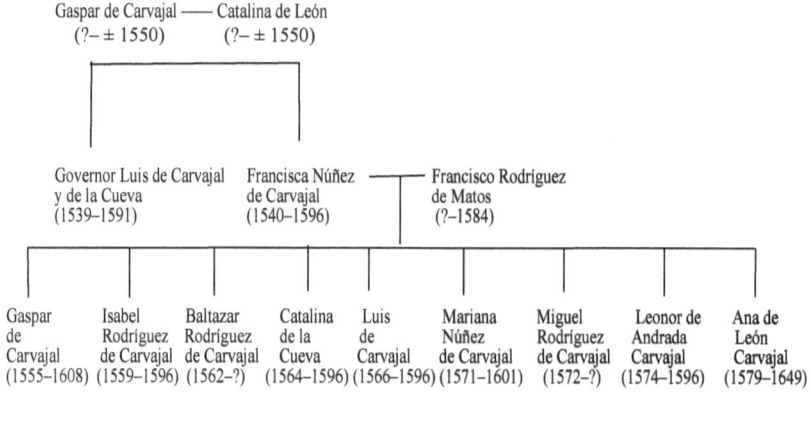

well-known that to allege that someone was a friend of the Carvajals was enough to taint him or her prima facie with the stain of Judaism.[18]

The bare outline of the coming of the Carvajals to Mexico is this:[19] Luis de Carvajal y de la Cueva, born into a well-placed family of conversos who were active in the Raya de Portugal, first made his mark as an accountant to the Portuguese monarchy, serving for thirteen years in the Cape Verde Islands in the lucrative trade of shipping slaves to the Iberian colonies in America. In 1568, as captain of his own ship and as second in command of Spain's Indies fleet, he sailed to Mexico, where he was named municipal magistrate (alcalde) of the rapidly growing port of Tampico on the northern Gulf Coast. When a company of English pirates led by John Hawkins was stranded on the coast in the fall of that year, Carvajal successfully rounded them up and turned them over to viceroyalty officials. With Carvajal's military competence thus established, the viceroy commissioned him to open a road from the port to the mining district of Mazapil, some four hundred kilometers inland, across the forbidding, tangled mass of the Sierra Madre Oriental. This Carvajal did, and in the process he began to subdue the hostile indigenous groups that were obstructing Spanish efforts to settle Mexico's vast northeast. He may also have participated financially in some of the Mazapil mines.[20] He also was rumored to have used his authority to illegally import African slaves into the northeast region and to have bought and sold Indian slaves. Recalled to Mexico City and chastised, Carvajal y de la Cueva was sent back to Spain.

From these lemons the able soldier made lemonade, persuading the Council of the Indies in Sevilla in 1579 to appoint him governor and captain-general of northeastern Mexico, which was to be named Nuevo León. In return, Carvajal promised to recruit one hundred soldiers and sixty married families, at his own expense, to develop the region's Gulf and river ports, to subdue the Native inhabitants, and to populate the region between Tampico and the Mazapil mines. But Carvajal also imposed one further condition on the council: that his recruits be exempted from having to prove their Old Christian lineage to pass to the Indies. Surprisingly, this exemption was formally granted, apparently for the first and only time in the history of the development of New Spain. With his orders in hand, Carvajal scoured the Raya de Portugal for his pioneers. At least eighteen of his recruits were members of Carvajal's own extended family,[21] and others were his personal friends. Many of the recruits were conversos, eager to put distance between themselves and the increasingly threatening conditions in the Raya.

In the close quarters of the long sea journey on the governor's ship *Nuestra Señora de la Luz*, members of the governor's party opened up to each other and began to forge the bonds that would lead to their becoming a community. Three of their party fell ill during the voyage: Isabel López Pérez, the wife of Dr. Manuel de Morales; the doctor's brother Francisco Hernández; and one of Isabel López's sisters. The latter two died en route. The illnesses, and the deaths, also helped create a sense of intimacy. Doña Francisca de Carvajal took care of the doctor's wife and talked for hours with her and with Hernández's widow. Once Isabel had wormed out of Francisca that the Carvajals were Judaizers, the two families quickly bonded, and the doctor and his wife began to share information with her about their Jewish knowledge and practices. According to Francisca,

> Morales and his sister-in-law said that it was good to fast on Tuesdays and Fridays for the dead . . . and on Sundays and Mondays pray the Penitential Psalms for the people of Israel, and Wednesday and Thursday for one's own sins, and whatever other prayers one might know; and

on Friday evenings light a lamp in the name of the Lord because that would bring glory and rest to the deceased people of Israel; and it had to burn until it went out by itself. And keep the Sabbath after cleaning and decorating the house and putting on one's best clothes.... They asked me which of my people kept that law, and I said that all my children who were accompanying me did except Isabel, who did not yet know it.[22]

Doña Francisca de Carvajal was the governor's sister (also known as Francisca Núñez and Francisca Rodríguez de Carvajal). With her on board were her husband, Francisco Rodríguez de Matos, and eight of their nine children, who, in accord with a practice not unusual in late sixteenth-century Spain,[23] were known by a number of different surnames:

Isabel Rodríguez de Andrada (Isabel de Carvajal), who in 1580 was twenty-one and recently widowed
Baltazar Rodríguez de Carvajal, eighteen, who would one day flee Iberia and call himself David Lumbroso
Catalina León de la Cueva (Catalina de la Cueva), sixteen, who would become the wife of Antonio Díaz de Cáceres
Luis de Carvajal, fourteen, often called young Luis to distinguish him from his uncle the governor, who would come to play a catalyzing role in the religious life of the Judaizing communities
Mariana Rodríguez de Matos, (Mariana Núñez de Carvajal y de la Cueva), nine, a high-strung young beauty who would one day go mad
Miguel Rodríguez, eight, who years later would flee the Mexican Inquisition and in Pisa change his name to Jacob Lumbroso
Leonor de Andrada, six, who would marry Jorge de Almeida
Ana de Carvajal (Ana de León Carvajal), one, the youngest sibling. Anica, the diminutive form of her name, stuck with her throughout her life.

The couple's firstborn child, twenty-five-year-old Gaspar de Carvajal, who had taken holy orders as a Dominican friar, had arrived in Mexico three or four years earlier.[24]

In their hometown of Benavente (León) and in nearby Medina del Campo (Valladolid), where various members of the Carvajal family had resided from time to time, Francisca and her husband, Francisco Rodríguez Matos, had been enthusiastic, if not deeply knowledgeable, Judaizers. As their older children reached the age of reliability, their parents introduced them to the at-home religious practices of their immediate and extended families. The Carvajal family's Jewishness was further nurtured on the high seas. By the time they had disembarked in Pánuco, all but the two youngest children had some knowledge of Judaism.[25]

> In the sixteenth century, the name Pánuco denoted a river, a city, and a province. The Río Pánuco rises in the central highlands, meanders through the swampy lowlands of Veracruz, and disgorges into the Gulf of Mexico at the place today called Tampico. It is navigable nearly to the base of the Sierra Madre Oriental. Provincia de Pánuco, essentially the catchment basin for the river, was the early colonial designation for parts of today's Tamaulipas, San Luis Potosí, and northern Veracruz. The city of Pánuco, formerly called Santisteban del Puerto, lies on the bank of the river some sixty kilometers from the Gulf, safely inland from the pirates who plagued the Gulf Coast up through the eighteenth century.
>
> In the 1520s, Hernán Cortés and his faction and the governor of Jamaica contested jurisdiction over the *provincia*. By 1580, when Governor Luis de Carvajal y de la Cueva established his base for the exploration and conquest of what became known as Nuevo León, it pertained firmly to the Audiencia in Mexico City.
>
> In the 1500s, small towns in Sinaloa, Durango, and Zacatecas also bore the name Pánuco, and the reader of colonial documents must use context to decipher which Pánuco is being referenced: village, city, river, or province. To compound the confusion, the Carvajal family and their friends often used the name Pánuco to denote Tampico, the city that by then was emerging as the principal port along Mexico's northern Gulf Coast.

For the next few years, Governor Carvajal roamed the north, consuming much of his personal fortune in building roads and supporting his small army, while sending almost nothing back to his sister and her family. He was often accompanied by young Luis de Carvajal, whom he felt to be the ablest of his nephews and whom he was grooming to succeed him one day as leader of the northern territories. While Luis uncle and Luis nephew campaigned in the north, Francisca, Francisco Rodríguez de Matos, and the majority of their children remained in Pánuco, the adults eking out a living as best they were able: the women as seamstresses; the men selling small goods in the streets and nearby villages. A few other members of the party that had sailed with the governor to New Spain also remained in Pánuco, among them Morales, who continued to share with the Carvajal siblings—excepting Fray Gaspar and young Miguel and Anica—his extensive knowledge of Jewish practices and ritual, writing out for them additional prayers that would become a key source of the family's liturgy. In effect, in Pánuco and later in Mexico City, the Carvajal household, with Morales acting informally as rabbi, in the early 1580s came to function as a kind of synagogue.

Governor Carvajal, who appears to have been Christian observant, neither attended nor approved. Although undoubtedly knowledgeable about Judaism and aware of much of the rest of his family's commitment to the Law of Moses, the governor was not supportive of it and tried actively, if unsuccessfully, to persuade the most fervent among them—particularly his eldest niece, widow Isabel de Carvajal—to renounce their Judaizing practices. What the governor did not do, and what eventually caused him no end of grief with the authorities, was denounce his relatives to the Inquisition.

As long as members of this growing Jewish community did not give public voice to their beliefs and were surreptitious in their practice, they were relatively safe from being targeted for investigation. However, individuals who acted or spoke publicly in any way that hinted at Jewishness were at risk, and this risk was magnified when they came together in groups. Communal Judaizing required environments free of prying eyes and eavesdropping ears. It required association with people known to be of absolute confidence and unwavering commitment, people who were unlikely to crumble under the coercive pressures of the Holy Office. If there ever were safe environments that successfully protected the Mexican Judaizers from all outside observance, we have no way of knowing, for the Judaizers in such cases left no paper trail. For those about whom we have data, the thousands of folios in more than one hundred Inquisition dossiers make clear that safe environments were illusory.

But the illusion of safety was crucial for people to come together to worship, to exchange information about Judaism, to test individuals' commitment and susceptibility, to proselytize, and to socialize in a context that reinforced the solidarity and sense of in-group-ness of the Portuguese Mexican Judaizers. There were two types of preferred environments. One was interior rooms behind closed doors in private homes. For Judaizers in the mining towns, the principal indoor havens of the 1580s were the Mexico City homes of the Enríquez-Paibas, the Machados, the Carvajals, and the Lucenas; the Taxco homes of Jorge de Almeida and Tomás de Fonseca Castellanos; and the Pachuca home of Manuel de Lucena.

The Judaizers of the silver towns in late sixteenth-century New Spain, together with their associates, family members, and friends, were drawn together to Judaize by the magnetic pull of family and business, in accord with the rhythms of what they knew of the calendar of Jewish observances. Children visited parents, young married couples called on their parents-in-law, housemates pulled together their mutual friends. Life-cycle events such as Almeida and Díaz de Cáceres's weddings in 1586 to the Carvajal sisters brought people together, as did obligations to care for the sick, tend to the dying, and bury the dead. When Judaizers came together in secure environments under any of these circumstances, the conversation quite naturally might turn to their shared religious heritage. If a meal was served, a question about how the chicken had been slaughtered or a comment about the absence of pork might lead to a discussion of the Law of Moses. In the comfortable closeness of family or friendship, someone might disparage some detail of Christian iconography or observance. If someone with a proselytizing bent was present—someone like Luis Díaz, Manuel de Lucena, Antonio Machado, Manuel de Morales, or Luis de Carvajal and his brother Baltazar, who visited all of these households on a regular basis—any subject of conversation was likely to veer toward matters relating to Judaizing.

Jewish conversation was also likely to sprout when Judaizers came together to do business. Every male converso in New Spain in the late sixteenth century participated in the business community. Some were tratantes, importers, wholesale and retail merchants, and street vendors; some were artisans who in their homes and shops produced goods for sale; some were miners, owners and operators, and supervisory staff at *ingenios de beneficiar metales*; some were ranchers who provisioned the reales with food and carters who plied the highways. When Judaizing conversos came together to buy or sell, to lend money or collect loans, or to acquire or deliver merchandise, so long as no outsiders were present, the conversation was likely to include references to Judaizing beliefs or practices.

While most conversa women were not actively engaged in business—except as producers of cloth and clothing that they themselves did not tend to market directly[26]—they maintained intense social networks with their friends and members of their extended families. As the women sewed or spun or embroidered together, or worked with one another to prepare a meal, their conversations would range over the whole universe of family affairs, including, inevitably, matters relating to the maintenance of a Jewish home: koshering, cooking, cleaning, women's hygiene, and the education of their children. Because their menfolk routinely escorted them to and from the home where they were gathering, the women's social networks brought men together as well. The one trait that the men and women all seemed to have in common was their urge to gossip.

Judaizers were also drawn together by the magnetism of certain men deemed to have deep knowledge about Judaism and a reputation for steadfast observance of Jewish customs. In Mexico in the early 1580s, one of the most prominent learned men was Antonio Machado, an ancient, irascible, gout-ridden tailor from Lisbon who had been living in poverty in Mexico City with his wife and six unmarried daughters since at least the mid-1570s, most of the time confined to his bed. Machado's seventh daughter, Leonor, had married and was mother of twelve children of her own; his son Juan was a lawyer in the viceroy's employ. The eldest of the six unmarried daughters, Isabel de Machado, was as strongly committed to the Law of Moses as her father; she conspired with him to keep their religious practices secret from the other children in the family, whom they did not trust. One strategy was to lock them out of their father's room when any of his Judaizing friends came to visit, posting Isabel like a mastiff to guard the door.

Machado, who did not know Latin and thus had little direct access to the Bible, was not quite as knowledgeable as his physician and friend Dr. Manuel de Morales. In Pánuco, Morales had translated the book of Deuteronomy into Spanish for the Machados, as well as copying out for them a number of hymns. In the years prior to the trials, Morales's handwritten materials circulated widely among Judaizers in Mexico.[27] Antonio Machado kept at least two books secreted in his room: selections from Deuteronomy handwritten in Spanish and a bound copy of Fray Luis de Granada's *Introduction to the Symbols of Faith*.[28]

For a number of Judaizers of the 1580s, Machado's bedroom functioned something like a salon and something like an informal synagogue.[29] People came for the overt purpose of comforting the sick man and bringing his family charitable donations of money, food, and clothing. One fund-raising campaign circa 1587 was organized by Tomás de Fonseca Castellanos, who had been spurred to the effort when his friend Francisco Rodríguez told him that Machado was descended from Jews and was a "God-fearing man, meaning that he followed the Law of Moses." Young Tomás dispatched his trusted employee Marco Antonio to deliver the contributions to the Machados. The old man—as he always did when a person of confidence came to visit—had Isabel lock the door and then read to Marco Antonio some Psalms from one of Dr. Morales's books.[30] Other regular contributor-visitors to Machado's bedroom were Dr. Morales's wife, Isabel; Beatriz Enríquez la Paiba; her daughter Catalina Enríquez; her son-in-law Manuel de Lucena; Gonzalo Pérez Ferro and his wife, Catalina de León;[31] Luis de Carvajal and his brother Baltazar Rodríguez; and sometimes old Tomás de Fonseca's half brother Julián de Castellanos. Francisco Rodríguez and Luis Díaz the silversmith were frequent visitors too, as were Jorge Rodríguez and his brother Domingo.[32] The traveling Portuguese merchants Fabián Granados and Juan Rodríguez Pardo would stop by when they were passing through Mexico City.[33] Machado taught some of them to recite the opening worlds of the Shema in Hebrew (the only Hebrew he knew), pausing a long time after each word because, Machado said, that was what the Hebrew language required.[34] He talked to his visitors about the coming Messiah, the importance of following the handful of precepts that constituted his repertoire of Jewish practices, and the false theology of Christianity. Listening to his disquisitions with the community that had assembled in his bedroom helped them strengthen their sense of Jewish identity.

For Judaizers who made their homes in the mining towns and commuted to Mexico City, or for Mexico City merchants whose business took them to clients in market towns throughout New Spain, the highways provided a second safe zone. On Mexico's dusty roads, in the vast solitary landscapes of New Spain, out of eyesight and beyond earshot of strangers, small groups of

Judaizers could feel, for a moment, secure, sensing that the immensity of Mexico surrounded them like a protective curtain.

The number of travelers in a group determined the group's dynamics of confidence. True safety, of course, could be found only in a group of one, which is why some Judaizers fell into the habit of celebrating important ritual moments in solitary fashion out in the countryside. That is why Manuel Francisco Belmonte told inquisitors that for the fast of the Great Day (Yom Kippur) of September 1595, "I went out of the town of Sultepec, winding my way into the countryside and turning off the road into a valley, I tied up my horse and remained there until the afternoon when I returned to my house in Sultepec." When the inquisitors asked him why he had gone out into the fields, he replied, "So that my neighbors would not see me."[35] What he was really saying was "see me fasting or hear me praying." When Rodrigo Tavares advised his son Manuel to pull himself out of his depression by confessing to God and getting mud on his knees (*póngase de lodo*), Manuel's desire for the security of solitude moved him to go out alone into the countryside. There, falling to his knees and with tears streaming down his face, he cried out: "O Lord of heaven and earth, hear me in your great mercy. Look not at the sins I have committed against you, which are many, but forgive me and erase all of my sin and give me intelligence and understanding so that I may serve you."[36] There must have been many such solitary excursions into the countryside, though because there were no witnesses to them, they entered the written record only when some repentant Judaizer chose to make a clean breast of his transgressions to his interrogators.

A group of two, particularly two close friends or relatives who knew each other's religious convictions and fully trusted each other, was also deemed to be relatively safe. Pairs of travelers could avail themselves of the isolation of the open road to broach with each other charged topics that were likely to lead to heightened emotions and raised voices. This was especially true if the topics involved religious differences, as they did with Governor Luis de Carvajal y de la Cueva and his Judaizing nephew Luis de Carvajal. The elder Luis wanted the younger to shed his dangerously inappropriate religious habits. One day in 1583, the governor rode out with his nephew on the road from Pánuco to the hacienda of the governor's friend Diego de Torres, a little beyond the village of Cuzcatlán. The governor waved his soldiers to go ahead and then, to test how his nephew would react, challenged young Luis with a blunt question: "Are you aware that your father is living in the Law of Moses?" Luis, who indeed knew that and likewise knew that his powerful uncle was a committed Christian, pretended to be shocked. The governor, believing he had made his disapproval of young Luis's Judaizing activities abundantly clear, smiled at his nephew's reaction: "That is why I like you better than your siblings."[37] Young Luis's brother Baltazar Rodríguez, who was just as committed to Judaizing as his brother, was much less circumspect with his uncle and a year later tried to persuade the governor to join them in their Judaizing. Riding out with him on the road to Tamaulipa, Baltazar hung back to let his uncle's escort of soldiers go on ahead so that he and the senior Luis might have a private conversation. Baltazar opened the topic by confessing to the governor his doubts about the miraculous power of the Christian sacraments and his skepticism that at consecration the host truly became the body of Christ. The governor did not want to hear it and brusquely cut his nephew off. When Baltazar asked what he should do about his doubts, the governor told him to report himself to the Inquisition. Realizing that influencing his uncle was a lost cause, Baltazar rode back to Pánuco.[38]

Manuel de Lucena was another whose innate sense of caution led him to favor the open road for sensitive conversations about religion. Manuel Rodríguez reported that once in 1593, as he was walking with Lucena, their conversation turned to Rodríguez's alienation from Judaizing. As they entered the inn where Lucena was staying, Lucena cut his friend off: "I can't talk to you about this because people in another room might hear us. We will deal with these matters another day, because they are things that can only be said out in the countryside."[39] When Cristóbal López came from Sevilla to Mexico City in 1588, he brought letters for Manuel de Lucena from some of Lucena's family members and friends in Portugal. López said that he needed to talk with Lucena in secret, so Lucena took him out to the wooded hill of Chapultepec, an hour's walk west of the city. López's confidential message was that Lucena's brother Fernando Váez, now married and living in Fundão, had asked López to instruct Lucena in Judaism. Lucena replied with a smile, saying that he was already committed to following the Law of Moses. With that the two men embraced and, safe from prying eyes and ears, spent the rest of the day sharing details of their Jewish beliefs and assuring each other how the lamentable persecution of their people was a result of the Jews not adhering strictly to the Law of Moses and how their suffering in this world would win them a place in heaven in the next.⁴⁰

Even when a pair of Judaizers believed that no one else was observing them, they could never be completely sure. Fear was always their silent companion. One day around 1587, when Luis de Carvajal was on the road to Taxco with young Tomás de Fonseca Castellanos, the two men stopped at an abandoned inn. Luis took out from his saddlebags a little prayer book that Antonio Machado had given him and began to read aloud. Fonseca was moved to tears by the prayers Luis was reading, but he was also horrified: "Put that book away! Hide it! This is a public road; somebody might see!" Luis did as he had been asked, and once Tomás had calmed down, the two men began to compare biblical passages about the Messiah with what Tomás had read in *Mirror of Consolation*. Presumably while Carvajal was absorbed in his discourse, young Tomás kept one eye focused on their surroundings while he listened.⁴¹

In larger groups, the danger was multiplied, for a group of three or more Judaizers allowed the Inquisition to cross-check versions of an event.⁴² No member of a multi-person group could be certain that he would not be informed on by one of the others and that a second participant would not confirm the accusation, undercutting the accused person's attempts at denial. This is how we know, for example, that in the fall of 1590, Manuel de Lucena took his cousin Antonio López and Manuel Francisco Belmonte out into an empty area along the road to San Bartolomé to unobtrusively observe together the Yom Kippur fast.⁴³ In dozens of trial dossiers, the numerous multiple denunciations of a single Judaizing event demonstrate the effectiveness of the Inquisition's strategy of triangulation.

Mexican Judaizers felt that any open road extended them an invitation to express themselves openly to their trusted companions. Because the road from Mexico City to Pachuca could be traversed by a man on horseback in a day and a half, and was a common first stage in any journey to the mining reales farther north and east, it played a particularly important role in the lives of the Judaizing community. Traveling back and forth to Pachuca in the late 1580s, Lucena often talked about Judaism to his companion Manuel Gómez Navarro, citing biblical passages that spoke of the Messiah and teaching him prayers such as "Oh Lord, open my lips" (Psalm 51:15).⁴⁴ Sometimes Luis de Carvajal joined them.⁴⁵ On the Pachuca road in 1591, Lucena shared confidences with his father-in-law, Simón Paiba.⁴⁶ On the road in 1593, he discussed the Bible with his brother-in-law Diego Enríquez and Manuel Gómez Navarro,⁴⁷ and on another occasion with Luis de Carvajal and Antonio Rodríguez.⁴⁸ On his commute the following year, Lucena traded scriptural citations with Sebastián Rodríguez, Manuel Gómez Navarro, and Francisco Váez.⁴⁹ Even when the group was large, as was the party on the Pachuca road in 1589 (Manuel de Lucena, Diego Enríquez, Antonio López, Luis de Carvajal, and his brother Baltazar Rodríguez), the conversation inevitably centered on Law of Moses, with the five friends maligning Jesus, trading references to "authorities" (most frequently the Bible, *Mirror of Consolation*, *Flos sanctorum*, or works by Fray Luis de Granada), and occasionally breaking into song.⁵⁰

The road was an ideal environment for proselytizing for men like Manuel de Lucena and Luis de Carvajal, whom Justa Méndez characterized as "two preachers who never stopped persuading people to follow the Law of Moses."⁵¹ On the road, the more committed of a pair of travelers could bolster what he perceived to be the more tenuous commitment to Judaism of his companion. It was on a road around 1587 that Manuel de Lucena, just turned twenty-one, tried to persuade his cousin Antonio López, a native of Celorico, to take up Judaizing, although without notable success. Four years later, on another road, Lucena tried again with the help of Manuel Gómez Navarro. Lucena talked Bible, and Gómez Navarro explained to López how Jesus was not the Messiah for whom the Jews were waiting. At this attempt to convert him, López exploded: "Sir, I am a good Christian. Don't talk to me about those things, because I believe in God and in Saint Mary and in the Holy Mother Church." Gómez Navarro drew Lucena aside and gave him a look that said he was a fool to risk exposing himself this way to Antonio López. A little later Gómez Navarro, in a gentle voice, tried to smooth things over: "Promise me you won't expose us." But López would have nothing of it. Years later, when López was accused of Judaizing, he credited Lucena for having taught it to him.⁵²

Gómez Pertierra, Lucena's business partner in Real del Monte, was another target of Lucena's missionary zeal. On the several-hour climb from Pachuca to Real del Monte, Manuel Lucena would tell Pertierra stories from the Jewish Bible, with pointed stress, Pertierra later explained, on how God was waiting for the Jewish people to rededicate themselves to him—he used the heavily freighted term for conversion, *convertir*—after which he would admit them to Glory and shower them in this world with wealth and material possessions.⁵³

As Justa Méndez intimated, among the Judaizers of his time, Manuel de Lucena was one of the two most dedicated users of the highways as his pulpit and Luis de Carvajal was the other. With Antonio López in 1588 on the Pachuca road, Luis's exegesis centered on Deuteronomy, after which the two men bought some chickens, slaughtered them in the Jewish fashion, and had them cooked for their supper.⁵⁴ In 1589, returning to Mexico City in the company of Manuel de Lucena, Baltazar Rodríguez, and Antonio López, Carvajal leaned heavily on Diego Enríquez to accept the Law of Moses, making his point by citing numerous biblical passages and by maligning the Christian holy family by saying that Jesus was not the son of God but of an adulterous whore.⁵⁵ One day in 1591 on the Taxco road, Carvajal found himself in conversation with Héctor de Fonseca, who asked Luis to explain to him a Latin passage from the book of Esdras that appeared to indicate that God had turned his back on the Jews because of their sins. Luis told Héctor he had missed the point: the verse in question was not a condemnation but a warning from a loving Father that if the Jews did not faithfully follow the Law of Moses, there would be dire consequences.⁵⁶

In roadside conversations with their converso friends, Judaizers often gave vent to their skepticism about the miraculous properties of the Christian sacraments and what they interpreted to be inconsistencies and logical absurdities in Christian theology, attitudes they would never knowingly reveal to a committed Christian. Altogether typical was Manuel Tavares's question to Bernardo de Luna on the road from Caponeta to Guadiana (Durango): "Why did God have to come into the world in order to save humanity? It is a joke to say that Jesus Christ came and died to redeem the world. He has to be in Hell for calling himself the Son of God." Luna replied that Tavares was absolutely right.⁵⁷

Doubts about Christian beliefs and practices sometimes gave way to scorn. In the highway environment of total confidence and isolation, Lucena and his traveling companions of the moment felt comfortable giving vent to their negative feelings about the religious culture that they found so oppressive, a negativism that expressed itself as disparagement of the theology and rituals of Christianity, and acts that in Christian eyes would be sacrilege.⁵⁸ Every time that Manuel de Lucena and Jorge Álvarez rode together from

Mexico to Pachuca, they would joke with each other about the "sect" of Christianity. When they happened on some roadside crucifix, one of them would cry: "Hey, give him a towel! He looks exhausted."[59] One day near Texcoco, Lucena found himself on the road with the merchant Rodrigo Tavares, born in Fundão and then about fifty, who used to sell throughout Michoacán and had a store in Pátzcuaro. The two men confessed their Judaizing to each other, and Rodrigo told him that whenever he and his teenage son, Manuel Tavares, who carted supplies to the mining reales, would pass a roadside cross, they were in the habit of farting at it, and sometimes defecating at its foot.[60] This revelation did not surprise Lucena at all. Another time, traveling on the same road with Manuel Tavares to Texcoco (or perhaps to Pachuca—Manuel Tavares remembered the road but not the destination), Lucena and Tavares came upon a roadside cross. There were other people around, so Tavares took off his hat as was the custom. Lucena did not, and when they found themselves alone again, Lucena berated Tavares for not being a good Judaizer. "It's true I took my hat off," Tavares protested, "but not willingly." "When I encounter a cross," Lucena scoffed, "I always show it the respect it deserves: I fart at it."[61]

The road was also a place where Judaizers could share with one another their dreams, and their most common dream was to escape: to earn enough money to sail back to Spain and from there to make their way to the European havens in Italy, France, the Low Countries, and Turkey, where they believed they could practice Judaism openly without fear of the Inquisition. On the Pachuca road in 1589, Lucena's friend Fernán Rodríguez de Herrera, who was born in the Portuguese city of Sabugal and who had left his wife and daughter in the Spanish city of Antequera before sailing to Spain in 1588, told him about the large number of Portuguese Jews who had made their way to Bordeaux and how freely they were allowed to live among the French. If that is the case, Lucena asked him, why did you come here? "For the same reason you did," Rodríguez de Herrera replied, "to make money, enough to be able to take my whole family to France."[62] This dream of escape surfaced often in Lucena's conversations on the road. He told Jorge Álvarez how one day they would "emigrate together to better lands where they could freely serve the Lord."[63] Another day he told him, "Very shortly I plan to go to a land where I can freely observe the Law of Moses." And at that point, Álvarez told the inquisitors, "a man rode up on a bay horse and our conversation ceased."[64]

Even allowing for the fact that the Inquisition took note of only conversations that touched on sensitive religious topics, instances such as these are so numerous in the record that it appears likely that any time two or more Judaizers found themselves alone together on a Mexican highway, the conversation would turn to the Law of Moses. Gonzalo Pérez Ferro said that this was always the case when he and Antonio Díaz de Cáceres traveled together[65]—as it was when Francisco Díaz and Jorge de Almeida rode together[66] and when Jorge Váez traveled with Gonzalo Rodríguez or Manuel Rodríguez and the Lisbonite Gaspar Correa.[67]

Judaizing confidences on the road occurred according to the rhythms of the need to travel. Indoor gatherings were often timed according to the rhythms of the Jewish liturgical cycles. In the 1580s and early 1590s, Judaizing conversos in Mexico often came together on Friday nights for a meal and conversation. The following day they enjoyed some communal leisure while abstaining from work, at least when they felt they could do so without attracting notice. The Sabbath aside, it was the annual cycle of Jewish festivals that exerted the greatest force in bringing them together, even though few of the sixteenth-century Mexican Judaizers had a sophisticated knowledge of the complete Jewish festival calendar. The holiday best known to the conversos in Mexico, and thus the most frequently observed, was Yom Kippur, which they knew universally as the Great Day of the Lord (El Día Grande del Señor) and sometimes as the Day of Pardoning (Día del Perdón), the Great Fast (Gran Ayuno), and occasionally, to those most familiar with the Bible, Quipur.[68] While the Día Grande del Señor fast could be observed in solitude,[69] Judaizers generally came together on that day to fast and pray, concluding the fast with a communal meal of fish.

The second most frequently celebrated festival was Passover, the Festival of the Lamb (Pascua del Cordero). Since they knew that Jesus's Last Supper was a Passover seder, Mexican Judaizers inferred that the seven-day Jewish festival began on the evening of Holy Thursday.[70] The Christian community expected everyone to participate in the church-sponsored Holy Thursday street processions, either by marching or by observing the parade. Not to participate provoked comment and was therefore dangerous. Some Judaizers did indeed march; others gathered at someone's home and, if they felt confident that no outsider was listening, made disparaging comments about the credulous, superstitious practices of the Christians. Once the processions had passed, they would celebrate with a communal meal and a retelling of the events of Exodus.

The third most frequent observance was the Fast of Esther, which replaced the feast of Purim.[71] Also commemorated in Mexico, but much less frequently, were Shavuoth (Primicias de Flores) and Sukkot, the Feast of Tabernacles (Cabañuelos).[72] With rare exceptions, Mexican Judaizers of this period seem to have been ignorant of Hanukkah or the Rosh Hashanah commemoration of the Jewish New Year.[73]

The open road and the closed room, these were the environments that most often served the converso Judaizers of late sixteenth-century New Spain as synagogues. They were, in every sense, the locus of what constituted the Judaizing community—or communities—of those years.

The lives of the individuals who frequented these "synagogues" revolved around two poles: their need to make a living, and their need to express their identity as Judaizers.

Chapter 10

The Taxco Miners

> Héctor de Fonseca ... from Viseo, though his parents said he was born in Galicia, age 48, ... he has been a miner in the mines of Taxco since he came to this country.
> —PROCESO, MAY 1596[1]

> Tomás de Fonseca Castellanos, native of the city of Viseo in Portugal, miner and merchant in the Mines of Taxco.
> —PROCESO, DECEMBER 1589[2]

> Proceso against Jorge de Almeida, Portuguese, a miner in the mines of Taxco, resident there and in this city of Mexico.
> —PROCESO, APRIL 1590[3]

> Doña Mariana and Anica went with Antonio Díaz de Cáceres and his wife to the hacienda de minas that he owned in Tenango.
> —LUIS DE CARVAJAL, AUGUST 7, 1589[4]

THE MOUNTAINS AROUND Taxco, some 180 kilometers south-southwest of Mexico City in what is now the state of Guerrero, are extraordinarily rich in minerals. Long before the arrival of the Spaniards, indigenous Chontal people had been extracting tin and copper from surface outcroppings on the flanks of Monte Atache. After the conquest, the area quickly came to the attention of Hernán Cortés, who was building churches and establishing sugar haciendas in the fertile valley of Cuernavaca between Taxco and Mexico City. Learning of the copper and tin, and thinking bronze, Cortés sent two of his artillerymen, Francisco Meza and Rodrigo Martínez, on an expedition in 1524 to explore the area that the Indians called Tlachco. When the emissaries returned in the early autumn with information that people there were forging together small amounts of the two minerals, Cortés notified Emperor Carlos V of the discovery[5] and ordered mining to begin. Over the next decade, the tin and copper were used to cast the cannons that the Spanish army required as it expanded its area of control.

It was silver, not tin and copper, that put Taxco on the map. In 1534[6] two conquistadors, Juan de Cabra and Juan de Salcedo, accompanied by a miner named Muriel, made the first silver strike on Monte Atache, not far from a hacienda that Cortés had commissioned for himself on a spur of the mountain in Taxco, between two streams, Mulata and Chorrillo, that appeared to run wet year-round. Word spread, and the rush was on. Dozens, then scores of prospectors swarmed the Taxco mountains. In their wake came the Indian laborers to dig out the ore, the merchants, tavern keepers, missionary friars, government officials, prostitutes, and all the others who hoped to profit by providing goods and services to the miners. By the close of the 1530s, Taxco boasted both an Audiencia-appointed chief administrative officer and a magistrate.

Figure 7. Chorrillo arroyo cliffs, Taxco, 1960. Photograph by the author.

Figure 8. Chorrillo waterfall, Taxco, 1960. Photograph by the author.

Miners, as young Tomás de Fonseca told inquisitors many years later, are a rough and covetous lot, given to arguing, fighting, stealing, and cheating each other whenever they have the chance.[7] In the early mining camps, moral discipline was maintained, up to a point, by church officials acting under the inquisitorial powers of the bishop in Mexico City. Two Spaniards in Taxco ran afoul of this proto-Inquisition. One was Francisco Castro, who would not let his wife attend mass; the other a woman named Catalina who was accused of bigamy for having two living husbands.[8] Growth in the mining camps, including the mountains around Taxco, was so rapid and so chaotic that in 1542 the Real Audiencia in Mexico City issued stern regulations in an attempt to bring order to the cutthroat competition and rampant vice. The regulations stipulated that in each mining camp:

- No more than two stores could sell mining equipment, cloth and clothing, and so-called luxury goods;
- No more than one tavern could dispense wine and spirits;
- No intoxicants could be sold to slaves or Indians;
- There could be only one market, in only one place, and only on Sunday;
- No other commerce was permitted within four leagues of the camp.[9]

By mid-century the mining camps strung out along the mountains near Taxco had coalesced into three separate mining districts, formally constituted as reales. In the center, around what is the heart of the current city of Taxco, was the Real de Tetelatzingo (generally shortened to Tetelcingo; Nahuatl for "small mountain"). A few kilometers to the southwest, in a place now called Taxco el Viejo, was the Real de Tenango, with a preconquest Indian community that provided labor for the mines.[10] Northeast of Tetelcingo, and farther down the mountain, were the mines of Camixtla (now called Acamixtla, near Juliantla). A scant two kilometers to the northeast of Tetelcingo was the spur of the mountain where the Cortés hacienda was located. The Spanish miners had rechristened the place Real de Cantarranas for the abundance of frogs (*ranas*) that sang there. Today the site, now called Chorrillos, is property of the Universidad Nacional Autónoma de México, but for a time it belonged to Jorge de Almeida.

Tetelcingo, with an assay office and a few stores and taverns, asserted itself as the center of the Taxco mining district. A sturdy adobe parish church had been built where the Baroque gem Santa Prisca now stands. A second parish, la Santa Veracruz, accommodated miners farther down the hill. A small Franciscan community from Cuernavaca was building a monastery. According to a report to the Audiencia in 1569, the labor force of the combined Reales de Taxco consisted of six hundred black slaves, two hundred Indians assigned under the repartimiento system, and twenty-three hundred free Indian contract laborers. The 150 European-born male residents of the Taxco Reales included both the support community and the miners working Taxco's thirty registered mines.[11] Included in this tally was young Tomás de Fonseca Castellanos, who would be joined within the next few years by Héctor de Fonseca, Héctor's brother Jorge de Almeida,[12] and Antonio Díaz de Cáceres. These four men and their relatives and friends, most of them Portuguese, comprised the converso community in Taxco for the next quarter century. When between 1589 and 1596 the Mexican Inquisition targeted these four as Judaizers, their testimony, together with the testimony of their relatives, business associates, neighbors, servants, friends, and enemies, left us a minute and nuanced appreciation of both their commercial activities and their beliefs.

Tomás de Fonseca Castellanos

In 1568 young Tomás de Fonseca Castellanos left his uncle in Tlalpujahua for Taxco, which was said to be booming. Living in Taxco was Felipa de Fonseca, the daughter of his sister Guiomar and her first husband, the Old Christian Antonio Pérez Herrero. Felipa, who had been raised as a Christian, had married the silver miner Gaspar de Enciso, a well-established, wealthy, Old Christian widower.[13] When young Tomás showed up, Enciso hired him.

Tomás de Fonseca Castellanos worked in Gaspar de Enciso's mining operation for eight or nine years. During that time, Tomás sired three children with a woman or women he does not name in his testimony and who are not named in other documents. Young Tomás's son Francisco de Fonseca was born in 1572, María in 1578 or 1579, and Álvaro in 1581.[14] There is no indication that he ever tried to instruct any of them in Judaizing.

Young Tomás left Enciso's employ in around 1579 to purchase his own mine and hacienda de beneficiar near Cantarranas.[15] His son Francisco, though still a child, went to the mine to help his father. Simultaneously Tomás opened a general store in the central Taxco real of Tetelcingo. Young Tomás juggled these two professions for the rest of his life, describing himself to inquisitors in 1595 as "a resident of the Mines of Taxco, where I am a miner and a merchant."[16]

The fullest description of Fonseca's hacienda is found in the documents amassed by the Inquisition. In May 1595, the Inquisition tasked Alonso Pérez Serrano with arresting Tomás and making sure that his mines and his processing plant would not falter in any way that might diminish the flow of silver to the royal coffers. As Pérez Serrano noted, Fonseca's operation was "one of the best that there are in these parts." Pérez valued the operation at some two thousand pesos and noted that it was "very well equipped, and with a sufficient number of Indian workers, which is the most important thing."[17]

When Pérez showed up with his bailiffs, he found a full complement of workers grading chunks of ore, feeding them into the crushing machines, taking the pulverized ore to the amalgamation patio, mixing the powder with mercury and flux, assessing the ripeness of the tortas of silver amalgam stewing on the patio floor, and shoveling them into the furnaces, where the mercury and silver were separated. Other workers were packaging the refined and semi-refined silver for shipment to Mexico City. Another contingent was attending to the hacienda's principal working livestock of twenty-one mules and two black horses, all of which Fonseca owned free and clear.[18] In the kitchen of the hacienda's main residence, women were preparing food for the workers. Pérez wrote to his superiors that the arrest of young Tomás de Fonseca had put the hacienda into such an uproar that Pérez had had to spend the night there to calm everyone down. He assured the workers that their jobs were safe, for there would be a continuity of management and production. Young Tomás's foreman, Tomás Cardoso, who was already handling much of the hacienda's administrative work, would remain in charge.[19] Pérez promised the workers that Cardoso had enough cash on hand to pay them every Sunday after church, as usual. With regard to the piles of semi-processed silver that Pérez observed dotting the working area of the hacienda, Pérez assured his superiors that he would make certain that they were processed and that the silver was dispatched as soon as possible. As to the longer term, Pérez requested that Cardoso be confirmed, in writing, as the hacienda's executive administrator so that he could legally claim his mercury allotment from Taxco's alcalde de minas and negotiate an installment plan to pay for it. The formal confirmation also would permit Cardoso to enter into contracts for the flux, salt, mules, and everything else he needed to run the hacienda productively.[20]

Tomás Cardoso, a native of Casteloblanco, was related to young Tomás de Fonseca, but none of Tomás's friends seemed to know precisely how.[21] In Mexico since at least 1588, Cardoso had settled in Taxco, where he mostly worked for young Tomás as an administrator at the mine and a carter of goods for the store. Tomás tried to teach him something about the Law of Moses, but Cardoso rejected his proselytizing. Their relationship soon turned sour: Fonseca feared Cardoso might denounce him to the Inquisition, and Cardoso believed that Fonseca owed him money. It also seems likely, at least according to Pedro Múñiz, one of Fonseca's gossipy neighbors, that Cardoso got one of Fonseca's bastard daughters pregnant and then refused to marry her, even though Fonseca had given him twenty or thirty mules as an inducement.[22]

Shortly after Tomás de Fonseca Castellanos's arrest, Alonso Gómez de Castañeda, the Inquisition's agent in Taxco, wrote that as requested, he had investigated to see if Fonseca had any other assets in Taxco that might be of interest to the Inquisition. His prize find was another patio-process refining hacienda, owned by Tomás but registered in the name of one of Fonseca's neighbors, Baltazar de Cepeda. The commissioner turned this property over to Diego Hernández de Merlo as temporary administrator. Gómez de Castañeda also reported Fonseca's cash receivables, noting that he was owed substantial monies by Felipe de Palacios, Héctor de Fonseca, and Jorge de Almeida.[23] Gómez promised he would see to it that the debts were collected and that all this property would be held in escrow until Tomás de Fonseca's case was resolved, at which point his possessions would either be returned to him, less whatever his incarceration had cost, or sold at auction.

Fonseca's first *mayordomo* at the mining hacienda was a converso surnamed Rodríguez, whose first name is never given. After Fonseca's arrest, when Tomás's conspiracy with Rodríguez to hide some of the hacienda's processed silver came to light, Rodríguez fled the country.[24] Fonseca then hired his Portuguese relative Tomás Cardoso to fill the gap, paying him four hundred pesos a year plus a two-peso-a-week expense allowance, amounts that the alcalde mayor deemed to be on a par with what the industry was paying.[25] Cardoso had ample experience supervising the mine when Fonseca was absent or tending to his store. Though Pérez Serrano's decision to leave Cardoso in charge when he arrested young Tomás ran the risk of appearing to invite conflict of interest, Pérez assured his superiors that

Cardoso was "an honorable man, known for faithfully husbanding anything that was entrusted to his care."[26]

Young Tomás relied on Cardoso and trusted him enough to nominate him as a character witness in his 1590 trial. Later, friction would develop between the two men. Cardoso had trouble controlling his temper (as did Fonseca), and one time Fonseca's delay in paying him his annual salary sent Cardoso into a fit. An additional and not insignificant point of friction, if rumors were to be believed, was the business with Fonseca's daughter María.[27]

Another of the employees at Tomás's hacienda was Marco Antonio, a Portuguese converso from Casteloblanco.[28] From late 1583 through the end of the decade, Marco Antonio's principal duties for Fonseca were as groom and hostler, taking care of Fonseca's personal mare, and freighting supplies with the hacienda's string of mules over the dusty roads of central Mexico. Like so many other adventurous, entrepreneurial young men in New Spain, he also did a little business for himself, buying here, selling there, and applying the profits to building up his stock.[29] When Marco Antonio's brother Manuel Gómez de Casteloblanco stopped by the hacienda for a two-month visit in 1591, Tomás employed him too.[30] During his time, working at the hacienda, Marco Antonio developed a close friendship with Francisco de Fonseca, Tomás's illegitimate son, who was nine years his junior.[31]

Among Fonseca's other workers were a branded mulatto slave named Francisco Pérez and his free mulatto wife, María, who were on extended loan to Tomás from his cousin Felipa de Fonseca. Francisco worked at Tomás's hacienda as a muleteer, while María cooked for Tomás at his store and residence in Tetelcingo.[32] Although initially Tomás seems to have liked and trusted them both, and in fact designated both of them as character witnesses in his 1589 trial, by the following year he had come to appreciate that Felipa's loan was no bargain. The mulatto couple was a constant source of friction among Fonseca's other workers. Young Tomás, by then in his early thirties, was not the sort of man to suffer such things with equanimity. Here is what he said about the couple in 1591:

> I wrote to their mistress Felipa de Fonseca, telling her that I could not stand that mulatto of hers and I didn't want him to serve me anymore. She told me to send him to the Devil and boot him out of my house.

And besides, even beyond the fact they are mulattos, worthless low class people, Francisco and his wife Maria are troublemakers, and they have stirred up all my mineworkers to the extent that some have been wounded. When that happened I begged their mistress for the love of God to rid my house of such an evil beast, and she told me to kill the mulatto, and that she'd make it all right.... That Francisco is a thief, a murderer, a gambler, and a highwayman who caught Pedro de Soto's mulatta out on the road and stole three pesos and her blanket from her, and then raped her. And from some of Soto's Indians he stole the bread they were taking to sell up at the mines.... He's a pimp, too, for Indians and Blacks, and he induced one of my sons to take up bad habits.... He and his wife were always fighting, and María punched her husband with her fists and knocked him out; once to insult him she called him a cuckolded dog and he wasn't even bothered by that, but instead called her a whore and that the sash she was wearing had been given to her by one of her lovers. And when they came up to Mexico City they stole a horse from Juan Aguilar that was worth more than sixty pesos.... Everybody at the mines said that the both of them should have been hanged a long time ago.[33]

As the tone of this screed might indicate, bad relations between Tomás and his employees seem to have been endemic at the hacienda. Tomás had to fire two other servants, Marcos and his wife, Ana, for reasons that he did not specify, saying only that they were angry with him when they left.[34]

Tomás de Fonseca Castellanos owned and supervised his large mining hacienda, but unlike his uncle in Tlalpujahua, he appears not to have done any of the physical labor himself. Day to day, it was Tomás's retail store in Tetelcingo that engaged most of his attention; if he ever lifted a shovel, it was to sell it. The retail business fired his enthusiasm: "In the store I have in Taxco," Tomás told inquisitors, "there is every variety of merchandise that is found in the stores in Mexico City and abroad, which is why it is patronized by so many people, both Indians and Spaniards."[35] The store occupied the street level of a two-story building, with Tomás's in-town living quarters upstairs. These included a sitting room, a bedroom or two, and a dusty storage area. The two Judaizing Carvajal brothers, Luis and Baltazar, who spent a night there in 1588, reported that their room had two beds and enough ambient light that in the morning they could sit and pray from the books they had brought with them.[36] Downstairs in the store was a desk where Tomás worked on his accounts and a counter where he dispatched merchandise to customers. The store was not always busy, for sometimes when Tomás's Judaizing friends visited, they could discuss the Law of Moses there without fear of being overheard.

Like the hacienda, the shop bustled on the weekends. Tomás stressed this to inquisitors in justification of why, as a Jew, he did not always observe the Sabbath and, why as a Christian, he did not always go to Sunday mass: "It is because I was busy in my store and at my mines. Saturday is the busiest day in the whole week, since that is the day they smelt the metals and weigh what the Indians have produced and separate it and refine the silver so they can be paid on Sunday."[37] Francisco Domínguez, an astrologer friend who worked in Taxco for nine months in 1589, confirmed that he sometimes saw Fonseca put on a clean shirt on Saturday, but he thought it was because Tomás was working up a sweat at the hacienda, where Saturday was the busiest day of the week. Likewise, the Franciscan friar Francisco de Solís confirmed Tomás's harried schedule: "I noticed that he rarely heard mass on Church festivals and Sundays; and when I confronted him about it, he excused himself on account of being so busy dealing with things in his store.... But I know that he confessed and took communion, and as his vicar, that satisfied me."[38]

When the Holy Office arrested Tomás in 1589, he tried to undermine the Inquisition's case by impugning the objectivity of the people he presumed had testified against him.

> The Inquisition routinely offered accused persons an opportunity to declare who might have animus against them, and if the reasons for the enmity were clear, and there were independent confirmations of the bad blood, the witness's denunciation would be scratched out (*tachado*) and disregarded.

Employees who were close enough to the Judaizing community to know their secrets were always a risk, and if the employees turned sour, they could do the Judaizers serious damage. At the top of young Tomás's *tachas* list were the mulatto servant couple Francisco Pérez and his wife, María. Héctor de Fonseca's mine guard Felipe Freire made Tomás's list too. Freire was a violently jealous and spiteful man who was liable to lash out at anyone he suspected—often with good reason—of having had sex with his wife, whose alleged lovers included both Francisco Pérez and young Tomás's son Francisco.[39] Tomás told inquisitors that Freire hated him, both for not controlling his son and for not getting rid of Pérez. Freire also believed that Tomás had dissuaded the miner Felipe de Palacios from taking Freire on as a partner in one of Palacios's mines.[40] Tomás stated that Freire had been hanging around his house "with malicious intent in order to take vengeance on me" and had once openly threatened Tomás by telling him that his San Martín was coming.[41]

> November 11, the feast of Saint Martin of Tours, was in Spain the traditional day for slaughtering pigs that had been fattened up over the summer. By November the weather was cool enough that the meat could be processed into sausage before it spoiled. The sense of the well-known proverb "a cada puerco le llega su San Martín" (every pig has his Saint Martin's Day) is that every evil act or inappropriate deed is eventually punished.

Another on Tomás's tachas list was Mateo Ruiz, a Portuguese converso bachelor and former glass blower from Coimbra who worked for Jorge de Almeida at his Cantarranas hacienda. The enmity came about because one of Tomás's servants had called Ruiz a drunken thug. Another day, when Ruiz was in his cups, he attempted to kill one of Almeida's servants. Tomás restrained him, scolding him for his behavior. Ruiz blamed Tomás for Almeida's firing him.[42] Tomás also listed his fellow businessman Francisco de Cáceres, who came from Santalunga, near Coimbra in Portugal, and had a store in Taxco. He alleged that Cáceres hated him and refused to talk to him because Tomás had declined to testify on his behalf in a lawsuit. He added that Cáceres was scheming to take over Tomás's store by getting him banished.[43] Tomás put Diego Rodríguez del Monte on his enemies list because del Monte was convinced that Tomás had maligned him.[44]

Tomás was ambivalent about another of his mining colleagues in Taxco, Felipe de Palacios, whom he considered both a friend and a potential enemy. Like many top-level Mexican businessmen in the last quarter of the sixteenth century, Palacios had diverse financial interests, of which mining was just one. Palacios had come to Mexico prior to 1569, possibly from Italy, for in 1576 he is noted as using the alias Felipe Napolitano.[45] For a time in the late 1580s Palacios pursued a military career, raising troops to reinforce Spanish garrisons in the Philippines and Cuba. Along the way, he amassed capital sufficient to purchase a mining concession in 1590 in Hueyxtaca. Over the next twenty years, Palacios was active buying and selling mines and initiating and responding to lawsuits in the region of Taxco.[46] It was undoubtedly this aggressive, acquisitive nature that led Tomás to list Palacios among his potential enemies, accusing him, as he had accused Francisco de Cáceres, of wanting to take over his property.[47] He also tried to discredit any potential testimony by members of the Carvajal family, who were by then beginning to be embroiled in Inquisition proceedings.

By the late 1580s, forty-year-old Tomás de Fonseca Castellanos, as a proprietor of a thriving store, a substantial wholesale business, and a productive mining hacienda, was one of Taxco's most prosperous citizens, with a wide circle of associates, customers, friends, and acquaintances. In pondering his strategy in his 1590 trial, Tomás realized that the counterweight to the potentially damaging testimony offered by his enemies would be statements by people who could both confirm the animus of those on Tomás's tachas list and testify to Tomás's solidly Christian behavior. To this end, he nominated as character witnesses fifty-four individuals in the Reales de Taxco and Mexico City—people from all across social and economic spectra.[48] The list is a snapshot of the broad web of connections that a merchant-miner of Tomás de Fonseca Castellanos's day had to nurture to be successful.

In Tetelcingo there was Domingo de Alfonso, a wholesaler who often stopped by Tomás's store, the alcalde Cristobal de Tapia,[49] and Tomás's neighbors Luis de Saballos[50] and Luis Alonso de Mercado.[51] There was the astrologer Francisco Domínguez.[52] There were government workers such as the royal scribe Luis de Buitrago, Dr. Diego de Bonilla, the alcalde mayor Martín de Salinas, and the former alcalde mayor and royal scribe Cristobal de Tapia. There were soldiers such as Capitán Hernando de Mena.⁵³ There were members of the clergy, such as Padre Eugenio de Moratilla, the Franciscan friar Francisco de Solís, Padre José de Urbina, Padre Antonio de Ribas, and Tomás's sometime confessor Padre Francisco de Sotos. To these he added people who had seen him regularly at mass: Luis Martín de Molina, Blas Ruiz Agamara, Luisa de Morales, and Dr. Villanueva, his neighbor in Tetelcingo. Some were wealthy merchants and miners, such as Vicente Pereira and Juan López; as his guarantors, they backed up Tomás's promissory notes to purchase mercury for the hacienda and stock for the store.⁵⁴ He named others in the Taxco mining community, men such aa Gaspar Hernández, Pedro de Prado, who owned the Margarita Mine, and Diego Rodríguez, who mined in Real del Monte and was the sole Portuguese on his list. He listed Pedro de Soto, who sold bread to the mine owners and sometimes ate with Tomás at his hacienda. The serving classes were well represented too: he listed Martín Cerón, Antonio González's slave; Francisca, who served Juan Núñez de León; and his own servant Petronila, who had worked for him for a long time but who unfortunately, he noted, still spoke no Spanish. At his own estate and at homes where he had been a frequent visitor, such as those of the Dominican friars Pedro de Galarza and García de Saucedo, Tomás requested that the inquisitors interview entire households: masters, slaves, and Indian servants. Of all these character witnesses, only the merchant-miner Antonio Díaz de Cáceres, who was Jorge de Almeida's brother-in-law; Francisco Jorge; and the man Francisco Jorge worked for, young Tomás's cousin Héctor de Fonseca, were in his circle of close crypto-Jewish friends.

Héctor de Fonseca

Héctor de Fonseca was born in Viseu, an important market city in central Portugal. His paternal grandfather, Héctor Fernández de Abreu, a man of stature and wealth, was probably an Old Christian. His grandson remembered him as a hidalgo and knight of the honorary Order of Santiago. Héctor's father, Antonio Fernández de Almeida, served the Marqués de Villarreal.

On his mother's side, the Fonsecas descended from Jews. Fernández de Almeida and his wife, Felipa de Fonseca, produced two daughters who died in infancy and four sons—Héctor de Fonseca, Jorge de Almeida, and

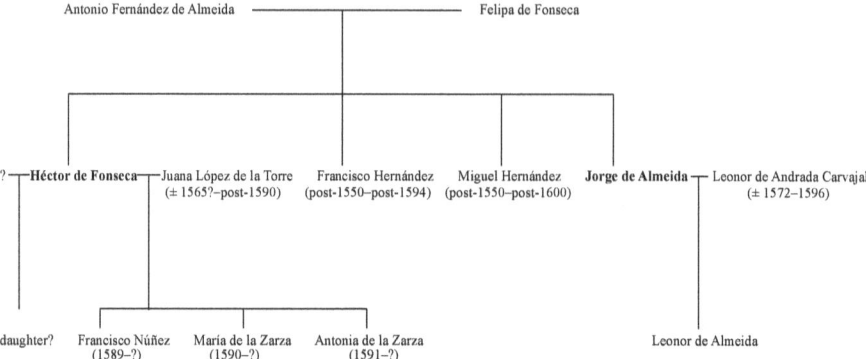

Francisco and Miguel Hernández; Héctor was the oldest. That siblings of the same parents would adopt different last names was sufficiently common at that time that nowhere in the copious documents that refer to the brothers did anyone draw attention to the fact.[55]

Héctor was still a child when the family moved to the border village of Almeida, in the Beira region, where his father served as chief administrator of the marqués's castle.[56] Somewhere along the way, Héctor acquired a solid reading knowledge of Latin. When Héctor was fourteen, his father secured a position for him as a page in the palace, hoping perhaps that this traditional first step on the ladder to government service would benefit his son and, through him, the family. But after only a year and a half, Héctor left to return to his family. Shortly after that, the family relocated to the Spanish hamlet of Saelices, fifteen kilometers from the Portuguese border on the road to the market town of Ciudad Rodrigo. In Saelices, Fernández de Almeida served as the customs inspector charged with keeping prohibited goods from being smuggled from Spain to Portugal. In 1571 Héctor sailed to Mexico with his family, most likely both pushed by the intensifying activity of the Inquisition against the Judaizing conversos in the Raya de Portugal and pulled by the promise of economic opportunity held out by the New World.[57]

When his parents brought twenty-three-year-old Héctor de Fonseca to Mexico City around 1571, it did not take him long to find that life in the capital did not suit him. Mining offered both opportunity and escape. Héctor set out for the north, wandering for two years from real to real, hoping to strike a lode that would make him rich. Although he tried his hand in

Mazapil, the Zacatecan town that Governor Luis de Carvajal y de la Cueva was using as his base for exploring and pacifying Mexico's northeastern territory, there is no record of the two men having made contact there. Héctor also prospected for silver in Tlalpujahua, but he seems not to have connected with his uncle old Tomás de Fonseca.[58]

After two years of minimal success as a miner in the north, around 1573 Héctor made his way to Taxco, where his cousin[59] young Tomás de Fonseca was working at Gaspar de Enciso's mining hacienda. In Taxco—excepting occasional visits to the capital and his final years in Mexico City in custody of the Inquisition—Héctor spent the rest of his life working a mine in Camixtla, a kilometer downhill to the east of the center of Taxco in Tetelcingo.

> Juliantla, as Camixtla or Acamixtla calls itself today, has built from the fact that Héctor de Fonseca mined there a legend that the village was a focal point of colonial Judaizing activity. Juliantla's native son and poet Francisco Luna blogs as fact that Héctor found there "silver, copper, gold, pearls, and precious stones." He adds that *Juliantla* is a corruption of *Judeanea* and that in its church the baptismal font was formerly a "Jewish ritual bath."[60] When I visited on January 31, 2009, a local guide explained that a beehive-oven-shaped mound in the village's small central plaza was the "crypt of the Jewish synagogue."

Surviving documents provide less information about Héctor de Fonseca's mine than they do about the mine of his cousin young Tomás de Fonseca. We do know that Héctor was an active and successful miner at least through March 1591, for on the ninth of that month he petitioned the alcalde mayor of Taxco, Martín de Salinas, to increase his mercury allotment from four to ten quintales, threatening that his hacienda would not be able to meet its habitual production targets unless the petition was granted. Salinas supported the request.[61] While mining for silver, Héctor had also located a valuable deposit of magistral, the copper-sulfite catalyst important to the patio process of amalgamation.

Figure 9. Juliantla "synagogue crypt." Photograph by the author.

Since miners held their license for only as long as they were actively working their mines, being jailed for lengthy periods presented serious obstacles. In May 1598, in his third year of incarceration, Héctor de Fonseca requested an audience to address the issue. His petition gives an idea of the extent of his holdings:

> In the Real de Taxco, within the boundaries of Camixtla, I have registered as sole owner a *magistral* mine. I have not dug it as deep as the ordinances require, so I request that this be done so that the mine will not be confiscated as abandoned and turned over to some other miner. This mine is underneath the hacienda's stamping mill. Likewise I have other very rich mines in that district that I have begun to exploit: three of *magistral* and three of silver. One of them is so rich that when I was arrested if they had offered me 100,000 pesos for it I would not have accepted it, because it is a very large and high quality vein. I am the only one who can tell you where it is, because I have not communicated it

with anyone because I did not want it seized to pay off some debts that I have incurred. I requested this audience because I do not want to lose it, and I do not want it sold for less than it is worth.

The inquisitors then asked Héctor if he owned any other mining property that might not yet have come to their attention. To their surprise, his answer was yes.

> I own five stakes in a mine called Mina la Margarita that Pedro de Prado has put out for shares. I hold five shares: Juan López de Obregón has bought two of them, as will be confirmed by a document signed before Juan García Parra, the scribe; Gaspar López, Juan López's brother, has two, as is also noted in the document; and the last is owned by Julián de Rebenes. . . . It is a very rich vein.[62]

All those mines and the stamping mill required a substantial workforce, but the surviving documents identify only one of Héctor's workers, Felipe Freire, who had sometimes been employed as a watchman and whom Héctor had hired as mayordomo. Eventually Héctor fired Freire for drinking, gambling, fighting, and shirking his responsibilities. Freire and his wife had a daughter, unnamed in the record, whom Héctor was considering marrying, until young Tomás talked him out of it. That undoubtedly soured Héctor's relationship with Freire as well.[63]

Although Héctor de Fonseca's sole, lifelong profession was mining, this is the sum total of what the records say about his mining activities.

Jorge de Almeida

The documents tell us a good deal more about the Cantarranas hacienda, for it has had a long and illustrious history, from its founding by Hernán Cortés through its current owner, the Universidad Nacional Autónoma de México. In the 1580s it belonged to Héctor de Fonseca's brother Jorge de Almeida.

Jorge was born circa 1550 in Almeida, a fortified town on the Portuguese-Spanish border, to which his parents had moved when his brother Héctor de Fonseca was still an infant. In 1569 his parents took him and his three siblings to Saelices, across the border in Spain. When two years later his parents sailed to Mexico, they took only Héctor. Jorge and his two younger brothers, Miguel and Francisco Hernández, made their way to the Italian city of Ferrara, where for the previous half century the Dukes of Este had encouraged the growth of a large, prosperous, and intellectual Jewish community.[64] In Ferrara's Portuguese Jewish neighborhood, Jorge was introduced to open, normative Jewish practices. There he became friends with Ruy Díaz Nieto, a Portuguese Jewish confeso from Oporto, and Ruy's son Diego, who had grown up in Italy.

> Ruy Díaz Nieto, born in Oporto around 1526, was living in Flanders in 1535. From there he relocated to Ferrara, where he took the name Jacob. In 1551, when Ferrara temporarily expelled the New Christians, he returned to Portugal to visit with family members, but in 1555 he was back in Ferrara, where he married Inés Núñez, whose Jewish name was Esther Nieto. Their son Diego was born around 1575. Two of Ruy's other children became businessmen in Istanbul; another was taken prisoner and held for ransom in the 1578 rout of the Portuguese in Morocco. Ruy Diaz, using Ferrara and Venice as his bases, traded widely and successfully throughout the Turkish Levant until a reversal of fortune ruined him. In 1590 fifteen-year-old Diego married a cousin who had been sent from Lisbon for that purpose. Soon after, leaving their wives behind, father and son set off to recoup their fortune by soliciting money to ransom the Jewish captives of North African pirates. After two years of constant travel between Italy, Spain, and Portugal, in 1594 father and son sailed to Mexico, where, until their arrest in 1596, the two Díaz Nietos played an important role in instructing the Iberian conversos in Judaism as it was practiced in the Jewish neighborhoods of Italy. Ruy was reconciled in Mexico in 1601 and included in the General Indulto of 1606. Diego's second trial lasted from 1601 to 1606.[65]

By 1580 the three brothers had split up. Almeida had left Ferrara for Madrid, where he rented a house on the Correo Mayor from a widowed doublet maker.

Almeida's housemate in Madrid was Juan Rodríguez de Silva, born in Portugal around 1560 and taken as a child by his parents to the Greek-Ottoman city of Salonica, where he was schooled in the Hebrew language and liturgy and circumcised. Before long, Almeida and Rodríguez de Silva were joined by Ruy Díaz Nieto and his son, who had returned from Ferrara. Ruy Díaz tempted the young men with stories of the economic opportunities waiting for them in New Spain, whereupon Jorge de Almeida informed them that his parents and older brother Héctor had been residing in New Spain for nearly a decade. Then Rodríguez de Silva surprised the others with the news that Almeida's younger brother, Francisco Hernández, was already in Mexico as well and that he had traveled there by a circuitous route: from Ferrara, Francisco had gone to Venice with a Jewish woman—Rodríguez de Silva did know her name or whether they had married—and from there to Salonica. In that Greek-Ottoman city, he had abandoned the woman. He had returned to Spain and finally made his way to the Indies.

Almeida and his friends resolved to go to New Spain. From Madrid the group traveled to Sevilla, where they lodged on the Calle de las Vírgenes with Blanca Lorenzo, the unmarried, tall, middle-aged woman who was Díaz Nieto's cousin. Her brother, Pelayo Álvarez, was already in Mexico. In Sevilla they reunited with Jorge's fourth brother, Miguel Hernández, a thin, white-faced man with a chestnut-colored beard who was missing one of his upper front teeth.[66] Domingo Cuello, a tall Portuguese confeso from Almofala, a small town near Lamego in the Beira Alta region, also joined their group. Years later, in the hearing room of the Inquisition in Mexico City, Diego Díaz Nieto related how in Sevilla this company of young men, all of them Portuguese confesos, most in their twenties and early thirties, all with some knowledge of Jewish practice, had drunk together and toasted their fortune. The elder Díaz Nieto volunteered to help them secure the necessary permits for crossing to the Indies.[67] They must have omitted giving any information about their Jewish ancestry or their previous residence among openly practicing Jews in Italy and Ottoman Turkey because, papers in hand, they were permitted to set sail for the New World.[68]

Almeida was not a handsome man. Diego Díaz Nieto described him as "of medium stature, of dark complexion, with a scar running across his face, pock marked, and with a patchy baldness."[69] Although Héctor was the oldest of the four brothers, Jorge was the alpha: entrepreneurial, decisive, willing to take risks; clever, beguiling, persuasive; impatient, intolerant; strong willed and often overbearing. During his years in Ferrara, Jorge de Almeida had honed the business talents that would soon make him an accomplished tratante, combining the skills of investor, jobber, and wholesaler. He had learned to monitor the pulse of supply and demand in the markets of foodstuffs and durable goods. When he could, he bought on credit and sold for cash, leveraging his credit to increase the volume of his transactions. Almeida lent money to others, too, and used the interest to build up his stock.

In Mexico City the young men separated. At first Almeida rented a suite of rooms in a house owned by Juan Rodríguez Sánchez near the monastery and church of Santo Domingo. The neighborhood was adjacent to the capital's main business thoroughfare, Calle Tacuba, and was a favorite of the merchant class, including the Portuguese conversos. Later he bought a house and purchased a slave, a Chichimeca woman named María, to run it for him.[70]

Almeida quickly made friends among the converso community, among them the fellow tratante Antonio Díaz de Cáceres, who had been buying, selling, and dealing in Mexico for nearly a decade. Almeida believed in the wisdom of diversifying his investments, and, in the context of his time and place, silver offered the greatest potential for profit. Díaz de Cáceres, too, seemed interested in acquiring mining property. The two men were well aware that success in the silver business could confer both power and prestige. Almeida's brother Héctor was making a decent living as a miner in Taxco, and the town was booming. The Cantarranas hacienda, in a prime location, and with the aura of having once belonged to the Marqués del Valle, Hernán Cortés himself, was up for sale. In 1586 Almeida bought it.

Cortés's Cantarranas hacienda was finished around 1534, about the time of the first significant silver strikes in the Taxco area. In 1539 the conquistador transferred title for the hacienda, together with its hydraulic system, three mills, tubs for sluicing away detritus that was devoid of minerals, stables, eleven mules, Indians, and thirteen slaves, to his legitimate son Martín.[71] By 1543 Cantarranas had become the property of the alcalde mayor of Taxco, Luis de Castilla. Sometime after that it passed to the powerful Mendoza family and then, around 1571, through Leonor de Mendoza to her husband, Pedro Ruiz de Alarcón.[72] At that time the hacienda comprised nineteen buildings; living there were twenty-seven European residents, 217 Indians, and 176 slaves.[73] Jorge de Almeida bought Cantarranas in 1586, along with an adjacent hacienda that had belonged first to Diego and Catalina de la Nava and then to Nicolás Ruiz de Valderrama; his wife, Leonor; and their son Nicolás.[74]

Over the centuries the hacienda has passed through many hands. In modern times it was sacked and largely destroyed by Zapata's troops during the 1910 revolution. In 1944 it was converted to a hotel, and several guesthouses were built over the ruins of the hacienda's processing plants. In the 1980s the government of Guerrero acquired the property, turning a portion of it into a culinary school and the rest into an arts center. In 1992 it was turned over to the municipality of Taxco, which ceded the central buildings to the Universidad Nacional Autónoma de México for its Centro de Enseñanza para Extranjeros (School for Foreigners).[75]

In the spring of 1586, Almeida purchased two neighboring haciendas from Nicolás Ruiz de Valderrama. Included in this second purchase, in addition to the buildings, machinery, tools, silver both in the ground and in the partially processed ore, were all the slaves and serving people and animals present on the property as of the date of purchase. Standing as guarantors if Almeida should miss any of the scheduled payments were Antonio Díaz de Cáceres, Héctor de Fonseca, and Tomás de Fonseca Castellanos.[76] These three men, either together or individually in combination with other Taxco miners, also figure as guarantors for the allotments of mercury that Almeida bought for his amalgamation patios.[77]

When Almeida purchased Cantarranas, he became, de facto, a miner. This does not mean that he ever hefted a pick and shovel like his brother Héctor and old Tomás de Fonseca, or that he knew how to distinguish a lump of silver-bearing ore from any other black-streaked chunk of quartz of the sort that abounds in the mountains of Guerrero. As a tratante, he saw the mine and its *hacienda de beneficiar plata* not as a career choice but as an investment to be held for a time, exploited for what it could produce and then, when the price was right, sold for a profit. For a tratante, owning a mine was like owning a ship: it was an instrument for creating value and conferring status, both key elements in the acquisition and wielding of power. The actual management of the mine could be delegated, technical expertise could be purchased, and the physical labor of extracting and refining the ore was the province of Indians, slaves, and wage-labor naboríos. Almeida's role was to hire the senior staff, oversee the costs of production, secure lines of credit, and manage the cash flow at Cantarranas and his other business ventures.[78] In other words, his job was to make money.

He was also not above cheating the government. The law required him to deliver his refined silver exclusively to the state. It obligated him to have it weighed at the assay office and to pay to the royal treasury a tax (quintal) of one-fifth of its value. When his ingots were stamped, indicating that the tax had been paid, they were then legal tender. Mariana Núñez de Carvajal, in her testimony of June 1600, said that her sister Leonor had told her that Almeida had an unauthorized quintal stamp that allowed him to legalize his silver without paying the tax. His friends Luis de Carvajal, Baltazar Rodríguez de Carvajal, and Cristóbal Gómez, who were in on the fraud with Almeida, said they incurred no sin in doing this because, after all, they were Jews.[79]

We know a good deal about the physical layout of Almeida's Cantarranas, both from contemporary documents and from the estate's visible architectural remains. Perhaps the most detailed description of how the hacienda was laid out in the 1580s comes from Francisco Díaz, a Portuguese shoemaker who in 1589 was employed by Jorge de Almeida as mayordomo for the modest salary of 150 pesos per year. Díaz wrote to the Mexican Inquisition from Peru in 1592 about the several months when almost the entire Carvajal clan was in residence in Cantarranas.[80] Documents relating to transfers of ownership of the estate and to its eventual confiscation and subsequent sale at auction fill out the picture.[81]

The industrial parts of the hacienda occupied a leveled stretch of ground a short distance uphill from the residences, on the south bank of the arroyo that brought water from high on Mount Atache. A millrace channeled the stream to the vertically mounted waterwheel of the stamping mill, constructed around 1580. The wheel powered a rotating shaft mounted with nine cams. Two water-powered grinding wheels reduced the lumps to powder, which was then moved to a boat-shaped basin, where the lighter, non-mineral-bearing powder was sluiced away. The remaining silver-laced powder was taken to the floor of the amalgamation patios. Other buildings stored salt and magistral. Nearby were the ovens for boiling off the incorporated mercury from the silver. Somewhere nearby there must have been a massive pile of wood to fuel them. Adjacent to this working core were several storage sheds that held the miners' picks, chisels, hammers, saws, pry bars, and strainers made of iron mesh.[82] Another shed stored tack for the pack mules and the working mules, whose slow plodding around another vertically mounted drive shaft powered the paddles that stirred the mud on the floor of the amalgamation patios (today the site of one of these is a swimming pool). Between the mills and the hacienda's main residence was the administration building, where the mayordomo had his office and where the containers of mercury, the scale and trays of weights, and the most valuable tools were stored. Farther up the hill were several cabins for the slaves, repartimiento Indians, and the naboríos. To one side of the hacienda's working core stood a chapel; once a week a priest came from Tetelcingo to say mass. There was a garden on the grounds, too, where Almeida and his guests like to stroll and sometimes recite their prayers.[83] The Almeida family and their guests lived in the main house, immediately downhill from the industrial areas. Since the residence was of less importance to the Inquisition than the hacienda's working components, the documents indicate only that it had two stories, several bedrooms, and a corridor for accessing the rooms on the first floor. There is no mention of its furnishings, nor of a kitchen, although they indicate that Isabel de Carvajal, during her visit to Cantarranas in 1588–1589, was in charge of preparing meals. Serving girls kept the house in order.[84]

Next door, the former Ruiz de Valderrama property also had a water-powered, nine-hammer crushing mill, as well as a horse-powered eight-hammer mill and a full complement of washing tubs, sheds, and workers' cabins. That hacienda was equipped with a bronze retort (*desazogadera*) for boiling off the amalgamated mercury and two pairs of bellows, made of wood and leather, to fan the ovens up to the correct temperature. Next to the stables stood a smithy with a fully equipped forge. Both properties were dotted by a number of mine shafts that the documents always refer to as *minas* in the plural, without bothering to note how many there were or precisely where the shafts were located.

Figure 10. Cantarranas aqueduct, Taxco. Photograph by the author.

Figure 11. Cantarranas amalgamation patio, Taxco. Photograph by the author.

The workforce of the two estates must have been very large. The assessor who inventoried Cantarranas prior to its being offered at auction in 1592 made note of nine of Almeida's slaves by name: Pedro, mulatto, age twenty-eight, captain of the mines; María, his sister; Manuel and his wife, Lucía; Juan; another Manuel; Francisco, age forty; another Juan; and Domingo. Almeida acquired these nine, who were all born in various parts of Africa, as part of the property he purchased six years earlier.[85] The anonymous uninventoried workers were most likely repartimiento Indians and naboríos.

One of Almeida's employees was Francisco Díaz, a converso shoemaker a few years younger than Almeida, who had found himself at loose ends when he first arrived in Mexico. He took lodging with Ana de Larios, the wife of Antonio de los Cobos, who at the time was serving as alcalde de minas in Sonsonete.[86] Cobos, an entrepreneur deeply involved in both Atlantic and Pacific maritime trade, was well-known to Almeida and to his brother-in-law Antonio Díaz de Cáceres. So when Francisco Díaz decided to seek his fortune in Taxco, it was probably Cobos who introduced him to Almeida.[87] At first Díaz worked at Cantarranas for free, but before long Almeida put him on salary for 150 pesos per year. He was the full-time supervisor at the hacienda in 1588 when the Carvajal family moved into the residence's upstairs rooms. Cobos, too, worked for Almeida at Cantarranas for a short time in late 1589 while the Carvajal clan was in residence.[88]

Francisco Díaz was himself an able businessman, with a head for numbers and a character that tolerated the risks associated with investment. He may well have learned during his time with Almeida how to increase wealth by keeping his assets in play. So, as Díaz wrote from Lima to the Mexican inquisitors, when he left Cantarranas and Almeida paid him his back wages in a lump sum, "I realized that by investing the money in imported Chinese clothing and taking it to the mines to sell, I would realize a greater profit."[89] That is precisely what he did.

Jorge de Almeida operated the Cantarranas mining complex for eight years. In April 1590, learning that the Inquisition had ordered his arrest, Almeida went into hiding, having already transferred title to the hacienda to old Tomás de Fonseca. Three months later Almeida slipped away on a ship bound for Spain. The Inquisition confiscated the estate and on September 26, 1591, sold it at public auction to Almeida's neighbor and sometimes friend Felipe de Palacios.[90]

Antonio Díaz de Cáceres

The fourth converso silver miner in Taxco was Jorge de Almeida's brother-in-law Antonio Díaz de Cáceres, a volatile, wealthy, politically astute, multi-faceted businessman and adventurer. Díaz de Cáceres was born around 1540 in the Portuguese village of Santa Comba Dão, halfway between Viseu and Coimbra. His mother, Leonor López, taught her son Antonio the rudiments of Judaism when he was a child.[91] His father, Manuel López, a comptroller in the royal Portuguese Exchequer, secured a place for ten-year-old Antonio as a page to the Count of Vimoso, who was a cousin to the king. Two years later he had him placed as valet to Prince Duarte.[92] Positions such as these were often used to train the sons of nobles for a life of service to the monarchy as counselors, senior bureaucrats, ambassadors, and military officers, which suggests that Manuel López must have had considerable cachet at court and was most likely not descended from converted Jews. Antonio continued on a typical career path to royal service that included, in his later teens, three long stints at sea on Portuguese warships, serving with the noted explorers and military commanders Gascón de Acuña, García de Toledo, and Francisco Barreto.[93] During a shore leave in Portugal, Díaz's parents arranged for him to marry a woman named Juana López, who soon gave him a daughter, whom they named Isabel. When both mother and daughter died shortly thereafter, Antonio Díaz de Cáceres went back to sea. He spent the next few years as a naval officer and merchant, gradually amassing wealth and getting to know the important commanders of Spain's and Portugal's Atlantic fleets. In the course of his service, he several times visited Mexico's Gulf Coast ports. In 1574, now a young man of thirty-four with capital to invest, political connections, and a solid knowledge of transatlantic trade, he began to sink entrepreneurial roots into the soil of Mexico.[94]

Although Mexico City was the largest and busiest city in New Spain, in the late 1570s it was in many ways still a small town. Members of the Portuguese Judaizing community, which was then just beginning to grow in earnest, inevitably knew each other. One of the first people Díaz de Cáceres got to know was old Tomás de Fonseca, who in the years following his father's death was making occasional visits to Mexico from his Tlalpujahua mine. The two men do not appear to have been friends—the twenty-year difference in their ages and the marked differences in their temperaments precluded that—but they probably did business together. If there was any cordiality between them, however, it soon evaporated. In his 1596 Inquisition trial, old Tomás—never a man to forgive or forget an injury—listed Antonio Díaz de Cáceres among his enemies, alleging that Díaz's putting up surety money for one of Tomás's competitors had spoiled a business deal that Tomás had been negotiating twenty years earlier.[95]

Another of Díaz de Cáceres's converso colleagues was Antonio de los Cobos, in whose house both Díaz de Cáceres and Francisco Díaz had lodged when they first arrived in Mexico City. Cobos, born in 1557, claimed to be a native of Cádiz, but that did not preclude his having Portuguese roots, as Cádiz, like Sevilla, was another of those Andalusian ports whose legitimacy-seeking "natives" were in fact transients on their way to the Indies.[96] Cobos was just twenty when in 1577 he entered into an investment partnership with Antonio Díaz de Cáceres. They remained close friends and business partners for the next two decades.[97]

Antonio Díaz de Cáceres met Jorge de Almeida shortly after Almeida's arrival in Mexico City in 1582, and the two men, of similar talents and ambitions, quickly bonded. When several years later Almeida purchased the Cantarranas hacienda and entered the mining business, Díaz de Cáceres followed suit, purchasing a hacienda de beneficiar metales in Tenango. While both men continued to base themselves in Mexico City, living in rented rooms and leaving the day-to-day operation of their mining haciendas largely in the hands of trusted employees, they appear to have made the 340-kilometer round-trip to Taxco frequently enough to remain in firm control of their estates' operations. Like Almeida, Antonio Díaz de Cáceres was first and foremost a man of finance and trade, importing, exporting, buying and selling, wholesaling imported goods to jobbers and to retail merchants in Mexico City and the mining centers. According to Antonio de los Cobos, testifying in July 1590, Díaz's dabbling ranged from macro to micro, from buying and selling shares in mines to leasing a "lady's bed" to María de los Apóstoles's daughter Mariana. His receivables as tallied by the Inquisition included five hundred pesos from a shoemaker named Rueda, four hundred pesos from Hernando de Vega, and other sums from Manuel and Cristóbal Gómez in Mexico and several people in Peru.[98]

Díaz's hacienda was undoubtedly similar to Almeida's at Cantarranas, although probably smaller in scope. At times he owned other mining properties as well, such as the one he sold to Pedro de la Piedra, Taxco's alcalde de minas, despite an uncertainty about its water rights. And then in 1590, having not been fully paid, he sued to get it back.[99] However, other than the fact that Díaz de Cáceres owned a hacienda and sometimes lived there with his wife, Catalina de la Cueva Carvajal, no descriptions of the property or its operation have come to light.

Chapter 11
The Jewish Life of the Taxco Miners

> Lots of Portuguese people have come to my house in the mines of Taxco;
> some of them were [Sebastián de la] Peña and Sebastián Rodríguez
> and Manuel de Lucena's friend Manuel Gómez [Navarro],
> Duarte Rodríguez, and Luis de Carvajal.
> —TOMÁS DE FONSECA CASTELLANOS, NOVEMBER 18, 1595[1]

Two Weddings

By the mid-1580s Antonio Díaz de Cáceres, who was in his forties, and Jorge de Almeida, ten years his junior, had become friends. Both were wheeler-dealer tratantes of similar disposition and accomplishment. Both were wealthy and well established, each with a house in Mexico City and a mining hacienda in the reales in Taxco. Both felt it was time for them to wed. Díaz de Cáceres suggested that they consider two nieces of Governor Luis de Carvajal y de la Cueva, Catalina León de la Cueva and Leonor de Andrada Carvajal.

In becoming one of Mexico City's wealthiest businessmen, Antonio Díaz de Cáceres had curried friendship with members of the top strata of colonial society, including Luis de Carvajal y de la Cueva. When Carvajal returned to Mexico in 1580 as governor of Nuevo León, Díaz de Cáceres came to know many of the people the governor had brought back with him, ostensibly to populate Nuevo León. Among them were the governor's sister Francisca Núñez de Carvajal; her husband, Francisco Rodríguez de Matos; and their nine children. By 1584 the bond between Díaz de Cáceres and the Carvajal clan was close enough that the family asked him to serve as a pallbearer at Rodríguez de Matos's funeral.

Díaz de Cáceres told Almeida that Catalina, who was in her early twenties, and Leonor, who was just reaching puberty, were pretty, well mannered, and faithful daughters of Israel. The fact that the widowed Francisca and her children were so poor that the Carvajal daughters could bring to the marriage no dowry whatsoever was of little concern to them.² Once Díaz de Cáceres and Almeida had made their decision, Díaz proposed the match to the girls' brother, young Luis de Carvajal, and Luis put the question to their mother. Francisca instantly grasped that a match with the wealthy businessmen, both of them Judaizing conversos,³ would bring her family's endemic poverty to an end. She realized that one potential impediment was the governor, who was hoping to marry his nieces to unimpeachable Old Christians, thus cementing his own bona fides as an observant Christian. All parties to the marriage negotiation agreed that it would be best not to inform the governor until after the ceremony, when it would be too late for him to intervene. In Pánuco, doña Francisca and Catalina began teaching twelve-year-old Leonor the rudiments of Jewish observance.⁴

In March 1586, just before Passover, the two men journeyed to Pánuco to claim their brides. With them in the wedding party were Almeida's brother Miguel Hernández, their friend Gonzalo Pérez Ferro, who was a cousin of the Carvajals, and Fray Gaspar de Carvajal, one of the brides' brothers. Francisca and her daughters rejoiced in the lively wedding music (the musicians hired by the grooms) and their fancy new clothes and jewels (gifts of the grooms). These sumptuous gifts were recorded as dowry provided by the brides' family. This allowed the Carvajals to save face by providing a wedding gift to the grooms, as was Jewish custom; the two savvy tratantes also believed that this fiction would shelter some of their assets in the event that any financial judgments were brought against them. In the midst of the joyful celebration, Fray Gaspar was torn between sharing his mother's happiness at seeing the girls well married and the family rescued from poverty, and his nervousness about the overtly Jewish flavor of the event and the consequences of what discovery of the family's Judaizing might do to them all.

Immediately following the ceremony, Díaz de Cáceres and Almeida took their brides, along with Francisca and young Anica, back to the capital. A few months later Baltazar and Fray Gaspar brought the rest of the youngsters. In 1588 Díaz de Cáceres and Almeida took their wives to live at their haciendas de minas in Taxco, and much of the Rodríguez-Carvajal family soon came to join them. The following year they all moved back to the capital.

With the wedding of Jorge de Almeida and Antonio Díaz de Cáceres to Leonor and Catalina, the fates of the two grooms and the Carvajal clan became inextricably linked. For the next decade—until all the principals had fled, perished, or been reconciled with the church as Christians—the Carvajals played a catalytic role in the Judaizing community in the reales of Taxco and Pachuca.

One reason was the indefatigable energy and proselytizing zeal of the Carvajal brothers Luis and Baltazar. In his 1589 trial, Luis volunteered his profession as tratante, though in his second trial, in 1595, he said that he had no profession at all. In truth, he and his brother Baltazar were itinerant vendors whose wares tended to be at the low end of the commercial spectrum. As Luis explained in March 1589:

> I have been making my living traveling to the mines, from Taxco to the Mixteca and Oaxaca, . . . Zacatecas and Michoacán. . . . The things my brother and I sell were my mother's. . . . Twenty-four days ago my brother Baltazar and I left Mexico carrying little things to sell, like blankets from Campeche, shoes from the Indian market, a net bed [hammock] and some Rouen cloth, some raisins and fruit preserves, and we took those up to the mines in Pachuca to sell.[5]

As Luis and Baltazar crisscrossed the high plateaus of central Mexico, sometimes individually and sometimes together, they took every opportunity to seek out the conversos who lived in the reales de minas. Lodging in refinery haciendas, in living quarters attached to conversos' stores, or in the rustic cabins of cattle ranchers and pick-and-shovel miners, the Carvajals talked incessantly with conversos about what Luis had taken to calling "the Law that God gave to Moses." When these outlying conversos came to Mexico City on business, they generally sought out the Carvajal household as a place where they could touch base with their religious heritage. There, too, they could always count on Jewish talk from the Carvajal siblings, since Luis, Baltazar, Isabel, and Mariana (when she was lucid) were all inveterate proselytizers, with Luis the most indomitable of the lot. Justa Méndez put it this way:

> Whenever anyone came into the room, it was Luis de Carvajal's custom

to greet them, ask them how they were doing, and then take out his book and preach to them and admonish them to follow the Law of Moses, and to die in that law. He told them they must do that if they found themselves jailed by the Inquisition, because then they would go straight to heaven. Mariana professed the same thing.[6]

The Carvajal siblings remained close to their married sisters, and they instructed, criticized, and bedeviled their cautious brothers-in-law with the openness of their Judaizing.

The Grooms: Jorge de Almeida and Antonio Díaz de Cáceres

Jorge de Almeida's Judaizing had begun in Portugal and had been nurtured in Ferrara. His mother, Felipa de Fonseca, had come to Mexico City around 1571 with her husband, Antonio Fernández de Almeida, and her other sons, Héctor de Fonseca and Miguel Hernández. Héctor almost immediately set off to the silver fields of the far north and eventually settled in Taxco. Jorge de Almeida came in 1580 or 1581, joining his mother and his younger brother Miguel in Mexico City in rented rooms in a house near the Church of Santo Domingo.[7] In April 1583 Jorge hosted a Passover gathering there. In addition to the three brothers—Jorge; Héctor, who had come up from Taxco; and Miguel Hernández, who had arrived in Mexico sometime previously—the family group included Felipa and her cousin Julián de Castellanos, who by then had resided in Mexico City for more than thirty years. The sole nonfamily member was Antonio Díaz de Cáceres. Felipa set her table in a long hallway and laid out her best silver implements. While her guests accommodated themselves and Felipa worked in the kitchen, the Chichimeca servant[8] carried to the table platters of roast and stewed chicken accompanied by mountains of fruit. Julián de Castellanos told inquisitors in 1590 that the two main topics of conversation around the table were the biblical story of Israel's escape from captivity in Egypt and how Jews must not venerate wooden images as the Christians do because that is idolatry.[9]

Like Almeida, Antonio Díaz de Cáceres had learned the rudiments of Judaism from his family in Portugal when he was a child. Unlike Almeida, he seems to have realized early that he was not comfortable with the risks involved in Judaizing. There is no hint of his engaging in any Jewish activity in the Portuguese court as a teenage page or at sea with the Portuguese navy in his late teens and early twenties. We do not know whether his short-lived first wife, Juana López, chosen for him by his parents, was a conversa.

The documents are all but silent about the two men's Judaizing activities between their arrival in Mexico and their marriage to the Carvajal sisters. In fact, despite the Inquisition's rigorous investigations into the later religious activities of both men, they do not record any Judaizing activities between the 1583 Passover dinner and the wedding. There is no doubt whatsoever that both Almeida and Díaz de Cáceres were well aware of their families' Portuguese converso heritage.[10] Before coming to Mexico, both men had traveled widely—Díaz de Cáceres on the Atlantic sea lanes and Almeida to Ferrara, where he had with mingled with the openly practicing Jewish community.[11] Both men clearly had some knowledge of the myriad rules that shape Jewish observance, although neither of them is recorded as having deep expertise or even curiosity about Jewish practice. Unlike so many of their contemporaries, there is no record of their asking questions of their more knowledgeable friends, participating in philosophical discussions, or speculating about the Messiah. They exhibit no sign of ambivalence in their religious identification or of wrestling with the conflicting theologies of Judaism and Christianity. But they thought of themselves as Jews, and it was important to both of them to choose wives from a Judaizing converso family.

Both Díaz de Cáceres and Almeida were men of vast ambition who depended on their wealth and their reputation as upstanding Christians to provide them access to the elite levels of government and commerce. They were skilled chameleons, what Thomas F. Glick called "cultural commuters," people who were comfortable in both Judaism and Christianity and adapted their behavior to the social context.[12] When functioning in the Christian world, they were adept at changing their colors to suit the circumstances and always reticent about letting their Jewish beliefs be known or their infrequent Judaizing practices be observed. Both men were self-aware and hypersensitive to their surroundings, characteristics that were often noted by their friends and associates. Given the number of people who reported seeing them going about their business on Saturday, neither man seems to have treated the Sabbath as a special day. Neither seems to have been fastidious about avoiding foods prohibited by the Jewish dietary regulations.[13] Both men seem to have avoided participating in communal Jewish religious observances: none of the more than two dozen gatherings for Yom Kippur, Purim, and Passover that are chronicled in Inquisition dossiers for the late 1580s and early 1590s list Almeida among the attendees. Only one mentions Díaz de Cáceres: a communal Yom Kippur fast in 1588 with Catalina, Mariana, and Ana Carvajal in Mexico City.[14]

As much as any of the Mexican Judaizers, and undoubtedly more than most, the two entrepreneurs were obsessive about polishing their Christian facade to a sheen that would deflect any inquisitive eye. Almeida went regularly to mass and made certain that he was observed entering and leaving the church and kneeling and crossing himself like the other parishioners. The Cantarranas hacienda that Almeida had purchased included a chapel, and Almeida took care to have a priest come out from the main Taxco real of Tetelcingo each Sunday to say mass.

Both men pressured their wives to fulfill their Christian obligations and to avoid communal Judaizing. For Catalina, who was knowledgeable about Jewish practices and committed to their observance, her marriage to Antonio Díaz de Cáceres and separation from the Judaizing nucleus of her family was a profoundly isolating experience. "After I was married," she said, "I almost always felt that I was alone. I kept some Sabbaths, but not as frequently as I did when I was young out of fear that my husband might see me or hear about it."[15] Almeida was well aware that his bride was inexperienced, naive, and not very bright, traits that, when she testified in 1589, Leonor acknowledged without any apparent embarrassment:

> I didn't know how to cook, not even what to throw into a pot, because I was a child and nobody had taught me. So he instructed me, he supervised everything, because I was so young, and he came right into the kitchen.... He told me what to say and how to answer when people came to the house.... He made me get up and go to mass on Sunday like he did, which is very different from what my mother and sister doña Isabel used to do."[16]

Leonor even went to confession in the company of her mother and her sisters—four times, she said, twice in Mexico City and twice in Taxco—limiting herself, per their instructions, to speaking only of her violations of the commandments. She told her inquisitors that she never mentioned her Judaizing because her family had told her there was nothing wrong about it.[17]

But if Díaz de Cáceres and Almeida had truly wished to keep any blemish from marring their Christian facades, their marriage to the Carvajal sisters had been inopportune, for most of their new Carvajal in-laws were ardent, committed Judaizers, openly observing the Sabbath and celebrating the festivals. Luis, in fact, encouraged Díaz de Cáceres to be more scrupulous in his Jewish practice. In Luis's recollection, on one occasion in 1588, Díaz de Cáceres, at Luis's urging and in the presence of Leonor and her daughters, opened up his heart to them, confessing that at his core he was a faithful Jew. Together he and Luis talked about how the Messiah had not come, how God was only one, not three, and how the statues of Jesus and the saints were idols. But, as Luis later lamented, Díaz de Cáceres openly acknowledged his Judaism only that one time. After that,

> with us he showed himself to the be world's biggest Christian. He taught his daughter Leonorica the four [Christian] prayers with so much enthusiasm that I could not stand it and had to remove myself from his sight because it was just too much. I think he did it out of fear that if we were arrested we would accuse him.... Since that time eight years ago [1588] when we confessed to each other we were Jews, I've never seen him fast or observe any ceremony, because in external things he is like an apostate from the Law [of Moses], careful never to keep the Sabbath nor the festivals, nor to abstain from eating dirty foods.[18]

After the 1586 wedding and before they moved to Taxco, Jorge de Almeida, with his wife, Leonor; Francisca; and little Anica, moved into a rented house in Mexico City's San Pablo district, just north of the new cathedral. By the end of the year, Baltazar Carvajal and Isabel had joined them. Antonio Díaz de Cáceres and his wife, Catalina, lived near the San Juan Market, a few blocks to the south.[19] Little Miguel was attending the Jesuit school and Mariana the School for Girls. When Mariana emerged after nine months at the school at age fifteen, her mother deemed her ready to be married and promised her to Jorge de León, Francisca's first cousin.

Mariana was an intelligent, beautiful, and charming young lady, but also given to bouts of antic raving and dark periods of depression. Despite the fact that Jorge de Almeida was already married to Mariana's sister Leonor, he was utterly smitten with her. Almeida demanded that Mariana's engagement to León be broken so that he could take her as a second wife. The Carvajal family reacted in shocked horror, but Almeida brushed aside their objections, arguing that there was precedent in that the biblical patriarch Jacob had taken the sisters Leah and Rachel as wives. Almeida told the family that just as soon as he could take Mariana to some European Jewry where plural marriage was permitted, the two of them would be wed. For this too, he said, there was precedent, because according to the apocryphal book of Esdras, God had commanded the children of Israel to put aside the wives they had taken while living in captivity and to take new Jewish wives once they had escaped to live in freedom.[20] Mariana's mother at first objected, but then, in the face of Almeida's overwhelming personality, and seeing the potential financial advantage of this new match to the always-needy Carvajal family, she relented and broke off Mariana's engagement to Jorge de León. This turned the León branch of her family into implacable enemies. When the remainder of Francisca's children and her close converso friends pointed out to Francisca that Almeida's marriage to Mariana would devastate Leonor (who had not yet been told of these plans for her sister), Francisca reversed her decision. A better solution, the family decided, without informing Almeida, and after improbably having persuaded Mariana to accept, would be for Mariana to marry Almeida's brother Héctor! They were all aware that Héctor was already married to Juana López de la Torre,[21] but they reasoned that, by the very passage in Esdras that Almeida had cited, Héctor's marriage was void because Juana was an Old Christian.

It seems that Héctor, too, had lusted after Mariana for some time. According to Antonio Díaz de Cáceres, Héctor used to hang around Almeida's hacienda trying to get something going with Mariana. Or maybe it was with her widowed older sister, Isabel—Díaz de Cáceres was not certain. Either way, he said, the Carvajal women felt uncomfortable around Héctor. But as long as they were all Almeida's guests at Cantarranas, they could not prevent Héctor from coming to the hacienda.

When the family broached with Héctor the idea of marriage to Mariana, for a moment or two he was elated by the possibility of exchanging his Old Christian harridan for a young Jewish beauty. But he quickly realized the folly of his marrying the woman for whom his powerful brother lusted.

Antonio Díaz de Cáceres, who was incensed by the original plan and its current permutation, said both schemes were an abomination, that Jews no longer practiced plural marriage, and that this tangle must be the work of the devil. In his rage, he took after Almeida with a knife. With the Carvajal family's rapidly cooling enthusiasm and the excuse that all these plans were moot until the family had relocated to Italy, the matter was shelved.[22]

Still, hard feelings remained. The strain of these negotiations sent fragile young Mariana into a deep depression from which she never recovered. The episode poisoned the relationship between Héctor and the Carvajal women. Jorge de Almeida fell out with Héctor too. Again according to Díaz de Cáceres, Francisca, her son Luis, and Almeida, all of them acting together, had asked one of Almeida's slaves to murder Héctor. In reward, Almeida had promised to grant the slave his freedom. That plot had never gone further, but according to various witnesses, the family was so angry at Héctor that the women threw stones at him and Díaz de Cáceres tried to knife him.[23] In Héctor's recollection, recorded in 1600 when he was sick with the pox and often delusional, he had never really wanted to marry Mariana, only to have sex with her, and that is why her brothers-in-law had tried to stab him. Mariana, also testifying in 1600, long after Almeida had gone back to Spain, said that the real reason he had done so was so he could bring the whole family to Europe, where he could make good on his promise to marry her. Relations did not improve between Héctor and the Carvajal women and their husbands until years later, when Héctor joined the effort to raise money to release the penanced Carvajals from having to wear their sambenitos.[24]

During the late 1580s, Almeida was making the three-and-a-half-day trip between Mexico City and Taxco frequently to supervise his hacienda. Sometime during the winter of 1588, perhaps because of the rumors of increasing activity of the Inquisition in Mexico City, or perhaps because he and Antonio Díaz de Cáceres were temporarily strapped for funds and it was less costly to live in a small town,[25] the two men decided to bring their Carvajal in-laws to their Taxco estates.

To Cantarranas came Leonor de Carvajal; her mother, Francisca; her widowed sister Isabel; and the Carvajal brothers Luis, Baltazar, and young Miguelito. To Díaz de Cáceres's hacienda in Tenango went his wife, Catalina, and her sisters Mariana (perhaps to keep her away from Almeida) and Anica. The conflicting degree of religious commitment within the two marriages—the men determined to avoid visible Judaizing; the women eager to practice—is clearly visible during their residence in Taxco. It inevitably gave rise to tension, as both Almeida and Díaz de Cáceres expected a greater degree of self-monitoring than their Carvajal in-laws were willing, or able, to practice.

The three Carvajal women residing in Tenango were deeply frustrated because Díaz de Cáceres barred them from any Judaizing activity whatsoever. When he was at home, the sisters walked on eggshells. They could talk about their beliefs only when they were visiting the rest of their family at Cantarranas. All the Carvajal women knew from experience how any overt Judaizing on their part made Díaz de Cáceres angry and how his rage often provoked him to violence. They recalled how he had ripped up the hair shirt that Isabel had chosen to wear in penance for not always observing the Jewish rites and how he had seized from her a small book of Jewish prayers and thrown it into a well while threatening to denounce her to the Inquisition.[26] Another time he actually punched his sister-in-law Leonor, which so provoked her Carvajal siblings that they attacked him with knives. Because of Díaz's acerbic character and standoffish attitude with regard to communal Judaizing, together with the fact that his hacienda lay on the far side of Taxco for people coming from Mexico City, Judaizers like Manuel Gómez Navarro and Duarte Rodríguez were more likely to lodge at Cantarranas or with young Tomás de Fonseca Castellanos in the central Real de Tetelcingo than they were with Díaz de Cáceres.

Cantarranas was the family social center. Luis de Carvajal later testified that the family would often gather there in the evening to talk about the Law of Moses while Miguelito slept in a corner.[27] In the autumn of 1588, when Díaz de Cáceres returned to the capital, Leonor's sisters Catalina, Mariana, and Ana found it a relief to move in with their siblings in Cantarranas,[28] although given that Almeida, too, had a violent temper, they also felt they had to hide their Judaizing from him. But in March 1589, with Jorge de Almeida conveniently away on business, the Carvajal family felt free to celebrate Passover at his hacienda, although even then they exercised a certain caution, substituting tortillas for the matzo that they feared might draw the attention of the hacienda staff.[29]

The women knew that Almeida could go overboard when he thought that his Christian facade was at risk or when one of his Judaizing friends was being threatened with exposure.[30] When one of Cristóbal Gómez's black woman servants threatened to go to the Inquisition about Gómez's Judaizing, Gómez confided his concern to Antonio López. López in turn told Antonio de Morales and Jorge de Almeida about Gómez's worry, at which point Morales and Almeida put an end to the threat by strangling the woman, using a towel so as not to leave any incriminating marks and then placing her in her bed to suggest that she had died of natural causes.[31]

Cristóbal Gómez, a Portuguese converso from a village just outside Fundão, had a store on the Calle San Agustín in Mexico City. He was Antonio López's cousin. An intimate of the Carvajal family who visited Francisco Rodríguez de Matos during his last illness, he often teamed with Luis in his efforts to deepen the Jewish education of the capital's Judaizing community. He contributed to the support of Antonio Machado. He was present at the wedding of Luis's two sisters to Almeida and Díaz de Cáceres. He ran up debts with Carvajal, Almeida, Díaz de Cáceres, and many others and went bankrupt prior to 1599, when the Inquisition tried him in absentia. His effigy was burned in the Mexican auto-de-fé of 1601. He died in Peru.[32]

Almeida inveighed the Carvajals to be cautious, but his warning fell on deaf ears. According to his one-time mayordomo Francisco Díaz, who wrote from Lima in answer to an inquiry from the Mexican Inquisition years after the facts, one day while the Carvajal family was at Cantarranas, Almeida came home and on a table found some Jewish prayers that Isabel had written out for Miguelito to give to Mateo Ruiz, one of Almeida's foremen. Almeida flew into a rage, ripped up the paper, burned the fragments, whipped young Miguel for leaving the paper in plain sight, and forbade anyone in his household from ever again committing a prayer to writing. For a while a pall settled over Cantarranas. The Carvajals hid their books and papers where Almeida would not be able to find them and agreed among themselves that even if they could not talk about their Judaism out loud, they could at least honor the Sabbath together in the house in silence by putting on clean clothes and abstaining from work.[33]

But in a large working hacienda, nothing could be kept totally secret. While the working parts of the hacienda were at some distance from the family quarters, the administrative offices were close by, and the hacienda's small cadre of administrators had access to everything. From the main hallway they could observe the rooms where the Carvajals were living. One time Mateo Ruiz confided to mayordomo Francisco Díaz that in the course of his work, he had noted how on Fridays the Carvajal women swept their rooms clean. He had likewise noted that although the priest whom Almeida had hired came every Sunday from the church in Tetelcingo to say mass in the hacienda chapel, none of the Carvajals ever seemed to get up early enough to attend the service. One Sunday, when not a single person showed up at the chapel, the disappointed priest turned around and left. Ruiz went upstairs to tell Isabel that he had gone and she sarcastically observed, "May that be our greatest loss." Ruiz said that after the priest left, the Carvajals partied all afternoon. Francisco Díaz reported how the family members prayed several times a day in their rooms, often on their knees, reciting prayers from memory or reading them from books. On Sundays, when casual observers might reasonably presume them to be reciting Christian prayers, they prayed openly in the hacienda's garden. Sometimes they also did this on Saturday night, loudly enough that Díaz could hear them beseeching God to free them from the captivity of living in Christian Mexico.[34]

When Almeida was absent, Luis studied and talked about the Law of Moses to any converso he could buttonhole. His prime targets were the estate's three administrators: Francisco Díaz, who supervised the refining process; Mateo Ruiz; and Antonio de los Cobos. The first two were Portuguese New Christians—Díaz a former shoemaker from Sabugal, near the Spanish border, and Ruiz from Coimbra. Cobos was probably an Old Christian. He was a sometime business partner of Antonio Díaz de Cáceres, who was at this time working for Almeida. Since Almeida employed all three men in positions of confidence, there seemed to Luis to be little risk in speaking openly with them. Luis often traveled with a small library of religious books in his saddlebags or hidden among his clothes, and at Cantarranas he also had access to Almeida's library, which included at least one very large volume that dealt with the generations of monarchs who ruled over Israel. Glossing passages from this book, Luis talked to the three men about Moses and Aaron, about the miracles that God had performed for the Jews, how because of their sins God had scattered the Jews across the world, and how faithful observance of the Law of Moses was the key to hastening the advent of the Messiah.[35]

Luis's widowed older sister Isabel, who cooked for the Carvajal family while they were resident in Taxco, only halfheartedly attempted to mask her Judaizing activities. Francisco Díaz told her not to bother trying to hide from him because he was well aware of what was going on. He did not openly state that he, too, was a Judaizer, but he made it obvious, and Isabel quickly warmed to him.[36] Díaz later recalled how one day when Almeida had gone to Mexico City, Isabel de Carvajal walked up to the amalgamation patios looking for him. She needed him to release one of his Indians to bring her some firewood. Isabel was surprised to find Díaz reading a small copy of *Mirror of Consolation* that he had probably borrowed from Almeida's library. Isabel remarked that she knew it was a very good book and that if he liked, she would also lend him a book of hours that he could pray from. When she brought the *horas* to him and he saw that it was in Latin, which he did not know, he handed it back to her. Isabel explained that the book contained some of the Psalms of David, and she dog-eared the corners to mark the pages of her favorites, telling him that if he read them many times, he would come to understand them.[37]

Two other episodes during the Carvajal residence at Cantarranas lodged indelibly in the participants' minds. One Saturday, in a corridor of the big house, Francisco Díaz was whipping a black slave who had tried to escape. The Carvajal women came out of their rooms and, horrified at the spectacle, tried to stop him. Díaz explained to them that he was only obeying Almeida's orders, but the women, with Isabel taking the lead, continued to berate him. When the whipping was finished and the women had gone, Miguelito explained to Díaz the reason for his sisters' explosion: "It's not because you were beating him, it is because today is a holy day." Díaz went to ask Miguel's older brother Baltazar Rodríguez for confirmation. "That's right," Baltazar responded "but don't talk about it to anyone." And then Baltazar, who rarely passed up an opportunity to proselytize, went on to explain to Díaz some of the basic tenets of Judaism, beginning with the Ten Commandments, Judaism's principal festivals, and some of the laws concerning diet and personal hygiene.[38]

The other memorable incident involved Almeida's brother Miguel

Hernández, who was staying at the hacienda with the Carvajals. Juana Núñez de la Torre, Héctor de Fonseca's Old Christian wife, came out to the estate to visit. Evidently the reason was to give her brother-in-law Miguel a large crucifix as a present and to hang it for him over the foot of his bed. As Luis de Carvajal later described the scene, once Juana had gone, he, Hernández, Francisco Díaz, Mateo Ruiz, and Francisco Jorge began to joke about the inappropriateness of the gift. "Look at this doohickey she brought me!" said Miguel. Then, to show his disdain, he farted, urinated on the cross, and proclaimed, parodying the liturgy of consecration of the chalice in the Catholic mass, "Take this and drink."[39] Almeida's mayordomo Francisco Díaz, pointing at some sacks of salt that were stored in the room, was moved to quip: "Hey, at least he won't go hungry for salt."[40] Luis knew that Francisco Díaz and Francisco Jorge were Judaizers, and the fact that Mateo Ruiz did not object to Miguel's sacrilegious comments was sufficient for Luis to conclude that Ruiz, too, must be a follower of the Law of Moses.[41]

Francisco Díaz, born in Sabugal, Portugal, in 1560, worked as a mayordomo at Cantarranas in the late 1580s before moving to Peru, where, according to Luis de Carvajal, he was tried and given penance by the Inquisition.

Mateo Ruiz, born in Coimbra around 1550, had been a glassmaker before coming to Mexico. He worked for Almeida in Taxco in the late 1580s.

Francisco Jorge, nicknamed *el tuerto* because he had only one eye, was the son of Francisco Jorge de Andrada from Benavente. He came to Mexico in 1580 with his distant cousin Governor Carvajal. In the early 1580s he roomed with Antonio Díaz de Cáceres for a while in Mexico City. He then moved to Taxco, where he worked for Héctor de Fonseca until January 1590, when he fled the country. Accused in 1590 of Judaizing, he was burned in effigy in the auto-de-fé of 1596. He died prior to 1600.[42]

Francisco Díaz related to inquisitors that when he first came to Cantarranas, "he was very Christian." Writing years later from Lima, in an effort to downplay his responsibility for his own Judaizing, Díaz blamed the Carvajal family with instigating it. He wrote that they used to mock him when he went to mass and had laughed at his rote recitation of church-sanctioned prayers like the Credo, the Ave Maria, and the Salve Regina. Instead they taught him to pray a number of Jewish prayers and songs, some of which they copied out so that he could memorize them at his leisure. Furthermore, Luis de Carvajal had brought him a book by Fray Luis de Granada and had instructed him to read about the prophecies concerning the Jews and the Messiah. He said that the Carvajals had always included him in their fasts (though he claimed that he always cheated and snacked) and invited him to their Passover seder. When none of the other workers were around, they had prayed with him, too, all of them together on their knees. This happened both in the hacienda's main house and in the garden.[43]

In December 1588, Díaz de Cáceres moved his wife and her two sisters back to the capital, to a suite of rooms that he rented from Hernando de Ávila in the San Juan district. Jorge de Almeida brought the rest of the family back in January. The two men continued to have a tentative, contradictory relationship with their Jewish heritage. Mariana recalled that at Yom Kippur in 1589, Díaz de Cáceres had fasted with her, Catalina, and Ana. The women spent the entire day at home praying, but Díaz de Cáceres, after reciting a few morning prayers and reading from one of their religious books, went out to conduct business all day before returning to have dinner with them.[44] In Mexico, as in Taxco, the husbands tried to keep their wives from publicly manifesting their Jewishness in any way. And Díaz de Cáceres's violent behavior toward the women persisted. Once, when Mariana had sunk into one of her delirious states and was ranting dangerously about her religious beliefs, he tried to whip her into silence. When her mother and sisters Isabel and Leonor protested, he threw them all down the stairs. Another time he chained Mariana to her bed and beat her and broke her arm.[45] Months after the incident on the stairs, when his wife, Catalina, fell ill, the Carvajal women came to visit her, but her husband barred the door and would not let them in. When Catalina complained, Díaz beat her and dragged her around the house.[46] Catalina was so afraid of him, she said, that she even stopped observing the Sabbath out of fear that he might notice.[47]

Leonor and Catalina, who were Carvajals through and through, did what they could to get around their husbands' strictures. On Jewish fast days they sometimes they pretended to eat and then slipped the food out of their mouths and surreptitiously threw it under the table.[48] When she could manage it, she joined the rest of the Carvajal family at their holiday celebrations. This was easier after her husband had fled to Spain; she attended a 1592 Passover gathering at Clara Enríquez's house and a 1593 Yom Kippur meeting with her siblings. Catalina, on the other hand, had been so cowed by her husband that she stopped observing the Sabbath, even when she was home alone—which was generally the case—out of fear that her husband might find out. He forbade her to Judaize with her siblings, so that even after her return to Mexico City, she tended to spend the holidays in lonely solitude. She did not join her family for the Fast of Esther, even though Antonio had gone to Taxco, leaving her at home with only her Chichimeca servant. A month later, at Passover, she made matzo for herself, since it was too dangerous to ask the servant to prepare it for her, and ate it without any ceremony whatsoever because she did not know the prayers. "My mother and my sisters must have observed the holiday," she told the inquisitors in December 1589, "but I do not know it for certain because they did not communicate with me because my husband considered them his enemies."[49] Even after her husband had departed for a three-year business trip to Asia, one step ahead of the Inquisition, Catalina attended communal gatherings only twice: Purim in 1591 and Passover in 1592, both at Clara Enríquez's Mexico City home.[50]

Héctor de Fonseca

Héctor de Fonseca's parents had given him and his three brothers a basic Jewish education by the time they had reached their early teens.[51] But during the twelve years following Héctor's arrival in Mexico—his wandering through the northern reales and his early years in Taxco—there is no evidence of his having Judaized with anyone or in any way.

Héctor's refresher course in Judaism seems to have begun early in 1583, when on a visit to Mexico City he became friends with silversmith Luis Díaz, who had lived for a time in Venice and was one of the circle of Judaizers who were taking inspiration from Antonio Machado and Dr. Manuel de Morales.[52] Díaz approached Héctor, saying he wanted to broach a subject that was important to the salvation of Héctor's soul, which was that Héctor needed to cease his Christianizing and return to his Jewish roots. Díaz and Morales informed Héctor about the Sabbath and the Jewish festivals and made him swear to keep their discussions secret. In relating these events to the Inquisition thirteen years later, Héctor said that the two men had left him in deep confusion about which law was better, that of Moses or that of Jesus. It was not unusual for people accused by the Inquisition of Judaizing to attempt to curry sympathy by claiming that even though they Judaized, they always felt some attraction for Catholicism. However, in Héctor de Fonseca's case, the assertion of ambivalence appears to ring true, for his open expressions of doubt and his wavering between the two faiths is confirmed by more than one independent witness.

Some months after his first conversation with Luis Díaz, Héctor ran into him again in Mexico City. Díaz, sensing his protégé's hesitancy to embrace Judaism, redoubled his efforts, citing biblical passages to reinforce the truth of his message. This led Héctor to determine to commit himself to Jewish observance, and in April 1583 he joined his brother Jorge de Almeida and other family members and friends at Almeida's apartments for a Passover dinner.[53] With them were Almeida's mother, Felipa de Fonseca, and two of Almeida's siblings, Miguel Hernández and Héctor de Fonseca. Old Tomás's half brother Julián de Castellanos was there too.

About this time, Héctor opened up about his Judaizing to Marco Antonio. They talked about Judaizing customs and about how Jesus was not the Messiah, for whom the Jews were still waiting.[54] But Héctor began to have second thoughts about his commitment. Not long after these events, as he examined his soul on the long road to Taxco, he flip-flopped again and, resolving henceforth to adhere to the law of Jesus, stopped at the Augustinian monastery of Malinalco to make confession, though he did not dare go so far as to confess that he had been Judaizing.[55] Back in Taxco, he began attending mass faithfully.

Another of the men working for Héctor was Francisco Jorge—el tuerto. Like Marco Antonio, he was always referred to by his full name. One day Héctor stumbled upon Francisco Jorge when he was praying and told him he recognized the words as belonging to Jewish ritual. Francisco Jorge, in a panic, fell on his knees and begged Héctor, whom he assumed was a Judaizer, not to reveal his secret. When Héctor pushed him off, protesting that he believed in the law of Christ and was even planning to denounce Luis Díaz for Judaizing, Francisco Jorge berated him as being blind to the truth, which was that only Judaism offered salvation for his soul. The upshot, in Héctor's recollection, was that his ambivalence about which was the true religion grew even deeper.[56]

Time passed. One day around 1588, Héctor found himself on the road to Taxco with Luis de Carvajal. Héctor confessed his quandaries to Luis and explained the trajectory of his religious confusion. He was especially disturbed by the passages in Esdras that talk about God abandoning the Jews because of their many sins. Luis reassured him that these verses were merely the "threat of a most loving father to his son that if he did not behave he would come to pay for it."[57] These talks had a profound influence on Héctor, and once more he resolved to commit to Judaism. Shortly afterward Héctor revealed his Judaism to the Carvajal women staying at Almeida's Cantarranas hacienda. In subsequent meetings—in Taxco, at the Carvajal home in Mexico City, on the road—Luis engaged Héctor in conversations about the Law of Moses. Luis was delighted to find in Fonseca a man fluent in Latin and well versed in scripture, a man with whom he could bandy biblical citations and who was receptive to learning those portions of the Jewish liturgy that Luis knew by heart.[58] Though Héctor rarely contributed to discussions in larger groups, he loved to hear Luis de Carvajal preach and enjoyed following the theological debates that swirled around his table. Mariana de Carvajal said that during the three months that she spent at Cantarranas, Héctor had come to visit the Carvajals almost every day. Justa Méndez, still in her mid-teens and a frequent guest at the Carvajals' Mexico City home, was initially nervous about talking openly about Judaism when Héctor was present. She later told inquisitors that Francisca, Luis, and all her sisters had reassured her that Héctor was a practicing Jew and could be trusted.[59]

Francisco Méndez and Clara Enríquez, from the small cities of Crato and Fundão in the Raya de Portugal, were passionately committed Judaizers. In 1588, after Francisco died, Clara brought her two surviving children, Gabriel Enríquez and Justa Méndez, to Mexico City, where Clara's sister Beatriz Enríquez lived with her prosperous merchant husband, Simón

Paiba. Gabriel found work as a carter, transporting goods to and from the burgeoning city of Querétaro, while Clara and her daughter Justa Méndez earned their living in the capital with needlework. Though Clara was shy, and reticent about speaking in public, Justa was just the opposite, and as a beautiful young unmarried woman in her early teens who was knowledgeable in Jewish matters, she attracted the attention of many, including Luis de Carvajal, who appears to have been one of her several suitors. From the moment of their arrival, the two women played an active role in the city's Judaizing community.

Twenty-year-old Justa Méndez was arrested in 1595. Early in the interrogations she confessed that she had Judaized but that she was trying to believe in Jesus Christ and his law of grace. To prove her sincerity, she was required to detail her Judaizing beliefs and practices and to disclose the names and particulars of everyone she knew of or had seen Judaize. She had a prodigious memory, and her proceso is one of the most complete in describing the practices of the Judaizing conversos of that period. In the auto-de-fé of December 8, 1596, Justa was sentenced to three years' incarceration, to wear the penitential sambenito, and to receive instruction in Catholicism.

Whether Justa Méndez had been insincere in stating her attraction to Catholicism, or whether she later changed her mind, her actions subsequent to her release make clear that she was neither Christian nor repentant. For example, as a reconciled Judaizer, she was forbidden to wear costly clothing or jewelry or engage in any act that hinted at wealth or status, conditions that she not only ignored but flouted. When charged with wearing silk dresses and gold jewelry, she protested to the Inquisition official that any black slave on the street dressed fancier than she.

At some point in the early 1600s, Justa married the Portuguese converso merchant Francisco Núñez (aka Rodríguez), who had been penanced in the same 1596 auto-de-fé as she. The couple had three children—Luis Pérez Roldán, and Isabel and Francisca Núñez—each of whom married and had large families. Justa died around 1633, and her children and many of her grandchildren appeared as Judaizers in the autos-de-fé of the 1640s.[60]

During his visits to Mexico City in the late 1580s, Héctor called frequently at the Carvajal home, where he soon came to know most of the people who comprised the Judaizing community in the capital. Luis taught him songs; Jorge de Almeida's teenage wife, Leonor, taught him Spanish versions of the Penitential Psalms.[61] Clara Enríquez's daughter Justa Méndez and Manuel Gómez Navarro were frequent guests. While Luis was initially serving his penance in Tlatelolco, for a time Héctor shied away from their relationship, fearing that his association with Luis would taint him as a Jew; but soon he was again visiting the Carvajals.[62] In 1592, once the Luis had served his sentence and was back in Mexico City, Héctor stayed with the Carvajals whenever he visited the capital. Once he coincided at their home with Manuel de Lucena and young Tomás de Fonseca Castellanos, but that was unusual because, since Héctor and young Tomás were not on the best of terms, the Carvajals felt more comfortable with only one or the other of them at their table—not both.[63]

In the view of many of his colleagues, Héctor de Fonseca was not a pleasant person. Antonio Díaz de Cáceres characterized him as "an uneasy man who does not know how to get along and deals roughly with people."[64] Yet, despite his occasional outbursts, other people thought him reserved, a man whose emotions and commitments were hard to read. Leonor de Carvajal was initially uncertain whether or not Héctor was even a Jew.[65]

Once Héctor began to Judaize in earnest, he was quick to criticize in others what he thought were lapses in their observance. Once in Mexico City in 1588, on a day when Héctor was fasting, Héctor and his brothers Miguel and Francisco Hernández dropped in on their cousin Julián de Castellanos. When Julián invited them to lunch, Héctor refused to sit down. When Julián insisted, he brusquely stalked out of the house.[66] One Saturday in Tlatelolco in 1592, Héctor scolded Luis and the Carvajal women for having been moved to tears while they were praying, chiding them that the Sabbath was not a day for lamentation and that their tears were out of order.[67] That same year, when Héctor went to visit Sebastián Rodríguez and found him reciting with his family a Jewish hymn of praise, Héctor's only reaction was to scold Rodríguez "for having so little sense of caution as to pray a Jewish prayer with the door open to the street." He criticized Luis de Carvajal for the same reason.[68]

The intermittency of Héctor's commitment to Judaizing was undoubtedly motivated as much by fear of being discovered as by true religious indecision.

Luis de Carvajal said that he had never seen Héctor engage in any Jewish practices because "he is so afraid of being observed that he exercises great caution."[69] He confessed that he had never been brave enough to inform his confessor of his Judaizing. Even during his seasons of fervent Jewish commitment, Héctor never stopped going to church, taking communion, or even making confession, because if he did stop, he explained to inquisitors, his neighbors would notice. Héctor seemed always to be watching himself from a perch on his own shoulder.

In 1585, during one of his Christian periods, Héctor married Juana López de la Torre, an Old Christian woman in Taxco, which before long he bitterly regretted.[70] Most Judaizing conversos were well aware that endogamy, which in the special circumstances of the crypto-Jewish Catholic world meant not only marrying someone of Jewish descent but marrying someone who shared one's Jewish beliefs and commitment to Jewish practice, was the most important factor in ensuring that the tradition would pass from generation to generation. This explains the antipathy that many conversos felt toward marriage with Old Christians. Simón Rodríguez once boasted to Manuel de Lucena that "he would never sully his bloodline by marrying an Old Christian."[71] Lucena and many of his friends clearly felt the same way. Lucena told Beatriz Enríquez la Paiba that Antonio Díaz Márquez's Old Christian wife "was a bitch, meaning that she was a Christian." Lucena added that because of her, Díaz Márquez was afraid to observe any Jewish customs,[72] and Luis de Carvajal reported how Díaz Márquez used to break into tears of guilt for working on the Sabbath and having to eat pork with his wife. Díaz Márquez claimed that even though he did not observe any Jewish customs, he expected to be saved in the Law of Moses, because in his heart he was just as good a Jew as any of them. He said that "if he could take his son to a Jewry somewhere, he would, just to get him away from his mother who was an Old Christian."[73]

Antonio Díaz Márquez, born in 1546 in a small town near Lisbon, came to Mexico around 1560 and served for a short time as a soldier. Still a teenager, he settled in the newly developing mining down of Sombrerete (Zacatecas), where he made his living for thirteen years as a tailor and a storekeeper. In the mid-1570s he moved to Mexico City, opened a clothing store on Calle San Agustín, and married an Old Christian named Francisca Rodríguez. Between 1580 and his arrest in March 1596, they had nine children. The back room of his store became one of the favored meeting places for several of the more observant members of Mexico City's crypto-Jewish community. Despite the way his wife made it all but impossible for him to Judaize at home, Luis de Carvajal characterized him as one of the city's two perfect observers of Jewish ritual, the other being Justa Méndez. Díaz Márquez was arrested in 1596. In the auto-de-fé of March 25, he was penanced and condemned to perpetual confinement in the Inquisition prison, where he died three years later.[74]

Crypto-Jews in mixed marriages almost always found their religious life circumscribed. Although some conversos, such as Antonio Méndez and Simón Rodríguez, continued to Judaize even after they married Old Christian women,[75] mixed marriage generally meant an end to Judaizing practice. The threat of denunciation to the Inquisition was a potent weapon in the hands of an Old Christian spouse. And because any denunciation could start a chain reaction, the fear of being revealed often led the whole Judaizing community to shun mixed married couples. Likewise, the converso partner in a mixed marriage sometimes estranged him- or herself from Judaizing former friends out of fear of being thought guilty by association. Beatriz Rodríguez felt unable to practice Judaism because of her Old Christian husband, Antonio Fernández.[76] Jerónimo Rodríguez, a converso who resided in Puebla in the early 1590s and had married an Old Christian, so vehemently rebuffed the attempts of his friends Jorge Váez and Rodrigo Tavares to persuade him to Judaize that they eventually stopped trying and spread the word never to speak of anything Jewish in his presence.[77]

Psychologically, for Judaizers, mixed marriage was a kind of prison, and prisoners tend to dream of escape from their stifling dilemma. Álvaro de Carrión's dream was that his Christian wife, Juana González, would eventually come around to his religious views. He assured Manuel de Lucena that once the couple had left Mexico and established themselves in the Jewish quarter of some European city outside of Iberia, "even though my wife is an Old Christian, it should be easy to teach her the Jewish law." When Lucena expressed skepticism, Carrión reassured him: "I knew what I was doing [when I married her] ... she's only a young girl, and I'll teach her to do things my way." He bragged that he had already taught her not to serve rabbit to his Judaizing friends.[78] For conversos in mixed marriages, even a short visit to a safe environment might bring a respite from the pressure to feign Christian observance. Lucena's house was such a place. Once, when Pelayo Álvarez was lodging with him in Mexico City around 1585, Lucena asked him to explain why a man as observant of the Law of Moses as he was had married a practicing Christian, and also why he had not taught their daughters to Judaize. "My wife used to be a saint and a God-fearing women," Álvarez replied, implying that formerly she had Judaized with him, "but I have not dared to teach the Law of Moses to my daughters because up until now our family has been living with Julián de Castellanos, whose wife is Christian, and also because the girls are so young [and thus not capable of keeping secrets]; but I would be pleased if you would teach them, since we are all living in your house now."[79]

Another way out of the prison of a mixed marriage was for the Judaizer to abandon the Old Christian spouse and run off to marry an observant Jew in some distant land. The moral issues were easily swept aside. Antonio Gómez reassured Manuel Tavares that it was perfectly legitimate for Tavares to walk away from his Old Christian spouse in order to marry a Judaizer, since "your marriage isn't worth anything because it is with an Old Christian; ... it is not even a marriage."[80] The Mexican Judaizers gossiped about the precedents for this practice: Manuel de Lucena reported that Jorge de Almeida's brother Francisco Hérnandez had left his Old Christian wife in Spain when he came to Mexico. Then, when he fled back to Spain after several of his Mexican converso friends were arrested, he again ran away from his Old Christian wife, this time taking their son with him. In Italy Hernández married a Jewish woman.[81]

All of these hypothetical escape routes buzzed in Héctor de Fonseca's head as his frustration with his marriage grew. Juana, though inevitably aware that her husband and his friends Judaized, persisted in being overtly, incessantly, and annoyingly Christian. When she was angry with Héctor, she threatened to denounce him to the Inquisition.[82] Years later, explaining to inquisitors his spotty record of Jewish observance, Héctor said, "I never performed any of the ceremonies of the Law of Moses, although I believed it in my heart; I did not dare to because I was married to an Old Christian."[83] His friends shunned him because they were afraid of her.[84] All in all, Juana drove Héctor to distraction. It was only when he found himself alone with other Judaizers that he allowed his frustration to bubble out. To his friends Héctor complained that "he was greatly vexed at being married to an Old Christian." To Isabel de Carvajal he said,

> I was a Jew who kept the Law of Moses. . . . I had a book of rhymed prayers that I had copied out with other things that praised the Law of Moses. But I was so upset at being married to an Old Christian who made me live a martyr's life and gave me no freedom to observe that Law, that I used to go out in the fields, up between the mountains, and shout and cry out to God to pardon my sins.[85]

Yet even though Juana frustrated him, Héctor continued to cohabit with his wife, and the marriage produced three children: Francisco Núñez, born in 1589, María de la Zarza, born the following year, and Antonia de la Zarza, one year after that.[86] Héctor also seems to have maintained a degree of trust in his wife, even if their emotional life was in shambles. When several Mexico City Judaizers were arrested in 1590, Héctor felt threatened enough to take steps to protect his assets and ensure that his mine and his processing hacienda would continue to function if he should be absent. After hiring the lawyer Toribio González to draw up the papers, on November 24 of that year he granted a power of attorney to handle his affairs not to a trusted converso colleague or a blood relative but to his wife, Juana.[87]

In 1594 Héctor found himself in the Inquisition prison.[88] When he was assigned minor penance and released, Juana sued him for divorce. It may be that she was as fed up with him as he was with her, but the reason for the divorce stated in the petition was that the shame of her husband being publicly identified as a Judaizer was intolerable to her and to their children. Despite the fact that divorce offered Héctor a way out of his frustrating marriage, he countersued, arguing that if the ecclesiastical court granted Juana's petition, it would set a bad precedent, since if the spouse of every penanced heretic were granted divorce, New Spain would be overrun with unprotected women and orphaned children. Not only should Juana's suit be dismissed, Héctor asserted, anyone who recommended divorce for these reasons should be excommunicated. The court's findings are not recorded, but there was no divorce.[89]

Given the unhappy circumstances of Héctor's marriage, it is not surprising that he sought comfort in other beds. He, like several of the conversos in the mining towns, acquired an informal second family in New Spain. Both old and young Tomás de Fonseca, for example, acknowledged to inquisitors that they had sired several illegitimate children, with whom they remained close and for whom they took responsibility. Héctor, too, sired a daughter outside of his marriage, and he took some responsibility for her, writing out a secret document that obliged his friend Jorge Álvarez to pay his bastard daughter fifteen hundred pesos from his estate when he died. However, he never recognized her publicly from fear of how his wife would react.[90] Somewhere along the way Héctor also contracted a venereal disease; during his later incarceration, he was twice transferred from jail to the Hospital de las Bubas, the syphilitics' hospital.[91]

Tomás de Fonseca Castellanos

Tomás de Fonseca Castellanos, like so many of the Portuguese confeso immigrants, had absorbed much of his Jewish knowledge from his family as a child in Viseo and Lisbon.[92] He probably Judaized during the years he spent with his uncle old Tomás de Fonseca in Tlalpujahua, though neither of them broached the topic with their inquisitors. Instead, young Tomás told inquisitors the improbable tale that he had only been initiated into Judaizing around 1585 in Taxco in conversations with Francisco Rodríguez.[93]

Tomás worked in Gaspar de Enciso's mining operation in Taxco until about 1579, when he acquired his store and mining hacienda. There is little information about his Judaizing activities during his eight or nine years with Enciso, except for testimony by Enciso's foreman, Juan Álvarez, who worked with young Tomás in 1576 or 1578. He said that young Tomás sometimes observed the Sabbath, making certain that his house, his table and bed linen, and his body were clean. He observed the Yom Kippur fast and the Fast of Esther.[94] When possible, he had his meat slaughtered and trimmed in the kosher fashion, and he had his food fried with olive oil rather than with lard. Álvarez noted:

> Tomás de Fonseca instructed me that whenever I roasted a leg of lamb, I must remove the sinews, because that way the lamb would cook better. I've come in [to the Inquisition] to clear my conscience because I heard in an Edict of Faith that that was a Jewish custom.... Also I never saw Fonseca eat a piece of salt pork, though he did throw some into the stew pot, because he said it bothered his rheumatism.[95]

Sometime in the mid-1570s, as soon as he had amassed sufficient funds, Tomás brought his mother, Isabel de Fonseca, from Portugal. Though her husband, Tomás Méndez, had come to Mexico years earlier with their young son Diego, there is no record of Isabel having found, or even having looked for, them.[96] When she finally saw young Tomás, she told him to "remember those things I taught you in Spain," which he took to mean that he should remember to keep the Law of Moses.[97] It is likely that young Tomás continued to meet with his mother during his visits to Mexico City, though neither he nor any of his acquaintances ever refer to it; no one mentions seeing her in Taxco. She died in Mexico City around 1578.

By the mid-1580s, Tomás was talking frequently with the Carvajal brothers. From then until the mid-1590s, whenever Luis and Baltazar were in Taxco and were not lodging at Cantarranas they generally stayed with young Tomás de Fonseca, either at his mining hacienda or in the rooms over his store on the outskirts of the real of Tetelcingo.[98] During those years Tomás stepped up his reading in the Bible and *Mirror of Consolation*. By 1587 his command of this material was sufficient to impress Baltazar's brother Luis.[99] On repeated visits to Taxco, Baltazar talked with young Tomás about his obligations as a Jew and criticized him whenever he lapsed into Christian practice. Once in 1590, when he caught Tomás in his store praying the rosary to free a certain soul from purgatory, Baltazar challenged him:

> What are you doing? You are blind if you think that the Pope has the power to release souls from Purgatory. Only God can do that.... The Law of Jesus Christ is not the law in which people can be saved; that is only in the Law of Moses.[100]

Neither man seems to have been aware of the irony in Baltazar's having framed these concepts entirely in Christian terms.

One morning in 1588, while Luis and Baltazar Carvajal were in Fonseca's upstairs bedroom reciting their prayers, Tomás came up from the shop to join them. He did his best to follow the brothers as they recited the traditional opening phrases: "Our Lord Adonay, God of our fathers, have mercy on us and on all your people Israel, on your city Jerusalem and Mount Zion." When they had finished, young Tomás broke into tears and said to them: "I am like Saul among the prophets, because even though I am estranged from God and his holy service here in my worldly affairs, when I find myself among his lieutenants I am one of them."[101] In the late 1580s, as young Tomás became more and more observant as a Jew and more open about sharing his passion for Judaism with his friends, his house and hacienda in Taxco became centers of Judaizing activity: "Many Portuguese people visited my house in the mines of Taxco," he told the inquisitors, "people like Sebastián de la Peña,[102] Sebastián Rodríguez, Manuel de Lucena's friend Manuel Gómez Navarro, Duarte Rodríguez, and Luis de Carvajal." His blood relatives and diverse members of the Enríquez and Carvajal families frequented the house too, as did his former teacher Francisco Rodríguez. When he stayed in Mexico City he was visited by all these people and by Antonio Machado and his daughter Isabel, whose poverty Fonseca had helped alleviate with contributions of money he had sent to them via Marco Antonio. Whenever two or more of these conversos got together, talk turned inevitably to the Law of Moses, for behind closed doors they all freely acknowledged to one another their commitment to Judaizing.[103] When inquisitors asked young Tomás's friend and Pachuca business associate[104] Manuel de Lucena why Lucena believed Fonseca to be a Jew, Lucena provided no shortage of reasons:

> Because the way he behaves and talks is like a Jew, since he never calls on Our Lady nor on Our Redeemer but rather on the Lord and on God. ... Because he and I confessed our Judaism to each other.... Because he said that Christians are cruel and oppress people who worship the true God and jail them and take their property and put the badge of shame on them by making them wear *sambenitos*, saying they are idolaters, and it is blasphemy to say that the true God is in the sacred host.... [Fonseca]

said that the Messiah has not yet come, because the people of Israel are scattered and when he comes they will be gathered together and Jerusalem will be rebuilt. . . .[105] Because one Friday night I was at Luis de Carvajal's house and I and Tomás de Fonseca slept over and [we all discussed the Law of Moses]; . . . and four years ago eating with Luis de Carvajal and Tomás de Fonseca, Carvajal took out a book and read passages about the Law of Moses. . . . Carvajal fed us some very tasty stew, though it had no salt pork in it, and then we talked about the Law of Moses and recited some psalms and prophesies.[106]

While Tomás generally celebrated the Jewish holidays in Mexico City with his Judaizing friends, in 1589 for Yom Kippur he hosted a small gathering at his home in Taxco. His uncle old Tomás de Fonseca had come down from his mine in Tlalpujahua for the holiday. Young Tomás's son Francisco was there, and his friends Marco Antonio and Duarte Rodríguez,[107] along with Luis de Carvajal. After praying all day, the small group broke their fast together with fish, chickpeas, eggs, and fruit.[108] In the presence of other close converso friends who were living in or traveling through the Taxco reales, the conversation during dinner often turned to the precepts of the Law of Moses. When Tomás's visitors were numerous, they had to sleep more than one to a bed, and in the intimate dark room they felt free to share their innermost thoughts. Typical of these encounters was an evening in 1594 in Taxco that Luis de Carvajal described in testimony two years later:

> It was during the time I was going around collecting money to free us from wearing our sambenitos. I went to Taxco and stayed in Tomás de Fonseca's house for four days. One evening, walking back from the *real* to his house, I brought with me Sebastián Rodríguez and Sebastián de la Peña. After we had eaten dinner, all four of us went to sleep in Tomás's room. . . . I recall that Sebastián de la Peña and Tomás de Fonseca slept in one bed, and I and Sebastián Rodríguez in the other. And we all talked together like Jews who were observant of the Law that God gave Moses. I cited some passages of that law—I don't remember which ones in particular—and the others listened to me attentively. In the morning when I got up, I knelt down next to the bed facing east, bowing deeply and touching my head to the ground, thanking God for having sustained

me to wake up among [these men]. And Tomás de Fonseca said to me: "How can you do that here in the room that we sleep in and where there are unclean things? Jewish ceremony requires that place we pray in be clean." Sebastián de la Peña scolded him [for saying that].[109]

The next day the four men set out for Mexico City together, continuing their discussion as they rode.

Even a cursory reading of witness testimony in Inquisition procesos confirms that the merest shadow of a suspicion of Judaizing caused a person's friends, relatives, neighbors, business associates, and servants to scrutinize the person's every move. Felipe Freire, the mine guard at young Tomás's hacienda de minas, seems to have kept track of every one of his employer's questionable activities:

> He is a bad Christian because he has no images in his house. He seldom goes to mass; when he does he comes in late and only hears half of it. I have observed that he doesn't eat pork, because he says it is dirty food. People have noticed that he does not go to confession. When he prays he doesn't say the Gloria Patri. . . . During last year's Corpus procession he stayed inside eating lunch rather than coming outside to see the procession. Once when we were riding from Taxco to Tenango we passed in front of a cross and I took my hat off and Fonseca did not. . . . At mass when they elevate the host he looks at the floor and not at the altar.

Fonseca's abhorrence of pork was obvious to everyone who testified against him at his trial. Mateo Ruiz, who worked for Jorge de Almeida and was a friend of young Tomás, said,

> I have often eaten in his house, and I have never seen salt pork in his house, nor on his table; I've never seen him eat it; in the sixteen months I have known him, I've never seen him fry it or put it in his stew pot . . . but I never asked him why because I was a guest and it wasn't right to question him.[110]

Another acquaintance, Francisco de Cáceres, a Portuguese from Santalunga, near Coimbra, testified that Fonseca Castellanos "doesn't eat salt pork, and he says that it is because he has a bad eye that an accident many years ago caused to cloud up; though I did see him eat it once." Cáceres added that "some people, as a joke, say that he must be Jewish because he has such a large nose."[111]

In young Tomás de Fonseca's Inquisition trials, both the witnesses against him and his own confessions make clear that he fully embraced Judaism and observed its precepts, within his knowledge of them, as steadfastly as he was able. He honored the Sabbath by dressing in clean clothes. Even though as a storekeeper he could not abstain from work, he kept a Latin version of the Ten Commandments on the wall to remind himself and his guests that the phrase "benedixit Dominus diei sabbati et sanctificavit eum" meant that the Sabbath was to be observed on Saturday and that the church had gotten the day wrong.[112] He celebrated Yom Kippur and Passover, and when he could he fasted also on various weekdays with his friends.[113] His observance of the rules of kashrut was limited to avoiding salt pork, cooking with olive oil instead of lard, trimming the fat from meat, porging the sinew from his leg of lamb, and slitting the throat of the fowl that he was to eat rather than twisting its neck as the Christians did; in prison in 1595 he refused to eat meat that he knew had not been bled and salted.[114] In praying he always omitted mention of the Father and the Son, and he preferred the Penitential Psalms to church prayers; he kept with him a folded sheet of paper on which he had written a number of Jewish prayers.[115] He awaited the Messiah foretold in the Jewish Bible and believed that the salvation of his soul depended on his belief in the Law of Moses.[116]

Of course, to survive, he also had to present himself as a faithful and observant Christian. He worked hard at that, and he felt sufficiently confident of his masquerade that in his first trial in 1589 he requested that the inquisitors interview his neighbors about his Christian bona fides.[117] In his own hand, in a document he titled "Notes for my attorney," written on paper supplied to him by the inquisitors at his request for that purpose, he made a list of the main points of his defense. His list could easily serve as a précis for the program of dissimulation that was adopted by many of the Judaizing conversos of his day in Mexico.

> First of all I am a good Christian, fearing of God and his Holy Mother and all his Saints. All the residents of Taxco will confirm this.

Second, in my household I provide good doctrine for all my people—Blacks and Indians and the young serving people—making them go to mass and making sure that every night they recite the four prayers after first crossing themselves. I often lead them myself, all of us with our faces upturned to the images which I have hanging in the room where I sleep.

... I cross myself in my bedroom when I lie down and when I wake up and when I go to church and take holy water and when I take my seat and kneel down to pray.[118] Alonso Pérez can swear to this, because he is always at the door of the church when I go in, as can Father José de Urbina, and everybody else.

... [All the clerics] will tell you how I go to hear mass on Sunday in the morning and then every weekday at noon, so long as I am not caught up in work.

... I always walk in the Corpus Christi procession, and if I have ever missed one in the ten years I have been living in the *Real*, it would be that after I heard mass I was caught up in something, or that my whole household had gone to see the procession and it was necessary [that I stay home] to guard the house. The year they said I was absent I recall I marched along side of Luis Martin de Molina, and Pedro Núñez.

... I always say *Gloria patri et filio et spiritui sancto*. But my voice is low and not very resonant. ... Sometimes I was in my store doing business and someone came in and interrupted me, so I had to leave off the psalm in the middle, and perhaps they thought I had finished. ... My enemies [he lists them] will think what they want to think.

... I always buy salt pork and eat it as long as I am healthy. I ate it all the time I was taking my meals in Gaspar Enciso's house; the other boarders who ate at his table in the Real de Taxco [he lists them] will testify to that, as will Felipa de Fonseca and her Blacks and Indians. ... Doctor Diego de Bonilla [will tell you] that when I came to Taxco I was very sick with fever and in my eye, and he forbad me to eat fish or beef, and I haven't for eight years, though I do eat salt pork. I buy entire pieces and throw them into my stew pot as these people can testify [he lists them].

In a word, Fonseca Castellanos's program was to do Christian things where he could be certain people would see them, to publicly violate Jewish prohibitions, and to keep track of potential witnesses. In his first proceso he listed by name thirty residents of Taxco whom he expected to confirm that he was an upstanding Christian. García Rodríguez, the Taxco vicar whom the Inquisition tasked with interviewing all these character witnesses, wrote to complain of the difficulty of the assignment, since some of the nominated interviewees had gone to other Mexican cities and one was in Europe.[119]

There was, of course, no way for young Tomás to be certain how these interviews might turn out. Both the inquisitors and those they accused of heresy knew that for anyone holding a grudge, denouncing an enemy to the Inquisition—presuming there was a thread of truth in the accusation—was a simple way to exact revenge. In his 1589 trial, Tomás de Fonseca Castellanos prepared a long list of the people he considered his enemies, including the three whose denunciations were quoted above: Felipe Freire was on his tachas list because Tomás had fired him for doing the work he had been paid to do, whereupon Freire threatened to murder him; Mateo Ruiz because when he was drunk he had tried to kill someone and Tomás had stopped him and scolded him; and Francisco de Cáceres because he had refused to testify on Fonseca's behalf in a lawsuit Fonseca had lodged against Cáceres's uncle.

The Judaizers who gathered in Taxco around Jorge de Almeida, Antonio Díaz de Cáceres, Héctor de Fonseca, and young Tomás de Fonseca constituted, for a few short years, a community. Visiting members often lodged with Almeida or with young Tomás. They were in the habit of congregating at Almeida's Cantarranas hacienda or in young Tomás's store near Tetelcingo to discuss their religious beliefs. The Taxco Judaizers, and in Almeida's and Díaz de Cáceres's cases their wives, traveled frequently to Mexico City and interacted with the Judaizing community there. The groups in the two cities were in some ways one, a community of Judaizers without formal organizational structure, woven together by their common origin in the Raya de Portugal, their commercial interests, their family ties, and their shared religious culture.

Chapter 12

Pachuca and Manuel de Lucena's General Store

> Catalina Enríquez must not leave off the trading in silver, because this is the time that the profits will come in. Gómez [Pertierra] must do as I expect of him; he must not leave his store so that they won't rob him.... My wife must not come to Mexico City; she cannot miss the silver trading season.
>
> —MANUEL DE LUCENA, DECEMBER 19–20, 1594[1]

PACHUCA, WHERE THE plain that stretches north from the Valley of Mexico meets the edge of the silver-threaded Sierra de la Magdalena, was where in the 1550s old Tomás de Fonseca had dug for silver and Bartolomé de Medina had developed the revolutionary patio process. The hub around which the Pachuca Judaizing community revolved during the 1580s was Manuel de Lucena, a man who earned his living by investing in silver, lending to the miners, and, from his store, supplying the mining community with the goods they needed and with the luxuries that their successes in mining enabled them to acquire.

Lucena was born in 1564 in São Vicente da Beira. His mother, Clara Rodríguez, began his instruction in the Law of Moses when he was nine or ten years old.[2] Manuel's maternal grandparents and probably his parents, Clara and Simón Fernández, were from nearby Fundão, and it seems likely that sometime during Manuel's childhood years they took him and his siblings back there to live. About the time that Manuel reached puberty, the Portuguese Inquisition was beginning to focus on the Judaizers in the Beira region. Years later Manuel told Mexican inquisitors that as a child he personally witnessed the auto-de-fé in Fundão in which his family's friend Francisco Ferro was reconciled to the church.³ Not long after that, when Manuel was thirteen, his parents sent him to Sevilla to learn the storekeeping trade from their former Fundão neighbor Duarte Rodríguez, who owned a shop on the Calle de la Sierpe.⁴

Fundão was a village, albeit a large one. Sevilla must have caused thirteen-year-old Manuel de Lucena's eyes to pop in wonder. The streets bustled with commerce, and the newly built palaces that lined them spoke of wealth and power. The doors that opened to Manuel in the converso neighborhood were friendly ones; the cooking smells that wafted from their kitchens awakened memories of home. Many of the residents of these houses were Portuguese businessmen. Those with minimal capital hawked merchandise in Sevilla's streets or in the surrounding Andalusian villages. Those with modest means opened small retail shops in the commercial district that ran from the cathedral down to the riverside wharfs. The most successful tratantes built their emporiums on Sevilla's principal commercial thoroughfare, the Calle de la Sierpe.⁵

Young Manuel already knew many of these people by sight and by name. Manuel Álvarez, the father of Lucena's friend Jorge Álvarez, owned a store in the district. There he saw Álvaro González, ten years older than Manuel, a man whose heavy chestnut beard, small mouth, and protruding eyes gave him an air of intensity. Unlike many of the Beira immigrants, Álvaro González had quickly mastered the Spanish language, and by 1577 he spoke it with no trace of a Portuguese accent. Álvaro's uncle Enrique Méndez also had a store on Calle de la Sierpe; by the mid-1570s it had made him a wealthy man and had enabled his extended family to live well.⁶ Ana López and her husband, Diego López Regalón, Fundão émigrés, had relocated to Sevilla more than a decade earlier, when Manuel was still an infant.⁷ Though Ana was an old lady of forty-three by the time Manuel de Lucena met her, he quickly became friends with her son Antonio. Another Fundão boy, Manuel Rodríguez, who was six years Lucena's junior and would become a black-bearded man of average height, had two uncles with stores on the street.⁸ Not far from them was Andrés Rodríguez, a year younger than Lucena, whose aunt Catarina Enríquez was married to Francisco Manuel, proprietor of yet another store on Calle de la Sierpe.⁹ All these were people to whom Manuel de Lucena could bring news from loved ones left behind in Covilhã, São

Vicente da Beira, or Fundão, and from neighboring towns in the bishopric of Guarda.

Among the most successful Fundão merchants in Sevilla was Lucena's employer, Duarte Rodríguez, a tall, dark-eyed man with a blond beard.[10] His booming establishment was stocked with merchandise shipped to him from Mexico by his brother Simón Paiba, who had established a branch of the family business in Mexico City in 1576. Manuel boarded with Duarte and his wife, Clara, for a year and a half, learning the business while he reacquainted himself with old friends and made new ones among the Portuguese crypto-Jewish community in Sevilla. Young Manuel seems to have impressed Duarte as both able and trustworthy, for in 1578 Duarte sent him on an errand to New Spain. Unlike many young men in those years who were moved to strike out for the New World by their yearning for adventure and dreams of easy riches,[11] when fourteen-year-old Manuel de Lucena stowed his sea chest below decks, he had been tasked with a specific mission: go to Mexico City and help Simón Paiba in his store.

In Mexico Manuel lived for two years in the Paiba house on the Plaza del Volador while he worked in the family store. Simón Paiba, too, was impressed with the young man, for in 1579, when Simón returned to Spain to square accounts with his brother Duarte, he left Manuel in charge of the business. By then Lucena was living with Domingo López on Calle de los Ángeles.[12]

The following year Simón returned to Mexico, where he was soon joined by his wife, Beatriz Enríquez la Paiba, and their children Diego, Pedro, and Catalina Enríquez, who came as part of the group organized by Governor Carvajal.[13] The Paiba-Enríquez newcomers were all staunch Judaizers, and once they had settled in Mexico City, they welcomed Manuel into their family. In May 1582 he and their daughter Catalina, both of them still teenagers, were married.[14]

Manuel de Lucena worked in Simón Paiba's store in Mexico City for another two or three years. Looking to go into business on his own, he was attracted by the growing wealth of the nearby silver city of Pachuca. It was not long before Manuel, a "thin, well-proportioned man, with aquiline features and a slightly prominent nose," was a familiar sight on the road from Mexico City to Pachuca, where he was commuting regularly on business.[15] Among Lucena's other endeavors he was shipping *pipas* (barrel-like clay tubes) of wine to Pachuca, even though it was illegal to transport wine from

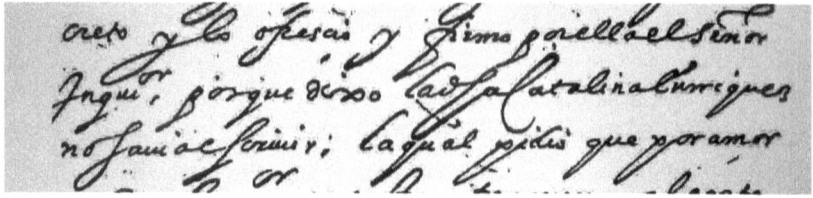

Figure 12. Inquisitor signs for Catalina Enríquez. Used with permission of the Archivo General de la Nación, Mexico City.

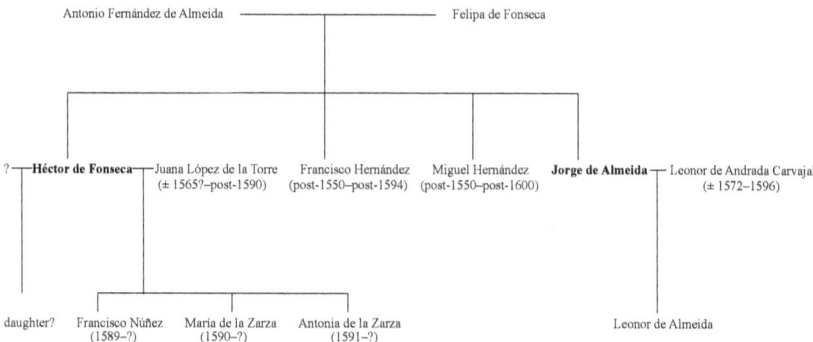

Mexico City.[16] Catalina and the couple's three-year-old daughter remained behind in Mexico City.[17] By the following year, Lucena was able to buy a building in Pachuca's central real of Tlaulilpa to serve as a store and a house for himself and Catalina.[18]

When the Inquisition arrested Manuel de Lucena in November 1594, it sequestered all of his assets. The Real Fisco (the Royal Exchequer) was the department of the Inquisition charged with ferreting out the accused person's assets, assembling them, accounting for them, and disbursing them as necessary to cover the expenses of the arrest, transportation, incarceration, and maintenance of the accused for as long as he or she was held by the Holy Office. The assets seized by Pedro de Vega, the Inquisition's agent, in addition to all of Lucena's available cash, included everything the Inquisition could locate of his possessions: real estate, both land and buildings; personal items like clothing and jewelry; household goods, both furniture and kitchen equipment; and livestock, including horses, mules, donkeys, and slaves.

Everything connected with Lucena's business was also sequestered, including all the real property and tangible inventory, as well Lucena's accounts receivable and all personal and business loans that were still outstanding.

While the Real Fisco's inventory does not describe the exterior or interior layout of the building that served Lucena as family residence and store, it enumerates the contents of both house and store with an attention to detail that aimed to establish each item's potential market value.[19] This inventory, together with the records of Lucena's interrogation, the documents the Holy Office collected from December 1594 through April 1595,[20] and an addendum found in documents collected in 1597–1598,[21] provides a remarkably comprehensive view of the material context of a well-to-do provincial colonial family of the late sixteenth century, shows the range of merchandise offered in a general store in a real de minas of that time, and gives a snapshot of a provincial businessman's professional activities. That both the Lucena household and the store included so many items produced in Europe and Asia as well as the Americas speaks eloquently of Mexico's position in the late sixteenth century at the nexus of world trade.

The Lucena Household

Pedro de Vega's report described the Lucena house, which was appended to the store, in considerable detail.[22] Adjacent to the shared wall was the home's wide entrance hall (*zaguán*), which doubled as the family's living room (*sala*). Next came a row of rooms, each sharing a wall with the next. Catalina and Manuel had one bedroom. Catalina's mother, Beatriz Enríquez, had another, which was large enough to accommodate overnight guests as well.

The *casas de morada*, the portions of the building in which the family lived, were furnished in a way that reflected Lucena's wealth and the family's custom of hosting visiting family members, important business contacts, and coreligionists. The mix of elegant items, frequently described as new, with items described as being worn or tattered, suggests a family enjoying newfound wealth while still preserving habits of prudence and thrift. The prices realized at the subsequent sale of many of these items at auction verify the family's position as comfortably well-off, if not in the stratosphere of great wealth.

Much of the Lucena household furniture was well made and colorfully decorated. They had many tables, two of them accompanied by benches. Several of the tables were covered with green or blue cloth. Their chairs numbered eight in the modern French style and one of the old-fashioned Spanish type.[23] That the Lucenas had so many chairs was somewhat unusual, for in houses in the Renaissance Spanish world, so heavily influenced by the prestigious Muslim culture, people commonly sat on cushions laid on low benches, called *estrados*, which were placed against the walls.[24] When the Lucenas had company, it was customary for the women to occupy the estrados while the men sat on the chairs. When overnight guests were many, the estrados doubled as beds.[25] People also sat on cushions placed on boxes or wooden trunks (eleven are listed in the inventory), which doubled as storage in houses that were, until modern times, devoid of closets.[26] A matched set of so many chairs, and the fact that the official making the inventory drew attention to their French nature, suggests that the chairs conveyed to visitors the family's international taste, their cutting-edge modernism, and their considerable wealth. The house offered pillows and cushions to sit on too. Two dozen of each are itemized in the inventory. Thirteen of the cushions were imported from China; each was covered with linen, canvas, or damask, and several of them were decorated with embroidered figures, their colors ranging from black to bright carmine. At the auction, the two Chinese damask cushion covers, unstuffed, sold for five pesos; two cushions and two pillows embroidered with figures in red went for thirteen pesos. By way of comparison, the Inquisition initially allotted the Lucena children's foster guardians only one hundred pesos for their full year's clothing and food expenses.[27]

The Lucena house had one writing desk, and it was both old and enormous. It seems to have been of the type known as a *bargueño*: a wooden box commonly set on either a two-door cabinet base or a trestle table. Designed to be portable, the bargueño often had iron handles on each side. The hinged front panel lowered to form a writing surface and to reveal an intricate array of box drawers and cabinets, many of them with locks and keys, which could be used for storing jewels, papers, and other valuables. In one of Lucena's desk drawers, Pedro de Vega found a diminutive barrel covered in leather; in another, a cluster of jet beads and some ribbons. But in the eyes of the Inquisition, the prize was several sheaves of paper listing Lucena's accounts receivable, with creditors' names and the amounts each person owed. Vega, not trusting these papers to be held safely with the rest of the house's contents, took immediate possession of them. He likewise took personal charge of an account book and a carved seal, in its case, used for impressing hot wax to close documents or envelopes.

The inventory lists several other containers in addition to the writing desk. There were a leather-covered chest and a painted chest from Michoacán, both with locks and keys. The family also had several reed-woven containers of the sort called *chicobites*. Somewhere, perhaps in the kitchen, stood a half barrel with its hoops.

As for the home's sleeping quarters, the inventory lists nine beds, two of them decorated with leather panels carved with scenes. The carved caryatid bedposts held up a draped ceiling of expensive cloth. One bed was painted green. Some of the featherbeds were sheathed with Castilian linen; others with native cotton and wool. The family had stacks of sheets made of finely woven cloth—the types called Holland (*olán* or *holanda*) and Rouen (*ruán*), indicating where in Europe they had been woven. On cold winter nights, the family's beds were piled with blankets woven in the Mexican highlands and in Campeche.

The Lucena house must have been well lit, for the inventory lists five pewter candelabras, and the couple had three sets of scissors for snuffing and trimming candlewicks. There were piles of candles—not cheap tallow candles, but beeswax. When their possessions were seized, all the family had for telling time was a sundial, though Lucena told inquisitors that he had "returned to a clock maker a clock that I'd originally bought from him for 72 pesos, and another, with an alarm, that cost me 40 pesos. . . . The prior of the Augustinians at Tezontepec offered me 120 pesos for it because he said it had the nicest bell in the Indies."[28]

On the home's floor were rugs, one of which is described as eight feet long, made of three strips sewn together. But the most eloquent testimony to Lucena's refined taste were his musical instruments: a Spanish guitar (*vihuela*) in its ebony case, a harp (*arpa*), for which he had paid four hundred pesos, and a clavichord (*clavicordio*) that was the very devil to keep in tune. Lucena was an accomplished musician who often accompanied his guests as they sang hymns or Psalms.

Because Manuel de Lucena and his wife and mother-in-law had been accused of Judaizing, it is not surprising that Pedro de Vega's inventorial eye went immediately to the religious icons displayed prominently in the house for the sake of Lucena's non-Jewish visitors. Right after the notation of eighty-seven pesos in cash, which Catalina Enríquez had handed to him when he entered the house, the very first household item Vega listed was a large painted statue of a lamb, an *agnus dei*, decorated with small offertory objects, standing in a black box that served as its frame. As the enumerator went from room to room, he noted other icons: a small statue of Christ; a Saint Michael, painted the way they did it in Portuguese India, with a headdress in the old style; a small carved *retablo* of Our Lady, with doors that were also fashioned in India; a retablo of Saint Jerome made from colored feathers, an art form perfected in pre-Columbian America and immediately put to the service of Christianity by the first generation of Spanish missionaries.

The most valuable items in the house, as befitted a wealthy household in a real de minas, were the family's silver table service. Many such items have been preserved; today they are prized by museums and collectors both for the quality of their workmanship and the artistic merit of their designs. Lucena's silver pieces were showy, impressive to his contemporaries, and for Lucena and his wife, a source of pride: "Come to my house to eat," Lucena told the priest Luis Díaz, "and you will note the fragrant odors of the cooking and the cleanliness and shine of the silver."[29] But the Inquisition had no interest in niceties of design, so Pedro de Vega enumerated the silver items only by their function and weight:

- Two pitchers, one small and one large; a flared bowl; a salt dish; and a large silver spoon and a couple of small spoons that together weighed seven marks, four ounces[30]
- A small pot and a narrow-necked vase that weighed three marks, six ounces
- Two plates, a serving platter, a medium-size plate, a pitcher and a jug, a cup, a small flared bowl, two salt dishes, and a large spoon and seven small ones that together weighed forty marks, five ounces
- A tiny gilded silver agnus dei, a gilded silver toothpick, and a little halo for an agnus dei, altogether weighing a little more than two ounces

Valuable items, to be sure, but they amounted to only a fraction of what the Inquisition expected Manuel de Lucena to have possessed. They surmised that Lucena, fearing that he might be arrested and his possessions sequestered, had hidden his most valuable silver items with friends or relatives. Their suspicion was bolstered by an event that occurred right after Lucena was arrested. Lucena's confidents in Pachuca wrote to the Inquisition that his house and store had been burgled in the night by some unidentified thieves, who, after boring a hole in the side of his house, had made off with cash, silver, jewels, and other valuable items.[31]

Suspicion remained, however, and a year and a half later, in the interrogation session of October 27, 1596, inquisitor Alonso de Peralta again took up the matter of the missing assets. He wondered aloud that perhaps Lucena had squirreled some of his valuable things away with his close friend and sometimes business partner Juan del Casal.[32] Lucena vehemently denied the allegation, but when pushed, he admitted the possibility that his wife, Catalina, had entrusted some items to Casal for safekeeping. Even after more than a year and a half in prison, Lucena spelled out, with a businessman's memory for financial detail, particulars of the silver items that Catalina may have given to Casal:

> a dozen silver plates that I had recently bought, which cost me 300 pesos, since each plate weighed fourteen or fifteen pesos. And a medium-sized platter that weighed three marks. And a pitcher that weighed five marks. And a jar that weighed four marks, and two plain salt dishes each of which weighed more or less eight pesos, and a white cup that weighed twenty pesos, and two round flared bowls that must have weighed ten to twelve pesos each, and a dozen spoons. I think there was a silver pot with a filigree handle that as far as I recall weighed more or less three marks.[33]

The Lucena kitchen was well equipped for cooking. The enumerator found pots—of iron, copper, and fired clay—of more than a dozen sizes and shapes. For supporting them over the fire there were forged iron tripods. The firebox itself was equipped with a bellows. The family had plates and platters, from small to large, made of glass, clay, and porcelain, and bowls and cups of the same materials, augmented by the wooden and gourd bowls that were preferred vessels in Indian kitchens. There were numerous spoons and knives, but no forks, for this innovative implement took another two centuries to enter into common use. The Lucenas had pottery jugs for water and ceramic bottles for vinegar and for the oil that the family cooked with instead of the lard used in Old Christian homes. The inventory lists a mortar and pestle for grinding chiles and another for grinding cacao. The kitchen maid whipped the family's chocolate drink to a froth with a wooden *molinillo* of the sort still for sale in every Mexican market. The tablecloths and napkins were acknowledged but were too numerous and of too little value to be listed individually.

The family's personal items included an ample selection of clothing, though the articles of male clothing listed on the inventory are neither numerous nor extravagant. Other than the clothes he had on when he was arrested, Lucena's wardrobe seems to have consisted of one pair of short breeches, a blue jerkin or doublet with gold braid along the seams, two short black capes of different cuts (a *capotillo* and a *ferreruelo*), some linen stockings, two pairs of leather shoes, a hat from India, a pair of fine mesh gloves, and a leather sword belt. No sword is listed, but he did own a pistol, a dagger, and a mold for making shot for a harquebus.

Catalina's sartorial collection, on the other hand, was large and colorful. She had three blouses, two of them embroidered with black silk thread, and two sleeveless blouses (*corpiños*), one of Chinese silk and the other of blue velvet. She owned six pairs of sleeves, which in sixteenth-century fashion were independent items that could be worn with any sleeveless blouse. One pair was taffeta and the others were of fine woolen weave (*telilla*). Some of them were embroidered; one, from Italy, in blue and gold. She also had two ruffled cuffs that could be attached to the ends of her sleeves. Her petticoats were cotton. She had five short dresses (*ropillas*), each of a different fabric: fine cotton sinabafa from East India, black tasseled taffeta, twilled serge (*tamenete*), and corded Chinese silk (*gorgarán*), which she could hold in place with a waistband (*pretina*).[34]

While Catalina's skirts and blouses were fairly plain, the sashes (*basquiñas*) she wore over them added notes of color and elegance. One was of fine quilted Holland cloth; another, of yellow Chinese damascene, was decorated with silver braid; a third, made of taffeta, was edged with black velvet and sported cloth pompoms; yet another was of bright red Chinese silk, sewn with brass-colored braid. Catalina could also wrap her waist with an extra-large, round, Chinese satin sash (*saya entera*). It was fashionable to wear these garments plump, so Catalina could bulk them up with one of her three Chinese farthingales (*verdugados*). Since modest women almost always covered their heads, Catalina could wear one of her eight wimples (*pañitos de toca de cabeza*), some of which were decorated with lace or appliqué points or chevrons (*puntas*). Over that she could place one of her seventeen delicate, transparent wimples (*tocas*[35]), all imported from China. Her shoes included a pair of cork-soled Valencian sandals (*chapines*) and two pairs of more delicate sandals (*servillas*). For the sniffles, or daintiness at table, she could take out one of her eleven handkerchiefs (*paños de mano*; *paños de narices*). The inventory also listed a baptismal cloth.

Many of the items in Catalina's wardrobe were clearly acquired readymade. Others were undoubtedly of home manufacture. The household inventory includes many bolts of cloth: serge, taffeta, fine cotton sinabafa, ruán linen, and wool. Although not every woman spun her own thread or wove her own cloth, in the early colonial world, women of all classes and occupations sewed, and the inventory lists a quantity of sewing supplies: needles and pins, small boxes and pincushions to hold them, silk buttons, spools of thread, and bundles of decorative bits that could be sewn onto clothing for adornment.

Well-to-do women normally complemented their clothing with jewelry, so the inquisitors were puzzled by how little of it Juan de Vega found when he inventoried Catalina Enríquez's things. What he did encounter was of little value: one necklace of coral and quartz; a number of small beads, presumably of glass and shell, which were the most common nonprecious materials in use for baubles at the time; a few loose coral beads; and one large blown-glass bead of many colors. But Catalina should have had more jewelry, and of better quality. When they asked Manuel de Lucena about it, a year and a half after the couple's arrests, he replied as he had with the missing silver:

> If some witness testified that Catalina had jewelry of great value, he is deceived. Because at that time she had only a gold chain that weighed 200 or so marks, made of tiny twisted links, which I sold because we needed the money. What she did have in jewelry was a seed-pearl necklace that must have weighed eight ounces, and a huge gold pear-shaped pendant from China, and another of amber. And one or two rings and sets of earrings, and a few more of those trinkets that women have.[36]

The remaining personal item on the inventory was Manuel de Lucena's box of tools. It contained everything needed for simple home repair. There were a hammer, nails, screws, a chisel, some knives, a pair of scissors, a couple of large iron spoons, a copper bowl, two lengths of pry bar, some bits of tubing, an ax, and a scale. Two saddles are recorded: a leather saddle with cloth trappings that was used by Manuel's wife; and another, cushioned with leather, with long stirrups. The inventory lists an unspecified number of pack mules and a horse but does not mention a stable adjacent to Lucena's house and business, so he must have quartered the animals elsewhere. When his property was seized, Lucena said that he had left a second horse with an innkeeper in Tezontepec to be fattened up.[37]

Lucena's Store

After tallying the family's personal possessions, Pedro de Vega turned to the stock of merchandise in Lucena's store. While many of the items for sale were similar to those in the living quarters, the quantities differed greatly. Vega ordered the durable merchandise to be sequestered and stored and the perishable items to be turned immediately into cash. "First of all," Vega's report began, "I found 5 *arrobas*[38] and 16 pounds of tallow candles, which I sold to Bartolomé de San Pedro for 22 pesos and 6 tomines . . . a cask which seemed to have 6 ¾ arrobas of wine as measured by a yardstick I sold to Juan del Casal at 8 pesos the arroba plus 3 pesos and 4 tomines for the cask."[39]

The largest category of durable merchandise in the store was ready-made clothing, both new and used, described in the inventory by color, place of origin, quantity, and condition. There were stacks of knee-length trousers (*calzones*) of wool, linen, and velvet, some made in Mexico and some in Italy. Fashion dictated that men cover their legs from the knee to the foot with stockings made of silk, wool, linen, or cotton. These snagged easily. They could be repaired, but for elegance they had to be worn in pristine condition. Lucena's store stocked at least twenty-seven pairs; the preferred color was black. Shoes seem to have been a big seller too: in stock were seventy-one pairs for adults, plus thirteen pairs of children's shoes (*botillas* and *zapatillos*) in both leather and sheepskin and nine pairs of slippers (*servillas*), some of them with insoles. There were ten pairs of locally made goatskin gloves. Both men and women carried handkerchiefs, which soiled and wore out quickly. The store carried them by the dozens, in a variety of textiles, the most elegant ones from China.

The store offered petticoats (*naguas*) in white and blue. There were shirts, new and used, for both men and women; embroidered red Indian blouses (*huipiles*), some with ribbons; sleeveless jerkins and doublets; and dozens of pairs of detached sleeves in black and in brown. For blouses with a low-cut décolletage, there were neckpieces called *gorguerillas*. There were capes, long and short, and hoods, some well worn and some new, cloth caps and wimples in gauzy silk and finely woven linen, both domestically produced and from China, in various colors, embroidered and ribboned. There were hats for men and for children, some felted and some woven, some made in Mexico and some imported from India, as well as twenty-three cheap cloth hats lined in taffeta to be sold to Indians.

The second largest category of durable merchandise in the store was cloth sold by the piece or by the Castilian yard (vara), often described in the inventory by color, place of origin, quantity (ranging from 1 to 152 yards), and condition. These included Castilian *bocací* (the Turkish word for buckram, a coarsely woven cloth), *crea* (semi-fine linen), holanda and *holandilla* (fine linen, often used for sheets), *jergueta* (coarse, twill-woven woolen material), *listón* (ribbon), *paños de camisa* (for making shirts), *randas* (for lining garments), ruán, *tafetán* (taffeta), and tellila (finely woven wool). The store also carried blankets from Campeche and from Castilla, and red-and-white *conga* blankets in the African style.[40]

It is not surprising that the Lucena general store stocked a large selection of sewing paraphernalia. There were uncountable numbers of needles and pins, along with thimbles, bobbins (*bollillos*), scissors, and twine of sisal (*pita*) and *henequén* fiber. There were decorative accessories such as ribbons; fancy cords; buttons made of silk, leather, shell, and glass; decorative braid (*pasamanos*); lace; and metal appliqués (*puntas*). There was indigo (*añil*) for dyeing. But most of all there was thread, sold by weight or by the skein: white thread from Sevilla and thread from Portugal in various gauges. Also for sale were silk fibers, both single filament and twisted, from China, Castilla, and the Mexican Mixteca.[41] In the sixteenth century, sewing supplies like these, imported from Europe or Asia or locally produced, were commonly hawked from village to village by traveling merchants like Luis and Baltazar

Carvajal, among many others. These *buhoneros*, *mercachifles*, or *vendedores ambulantes* would replenish their stock at stores like Lucena's in Pachuca or Tomás de Fonseca Castellanos's in Taxco.

To equip women's dressing tables, Lucena's store offered mirrors, ivory-tipped brushes, combs, hair bands, and ribbons, as well as *solimán*, a toxic, mercury-based cosmetic used for whitening the skin. To complete their personal decoration, shoppers could find a wide selection of mostly inexpensive jewelry, including some that served religious purposes, such as a gold-plated silver agnus dei and rosaries of glass and coral beads. There were cartons of loose beads, too, made of glass and coral and small seed pearls, and boxes of loose semiprecious stones, such as garnets, girasol opals, cat's-eyes, beryls, and a few larger pearls. There were several gold rings. The inventory describes a few of these creations in tantalizing detail: "a little golden snake encrusting a beryl carved with the Resurrection . . . a necklace of tiny grains of gold each hung with a small pearl."

In addition to personal items, Lucena's emporium offered lines of products to satisfy nearly every need or desire of a household in a colonial city. There was tack to equip the stable: saddles, stirrups, and cinches; trappings; halters, reins, bits, and spurs. Miners could equip themselves with hammers, knives, scissors, pry bars, picks, punches, awls, pliers, chisels, and measuring sticks, along with screws and nails and the pumice stone and powdered lead oxide (cendrada) used as catalysts in their smelters. Blacksmiths could find horseshoes, hoof trimmers (*pufabantes*), and barrel hoops, as well as the lighter metal rings (*argollas*) that the inventory describes as "those commonly placed around the necks of Chichimeca slaves."[42] For self-defense: a sword, a sheath, a sword belt, and a harquebus. For the musically inclined, there were vihuelas and sets of strings, as well as clavichord hammers (*macillos*). And there were several sizes of the scales and weights that were an absolute necessity in an environment in which valuable items were generally priced by weight.

Lucena's Employees

Manuel de Lucena had three full-time employees in his business in Pachuca. His store in the Real de Tlaulilpa was staffed by a manager, Francisco Váez, and a junior clerk, Juan de la Serna. Lucena's branch store in Real del Monte, high in the mountains northeast of Tlaulilpa, was managed by Gómez Pertierra under a formal partnership agreement.

Like Lucena, Francisco Váez had been born in the village of São Vicente da Beira. Among his many relatives in New Spain were two uncles: Jorge Váez, an active Judaizer and itinerant merchant who sold imported Chinese textiles and traded for cacao in southern Mexico; and Jerónimo Rodríguez, Jorge Váez's brother, who was a pastry chef in Puebla. Jerónimo was reluctant to Judaize and distanced himself from his Judaizing family members in so far as was possible.[43] Francisco Váez's job was to manage the Pachuca store in Lucena's absence, to keep the business's accounts in order, and to shuttle to Mexico City to buy stock for the store at Lucena's direction. Lucena treated the young, dark-bearded boy more like a relative than an employee, including him in his family's religious observances, reading him biblical stories from his copy of *Mirror of Consolation*, and instructing him in the basic tenets of Judaism as Lucena understood them.[44]

The store's junior clerk, Juan de la Serna, was in his early teens when Lucena hired him to help out in the store and run errands. De la Serna was born in Pedroche, a tiny village in the Sierra Morena north of Córdoba in Spain. Presumably an Old Christian, de la Serna was astonished by many of the things he witnessed in the course of his duties. Lucena and Váez took care not to let him draw too close. Nevertheless, at Lucena's 1594 trial, de la Serna, by then seventeen, described how Lucena, Váez, and Lucena's close friend Manuel Gómez Navarro would lock themselves in a room together, presumably to pray. He was keenly aware of how these three and Lucena's wife, Catalina Enríquez, slaughtered their chickens by cutting their throats and how the couple abstained from eating pork but were nervous about not setting it out on the table.

Lucena's third employee, Gómez Pertierra, from the northern Spanish region of Asturias, had been brought to Mexico by his mother, Balaguida de Mesas.[45] In March 1594, when Pertierra was twenty-one, Manuel de Lucena and he cut a deal: Pertierra would open a branch store in Real del Monte, a prosperous and rapidly growing real a league northeast and 250 meters higher than Tlaulilpa. According to the terms of their partnership, which was to be in effect for one year, Lucena would advance the partnership one thousand pesos in cash and merchandise. Pertierra put up 108 pesos of his own money. Pertierra would keep accurate books, and at the end of the year they would divide the profits: two-thirds to Lucena and one-third to Pertierra. During the year, Pertierra would use the cash flow to replenish the store's stock and to invest, judiciously, in ventures that were sure to yield a good gain. Since the miners in Real del Monte, like those in Real de Tlaulilpa, needed tools, food, basic household supplies, and amalgamation catalysts to produce the refined silver that was the cash product on which they lived, storekeepers like Lucena, Pertierra, and Tomás de Fonsca Castellanos in Taxco routinely advanced equipment, clothing, and food staples to the miners on credit, which the miners paid off in due course with cash, bars of refined silver, and in some cases unprocessed silver-rich ore. Shortly after Lucena's arrest, Catalina, in Pachuca, asked Gómez Pertierra for an accounting of the branch store, which Pertierra produced and turned over to Catalina's advisers, Juan López Tavera and Juan del Casal.[46] During the year in which Lucena and Pertierra did business together, the original 1,108-peso investment had grown to 1,643 pesos. But in fact, Pertierra reported, estimating the value of stock in hand and accounts still receivable, it was closer to two thousand pesos.[47]

Lucena and Pertierra did not dig their silver out of the earth, but in a very real way they were part of the colonial mining industry.[48] They supplied miners with their necessities, usually on credit, and they received their payment in silver in any of its many forms, from coins to lumps of unrefined ore. They also bought and sold silver outright.

Most legal silver followed a straight path from the mine to the royal mint. As we have seen, the last step in the refining process was to heat the amalgam in an oven to pry apart the mercury, the silver, and whatever other minor impurities remained. The liquid silver would be poured into a mold to form an ingot or small flat cake known as a *plancha*. The value of the planchas was determined by their weight in pounds (*libras*), half pounds (*marcos*), pesos, or the various other measures that were current at the time.[49] The miner would bring the planchas to the assay office, where he would pay a tax of one-fifth of their value to the Royal Treasury and each plancha would be stamped with the quinta seal, which meant it was now legal tender, to be shipped to Spain or to be struck into coins.

Silver, in any and all of its forms, from raw ore to *planchas quintadas*, was fungible. Lucena, like any other storekeeper or tratante in colonial Mexico, could lend it out in one form and take it back in another as payment.[50] People carried coins, bars, and lumps of silver in their purses to make their purchases.[51] Storekeepers, perforce, kept a balance and a box of weights handy on the counter, so it was not unusual for people entering Lucena's shop to see him "weighing some piece of silver, watching the scale swinging."[52]

One way for a merchant like Lucena to invest in silver was to buy unrefined or partially refined silver from miners who did not have the wherewithal to convert their raw ore into planchas. Buying this so-called plata de rescate (recoverable silver) was a regular and necessary part of Lucena's routine. As early as 1585, when he and Catalina were still living in Mexico City, he was traveling to Pachuca to *rescatar* plata.[53] Often the raw or semi-refined ore passed through several hands before it ended up converted into coins or planchas, and Lucena might buy it at any step along the way.[54]

The shopkeeper-investor, acting alone or in partnership with others, needed a keen eye to estimate the quantity and the quality of the silver in a particular batch of ore. He needed either to own or to have access to an amalgamation patio and an *ingenio de moler metales* to turn the raw ore into spendable silver. He needed a string of mules and a hostler for transporting the ore. If he could not do those things himself, he had to subcontract to an agent who had those skills and resources. He needed to be as shrewd a judge of character as he was of silver ore, for there were opportunities for him to be robbed or cheated at every step of the process. Even a close confident to Lucena such as Jorge Álvarez, a Portuguese Judaizer from Fundão who in Mexico City had lived for a time with Lucena's mother-in-law, could be a risk. When Manuel de Lucena tendered him a sum of money to buy silver for him, Jorge Álvarez spent it, probably on drink, women, or gambling, which were his preferred vices.[55]

A second investment that went sour about the time the Lucena family was being arrested will illustrate another kind of risk to the shopkeeper-investor. On November 9, 1594, Gómez Pertierra, acting for Manuel de Lucena, gave the agent Juan de Miranda cash and merchandise with a total value of 622 pesos as prepayment for acquiring and processing a certain quantity of ore on Lucena's behalf.[56] Miranda bought the ore and had it taken to the ingenio of the Tlaulilpa miner Hernando de Castro[57] to be crushed, incorporated, and refined. Unfortunately, just before the amalgam was to be smelted, Miranda found himself the target of a lawsuit brought by one

Gonzalo de Angulo. The authorities seized the amalgam and would not let Castro complete the refining process.[58] Pertierra tried to have Miranda held responsible for the loss, but Miranda fled and could not be found. In the words of Antonio Trancoso, a Pachuca tratante whom the Inquisition called to testify about the muddle, "With Miranda's departure, Gómez Pertierra has not been able to recover the money he gave Juan de Miranda from the assets of Manuel de Lucena; and that is the truth."[59] On January 13, 1595, inquisitors Bartolomé Lobo Guerrero and Alonso de Peralta intervened, ordering Hernando de Castro to deliver the 622 pesos that ultimately belonged to Lucena directly to the Real Fisco's agent in Pachuca. When this order reached Pachuca five days later, Castro refused to comply. He alleged that Miranda had purchased the ore not from the owners but from naboríos who had stolen it from their employers, reporting that the mine owners had filed suit, arguing that the proceeds of the ore on Castro's amalgamation patio belonged legitimately to them. He stipulated that the judge had ruled that if he did not turn the money over to the owners immediately, he would be required to pay them double the amount. Under the circumstances, Castro wrote, he could not surrender the money without a written order from the Inquisition overturning the local judge's ruling.[60] There appears to be no record of the resolution of this legal tangle.

A third risk was the Real Fisco's allegedly sticky hands. Fear of sequestration led many converso businessmen to devise precautionary plans to hide their assets. But despite the endemic fear of arrest and sequestration, for the converso mining community, the rhythms of silver never abated. In May 1594, as the second phase of the great purge of Judaizers was gathering momentum, Lucena sent Francisco Váez to the mining community of Sichú to collect some silver for him.[61] Even after Lucena's imprisonment in early November of that year, he was still concerned about his store, his accounts receivable, and his investments in silver. From his cell he wrote to friends in Pachuca: "Catalina Enríquez must not come here from Pachuca, even if I am here for two years.... She must not leave off the trading in silver, because this is the time that the profits will come in.... My wife must not come to Mexico City; she cannot miss the silver trading season."[62]

Buying *rescate* silver was an important part of Manuel de Lucena's business ventures, but the core was his emporium in Pachuca and, to a lesser extent, his branch store in Real del Monte. Lucena's Pachuca store, similar to the one Tomás de Fonseca Castellanos operated in Taxco, functioned as both a general retail and wholesale emporium and a bank. In his account books, Lucena recorded transactions involving the buying and selling of merchandise and the loans he extended to customers, local miners, and other members of the business community. Sales and loans were often one and the same, since merchandise was often—perhaps nearly always—sold on credit, sometimes on the installment plan, sometimes for settlement after a crop was sold or some quantity of silver ore—in the ground or somewhere in the processing chain—was successfully turned into planchas of silver.

When the inquisitors pressed Lucena for details about his outstanding creditors, his answers revealed a complex portfolio of due bills—generally but not exclusively for sales of cloth and clothing, both to wholesalers and to individuals. Manuel Gómez Navarro, who had a store in Sichú, regularly bought merchandise from him. A typical Gómez transaction included eleven pesos worth of undyed finely woven cloth sheeting; two pesos worth of damask, two of silk, two of ribbed silk cloth; and eighty-three pesos worth of miscellaneous items, all of which Francisco Váez transported from Pachuca to Sichú. Gómez Navarro was not only a creditor; he also acted as Lucena's agent in brokering sales to small merchants in other towns. Catalina's young brother Diego Enríquez, on a much more reduced scale, also sold for Lucena, relying on Gómez Navarro to keep all their financial records in order. In one instance, Diego sold one of Lucena's packhorses on credit to a man named Pedro Montezuma. In another instance, Diego bought a horse in Quichiapa for seventy pesos and gave it to Lucena, who reimbursed him that amount. Lucena then sold it on credit for seventy-five pesos to Gómez Navarro, who promptly lost the horse to thieves. Lucena listed Gómez's outstanding seventy-five-peso debt as one of his assets.[63]

Many documents assembled by the Inquisition in its attempts to seize Manuel de Lucena's far-flung assets provide information about his creditors. More than 144 of them are listed by name, many with multiple purchases or in receipt of multiple loans.[64] Juan Alfaro and Francisco García each owed a year's rent on one of Lucena's properties. Juan de Arriarte owed for some silk stockings and a hat. Fortunio Cevallos owed on a clock he had purchased. Francisco Domínguez had purchased a head scarf for his wife; Diego Enríquez, a horse; Domingo de Peñarrieta, a mule; María García de Inclán, a gold ring. Elías Pereira, a silver miner in Pachuca, had purchased a clavichord. Young Tomás de Fonseca Castellanos, with whom Lucena had frequent business dealings, owed him for some sinabafa cloth.[65] Antonia Guiral, the wife of Alonso de la Torre, owed for merchandise and left a large gold agnus dei with Lucena in pawn.[66]

Lucena's creditors represent a broad swath of colonial society. They lived in the reales and in Mexico City. Only a few of their professions are listed or readily apparent in other documents, but they included government officials, a baker, a shirt maker, a cattle rancher, a cleric, and several miners. Eighteen were women, and several of the men were husbands who owed money on their wives' accounts. At least nineteen of his clients, judging from other sources, were probably conversos, and at least half of these are known to have Judaized.

Manuel de Lucena may have practiced his religion only with people from his own caste of Portuguese Judaizers, but he did business with everyone.

Chapter 13

Lucena's Judaizing Community in Mexico City and Pachuca

> My husband Manuel de Lucena, Baltazar Rodríguez, Luis de Carvajal, Miguel [de Carvajal], Antonio López, and Diego Enríquez . . . fasted a three day fast of the Law of Moses and at night came to my house to eat. . . . I didn't fast because I was pregnant then, nor did my mother Beatriz Enríquez because she was ill. . . . [The men] prayed prayers of the Law of Moses in a bedroom, but my mother and I were not there because since this is both a house and a store, we had to attend to the people who came to buy merchandise and trade silver.
>
> —CATALINA ENRÍQUEZ, FEBRUARY 23, 1596[1]

SIMÓN PAIBA AND his wife, Beatriz Enríquez la Paiba, were the children of Jews who had fled from Spain to Portugal in 1492 only to be forcibly converted in their new homeland. They and their siblings had been raised as Judaizers, and they in turn made certain that their own children, now third-generation New Christians, were well grounded in Jewish traditions.[2] From the moment of Simón's arrival in Mexico City in 1576, his home had become a gathering place for Judaizers, and when Beatriz Enríquez and the children joined him there in 1580, the home quickly exerted a similar attraction for the conversa women of the capital.

Manuel de Lucena, by contrast, was the only member of his immediate family to come to Mexico. It was natural that as a newcomer to Mexico City in 1578, he would lodge initially with his employer, Simón Paiba. By the time Simón's family arrived in 1580, Lucena had taken rooms on Calle de los

Ángeles in a house owned by Miguel Rodríguez de Acevedo, across the street from another Portuguese converso, Domingo López, who was probably from Lucena's hometown of São Vicente da Beira. López, some ten years Lucena's senior, was a thin, asthmatic man with light-brown hair and a dark beard. López liked to talk with Manuel about their common religious heritage, arguing that since God had scattered the Jews because of their sins, it behooved Jews in the Diaspora to observe the commandments, such as fasting, as strictly as they were able.[3]

When Manuel wed Simón Paiba's daughter Catalina Enríquez in May 1582, he married into an extended family of enthusiastic Judaizing conversos from Covilhã, Fundão, and Manuel's hometown of São Vicente da Beira, the seminal triangle of towns in the Raya de Portugal. The wedding of Manuel and Catalina signified not so much the union of two families as the absorption of Manuel de Lucena into the Enríquez clan.

Manuel was eighteen, a year older than his bride.[4] At first the young newlyweds lived on the Plaza del Volador with Catalina's parents and Catalina's younger brothers Pedro and Diego Enríquez.[5] The newlyweds fit easily into the community of friends that often joined the Enríquez-Paiba family on the Sabbath or for the principal Jewish festivals. Shortly after their wedding, for example, in an event that was representative of the family's pattern of Judaizing, the young couple observed the Yom Kippur (Dia Grande) fast with Catalina's parents and seven of their friends. One was Álvaro González, from Fundão, who had known Lucena in Sevilla and in Mexico City owned a store in the Casas del Marqués.[6] Another was Álvaro Rodríguez, from Monforte de Lemos, who worked for Hernando de Castro at Castro's mining hacienda in Pachuca and who liked to gamble at cards.[7] Also fond of gambling were the bachelor Baltazar González, who lived in the small sheep-ranching town of Guachiapa,[8] and the Mexico City street vendor Manuel Rodríguez, whom Clara Enríquez thought might be Lucena's cousin. Everyone knew Manuel Rodríguez to be a womanizer, and some thought he was a crook.[9] Also fasting with them that Yom Kippur was Catalina's cousin Jorge Álvarez, who had come with her to Mexico on Governor Carvajal's ship.[10] Of these five men, all but Álvaro González had been born in Fundão, and in 1582 all were in their late teens or early twenties, suggesting that their friendship had formed when they were children back in Portugal. Also fasting with them was Manuel Francisco Belmonte, a Judaizer in his mid-thirties from

Covilhã, who at that time was living with the Paibas.¹¹ The merchant Jorge Rodríguez also fasted with the group. He claimed to have been born in Sevilla, but he was thick with the Portuguese community and had likely been born in Portugal. Years later he sailed to Asia to trade.¹²

At this Yom Kippur gathering, Manuel de Lucena, who even at age eighteen seems to have been the most knowledgeable and most assertive of them all in things Jewish, stood on a bench and read to them prophetic passages from the copy of the book of Esdras that Dr. Morales had given to the Paiba family. In the late afternoon, several of the attendees stretched their legs with a walk to the Tianguis de San Hipólito, an open-air Indian market on the western outskirts of the city.¹³ Afterward, back at the Paibas, the majority of the party broke their fast together with stewed chicken and fruit.¹⁴

By the following year, the young marrieds had moved to rooms rented from the silversmith Dionisio de Citola in the Plaza del Volador, two houses distant from Catalina's parents.¹⁵ Lucena fasted there with Manuel Álvarez (Jorge Álvarez's father), who had just recently come from Spain and was living with them. Álvarez spent the day playing cards with Álvaro Rodríguez while Lucena recited the morning prayers and Catalina watched. Because of her pregnancy, Catalina did not fast. When Lucena had finished praying, he spent the rest of the day walking around the city, stopping for a brief visit with his parents-in-law, who were fasting in their house with Manuel Francisco Belmonte. Once the sun had set, the entire group, including Simón and Beatriz, gathered at Manuel and Catalina's to break the fast ceremonially with chicken, both roasted and stewed, and fresh fruit. Joining them at the meal were Catalina's brothers Diego and Pedro, the merchant Jorge Rodríguez, and Álvaro and Baltazar González, Lucena's Fundão friends in Sevilla. When Jorge Álvarez appeared a little later, Lucena invited him to come listen to some things that would give him much pleasure. Álvarez took off his cape and hat (covering one's head was not generally part of the male Judaizing repertoire in Mexico) and sat down. Lucena began to read aloud some prophetic passages from the book of Esdras. When he was halfway through, Pedro Rodríguez Saz (from Fundão) came in and sat down. Years later, Lucena told inquisitors that he had glossed the verses as he read, telling the gathering "how the Messiah had not yet come, how Jesus was not the Messiah, and how the Messiah would come to redeem the people of Israel. They all listened to me with great attention. Finally Pedro Rodríguez Saz stood up and, making castanet sounds with his hands, laughed and said: 'Yes, and then all these Christian dogs will be dead.'"[16]

Manuel Álvarez later characterized the event as one of "pomp and ceremony."[17]

The couple's Jewish life continued to center on the Paiba-Enríquez household. In 1584 they again observed the Yom Kippur fast with Catalina's parents and siblings; the only non–family member present this time was Sebastián de la Peña (from São Vicente da Beira), a short, stooped man with a curved nose and a salt-and-pepper beard.[18] The pattern of Manuel de Lucena and Catalina Enríquez's festival Judaizing community had been set: a core of Enríquez-Paibas and as many of their friends as could be gathered, the majority of them from the same cluster of three Portuguese towns along the Spanish border.[19]

Members of the Portuguese community in Mexico City who owned houses or rented sets of rooms were in the habit of sharing them with newcomers. Conditions were crowded, and there was little privacy. Manuel de Lucena reported that when he was living with the Paibas before his marriage, Álvaro González, Gonzalo Rodríguez, Pedro Méndez, and Manuel Francisco Belmonte were living there too.[20] Manuel Gómez de Casteloblanco told inquisitors that "when the Portuguese came up to Mexico City they all used to lodge together in one room in the house of a baker woman ... and later they separated."[21] During their first three years of married life, while Catalina and Manuel were living in a succession of rented rooms before they moved to Pachuca, they often shared their space with new arrivals from Spain, almost all of them Judaizers from the Portuguese border towns. By 1584 Manuel and Catalina had moved to an apartment in a new building on Calle San Francisco owned by Diego Alonso Larios, an investor, cattle rancher, and probably land speculator, who, in addition to his house in Mexico City, at one time owned estates in Veracruz, northern Michoacán, and several parts of what is now the state of Mexico.[22] Larios was an Old Christian, and Lucena, now a prospering young man of twenty, was expanding his own circle of friends beyond the Portuguese Judaizing community, even while his Jewish life continued to center on the Paiba-Enríquez household.

The couple's next home was on the Calle Donceles. In 1585 they moved three times: to the Calle de la Inquisición, where they shared their house with Jorge Álvarez, Domingo Rodríguez, and two Portuguese men whose names

Catalina's mother could not later remember;[23] from there to a house owned by Rodrigo Pérez near Santa Catalina Church; and subsequently to another on the Calle de la Puerta de los Carros de Santo Domingo.[24] The following year the couple took rooms in the house of Diego de León, a merchant from Nájera in the Spanish Rioja who was fluent in Náhuatl and earned a living as an interpreter. "When I lived with Diego de León," Lucena later told inquisitors, "Domingo Rodríguez and Jorge Álvarez lived with us. We all celebrated the Día Grande del Señor with Simón Paiba and Beatriz Enríquez. I bathed with Domingo Rodríguez in his room, and I think Jorge Álvarez did too."[25]

Supplementing their housemates was a regular crowd of visitors, especially on the Sabbath and on Jewish festival days. Often groups would gather to fast together during the week as well.[26] In addition to most of those already mentioned, their visitors included Manuel Gómez, who later drowned while on his way to Spain;[27] Sebastián Nieto and his brother Antonio Núñez from Covilhã, slavers in the Guinea trade, who were particularly knowledgeable in matters pertaining to Judaism;[28] and Francisco Rodríguez Ledesma, a handsome, chestnut-bearded Spaniard from the province of Salamanca, who dealt in slaves and pearls that he brought to Mexico from Cartagena, once selling a selection of the latter to Manuel de Lucena.[29] The ritual included reading, reciting, and sometimes singing Psalms, or reading from one of the handful of books that some member of the group had brought with him. The gatherings were punctuated by light moments of poking fun at Christian doctrine and scoffing at the Christian worship of carved images that the Judaizers termed idols. The women prepared a meal, favoring either chicken or, during Lent, fish. Almost always the group's leader was Manuel de Lucena.

When overnight visitors were many, it was common practice for the guests to sleep two to a bed. Lest this raise questions about their sexuality, they were always careful to report that the men had been fully dressed.[30] Despite the inconvenience, this sharing of beds strengthened communal ties and fostered the sense of in-group-ness that was one of the salient characteristics of the Mexican Portuguese converso community. It also provided a hothouse environment for proselytizing and for mutually reinforcing consciousness about Judaizing beliefs and practices. Catalina Enríquez told inquisitors how

> eleven or twelve years ago [1585] when I was living on Calle Donceles...

Jorge Álvarez and Duarte Rodríguez came to the house. We ate stewed chicken and fruit, and afterwards Jorge Álvarez and Francisco Rodríguez lay down together in one bed, and Duarte Rodríguez lay down on the *estrado* with Diego Enríquez, my brother, who had been wounded in a hunting accident, and Jorge Álvarez and Francisco Rodríguez began to talk about the next day being the Sabbath, . . . and Álvarez said that it hurt him to have to work that day so that he could not observe the Sabbath, and Rodríguez told him to put the work off until Sunday.[31]

Manuel de Lucena's pleasant character and his knowledge of and enthusiasm for Judaism garnered respect among Mexico City's Judaizers. His wife, Catalina, was held in similar repute. It is therefore no surprise that Pelayo Álvarez, who, because he had married an Old Christian, felt that he could not teach his daughters Ana and Felipa to Judaize, asked the couple in 1583 or 1584 to take the young teenage girls into their household to instruct them in Judaism. Catalina and Manuel reluctantly agreed. The girls lived with them for several months, but the arrangement did not work. The two girls were unshakably Christian, and their presence put an intolerable crimp in the couple's routines of Jewish observance. In 1596 Catalina explained to inquisitors their decision to revoke their invitation:

The main reason Manuel and I threw them out of our house was to be able to live freely, and to keep them from seeing us observe the Sabbath and not eat bacon or lard or any pork. Ana asked me, "Why don't you eat lard? Why do you eat everything at your house with olive oil?" And I told her that lard makes us sick and we were not accustomed to eating pork. And then I saw Ana talking with her sister, telling her that she didn't understand me and my family because we didn't eat pork and we didn't go to hear mass on festival days. I told Manuel about it, and we threw them out. That not going to mass that Ana and Felipa noticed, I told them I was sick and that is why I didn't take them to hear it, and that they couldn't go by themselves because they were young unmarried girls. So to comply with custom [my mother] Beatriz Enríquez la Paiba took them to mass once every three months.[32]

By 1585, twenty-one-year-old Manuel de Lucena was commuting regularly to the towns north and east of Mexico City to explore business opportunities. Catalina, pregnant with their second daughter, Clara, and later nursing, remained in the capital. In the spring of that year, just before Purim, Lucena bought three casks of wine from Manuel Francisco Belmonte and carted them to Pachuca to sell. Shortly after that he acquired the property in the center of Pachuca's central mining district of Tlaulilpa that served as both a home and a general store. For the next couple of years, while Manuel commuted to Pachuca and built up his business there, the family's houses in both cities functioned as centers of Judaizing activity. Though Manuel and Catalina were often apart, they usually managed to celebrate the major Jewish holidays together in one or the other of their homes.[33]

Pachuca is only ninety kilometers from the capital—half the distance that separates Taxco from Mexico City—with a road easily traversed in a day and a half on horseback. The community of Judaizers that gathered in Manuel de Lucena's Pachuca house and store always remained close to their coreligionists in Mexico City, even more so than the community that coalesced around Jorge de Almeida, Tomás de Fonseca Castellanos, and the others in Taxco. The converso merchants doing business with the northern reales, such as Zacatecas, Guanajuato, Tlalpujahua, Mazapil, and Sichú, generally passed through Pachuca. They invariably visited Manuel and Catalina and often stayed with them, as the couple's home was a convenient stopping place, with meals that met their dietary restrictions and conversation that enhanced their sense of Jewishness. In January 1588, Luis de Carvajal, traveling on business to the northern mining towns with his brothers Miguel and Baltazar, lodged in Pachuca with Manuel and Catalina. The four men, all in their mid-twenties, revealed their enthusiasm for Judaism to each other. Luis read aloud from the Spanish Deuteronomy he had copied from Dr. Morales and gave Manuel a written copy of the Amidah prayer that begins "Adonai, open up my lips."[34] With that, the two young men realized that they had become fast friends.

Manuel de Lucena's core of religious convictions, like those of the more intellectual of his Judaizing contemporaries, consisted of affirmations of some fundamental and widely held Jewish beliefs, a scornful rejection of many central tenets of Christian theology, and a syncretic melding or hybridization of the two religions, what Jacob Marcus called a "distorted twilight version of Judaism."[35] At the top was belief in a single, unique, incorporeal deity, in contrast to the three-part Christian divinity. Lucena believed that the Messiah had not yet come and often told his friends that Jesus could not have been the Messiah because he had not removed sin from the world. He believed that the Messiah, whom he thought of as a kind of Antichrist, would come soon to redeem the people of Israel; although neither he nor most of his contemporaries endeavored to explain what they understood by "redeem." Lucena also believed in the truth and the rightness of "the Law that God gave to Moses," to use Luis de Carvajal's habitual formulation. His knowledge of that law was limited to what he had heard read aloud from the Bible (as he knew no Latin himself); information given to him by his friends, none of whom had access to the Talmud, the Mishna, or to the vast corpus of later rabbinical interpretations of the law; and what he gleaned about Judaism from Christian literature that dealt with Old Testament topics. He was committed to observing that law, at least insofar as he was aware of its details. But at the same time he realized that the Mexican environment in which he lived forced him to make compromises in his observance.

Lucena held many Christian theological concepts to be absurd and thought that the way the church put them into practice was ludicrous, if not scandalous. He told Luis Díaz that it was silly to say that God was physically present in the consecrated host, adding that the images that proliferated in churches were idols.[36] At the same time, Lucena accepted certain Christian ideas that were alien to the normative Judaism of his time. One was that the salvation (undefined) of his soul required his belief in the Law of Moses. He accepted without question the Christian formulation of hell and purgatory, telling Luis Díaz that the holy fathers were still in limbo and that it was a joke to say that Christ had taken them out of limbo. For Lucena it was "true and certain that the Pope, the King, the grandees of Spain, the inquisitors, and all Christians are in Hell."[37]

The Sabbath was the most important touchstone of identity for the Lucena family, as it was for most observant Mexican Judaizers of his time. In 1595 Lucena told inquisitors:

> I, my wife Catalina Enríquez, and my mother-in-law Beatriz Enríquez always observed the Sabbath when we were in Pachuca. On Friday Beatriz Enríquez would order the house to be swept and clean linen placed on the beds. [We] wore clean shirts on Saturdays. And if . . .

Catalina Enríquez ever worked on a Saturday, ... it was to dissemble; but she, I, and my mother-in-law ... kept [the Sabbath] in our hearts.[38]

Manuel often went to Mexico City during the week to conduct business, arriving exhausted back in Pachuca late Friday afternoon. After their baths, both Manuel and Catalina would trim their nails and dress in clean clothes, which for Manuel always included a clean collar.[39] Before their dinner they would light a beeswax candle, which they would let burn all night, until it went out by itself.[40] Whenever possible they would gather a group of Judaizing friends to celebrate the Sabbath with them at their house in Pachuca.

In Mexico City, when the Lucenas were not at home or with their in-laws, they sometimes celebrated with the Machados, who liked to pray in Portuguese, or with the Carvajals.[41] One Friday night when Manuel had come to Mexico City from Pachuca, he slept over at the Carvajal house along with Manuel Gómez Navarro and Tomás de Fonseca Castellanos, who had come up from Taxco. The four men spent the evening discussing the Law of Moses, singing songs, and listening to Lucena read to them from the apocryphal *Book of Wisdom*.[42] Occasionally Héctor de Fonseca joined the group at these gatherings.[43] On these evenings, often one of the men would read to the others from religious texts, such as *Mirror of Consolation* or Fray Luis de Granada's *Symbol of Faith*.[44] If the only Bible available was in Latin, the most knowledgeable among them would translate or gloss the passages into Spanish for the others. They often began their worship with the traditional opening of Sabbath prayers from Psalm 51:15 in Spanish: "Adonai, open my lips and my mouth will proclaim your praise. Blessed art thou, Adonai, our God and God of our Fathers Abraham, Isaac, and Jacob."[45] Manuel Gómez taught Lucena a prayer he called the Shema, which he said had to be recited standing with one's eyes closed.[46] The prayers Lucena's friends recited most often were Psalms, particularly the Penitential Psalms, often in Latin and always concluding with "Gloria Patri" while generally omitting "et Filio et Spiritui Sancto."[47]

Another frequent attendee at Lucena's gatherings was Manuel Francisco Belmonte, who had been born in Covilhã and in Mexico ran a store in the mining community of Sultepec. His Jewish life, like that of old Tomás de Fonseca of Tlalpujahua, was centered on Mexico City.[48] A man in his late thirties, he was held in high repute for both his knowledge in the ways of

Judaizing and his wisdom. Antonio López told Lucena's wife, Catalina, that Francisco was a "Séneca en la Ley de Moisén,"[49] and Catalina's daughter Clara considered him instrumental in her instruction in Judaism.[50] If Francisco Belmonte had a flaw, it was his moral character. When questioned by inquisitors, Francisco Belmonte recalled vividly the night that Beatriz Enríquez la Paiba scolded him at her house in front of a crowd that included Lucena:

> She told me I should be ashamed of myself, that I was a grown man now and should stop visiting brothels and come to know the Lord, and that God would forgive me my sins. . . . She said this in front of Simón Paiba, Manuel de Lucena, Jorge Rodríguez, Álvaro Rodríguez (who was hanged), Catalina Enríquez, Baltazar González (he went to China and he never married), and Diego and Pedro Enríquez.[51]

Despite their firm commitment to Judaizing, fear of being observed required the Lucena family to be circumspect. The rhythm of work in colonial Mexico, in which Saturday was a workday and Sunday the day of rest, complicated both days' routines. Though Manuel and Catalina observed the Sabbath with rigor when circumstances permitted, sometimes overt observance proved unacceptably risky. "I kept the Sabbath when I could," Lucena told inquisitors, "though it was not very often because there was no place to do it and I was afraid that people in my household and outside would notice."[52] Lucena's friend Sebastián Rodríguez empathized with him: "When [Lucena] could not [keep the Sabbaths], he kept them in his heart; it troubled him when he had to work on the Sabbath because it seemed to him like he was sinning and offending God."[53]

The Lucena family's most frequent and faithful visitors in Pachuca were Luis de Carvajal and his brother Baltazar.[54] As he did with the Taxco Judaizing community, Luis de Carvajal served Manuel de Lucena and the conversos in the region of Pachuca as a catalyst for their Jewish identity. On his business trips north, Luis often rode in company with Lucena, and sometimes with his brother Baltazar or Manuel Gómez Navarro as well, filling the long hours on the road with talk of the Law of Moses. When one of the Jewish festivals coincided with these trips, Luis generally observed it in the Lucena home. For the Yom Kippur fast in October of 1588, he was one of the seventeen conversos who crowded into Lucena's house to observe the Día Grande del Señor together.[55] Luis was also there for Purim in 1588, 1592, and 1593. These holiday celebrations in Pachuca generally included Catalina's parents, her two brothers, Luis de Carvajal's brother Baltazar Rodríguez de Carvajal, and Lucena's friend and sometimes creditor Antonio López. At the latter two celebrations, Justa Méndez joined them, as did Francisco Rodríguez Ledesma and his brothers Jorge and Domingo Rodríguez.[56]

Though when Manuel de Lucena was in Mexico he usually stayed with his in-laws, sometimes he lodged with the Carvajals. Luis's sister Leonor de Andrada Carvajal, who became Jorge de Almeida's wife, recalled how when Luis used to read to her and her siblings, Lucena would often join them. Sometimes this group stayed for dinner, where they might well coincide with any of a large number of Mexico City Judaizers: Sebastián Rodríguez and his wife, Costanza Rodríguez; Clara Enríquez and her daughter Justa Méndez; Pedro Rodríguez Saz; Manuel Rodríguez Silguero; or Manuel Gómez Navarro. Sometimes young Tomás de Fonseca Castellanos and Héctor de Fonseca came up from Taxco.[57]

During the period between 1591 and 1593 when Luis served his Inquisition sentence in the monastery library in Santiago Tlatelolco, Manuel de Lucena often visited him. One day in the summer of 1593 he found Luis copying out moral exempla from the Bible. Luis told him that the passages would open the eyes of any believer and would move Lucena to strictly observe the Law of Moses. Lucena began to question him about certain doubts that he was harboring, and he found Luis's replies so enlightening that he returned on several occasions to continue their conversations. Together they discussed passages from *Flos sanctorum* and Fray Luis de Granada's *Symbol of Faith*. One Friday afternoon, Carvajal invited Lucena to come home with him for dinner to the house where his mother and sisters were serving out their sentences. The two men talked so late, listening to Francisca and her daughters in the next room praying and reciting Psalms, that Lucena ended up spending the night.[58]

For his part, Lucena held Luis on a pedestal as an accomplished scholar, great teacher, and paragon of an observant Jew, a young man who "is more knowledgeable than anyone else here or in Castilla."[59] Likewise, it is clear that Luis considered his friend a soul mate and his match in knowledge of Judaism. As Luis told Manuel Gil de la Guarda, "Lucena and I are one and the same, we understand each other, and together the music of our souls is like a symphony."[60] The simile was apt, because in addition to their other affinities, the two men quite literally made music together. "In my house in Pachuca," Lucena told the inquisitors, "I played the harp and Luis sang a song about the commandments of the Law of Moses."[61] When Carvajal was not present, it was Lucena who would lead his gathering in a familiar hymn. Lucena laid out the verses—"Let us all sing with joy / our praises of the Lord, / for all who trust in him / will receive his reward"—and the others chimed in on the chorus while Lucena accompanied them on his vihuela.[62]

The other members of their company were well aware of the influence that the two men had on each other. Catalina's brother Pedro, in prison early in 1595, damned Manuel de Lucena for having pushed him into Judaizing and damned Luis de Carvajal for having pushed Lucena:

[I swear by] my father, if they had burned this Luis de Carvajal, then Manuel de Lucena would not have come to this, nor I, nor Manuel Gómez [Navarro]. Luis de Carvajal has taught Lucena everything he knows. . . . Whenever [Lucena] came to Mexico, he wouldn't stay anywhere but Luis de Carvajal's house in Santiago. For him, seeing Luis was glory.[63]

In Justa Méndez's view, "when Manuel de Lucena got together with Luis de Carvajal they were like two preachers who never stopped persuading people to observe the Law of Moses."[64] Her simile, too, could not have been more accurate. Lucena, like Luis de Carvajal, never missed a chance to preach and had the habit of engaging in conversation about religion with anyone he thought might be receptive, meaning anyone he supposed might have converso roots.[65] Both Carvajal and Lucena thought of themselves, and were regarded by others, as teachers. Lucena, in fact, told Justa Méndez that "the Law of Moses is so clear and plain that, if I did not have children, I would travel the whole world teaching it."[66] At one time or another, Lucena took credit for having brought Jewish instruction to Luis Díaz, Manuel Francisco Belmonte, Manuel Gómez Navarro, Felipa López, Sebastián de la Peña, Manuel Tavares, Francisco Váez, Diego Enríquez, and Andrés, Duarte, Francisco, Manuel, Pedro, and Sebastián Rodríguez.[67] Among those he had failed to persuade to Judaize was his brother-in-law Pedro Enríquez.[68]

It was at Lucena's home in Pachuca that Luis de Carvajal met Álvaro de

Carrión.⁶⁹ Carrión's ancestors had followed the border-hopping pattern of so many conversos of their time: his grandparents, and probably his parents, had migrated from Spain to the northeast corner of Portugal in the diocese of Bragança, and his parents had returned to Spain to Cervera del Río Pisuerga in the mountains of northern Palencia. Though Cervera was known for its sheep and goat farming, as a young man Carrión trained as a shoemaker. That was the profession of his father and all of his paternal uncles, and that is how he supported himself initially when he came to Mexico in 1580. There he became friends with Manuel de Morales and his son and the community of Judaizers that gathered around them.⁷⁰

Carrión was thirty-nine years old when a Portuguese converso named Alonso González, who raised goats near Pachuca to supply the reales de minas with meat and hides, proposed that if Carrión would marry his daughter Juana, he would set Carrión up in the goat farming business.⁷¹ González was apparently not in the habit of Judaizing. He had married an Old Christian woman, María de Aguilar, and they had raised Juana as a Christian. Still, Carrión felt confident that once they were married, he would be able teach his young wife to follow the Law of Moses. The marriage took place in Tilcuautla, in the foothills a few kilometers west of Pachuca, on the estancia that González provided as Juana's dowry. Present were Juana's Christian family and Carrión's Judaizing friends: Manuel de Lucena, Catalina Enríquez, Beatriz Enríquez la Paiba, Diego and Pedro Enríquez, and Lucena's friend Domingo Rodríguez. Juana's sister, who like her mother was named María de Aguilar and was summoned by the Inquisition in 1597 to testify against Carrión, felt that Carrión's wedding guests had behaved in very peculiar ways. She said that before they roasted the lamb, Catalina Enríquez had held it while her mother, Beatriz, had cut out something she could not identify. When María had asked what it was, Beatriz had told her only that it made the meat taste better. Then, María said, four or five times the Enríquez family had gone into a side room and Beatriz had taken a book from her sleeve and handed it to Manuel de Lucena, who had read from it to his family and her new brother-in-law Álvaro de Carrión. María had noticed that whenever she walked by that room, Beatriz grabbed the book from Manuel's hand and hid it in her sleeve. She said that now, of course, a year after most of those people had appeared in an auto-de-fé, she realized that those were Jewish customs.⁷²

On his estancia, Carrión had no one to talk with about the Law of Moses, so he relished his time with Lucena. He often rode along when Lucena was traveling to nearby towns on business, and when Manuel and Catalina were at home in Pachuca, once a week Carrión brought them goat's milk and cheese from his ranch, some of which Lucena then retailed in his store. Lucena liked to visit him on the ranch as well. For Catalina Enríquez, who spent most of her time indoors in Mexico or Pachuca, Carrión's estancia was like Eden. In October 1590 she begged her husband to take her there for the Festival of Booths (Cabañas; Sukkot), and the couple spent four idyllic days with the Carrións in the country air.[73]

Sometimes Carrión arrived at Lucena's house when Manuel was reading to his wife from *Mirror of Consolation*, and he stayed to listen. Lucena would talk to Carrión about how Jesus was not the Messiah and that the real Messiah would come at the end of days to redeem the people of Israel. Another favorite Lucena theme was how Carrión's soul could be saved only by his strict observance of the Law of Moses. Together on the road from Atotonilco on July 6, 1591, the two men dreamed about going back to Spain and from there to a land where they could practice their Judaism openly. Carrión acknowledged that if they did reach such a place, it would be necessary that his wife learn to Judaize, and he asked Lucena to help him with her instruction.[74] At his trial, Álvaro blamed Lucena for his Judaizing, saying that if it were not for Lucena, he never would have deviated from Christian practice. He added that when Lucena came to his estancia on a Jewish fast day, he fasted, but that when Lucena left, he went back to eating blood sausage (*morcilla*).[75]

Despite the dangers inherent in Carrión's mixed marriage and his inconsistency of observance of Jewish customs, Luis de Carvajal considered him a friend and visited him from time to time at his farm. In September 1594, Carvajal decided to observe the fast of El Día Grande del Señor and the entire week leading up to Yom Kippur by himself in the countryside near Carrión's farm, fasting during daylight hours and eating only after dark. Lucena had provisioned him with two candles, a box of fruit preserves, and a dish of fried eggs and cheese called *frutas del sartén*. This food evidently proved insufficient, because Carvajal sent a message to Carrión asking him to send him more fried eggs, fresh cheese, and tortillas, cautioning him that they must not include any bacon, lard, or other pork product.[76] After the Día Grande ended, Luis rode to the estancia to break his fast with Carrión, but when

Juana brought out some stewed cabbage, Luis sensed it had been prepared with pork and refused to eat it. So Carrión had Juana fry their guest a couple of eggs in olive oil.[77]

In Pachuca many of the men Manuel de Lucena hired to work for him were Portuguese conversos. His clerk Francisco Váez, a nephew of Jorge Váez, came from São Vicente da Beira. Francisco, a short, plump, light-bearded man with one lazy eye, was seven years younger than Lucena.[78] When Lucena began to instruct him in Judaism, Francisco informed him that he was already a Jew and that in Portugal an aunt had taught him about the Law of Moses.[79] Before long Váez was regularly observing the Sabbath with Manuel, Catalina, and their Judaizing friends, although Lucena had to keep reminding him not to ride a horse or go out selling on the day of rest.[80] Among friends in Lucena's Pachuca house and in his store, Váez felt he did not have to be circumspect about talking about the Law of Moses or reading Old Testament stories from books such as Fray Luis de Granada's *Symbol of Faith*; nor did he have to worry about someone seeing him slaughter chickens in the Jewish fashion. But this comfortable sense of security could be dangerous. Once, when he openly criticized another converso for eating a piece of salt pork in front of Juan de la Serna, one of Lucena's house servants who was not a member of the Portuguese Judaizing community, Lucena called Váez an ass and scolded him for his lack of caution.[81]

Although it is questionable whether Lucena's young employee Gómez Pertierra was of Portuguese or Jewish descent, Lucena had confidence in the young man's discretion.[82] On days when they walked together up the mountain from Tlaulilpa to Real del Monte, Lucena related Bible stories to his assistant, explaining how the Jews were God's chosen people and that if they would only turn to him and observe his commandments, he would reward them both in this world and the world to come. Often Pertierra would join Lucena, Francisco Váez, and Manuel Gómez Navarro at dinner in Lucena's house in Pachuca, and there he would listen to one of them reading about Old Testament heroes from Lucena's books and their subsequent conversations about the Law of Moses.[83]

Beyond Manuel de Lucena's circle of employees, one of his closest friends in the early 1590s was the merchant Manuel Gómez Navarro, a man of his own age and similar background, raised in San Martín de Trevejo, a village in the province of Cáceres, an hour's walk from Portugal's eastern border.

Though his father and paternal grandparents were from the Galician village of Salceda in Pontevedra, an hour from the Portuguese northern border, his mother had been born in Castelobranco and his maternal grandfather was from Fundão.[84] Coming to New Spain in the late 1580s, Gómez Navarro established his base in Mexico City and began trading in the area of the Real de Sichú in Guanajuato, in territory only recently pacified after a bloody war with the Chichimeca Indians.[85] On his journeys north from Mexico City, he often accompanied Manuel de Lucena as far as Pachuca.

Though of converso background, when Gómez Navarro arrived in the New World he seems to have been a practicing Christian. At first he resisted Lucena's attempts to turn him back to the Law of Moses, but during their long hours of travel in 1590, Lucena kept at him, speaking to him of his salvation, teaching him to sing Psalms, and reading to him from his "book of hours," almost certainly *Mirror of Consolation*. As Lucena told inquisitors: "Although Manuel Gómez Navarro was stubborn in not drawing away from the Law of Jesus Christ, at the end, after about a month of my teaching, he did so."[86] From then until their arrests, the two men were frequent, if not constant, companions. Together they attended at least five major Jewish holiday gatherings in Mexico City and Pachuca in the early 1590s.

When Manuel Gómez Navarro's younger brother Domingo Gómez arrived from Spain, Gómez Navarro tried to induce Domingo to join him in observing the Law of Moses. Gómez Navarro admired Lucena's commitment to Judaizing and his ability to inspire others with his enthusiasm, so when his own efforts to convert his brother fell on deaf ears, he tried to persuade Lucena to give Domingo a few pointers to draw him away from the law of Jesus. Lucena, recognizing the danger in preaching Judaism to a practicing Christian, tried to persuade Gómez Navarro to leave his brother to go his own Christian way, but Gómez insisted that conversion was crucial for the salvation of his brother's soul. Eventually, despite his reservations, Lucena agreed to try, and when he did, Domingo exploded, clapping his hands over his ears to shut out the talk of Judaism and screaming at Lucena:

"Don't talk to me about that. I believe what the Holy Mother Church believes."

"Impossible," shouted Gómez Navarro, bursting in from the next room, "you know I wouldn't tell you this if it wasn't for your own good."

"Don't talk to me about this stuff, because we"—he said that meaning the new Christians—, "we killed Christ and He died for us."[87]

Even after this outburst, with its implied threat of reporting them to the Inquisition, Manuel Gómez Navarro approached his brother once more, this time at Lucena's home in the presence of Luis de Carvajal and Francisco Váez. As Carvajal recalled it, when Manuel Gómez attempted to plead his case, Domingo pointed to an image of Jesus on Lucena's wall and said, "Come what may, that is my flag and I am sticking with it." This caused Francisco Váez to burst into laughter and tell the men: "I used to know a man who whenever he swore by Jesus's name would say in Portuguese: *Jhú quanta merda* (Jesus, what shit)."[88]

Manuel Gómez Navarro's head and heart may have been committed to Judaizing, but his observance of Judaic custom was at best sporadic. Like other Judaizing conversos, often his lapses in Jewish observance were often caused by a desire to prevent detection by his Christian neighbors. But other times it seems that he did not care about the Jewish rules. Even at Lucena's house in Pachuca, he sometimes flaunted his fondness for pork, which evoked disgust from Lucena, who would ask him why he ate that filthy stuff. Francisco Váez's reaction to their friend's eating pork was nausea. Sometimes, when Gómez Navarro thoughtlessly added a slab of bacon to the beef that Lucena was cooking for himself, Lucena went hungry and his disgust turned to anger.[89] Despite these lapses in behavior, the household continued to treat Gómez Navarro as a friend.

Another frequent visitor to Lucena's homes in Pachuca and Mexico City was Sebastián Rodríguez, from São Vicente da Beira, a man a few years younger than Manuel, who had come to Mexico on the ship that had brought Justa Méndez, Manuel Álvarez, and Manuel Gómez de Casteloblanco.[90] At home and on the roads of central Mexico, Lucena tutored Rodríguez in Judaism, as he did so many others, insisting that Jesus was not the Messiah, that the statues in churches were idols, that priests had no power to forgive sins, and that the mistreatment of the Jews stemmed from their incomplete adherence to the Mosaic Law.[91] He said that if Sebastián and all the Jews would properly honor the Sabbath and follow the basic Jewish dietary rules, God would come to redeem the people of Israel. At home Lucena read to him passages from *Mirror of Consolation*. Out on the road, in company with Manuel

Gómez Navarro, Lucena taught him the tune for Psalm 96, "We sing to God every day," and Psalm 137, "By rivers in Babylon," a perennial favorite of the Mexican crypto-Jews, who in their "Mexican Babylon" took solace in the charge to remember Zion in their exile.[92] Lucena's barrage of encouragement had the desired effect: "I decided to leave the Law of our Redeemer Jesus Christ and pass to the Law of Moses," Sebastián Rodríguez told inquisitors, "because Manuel de Lucena was entering into my beliefs on many different days."[93] From 1588 to 1592, Rodríguez was a regular guest at the Lucena-Enríquez Jewish festival celebrations.[94]

Although Manuel de Lucena routinely worked with Pachuca's silver mining community, he appears to have had few actual miners as friends. One exception was Miguel Gerónimo de León, who often joined Lucena's group in Pachuca in the late 1580s and early 1590s, along with his wife, Catalina López. It is unclear whether Miguel Gerónimo was a Judaizing converso, though it is almost certain that his wife was not. In April 1592 a large group of conversos gathered at Jorge Álvarez's house on Calle Tacuba in Mexico City for a Holy Thursday Passover celebration. While they were watching the processions from the window and joking about the idolatrous statues the marchers were carrying, Miguel Gerónimo and his wife, Catalina López, came in. Immediately everyone fell silent and Antonio López stopped playing his guitar. It appears that only after signals of acceptance were circulated did conversation resume. That afternoon the Gerónimos, Antonio Méndez, and his Old Christian wife, María de los Ángeles, went out to observe the processions and then came back to Álvarez's house, where Méndez and Gerónimo stood at the window with the others and jeered in Portuguese at what they termed the "credulous" Christians.[95]

A close colleague of Lucena for a few years in the early 1590s was Manuel Gil de la Guarda, whose father was from Guarda, an important commercial city in the Beira region of northern Portugal. Gil's mother's family was from Fundão. Gil had learned Latin in his natal city and learned Judaism as an eighteen-year-old in Talavera de la Reina in Spain.[96] After some years as a traveling merchant in Spain, and a few more as an Atlantic trader to Caracas and Cartagena, in 1592 he sailed to Mexico on a boat captained by the Portuguese converso mariner-merchant Feliciano de Valencia.[97] In Mexico City Gil lodged first with Valencia and then with Felipe Núñez, a Portuguese converso from Lisbon, a relative of Governor Carvajal's wife, who had come to Mexico in 1580 in the governor's group and had served him as adjutant in the northern expeditions. Núñez, a man well connected in the Judaizing community of the capital, was a close friend of various members of the Álvarez family, Ana Váez, Justa Méndez, and Manuel Tavares. He was about five years older than Manuel de Lucena and Luis de Carvajal. In testimony in 1596, Luis de Carvajal suggests the intensity of his friendship with Gil and Lucena. Back in the autumn of 1592,

> One Sunday morning Manuel Gil de la Guarda came to my house in Santiago [Tlatelolco] with Manuel de Lucena, and when they found me at the doorway to my house, they came in and went up to the room where I had my bed and there the three of us chatted about the Law of Moses, saying that it was the right law, the one in which men could be saved. I read them Chapter 31 of Jeremiah, translating from the Latin into Spanish. It is the chapter that deals with the last gathering of the people of Israel. And when Manuel Gil and Manuel de Lucena had heard it, Gil responded saying that even if the whole Bible were lost, as long as Chapter 31 remained it would be enough to make one understand that the Jews were right in observing the law that God gave to Moses. And Manuel de Lucena stood up and came over to hug me and embrace me, calling me a good Jew and a good student, and saying that he would trade all his music to know a little Latin.[98]

On another occasion, again at Luis de Carvajal's house, it was Manuel Gil who read to Luis and Manuel de Lucena the story of Balaam and his ass, bragging to them that back in his town in Portugal, he had served people as rabbi.[99]

In 1594 Manuel Gil set sail for Philippines. In Manila the following year, he took an Old Christian wife, María de Tovar. In 1597 the Inquisition, with information gleaned from the trials of Judaizers of the previous year, sent out an order for his arrest. On Gil's arrival in Acapulco late in December of that year, he was brought to Mexico City for trial. Now ostensibly a Christian, Gil ingratiated himself with the inquisitors by denouncing—eagerly and with much incriminating detail—all the Judaizers he had known before sailing to the Orient.

A latecomer to Lucena's community was the Portuguese converso Domingo Cuello, who was thirty-six when he went to Mexico in 1594 along with Ruy Díaz Nieto and his son Diego.[100] Cuello met the Carvajals through Díaz Nieto and shared with them his commitment to Judaizing. In the presence of all the Carvajal women and Ana Váez and her children, Cuello told Luis de Carvajal the story of Joseph's brother selling him into slavery, and Luis gave him a paper with two Psalms in Spanish that he had translated into rhyme. Cuello credited Luis de Carvajal with having enriched his knowledge and observance of Judaism, which had in turn had led God to shower him with material and spiritual rewards.[101] In Mexico City Cuello often ate with the Carvajals and through them got to know Manuel de Lucena and the Pachuca community of Judaizers. Riding back and forth from the Real de Tlaulilpa to Mexico, they shared their knowledge of Judaism and their disdain for Christian idolatry. One day, as Lucena, Cuello, and Duarte Rodríguez were riding to Tulancingo, they happened on a roadside cross. According to Rodríguez, Lucena and Cuello spit at it and began to insult it, saying that Jesus was not the Messiah, that the whole crucifixion story was a lie.[102]

Lucena, like the other Judaizing conversos of his time in Mexico, generally opened up about his religious beliefs only to other conversos. Bonded by shared complicity, these men on the whole felt comfortable in trusting their associates to keep their religious beliefs and activities secret. And for the most part their trust was honored, at least up to the time of their colleagues' arrests and sometimes well into their long and sometime tortured interrogations. But occasionally Manuel de Lucena's zeal for proselytizing led him to approach an Old Christian who he thought might be receptive to converting to the Law of Moses. Juan de Casal was such a person.

Casal was employed as mayordomo at the Atotonilco mining hacienda of Agustín Guerrero, a wealthy businessman who also had a house in Pachuca and an estancia in Pánuco.[103] Even though Casal was not of Jewish ancestry, Lucena considered him a man of substance and a good friend, so when Casal shared with Lucena some of his doubts about Catholic theology, Lucena decided to risk talking to him about the Law of Moses. Casal was so excited by Lucena's reading from *Mirror of Consolation* that he came back repeatedly to hear him read more. Sometimes Lucena went to Casal's house to read to him, and eventually Lucena lent Casal his copy of the book. When he told Casal that he should also read Fray Luis de Granada's *Symbol of Faith*, Casal asked Lucena to buy him one, whatever it cost.[104] Lucena did, and Casal would bring the book with him to Lucena's house to discuss with him passages that he had marked with braided string, so he would not have to turn down the corners of pages. Casal particularly liked the passages about the creation of the world and the stories of Judith and Esther. Riding together to Atotonilco or to Álvaro de Carrión's goat ranch, Casal would quiz Lucena about the finer points of Jewish observance.[105]

Although Manuel de Lucena accepted Casal despite his Old Christian heritage, other members of the Judaizing community were wary of him. At the Passover gathering at Jorge Álvarez's Mexico City home in 1592 that Miguel Gerónimo and his wife had attended and where conversation had stopped, Juan de Casal's entrance cast a similar pall.[106] Still, when the community of Judaizers got to know him, and with Lucena's obvious confidence in the man, they agreed to accept Casal as part of their community. When Casal visited Mexico City he often lodged with Lucena's brother-in-law Diego Enríquez, with whom he liked to play cards, and sometimes with Ana López. Lucena had such faith in Casal that he told Justa Méndez one day in 1596 that if her other wedding prospects did not work out, he would arrange for her to marry Casal. When she protested that the match was impossible, since Casal was not of Jewish descent, Lucena shrugged off her objection, telling her that he would make Casal become a Jew, which would be easy because he was halfway there already. Justa Méndez started to laugh and told him he was crazy.[107] Later that year, when Lucena thought that his own arrest was imminent, he gave many of his valuables to his friend for safekeeping.[108] Curiously, and to the inquisitors unconvincingly, after his arrest Lucena denied that he had ever trusted Juan del Casal and that he had ever hidden any assets with him, saying that he was afraid of Casal because he was an Old Christian who considered himself a hidalgo. He even went so far as to protest, "It is wickedness to say that I have ever taught Judaism to someone who was not a Jew."[109] There appears to be no record of Casal ever testifying against Lucena or any of his Judaizing circle.

Lucena was less well served by the traveling peddler Duarte Rodríguez.[110] This young man from Fundão or Covilhã (people who knew him were not certain which) often met with the Judaizing communities that convened in Taxco, Mexico City, and Pachuca. He sometimes rode along with Manuel Gómez Navarro to Taxco, Esquimilpa, Guachiapa, and Zimapán and with Manuel de Lucena back and forth to Pachuca and other nearby towns.[111] In Taxco, Duarte usually stayed with Tomás de Fonseca Castellanos, who bragged to Luis de Carvajal that he had taught Duarte the basics of Judaizing. At Fonseca's, Duarte sometimes coincided with Sebastián de la Peña and Sebastián Rodríguez.[112]

Duarte had come to Mexico with Governor Carvajal in 1580 as a ten-year-old. By the time he reached his late teens, he was known throughout central Mexico as a foolish and dishonest man of little substance[113] who liked nothing better than a good card game.[114] He found friends among the Enríquez family, whose Mexico City home was a Sabbath gathering place whether Manuel de Lucena was in Mexico or Pachuca. In 1586 he sat at Beatriz Enríquez la Paiba's Sabbath table in her rented rooms on Calle Donceles. At the table with him were young Diego Enríquez; Jorge Álvarez, who was living with the Enríquez family; Domingo and Jorge Rodríguez; Francisco Rodríguez Ledesma; Sebastián Nieto; Antonio Núñez; and Hernán López, all of them Portuguese. A similar group is recorded at an Enríquez Sabbath in 1588.[115]

Ana López's daughter Leonor Díaz confirmed to inquisitors that the Enríquez house was always full of people such as Francisco Rodríguez Ledesma, Nicolas Pereira, Manuel Fernández Cardozo, Simon Cuello, Manuel Rodríguez Silgueiro, Duarte Rodríguez, and his brother Manuel Gómez Navarro. But they had many other visitors as well. Often the women came to chat, while the men came to play cards and to listen to Manuel de Lucena read and preach.[116] Groups were larger on the major Jewish festivals, and their activities were more focused on religion. Duarte Rodríguez attended the Lucena-Enríquez Passover or Yom Kippur observances (and sometimes both) every year from 1589 through 1594.[117]

Only five days after his arrest in May 1596, Duarte Rodríguez began to tell inquisitors the particulars about his friends' Judaizing practices. Among the people he fingered as Judaizers in both those early and later interrogations were Domingo Cuello, Luis de Carvajal, Manuel de Lucena, Antonio Méndez, Manuel Gómez Navarro, and Jorge Álvarez.[118]

The nucleus of Manuel de Lucena's Judaizing community in Pachuca was comprised of Catalina's Enriquez relatives and a handful of men: Manuel Gómez Navarro, Francisco Váez, Gómez Pertierra, Álvaro de Carrión, and, when they were in the north, Luis and Baltazar de Carvajal. With the exception of Carrión, these men gathered in Mexico City as well, sometimes at the homes of one of the Enríquez family and sometimes at the Carvajals'.

Often as not, the groups that gathered at the Carvajals' house to share their Jewish knowledge and interests were larger—sometimes much larger—than these few individuals. According to Manuel González de Casteloblanco, a tratante who often shuttled from Mexico City to the Real de Sultepec, at the Carvajals it was common to find—in addition to Lucena and Gómez Navarro and the extended Enriquez and Carvajal families—Manuel and Jorge Álvarez and Jorge's wife, Ana Váez; Catalina, Costanza, Manuel, and Sebastián Rodríguez; Justa Méndez; and Manuel Jorge. Justa Méndez reported similar gatherings at the Carvajals' in Santiago Tlatelolco. Lucena's catalog of visitors to the Carvajals' added Pedro Rodríguez Saz, Manuel Rodríguez Silguero, and the Taxco Fonsecas, Héctor and Tomás.[119] Jorge de Almeida's wife, Leonor de Carvajal, said that once her husband had left for Spain and she was back living with her Carvajal siblings, all of these people were dinner guests at her house.

The majority of people who met regularly with Manuel de Lucena and his wife, Catalina Enríquez, were New Christian Judaizers of Portuguese origin. The holiday gatherings between 1580 and 1594 hosted by Manuel and Catalina in Mexico and Pachuca, and the gatherings hosted by Catalina's Enríquez relatives in Mexico City, consistently drew the largest attendance of any Judaizing events in New Spain during this period, topping even those hosted by the Carvajal clan in Mexico City and Santiago Tlatelolco.[120] The groups gathering at the Carvajal and Lucena-Enríquez homes—groups that overlapped to a considerable extent—were driven by enthusiastic proselytizers, men of engaging personality. Rarely were these groups sundered by personal animosities.

By contrast, the Judaizing miners and merchants clustered in Taxco rarely came together for the holidays, although occasionally in Mexico City they joined the Carvajals or less frequently the Enríquez-Paiba-Lucenas. There are several reasons for this. Two of the four major Taxco figures—Jorge de Almeida and Antonio Díaz de Cáceres—took extravagant care to hide their rare Judaizing activities and generally shunned communal gatherings. Their wives, Catalina de la Cueva and Leonor Andrada, frustrated by their husbands' paranoia and refusal to socialize, generally chose to express their Judaism with their Carvajal siblings and other close relatives back in the capital rather than with their husbands in Taxco. Almeida's brother Héctor de Fonseca had a prickly personality and was married to an Old Christian. Jorge and Hector's cousin young Tomás de Fonseca Castellanos often hosted visiting conversos in his store or hacienda, but he was not at all close to his Taxco relatives. When young Tomás wanted to celebrate a Jewish holiday with a community, he did not tender an invitation to the Taxco Judaizers; he went to Mexico City to join the Carvajals.

Chapter 14
Judaizing from Tlalpujahua

> I do not recall having done or said anything [to cause my arrest] . . . because I have lived Christianly, as everyone in New Spain knows. And if I think of anything that I might have said I will submit to being corrected by the Holy Office. . . . I don't know anything about the rites of Mohammad, or of Moses, or of Luther, nor, as far as I know, do I have anything to do with people who are Jews, Moors, or Lutherans.
>
> —TOMÁS DE FONSECA JULY 14–17, 1590[1]

THERE WAS NO crypto-Jewish community in Tlalpujahua, and old Tomás de Fonseca seems to have been the only converso resident of the town. Unlike the reales located on or near major transportation routes, Tlalpujahua was not a convenient stopover for converso businessmen on their way to somewhere else. Unlike Taxco and Pachuca, where a number of mining camps coalesced around a central real that by the mid-1550s had become a regional market center (Tetelcingo for the Taxco district, Tlaulilpa for Pachuca), the town of Tlalpujahua was small, and it developed relatively late. High in the mountains on the northern border of Michoacán and the state of Mexico, it was an isolated place—cold, windswept, and sparsely populated. Although an occasional crypto-Jewish merchant did visit the real on business, there is no record of their having met with old Tomás.[2] In Tlalpujahua old Tomás kept his Judaism alive by reading his books. If he wanted to share a Judaizing experience with living persons, he would have had to go to them, and not expect them to come to him.

In 1568, ten years after old Tomás had begun mining in Tlalpujahua, his father, Gabriel de Castellanos, fell ill in Mexico City. During the two years his father lingered, old Tomás went down from the mountains several times to stay with him and Blanca Rodríguez. The only other Judaizer with whom Tomás associated during that period appears to have been his half brother Julián de Castellanos, for whom he bore little love. After Gabriel died in 1570, Tomás evidently felt no compunction to maintain any connection with Julián or Blanca, who died in 1572.[3]

During the two years before his father's death and for the following decade and a half, old Tomás occupied himself with mining in Tlalpujahua and with defending his water rights for his properties. His other interest during those years was a woman named Ana Jiménez, whom he may have met during one of his visits to Mexico City. Between 1570 and 1575 he and Ana produced four children: Beatriz, Lope, Ana, and Gabriel.[4]

I have found no record of Tomás having engaged in any Judaizing activity during the 1570s through the mid-1580s. Not to be immersed in a community of practicing Jews may have suited him, for old Tomás was a loner from the day he walked away from his father's mine in Ayoteco. Marco Antonio characterized him as a guarded, suspicious man, averse to attracting any sort of attention to himself, a man who dealt with very few people and talked little.[5] Luis de Carvajal believed that "he lives such a secretive life because of his fear that someone might notice him; yet even so, he believes in the Law that God gave to Moses and he is confident of being saved in it just like any other good Jew."[6]

It was not until late in the 1580s that old Tomás de Fonseca began to participate regularly with Portuguese Judaizers in Mexico City. He explained to inquisitors on June 2, 1596, in his first (largely fictitious) full confession, that his introduction to Judaizing had taken place during the winter of 1589. He had been strolling through Mexico City's busy main plaza, the large rectangular open area on the west side of the cathedral, which was slightly smaller than today's Zócalo, when he chanced to bump into Baltazar Rodríguez de Carvajal, who was then about twenty-seven years old. Without any preamble, at least in Tomás's recounting of the event, Baltazar had launched into a proselytizing sermon:

> "Be aware that the Messiah has not come, that Jesus Christ is not the Messiah, that you must await the Messiah's coming as the Jews do." I told

him not to talk like that, that he must report himself to the Holy Office, and that if he didn't, then I would. He calmed me down and begged me not to report him.

Old Tomás went on to say that eight days later Baltazar and his brother Luis de Carvajal had accosted Tomás on the Calle de San Agustín and, sandwiching him between them, had gone at him again:

"The Messiah that the Jews are waiting for has not come; still, they hope for him every day. You must observe and believe in the Law of Moses, which is the good law in which you can be saved, and is the law that God gave to the Jewish people, written by His hand. And if you want, we can teach it to you."

Tomás, who was trying to represent himself to his inquisitors as an innocent, said:

I told them that I was a Christian, the child of Christian parents, and they must not talk about those things with me, and they must go and report themselves, and if they didn't, then I would report them.[7]

According to the taradiddle that Tomás was relating to the inquisitors, the Carvajal brothers, undeterred by his reaction, had kept on with their efforts and over the next weeks had given old Tomás a detailed tutorial on the rudiments of Jewish observance as they understood them: keeping the Sabbath by not working; praying the Psalms while omitting the closing "Glory to the Father, the Son, and the Holy Spirit" so as not to profess a belief in the Trinity; and keeping the Jewish fasts by abstaining from food from sundown to sundown.

Tomás told inquisitors that after these conversations he had followed these customs for a while—perhaps a year and a half—but then, moved in large part by a vision he had had on the road from Mexico City back to Tlalpujahua, he had come to realize his mistake in having let a couple of stripling kids mislead an old man like himself. So he had gone back to being a Christian.[8]

In trying to blame his brief Judaizing on his proselytization by the Carvajal brothers, old Tomás omitted the fact that he had grown up in a

Judaizing family and had been aware of the basic beliefs and practices of Judaism for more than half a century. Parts of his tale may have been true, at least with regard to what had been said on those two occasions, as it reflected the Carvajal brothers' eagerness to incorporate Tomás into their Judaizing circle and the basic outlines of their brand of observance. But the inquisitors must have known that the rest was hooey. The conversation would never have taken place unless the Carvajal brothers had known of Tomás's background and felt that he was at least potentially receptive to their message. Otherwise, to broach such mortally risky subjects with him on a public street would have been folly.

Tomás went on to say that four or five days after these encounters with the Carvajals, he had run into Jorge de Almeida and warned him to be wary of his brothers-in-law because they were Jews. According to Tomás, Almeida had feigned shock at this news.[9] Tomás repeated to the inquisitors that shortly after that, as a result of the Carvajals' teachings, he had begun to follow the Law of Moses.

These conversations corroborate how in the 1580s old Tomás began to seek out conversation with his friends about Jewish topics. The Carvajal brothers and Manuel de Lucena, who were in their twenties, and Jorge de Almeida and Antonio Díaz Márquez, who were in their thirties, comprised the nucleus of old Tomás de Fonseca's circle of Judaizing associates in New Spain, even though Tomás was by then in his late sixties. He seems to have felt comfortable with them, and they with him, to the extent that they did not hesitate to inform him about which other members of the converso community were active Judaizers.

One afternoon in 1589, while Tomás was talking with Manuel de Lucena and Antonio Díaz Márquez in the latter's shop on the Calle de San Agustín, a procession led by a priest carrying a consecrated host passed by on the street, and the three men had all kneeled in obeisance as custom required. As old Tomás related it, Díaz Márquez then turned to his two friends and, cupping his hands around his face, whispered to them:

> "You know that it's only a piece of bread; . . . in Lisbon they subjected a woman to an *auto-da-fe* only for saying that the Holy Sacrament was just a piece of bread." So when I heard those words I knew that Antonio Díaz Márquez was a Jew. And what startled me was that even though Díaz

Márquez and I had not openly confessed to each other that we were Jews, he dared to say those words, unless maybe Baltazar Rodríguez and Luis de Carvajal had told him that I was a Jew.¹⁰

Luis de Carvajal remembered his initial interactions with old Tomás de Fonseca somewhat differently. He said that Tomás had come out to him about his Judaizing a full year earlier, when they were alone together in Luis's house near Santa Ana in Mexico City.

[Fonseca] told me that he kept the Law that God gave to Moses, saying that it was the true law in which men would be saved; he said that God is one, and not in three persons, making fun of that Trinity business and that there could be persons in God. He knows Latin and is knowledgeable about the Bible. The second time that he revealed that he was a Judaizer was in Cristóbal Gómez's store about seven years ago [1589] in the presence of Antonio López.¹¹

Luis de Carvajal had great respect for the knowledge of Judaism that old Tomás remembered from his youth and had gleaned from the books in his collection in Tlalpujahua. Luis Díaz, a cleric planted as cell mate to various conversos accused in the mid-1590s of Judaizing, reported that Carvajal had told him that "Tomás de Fonseca of Tlalpujahua kept the Law of Moses better than the one in Taxco because he was a good student."¹²

Marco Antonio reported in 1596 that back in 1588, old Tomás had recited for him his basic repertoire of Judaizing: keep the Saturday Sabbath, on fast days eat nothing until the first star can be seen in the sky, eat fowl only if it has been killed by decapitation, do not eat pork. There might have been more, Marco Antonio said, but Fonseca broke off because he had to leave.¹³ With only one exception, no one reported having seen old Tomás actually *do* any of these things. In the fall of 1588 or 1589, old Tomás spent Yom Kippur at the home of his nephew young Tomás de Fonseca in Taxco. According to Duarte Rodríguez, present were young Tomás's son Francisco, his friend Marco Antonio, and a Luis de Something-or-other whose surname he could not remember.¹⁴ After a day of praying, the men broke their fast with fish, chickpeas, eggs, and fruit.¹⁵

While old Tomás was, with respect to most of his contemporaries, relatively learned in the Bible, his core beliefs were few and easily put: The Law of Moses is the right one and the only one in which human beings can be saved. Jesus is not God. The Messiah has not come but will come to save the people of Israel.[16] Accompanying these beliefs was a categorical disbelief in the Christian sacraments and rejection of most aspects of Christian worship. Tomás seemed to have reserved his greatest scorn for what he called the Christian obsession for worshiping idols.

> How could a person adore those images, which were only men made by the hands of men. . . . They ask you to believe that an Our Lady of this city or of Guadalupe has done miracles. How could that be if she is just a piece of wood? And of another image of Our Lady that an Indian named Miguel painted, they say it worked miracles, and that the Indian had said in his language, "I'm not the one who made it." And they said it had come down from heaven. And they made to believe that a Christ that is in San Agustín blessed people, and it was because it had a hinge in one arm.[17]

In 1599, when old Tomás's cell mate, the English Protestant Thomas Day, told him that in England they had banished all of the statues and images from their churches with the exception of a bare cross, old Tomás was deeply impressed.[18]

The credulity of Christians for miracles never ceased to amaze old Tomás. He stored up tales and relished telling them to his friends.

> I remember telling Manuel Tavares . . . how when a niece of mine named Juliana de Castellanos, Julián's daughter, was sick because her belly swelled up, they took her to Our Lady of Guadalupe in a canoe. On the way, the movement of the boat make her spew out everything she had in her belly, both from her mouth and from down below, after which she got well. And all over Mexico City they were saying that it was a miracle.[19]
>
> Back in Spain, when there was a shortage of water or of sun, the farmers took the statues of the saints out of the hermitages and said that they would not bring them back until they had granted them what they were asking for.[20]

It is clear that by the time the first great purge of the Mexican Judaizers began in 1589, old Tomás de Fonseca had made himself part of the central Mexican Judaizing community. He knew Manuel de Lucena and Catalina Enríquez's friends in Pachuca, the circle that gathered around the Carvajal brothers in Mexico City, and the converso miners and shopkeepers in Taxco, among them several of his relatives. It was the Taxco miners, particularly Jorge de Almeida and young Tomás de Fonseca Castellanos, who developed particularly close bonds with old Tomás. Their trust in the old man was such that in April 1590, when Almeida began laying his plans to flee Mexico for Spain, he transferred the title of his Cantarranas hacienda to old Tomás.[21] In January 1591, Tomás de Fonseca Castellanos gave his uncle a power of attorney to handle his interests in the Inquisition's suit regarding Jorge de Almeida and Leonor de Carvajal's dowry.[22]

Chapter 15

Destruction and Survival

> We poor souls cannot confess [our Judaism] to each other because they drag us from Herod to the House of Pilate (he meant by this the Holy Office). And when they arrest us they take away our livelihood and they bring us in chains. And when the inquisitors have had their fill of chicken they sit down to judge us, thinking that they themselves will never be judged. And they seize what we have earned with our sweat and labor. And if they want to do us a favor they make [galley] slaves of us. As priests they judge us and smear mud on us, and when we are muddy they turn us over to the Secular Arm to do justice. They say they have treated us mercifully, and that God will one day reward us.
>
> —JUAN DE LUNA TO MANUEL TAVARES, 1593[1]

Dominos

In December 1586, Captain Felipe Núñez dined with Francisca de Carvajal and her children in Mexico City. Núñez, a converso from Lisbon, had come to Mexico in 1580 with Governor Luis de Carvajal and had ridden with him in the exploration and pacification of Nuevo León.[2] At the dinner, Isabel de Carvajal, the most outspoken of the sisters, attempted to convince Núñez that Jesus was not the Messiah and that he should return to the religion of his ancestors. Núñez, scandalized, told Isabel to watch her tongue. This veiled threat frightened Isabel into backing off. Núñez knew that he was under obligation to report the conversation to the Inquisition, but his loyalty to the governor and the governor's relatives persuaded him to hold his tongue. Still, the incident festered in his mind, and twenty-seven months later, on March 7, 1589, Núñez went to the Holy Office and assuaged his conscience by telling them about Isabel and the rest of the Carvajal family's Judaizing.

Five days later, the Inquisition arrested Isabel.

The news of her arrest disseminated rapidly, convulsing the converso community, since almost all the Judaizing conversos had interacted in some way with the Carvajals.[3] The Carvajal family members were the most frightened, for Isabel had been privy to their most intimate secrets. Fray Gaspar, well aware that he had shirked his obligation to denounce his siblings to the Inquisition, went to confer with his uncle the governor. He likewise had not reported what he knew of his nephew's family's Judaizing habits. Doña Francisca and Mariana were living in Almeida's rooms near the School for Girls in Mexico City. Luis was in Zimapán collecting some silver that he and his brother were owed. Baltazar was in Pachuca, observing the Fast of Esther with Manuel de Lucena; his wife, Catalina Enríquez; and most of Catalina's family.[4]

Jorge Álvarez, a close friend of the family, galloped eighty-six kilometers to Pachuca to deliver the news. He warned them to look sharply to their assets.[5] When Luis got back to Pachuca with the silver he had collected in Zimapán and Baltazar told him about his sister's arrest, both realized that if Isabel should begin to wag her tongue, they would all soon find themselves in jail. Their first thought was to hide the silver to prevent its being sequestered.[6] They gathered up their silver coins, planchas, and artifacts and rushed to the Lucenas, where they found Catalina and her brother Diego Enríquez playing cards with Antonio López. Luis began to cry as he broke the news of Isabel's arrest. Manuel de Lucena and the others tried to console him. Catalina and the five men told each other that their best hope for preserving their property and their lives lay in fleeing New Spain as quickly as possible.[7] The men spent that night tying up their silver into bundles and loading the packs onto mules. At dawn they set out for Mexico City.[8]

In the following months, under intense psychological and physical duress, Isabel de Carvajal detailed everything she knew about her family and their vast network of Judaizing converso acquaintances. One by one the Inquisition brought them in, and over the next few years, one by one they told their stories. By the early 1600s, the communities of crypto-Jews in the mining towns of Tlalpujahua, Taxco, and Pachuca ceased to exist.

Of the people profiled in depth in this book, the two richest and most

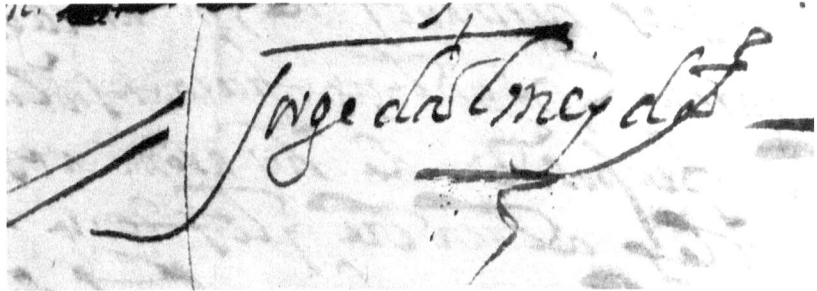

Figure 13. Signature of Jorge de Almeida. Used with permission of the Archivo General de la Nación, Mexico City.

powerful—Jorge de Almeida and Antonio Díaz de Cáceres—managed, in very different fashions, to survive the purge. Others, such as old Tomás de Fonseca and Lucena's wife, Catalina Enríquez, died in prison. Most of the rest—young Tomás de Fonseca, Manuel de Lucena, Luis de Carvajal, Isabel de Carvajal, Mariana de Carvajal, and Antonio Díaz de Cáceres's wife, Catalina de Carvajal—were executed after appearing in autos-de-fé. A few, such as Héctor de Fonseca, survived in prison and eventually returned to Spain. The stories of their downfall vary so widely in detail and resolution that we will consider them one by one.

Jorge de Almeida[9]

Following Isabel de Carvajal's arrest, her brother-in-law Jorge de Almeida felt it his duty to deal with the immediate practical problems of keeping the family afloat. Isabel had been living with Almeida and administering his household, since his wife, Leonor, was an immature fifteen and did not exhibit her sister's natural talent for managing complex tasks. With Isabel's arrest, Almeida felt that he had no recourse but to put Leonor in charge. He told her that this was the moment in which she had to take on the responsibilities of an adult, or at least "keep the house in order, prepare my meals, and clean my shirts."[10] Leonor, though well intentioned, very quickly proved incompetent, so her mother moved into Almeida's house to help. But Francisca got along so poorly with Almeida that she moved out again almost immediately.

One stressful week after Isabel's arrest, Almeida went to the Inquisition adjacent to the Santo Domingo Monastery and deposited fifty pesos to support his sister-in-law in what he hoped would be reasonable comfort during her incarceration.[11] In one way this was a bold move, for it drew attention to Almeida's support of a conversa who had undoubtedly been accused of Judaizing. In another way the visit was expected of him, for he was a man of means and a relative of Isabel's by marriage, and it was well-known that anything beyond the clothes a prisoner was wearing when arrested and minimal food and drink had to be paid for by the prisoner's personal resources or supplied by the prisoner's family and friends. *Not* to have come to her support might have raised questions about whether Almeida's fear of being tainted by association might indicate that he, too, was a Judaizer.

Almeida had a sophisticated sense of how the world worked. He knew that arrests of other family members were both inevitable and imminent, and that he himself was in grave danger, for any of the Carvajal tongues could spill out his doom. He and his brother-in-law Antonio Díaz de Cáceres needed to ensure the family's silence. Passover began the week following Almeida's depositing the support money, and despite his customary reticence about observing Jewish holidays in any public way, he invited Díaz de Cáceres, Francisca de Carvajal, and Francisca's sons Baltazar and Luis to his rooms in Mexico City for the festive meal. Almeida and Díaz reminded the Carvajals that the two of them were the principal financial support of the family. They warned the Carvajals that if any of them should be arrested and interrogated, they must not attribute any Judaizing activity to the two men if they wanted that support to continue.[12]

Then Almeida assigned Luis a task: to go to Taxco to collect the money that Tomás de Fonseca Castellanos owed him.[13] Almeida knew that the greater the liquid assets he had on hand, the wider would be the options open to him should the need arise.

On April 14, 1589, the Inquisition arrested Governor Luis de Carvajal y de la Cueva. It also took in Isabel's brother Fray Gaspar, accusing him of knowing about his siblings' Judaizing but failing to denounce them to the Inquisition. On May 9 Francisca and her son Luis were arrested.[14]

For nearly a year, Almeida managed to stave off the inevitable. Outwardly he continued to behave as a Christian citizen of substance and influence.

Gradually he turned what assets he could into cash. His wife, Leonor, and her sister Catalina were not touched for another seven months, but on December 2 they and their sister Mariana were also seized and lodged in the Inquisition's Cárcel Secreta.[15] For Almeida, Leonor's arrest must have been deeply unsettling, both because of his affection for his wife and concern for her well-being, and because of his fear for his own safety.[16]

Over the next few months, all the incarcerated members of the Carvajal family were interrogated, several of them under torture. The trials were handled with dispatch and brought quickly to conclusion in the public auto-de-fé of February 24, 1590. The inquisitors, believing that the incarcerated Carvajals had made full confessions, had expressed remorse and repentance, and had promised to live and believe henceforth as Catholics, ordered that they be formally reconciled with the church. Luis de Carvajal was made to abjure publicly in the auto-de-fé and was sentenced to confiscation of his property, perpetual incarceration, ineligibility for public honors or offices, and, for the length of his sentence to wear a sambenito whenever he appeared in public. The women were treated similarly, with lengths of imprisonment that varied according to the severity of their Judaizing: Francisca and Isabel in perpetuity, Mariana and Catalina for two years, and Leonor, because of her youth and naïveté, for one year. Even those unavailable to be jailed did not escape: Francisca's long dead husband, Francisco Rodríguez de Matos, and the fugitive Baltazar Rodríguez de Carvajal were declared guilty of Judaizing and were sentenced to be burned in effigy.

As a tratante of wealth and stature, Almeida dealt routinely with the upper levels of the government, the business community, and perforce the church. It is apparent that his connections reached into the upper echelons of the Inquisition, although precisely who his contacts were has never come to light. Almeida learned that the Holy Office planned to release the Carvajal women separately into several convents, where they would work off their penance as they received instruction in Catholicism. He convinced the inquisitors that it would be wiser to lodge them all together someplace where Almeida himself could take responsibility for them, thus avoiding the risk of the women being a pernicious influence on young impressionable nuns. The inquisitors transferred the women to a house in the nearby village of Tlatelolco that was adjacent to a Franciscan monastery and its school, the Colegio de Santa Cruz.[17] Not long after, Almeida succeeded in having Luis de Carvajal reassigned from his service in the Hospital de San Hipólito to the same Franciscan monastery to work in the scriptorium.

Ironically, it was already clear to the inquisitors from the testimony of Isabel and others that Almeida had participated in several Judaizing activities. Evidence against him mounted as the arrests and interrogations of members of the capital's Judaizing community continued. Among those arrested was Julián de Castellanos, old Tomás de Fonseca's half brother.[18] With the detail he provided, the Holy Office felt it had enough to move.

On April 9, 1590, the Inquisition ordered Almeida's arrest and sent a bailiff to his Mexico City lodgings. When Almeida recognized the official approaching his door, he slipped out the back and bolted for Taxco. The Inquisition then sent Luis Marván de Fontiveros to Taxco to arrest Almeida, instructing Marván to tread cautiously and not seize the Cantarranas hacienda until Almeida was securely in jail, since at the first hint of impending arrest, Almeida was likely to flee. But Marván was already too late. People in Taxco informed him that Almeida was hiding somewhere and sneaking into Cantarranas to tend to business only at night. Marván laid traps, but Almeida proved elusive. For three months they played cat and mouse. Then, on July 13, in a freak accident, Marván was trampled to death by a runaway bull.[19]

Pedro de Medinilla, the bailiff sent by the Inquisition to replace Marván, could not find Almeida either, probably because by then Almeida had left Taxco and was hiding with his brother Miguel Hernández in a small house behind the market in Tlatelolco, a stone's throw from the house and monastery where the Carvajal women and Luis de Carvajal were confined.[20] The prior had granted Luis occasional freedom to visit his mother, doña Francisca, and his sisters and Luis used the time to visit Almeida in his hidey-hole as well. He took Almeida books, including the well-thumbed copy of Fray Luis de Granada's *Symbol of Faith* that Luis had successfully hidden before his own arrest. Together he and Almeida read passages aloud and discussed their mutual commitment to the Law of Moses.

Unexpectedly, on July 30, 1590, the Inquisition suspended its order to arrest Almeida because Julián de Castellanos had recanted his testimony.[21] Almeida breathed a temporary sigh of relief. Still, he knew that despite Julián's about-face, and despite the care he had always taken never to allow his rare Judaizing activities to be observed, the Inquisition would be able to build a case against him with relative ease. His best chance at safety was to flee Mexico. Gathering all his available liquid resources, he made his way to Veracruz and set sail for Spain in the company of his brother Miguel and Francisco Díaz, whom he had employed as mayordomo at Cantarranas. In August 1590, Leonor told an Inquisition official in Tlatelolco that she could not speak to her husband's whereabouts because she had not seen Almeida in three months.[22]

The circular patterns of winds and currents mean that eastbound convoys between Mexico and Spain put in for water and supplies in Havana and again in the Azores, while westbound convoys are provisioned in the Canaries and Hispaniola. From very early in the Indies trade, Havana, with its superb harbor, had become the dominant commercial hub of the Caribbean. For businessmen like Almeida, it was a good tarrying point, a place to meet friends, exchange news, and do business. However, his escape had cost him dearly, and what money he had managed to take with him from Mexico was nearly gone.

From Havana, in early February 1591, Almeida sent a packet of letters to his brother-in-law Fray Gaspar de Carvajal, who, after his release from prison, had been assigned to the Dominican monastery in Oaxaca. The packet included a note to Leonor and other letters to business colleagues and friends. Despite the fact that Fray Gaspar had been both open and adamant about his opposition to his family's Judaizing, Almeida seems to have trusted him, at least up to a point. The main purpose of his letter was to ask Gaspar to urge Almeida's inner circle of business colleagues to find a way to send him money, which in practical terms meant not to ship coins to him in Cuba but to secure a line of credit for him back in Spain. Writing with tact and circumspection, Almeida couched his request as a chatty, newsy family letter:

> Here I have learned that your brothers have arrived in Castilla and disembarked in Galicia. They went to Sanlúcar with the intent of going to Rome to seek absolution. May God grant them light and preserve them with his holy hand.[23]

If the letter were to fall into the wrong hands, on the face of it these words could suggest that Baltazar and Miguel were planning to embrace Catholicism, though any discerning member of the Judaizing community would realize—from Almeida's reference to Rome rather than the Pope, and to God rather than to Christ—that the brothers intended to reincorporate themselves into Rome's Jewish community.

Almeida went on to write that in Havana he had run into two colleagues, Duarte de León, who was also headed to Spain, and Francisco Rodriguez—the one whose father was the silk merchant Simón Gómez, with a store in the Zócalo[24]—who was on his way to Mexico. Almeida had asked Rodríguez to carry two small packets of scent for Leonor, an ounce of musk and another of ambergris. He would like to send her a million more presents, he wrote, for she had always been such a model sister to her siblings and daughter to her mother, which is the highest compliment one could pay to a woman. The letter seems to convey more esteem than love: it praised Leonor as a sister and a daughter, not as a wife; it expressed Almeida's respect, not his pain at being separated from his beloved. Still, he promised to use his time in Spain "in the service of doña Leonor, my lady [doña Francisca]," and the sisters. What he meant, but could not overtly write, was that he would use his influence and money to secure for the Carvajals who had been penanced by the Mexican Inquisition a dispensation that would release them from the obligation to wear their sambenitos in public.[25] Almeida's underlying message was his husbandly allegiance both to Leonor and to the Carvajal family.

After these preliminaries, Almeida's letter got to the heart of the matter. He had spent all the money he had brought with him. The people in Spain who owed him money were all as broke as he was. He instructed Fray Gaspar to tell Antonio Díaz de Cáceres to send him a letter of credit for the four thousand pesos that Díaz owed him and to include the original promissory notes that the two of them had signed. Likewise Gaspar should have Cristobal Gómez send Almeida the money he owed him. The money should go to Almeida in Sevilla in care of Diego Pinero. We know these details because Fray Gaspar, out of concern to maintain his own bona fides as a solid Christian, ignored his brother-in-law's instructions and gave Almeida's letter to his superior, who was also the Inquisition's *comisario* in Oaxaca.[26]

Almeida also sent Antonio López a letter from Cuba with instructions to deliver it to Luis de Carvajal. Luis received it, but after his arrest, he too revealed its contents to the inquisitors. In it Almeida had written that in Spain he was planning to raise money from his relatives to go to Cape Verde to buy slaves to take to America. Almeida's brother Héctor de Fonseca and his cousin young Tomás de Fonseca Castellanos also received letters. In these notes Almeida reiterated his intention to seek the dispensation for the Carvajals.[27]

Though his letters pleaded poverty, Almeida apparently had sufficient resources to sail from Cuba to Spain and to rent a house for himself and his brother Miguel Hernández on the fashionable Correo Mayor in Madrid. Ironically, given the care he took in Mexico to hide his Jewish heritage, their home became a favorite stopping place for traveling crypto-Jewish merchants with business in southern Europe and the Americas. Among the visitors was Juan Rodríguez de Silva, a man well versed in Judaism who had lived for a time in Salonica.[28] Another was Ruy Díaz Nieto, a well-educated Jew whose family had lived in Flanders and Ferrara, where he had met Almeida years earlier. A recent bankruptcy had caused Ruy Díaz to set off with his young son Diego Díaz Nieto in search of business opportunities. Almeida told them of the property he had left behind in Taxco and extolled the success of their cousin Fernando Cardoso, who lived in Querétaro. Mexico was a rich land, he told them, and they could easily make a new fortune there. Early in 1594 the Díaz Nietos sailed for Mexico, carrying with them another packet of letters from Almeida to his relatives, friends, and business contacts. In Mexico City father and son lodged with Antonio Díaz de Cáceres, who had recently returned from a business venture in Asia in which Almeida had invested some sixteen hundred pesos that he had yet to recover.[29] Taken together, all these things suggest that Almeida was planning to return to New Spain.

While Jorge de Almeida was pursuing business interests in Madrid, he did not forget his Carvajal relatives. Although the details of his negotiations with the Supreme Council of the Inquisition have not all surfaced, Almeida succeeded in securing an arrangement whereby, in return for a contribution of thirteen hundred ducats, the Holy Office would issue a dispensation freeing the penanced Carvajals from having to wear the shameful sambenito. Almeida sent the relevant documents back to Mexico with Ruy Díaz Nieto, advising Luis that the dispensation depended on Luis being able to raise the money.[30] Luis set to work, but by early autumn 1594 he had only put together contributions of 850 pesos, some of which were promissory notes. He delivered these to the Holy Office on October 10 and the sum was deemed sufficient. A letter from the Mexican Inquisition to the chief inquisitor in Madrid in March 1595 confirmed that

> in accord with your order regarding Luis de Carvajal and his mother

and sisters . . . that their penitential habits be removed upon their contributing a certain sum of money for the needs of this Inquisition, the habits were removed and the money was received.[31]

The Mexican Inquisition knew full well that Jorge de Almeida was living in Madrid, but it put little energy into taking him into custody. Instead it concentrated on seizing the assets he had left behind. His most substantial holding was the Cantarranas mining hacienda, which he had purchased in 1586 on installments. Several payments were still outstanding; moneys for which both he and his guarantors—Antonio Díaz de Cáceres, Héctor de Fonseca, and Tomás de Fonseca Castellanos—were liable. Almeida had presumed that if he were arrested and his cousin old Tomás de Fonseca remained free, old Tomás could safeguard the property for him. Of all his relatives, close friends, and business colleagues, old Tomás seems to have been the man whom Almeida most trusted. The decision made, he had transferred the Cantarranas title to his cousin.[32] The effort was in vain. When Almeida fled Mexico for Spain, the Inquisition seized Cantarranas; it was sold at public auction on September 26, 1591, to another Taxco miner, Felipe de Palacios. Almeida's representatives fought for years to collect the purchase price. Though Palacios made a partial payment in March 1607, the legal proceedings against Palacios and his heirs on behalf of Almeida's many creditors continued until July 1783.[33]

After Cantarranas, Almeida's second largest asset was his cash receivables. Years previous, with remarkable foresight, he had taken steps to shelter a portion of his liquid assets legally by disguising them as property of his bride, Leonor de Carvajal. The ruse was this: the lavish gifts of clothing, jewels, and silver plate that Alemeida presented to Leonor were attested to have been provided instead by the Rodríguez de Matos family as Leonor's dowry. In the event that Almeida should be sued, or an attempt made to sequester his belongings, in theory the value of the dowry would, as property of Leonor, be legally exempt. Then Almeida could stipulate that although the dowry goods were long gone, his cash on hand and receivables were the equivalent of the value of the faux dowry and thus belonged to Leonor and not to him. As long as Leonor remained safe, that money would be safe as well.

But Almeida had missed one crucial possibility. Leonor had been arrested in the spring of 1589, found guilty of Judaizing, and reconciled to the church in the auto-de-fé of February 24, 1590; her sentence included confiscation of all her possessions. After her release, the Inquisition sued the absent Almeida for 6,535 pesos, the attested value of the faux dowry that Leonor had allegedly brought to the marriage.[34]

But there was no extant cash. It all lay in uncollected debts. So the Inquisition's Real Fisco worked diligently to collect for its coffers the moneys owed to Almeida by his various creditors. Greatly complicating the matter were the debts that Almeida had not yet paid off when he fled the country, obligations that constituted first liens against his estate.[35] Not only was the web of his financial entanglements exceedingly complex, the fraudulent dowry cast a shadow on everything. Old Tomás de Fonseca put the matter straightforwardly in the suit that he brought against the Real Fisco:

> I understand that you have sequestered Leonor's share of Jorge de Almeida's Cantarranas hacienda. . . . Almeida is in debt to me and I hold a first lien. . . . The said hacienda is explicitly mortgaged to those outstanding debts. In addition, the document of the dowry of the said Leonor on which the Real Fisco bases its claims was false, not certain or true, and intended to indicate that Jorge de Almeida acquired those goods in that way, even though he never received anything at all as dowry.[36]

The Inquisition chose to let Leonor's faux dowry stand, because since she had been judged guilty of heresy, Almeida—or his executors—was obligated to deliver the dowry's declared value to the Real Fisco. If subsequently Almeida were to be convicted of heresy, the money could be taken from him; if not, it would have to be taken from her, or from him in his role as her guardian.

The Inquisition's attempts to seize Almeida's assets dragged on for years. In June 1594 Almeida, from Madrid, delegated power to Luis de Carvajal, by then a free man, to defend the assets on Almeida's behalf. The authorizing document suggests that despite the outstanding arrest warrant for Almeida, and despite the fact that his wife and in-laws had been prosecuted as Judaizing heretics, Almeida still had the wealth, the connections, and the gall to deal openly as an international businessman:

I authorize . . . Luis de Carvajal or his representatives . . . to demand, receive, collect, and hold . . . all the *maravedís, reales, escudos, sueldos, libras, dineros* and *pesos* of gold and silver, merchandise, and any other kind or quality of thing. . . . Luis de Carvajal should make an accounting of anything that he recovers or collects of my estate; he should load it onto one or two or three ships at my command in silver or in merchandise consigned to me or my designees and send it to the *Casa de la Contratación* in Sevilla so that I can take possession of it.[37]

In 1607, seventeen years after Almeida fled Mexico, the Inquisition's prosecutor, Martos de Bohórquez, acknowledging that the Holy Office was unlikely ever to find Alameida, moved to proceed against him in his absence. Bohórquez detailed eight charges:

Though Almeida was a baptized Christian, he had Judaized.
He did not believe Jesus was the Messiah but rather that the Messiah was still to come.
He observed the Sabbath on Saturday with various Jewish practices.
He fasted on Yom Kippur with other Jews.
He believed in plural marriage and wanted to go to an Italian judiaria to wed his sister-in-law.
He mocked Christ and Christians.
He sent secret letters to Mexican Judaizers.
He had not responded to the Inquisition's summons to appear.

The declaration of Almeida's rebelliousness was read out in Mexico City's cathedral on March 18, 1607, the third Sunday of Lent, and again on April 21 and May 16. The summons commanded him to appear within sixty days. If he did not, as a fugitive, unrepentant Judaizer, he would be burned in effigy, all his property would henceforth belong to the king, and his heirs would be ineligible to lodge any claim against his estate. Almeida did not appear during the sixty days. The last documentary evidence of the life of Jorge de Almeida attests that in a private *autillo* in the cathedral on the third Sunday of Lent in 1609, his effigy was consigned to flames.[38]

Figure 14. Signature of Antonio Díaz de Cáceres. Used with permission of the Archivo General de la Nación, Mexico City.

Antonio Diáz de Cáceres[39]

From the day they met in Mexico City early in 1582, the careers of Antonio Díaz de Cáceres and Jorge de Almeida had run parallel courses and in many ways were inextricably linked. Both came from well-traveled, educated families. Both had been initiated in Europe into the ways of Judaism. Both were successful tratantes with substantial capital and multiple business interests. Both developed important government, business, and church connections in Mexico City. Both bought into the mining business, purchasing haciendas de beneficio in Taxco in 1582. Together they decided to marry the impoverished but well-connected conversa sisters Catalina and Leonor de Carvajal. Both used the faux dowry ruse in an attempt to shelter some of their assets. In many ways the two men were of similar character: aggressive, not afraid to take a business risk, but at the same time protective of their investments; adept at multitasking; rational, far-thinking, and calculating; private in their personal affairs, which included their religious practices; not given to public displays of emotion—with the exception of anger and, in Almeida's case, lust—and rarely given to expressions of affection.

For both men, matters of business were their second-highest priority, ranking just below assuring their personal safety. It is not surprising that among the men profiled in this book, it was these two who developed concrete escape plans for themselves—plans that combined safeguarding their bodies with advancing their business interests; plans that required taking certain preliminary actions long before the threats against them materialized. Nor is it surprising that when the time came, they acted on those plans decisively.

When Antonio Díaz de Cáceres learned of Isabel de Carvajal's arrest in March 1589, he joined Jorge de Almeida in warning the Carvajals who were still free to keep their mouths shut with regard to their brothers-in-law, threatening to withhold the financial support that had sustained Francisca and her children ever since the weddings. He gave his longtime business partner Antonio de los Cobos a power of attorney to handle his affairs should he be unavailable to do so himself.[40] As the first Carvajals were taken prisoner, Díaz de Cáceres, who was always aware of how he appeared to others, took extra care in burnishing his Catholic facade. Now he scrupulously avoided any activity that might emit the faintest scent of Judaizing or of sympathy with the Judaizing community. Unlike Almeida, he did not contribute to Isabel's maintenance in prison. He built a wall between himself and the Carvajal siblings who still remained at liberty. Carrying this tactic to an outrageous extreme, he cut off all contact with his wife of three years, Catalina, and their infant daughter, Leonor, born in the spring of 1587.

Somehow—through his high-level connections in the capital? Through Almeida?—Díaz de Cáceres learned that the Inquisition was preparing to issue arrest warrants for Catalina; Almeida's wife, Leonor; and their sister Mariana. When he learned that the Holy Office had indeed arrested his wife and sequestered her property, he fled.[41] Unlike his brother-in-law Almeida, who, in the period between when Isabel Carvajal was arrested and his own arrest warrant was issued, did what he could to assist the Carvajal family, Díaz de Cáceres looked first, and solely, to himself. He tore off on the long road over the mountains and down the Pacific slope to Acapulco, with as much of his liquid wealth as he could muster in his saddlebags. Typically, he had already begun a new business venture that doubled as a contingency plan, forming a company with his partner of thirteen years, Antonio de los Cobos, and a man named Francisco Ibáñez to buy a ship for the Asia trade. He had already raised funds from investors in Taxco to purchase the goods he would trade. He found an appropriate vessel anchored in the Acapulco bay: *Nuestra Señora de la Concepción*. Its captain, Pedro Palacios, was willing to sell Díaz de Cáceres and his partners a half interest in the ship. Given his extensive experience at sea, Díaz felt comfortable assuming for himself the role of ship's master. On December 29, with a crew of forty-five and an additional twenty-five paying passengers, the ship weighed anchor for the long voyage to the Philippines. Its destination was Manila, the Iberian port of entry to the whole of Southeast Asia, a vast area that in the parlance of the age was called simply China.[42]

> Among the passengers was Felipe de las Casas, born in Mexico City in 1572, who as a teenager had professed with the Franciscans as Fray Felipe de Jesús, at seventeen left the order, and as a novice merchant sailed to Manila with Díaz de Cáceres. In Manila, after some years of excess, he sought to rejoin the order. In 1596, on his way back to Mexico to be formally ordained, his ship was blown off course and he and several friar shipmates found themselves in Japan. They, and several missionary friars who had been left in Japan by Saint Francis Xavier, were accused of preparing the way for a European conquest of Japan. Twenty-six friars were arrested and, in 1597, executed in Nagasaki. The twenty-six were beatified in 1627 and canonized in 1862. San Felipe de Jesús, considered the first Mexican-born martyr, is patron saint of Mexico City.[43]

A film treatment of Díaz de Cáceres's escapades in China over the next two years might well be dismissed as improbably exaggerated. On arriving in Manila, his ship capsized. In a daring rescue, the local populace saved all the passengers and most of the cargo. The ship was righted and consigned for repair. Díaz next decided to sail to the rich Portuguese trading colony of Macao on the Chinese mainland, and though authorities in Manila initially denied him permission to go, he hired an attorney and eventually secured authorization. When he arrived in Macao, he was arrested. The reason remains murky, though it may have resulted from Portuguese antipathy to the encroachments of Spanish businessmen or the prior arrival of notice that Díaz de Cáceres was sought by the Inquisition.[44] The Macao authorities sequestered his ship and cargo, clapped him in irons, and locked him in the brig of a ship bound for India. Somehow Díaz managed to file through his chains and hide himself in the recesses of the ship, where he avoided being seen even through the unloading of cargo in Goa and the reloading of Indian goods for the return voyage to the Philippines. When at last Díaz emerged on deck, he was again arrested. In Manila the captain turned him over to the secular authorities. There he petitioned to return to Mexico.

After considerable delay, during part of which he was employed as a notary by the office of the Inquisition in Manila,[45] he was allowed to retake command of his ship, which improbably was still manned by its original crew. At some point in this mercantile hegira, Díaz de Cáceres managed to purchase and crate a large quantity of Chinese porcelain for sale in Mexico.[46] The ship docked in Acapulco on November 24, 1592, not quite three years after Díaz had departed.

During the time Díaz de Cáceres had been away, the trials of the imprisoned members of the Carvajal family had been concluded and the sentences of all but Catalina de Carvajal had been proclaimed in the auto-de-fé of February 24, 1590. Catalina's proceso had dragged on, in part because of the Inquisition's inability to locate all her assets. Eventually she, too, was judged to be guilty, but with the mitigating circumstances of her having been initiated to Judaism as a child and having been unduly and constantly influenced by her seniors. In her favor were her apparently sincere conversion to Catholicism and her abjuration of her Jewish beliefs and practices. In 1592 she was reconciled with the church with the forfeiture of all of her property. She insisted that her absent husband, Antonio, had taken all her personal assets to invest in the China trade, including the dowry that she, like her sister Leonor, had allegedly brought to her marriage.

That being presumed so, the Inquisition wrote to the port captaincy in Acapulco in November 1592 with detailed instructions:

> [When Díaz de Cáceres's ship docks], before they unload anything you must make a general inventory of all of the merchandise and any other thing which is carried by said ship, noting everything that is registered under his name or the name of his wife. Only then you may unload them and inventory and tag them by item, identifying mark, and weight, as may be required, and deposit them with Alonso de Pareja, the chief shipping agent of that port.[47]

The letter concluded by instructing Pareja to engage a trustworthy wagoner to cart the goods to the Holy Office in Mexico City. If Díaz should have insufficient cash to pay for the freighting, it instructed Pareja to auction off some of the merchandise.

When *Nuestra Señora de la Concepción* tied up to the wharf, the Inquisition's agent in Acapulco arrested Díaz de Cáceres and impounded his ship and its cargo of Chinese porcelain. The immediate concern was the goods in which Catalina had presumably invested, goods over which the Royal Treasury exerted claim by virtue of Catalina's sentence. Díaz de Cáceres, deprived of both his liberty and his property, sent a letter to his friend the senior Inquisition official (unnamed in the copy in his dossier), requesting that the Holy Office order that the ship's cargo and his personal possessions be released to him. Although by this time the Inquisition, by virtue of the testimony of various members of the Carvajal family, was clearly aware of Díaz de Cáceres's Judaizing, astonishingly, the Inquisition did as he requested.

Almost immediately new problems surfaced. Díaz de Cáceres had not paid the ship's crew. Furthermore, although much of the porcelain cargo had been broken to bits during the voyage, Díaz de Cáceres was trying to pass it off as perfect goods. Over the next four months he found himself repeatedly in the Acapulco jail on one or another of these charges. He would pay a little of his debt on account, then default on subsequent payments, and again be arrested. Eventually, as the result of his partial payments, the sale of the cargo to raise money to pay the crew,[48] and the influence of Díaz's powerful friends, he was freed. Could it be possible that his alleged record of Judaizing was no longer an issue?

Back in Mexico City, the *tratante* resumed investing, buying, and selling.[49] He was surely aware that he would be watched and that any shadow of suspicion might land him in the Inquisition's Cárcel Secreta. He raised his habitual circumspection to the level of obsession. He adamantly refused to have anything at all to do with his sambenito-clad relatives, including his wife, Catalina, and their daughter Leonor. He chose instead to take up residence with his business partner Antonio de los Cobos. When the kerfuffle over the broken porcelain landed him in Mexico City's civil prison, the authorities made cohabitation with his wife a condition of his release. Díaz de Cáceres balked, insisting that he preferred to remain locked up. This scandalous rejection of his husbandly responsibilities so upset the senior inquisitor that he sent a committee of theologians to Díaz's cell to persuade him to do the right thing. With no other choice, late in the summer of 1593, Díaz went home to Catalina.

It is unclear to what degree Díaz de Cáceres's public rejection of his wife reflected his true feelings. From the moment he had married, his business concerns seem to have occupied most of his energy. He spent very little time at home, and when he was there he worked assiduously—if not always consistently—to quash the overt Judaizing of Catalina and her relatives. He was not a faithful husband: like many men of his class and circumstances, when he traveled he did not always sleep alone. At some point prior to 1596, he fathered a mulatta child named Agustina de Quiñones.[50] Nevertheless, Díaz de Cáceres must have harbored some affection for his Judaizing wife, for he never broke with her completely.[51]

He also felt some attachment to Judaism, for though he seldom risked participating in communal Judaizing activities, his abstention was never absolute. During the decade prior to the 1589 arrests, he occasionally took part in community gatherings, such as Jorge de Almeida's Passover celebration in 1583.[52] In choosing a wife, he sought out a girl from a family with a solid reputation among the converso community for Judaizing. In the opinion of her sister Mariana, the family only permitted the marriage because Díaz was an observant Jew.[53] And after his release from prison, living with Catalina in the house that she shared with her mother and sisters, he began, cautiously, to Judaize. The adjective that his relatives and friends most often used to describe him was *recatado*: guarded, self-monitoring, cautious.[54] His sister-in-law Mariana described his reticence this way:

> Once they were back together they began to collaborate in keeping the Law of Moses. When Antonio Díaz de Cáceres and his wife came to my mother doña Francisca's house, I went back to reading Psalms of praise to them from Licenciado Morales's book (without the "Glory to the Father") and some songs that Morales had extracted from the Holy Scripture. He kept the Sabbath with me, my mother doña Francisca, Luis de Carvajal, doña Isabel, doña Leonor, and doña Ana. Antonio Díaz de Cáceres begged us to do these things cautiously, warning us that since we had been reconciled [in the *auto-de-fé*], we would suffer the pain of death if we went back to keeping the Law of Moses. He said we were keeping

the Law with little caution, because we sang those songs without concern for the Indian woman in our house. He begged us for the love of God to wear our *sambenitos*. . . . Some Saturdays we went to his house too. . . . He liked to do those things but . . . he didn't keep the Sabbath as a festival. Rather, he went out to his business, and he did not wear better clothes, or clean shirts, or abstain from eating bacon, lard, and things made with pork. I believe he did this so as not to be noticed, because he was very guarded.

Mariana said that even though Díaz believed that Jesus was not the Messiah, he urged the Carvajal women to pray the Our Father, telling them that they were holy words and that praying them would ensure their salvation. And he was insistent in teaching his wife and daughter the Christian doctrine.[55] Mariana added that in 1595, he and Catalina had told her that they saw no need to abstain from eating on Yom Kippur.[56]

Although testimony by many of the conversos arrested in 1589 and 1590 had named Antonio Díaz de Cáceres as one of their Judaizing colleagues, he had managed to remain at liberty. Beginning with the next round of arrests, late in 1594, the inquisitors interrogated their converso prisoners about the Judaizing conversos who remained at large. Díaz de Cáceres, suspecting that he would soon be taken, gave his friend Diego Márquez de Andrada a power of attorney, enabling him to "collect, dispatch, buy, and sell any pesos of gold and silver, jewels, slaves, merchandise, beasts of burden, cattle, real estate, and any other goods."[57]

On March 12, 1596, the inquisitors voted that Antonio Díaz de Cáceres, Antonio Díaz Márquez, Simón Rodríguez, and old Tomás de Fonseca of Tlalpujahua be arrested. The following day Díaz de Cáceres sat in the Cárcel Secreta waiting to be called to the audience chamber at any moment to defend himself against the charge of Judaizing.[58] But the call did not come. During the next eight months, while Díaz de Cáceres stewed in his cell, inquisitors Bartolomé Lobo Guerrero and Alonso de Peralta concentrated on Luis de Carvajal and his siblings. Eventually Luis and four members of his family, including Díaz de Cáceres's wife, Catalina, were found guilty. On December 6, after the auto-de-fé in the plaza in front of the cathedral, they were executed at the burning grounds in the Plaza San Hipólito. One day after his wife's immolation, the inquisitors called Díaz de Cáceres to his first audience. His interrogation dragged on for the next five and a half years.

In the early audiences, Díaz de Cáceres professed to be a practicing Christian. When the inquisitors enumerated specific charges—that he associated with known Jews, talked with them about the Law of Moses, awaited the Messiah, and told people that he wanted to live and die as a Jew—he denied everything. "I have always been a Christian," he said, "well instructed in the law of Jesus Christ, and as such I taught it to my daughter before I went to China; and anything other than that is not true." In April 1597 they read him the mass of anonymized witness testimony to his Judaizing. Díaz, surmising the witnesses' identities, claimed that they were all his mortal enemies and denied any wrongdoing. In August the inquisitors read him summaries of a second round of testimonies against him, and again he claimed animus and denied having Judaized. And so it went, over the next forty-two months. On December 2, 1600, they read him the testimonies of nine new witnesses, eliciting from him the same response. Díaz de Cáceres went so far as to say that he had never even heard of Yom Kippur other than the fact that Catalina had told him that fasting on it was one of the reasons the Inquisition had given her penance after her first trial. If his sister-in-law Mariana sang hymns out loud, he protested, he thought it was because she was crazy, not that it was some Jewish ceremony.[59]

The Secret Prison was generally so crowded that prisoners had to share cells. During the summer of 1600, Díaz de Cáceres shared a cell with Alberto de Meyo[60] and Gonzalo Pérez Ferro. Antonio Gómez Silveira, in the cell next to theirs, tried to pick out a hole between their cells to make it easier to talk with them and pass small items back and forth. At first the wall proved to be too hard, and he quit a third of the way through. Manuel Tavares, from a cell on the other side, succeeded. One hole, at floor level, was large enough for them to pass a bottle of wine and two medicinal stones, a bloodstone of green chalcedony dotted with red jasper or iron oxide, and a bezoar to cure melancholy. Sometimes the men wrote out Psalms and passed them to one another. When the hole was not in use, they packed it with mud to disguise it. A second, smaller hole in a corner of the cell they masked with a chunk of brick. Ana de León Carvajal occupied a cell on the other side of Tavares's with her cell mate Isabel Machado. Díaz de Cáceres passed Tavares a note for Ana, informing her where he was and asking if she recalled him as the man who had once broken her older sister's arm. Ana wrote back saying that she wished Díaz well and often prayed for him, and Isabel too sent him her best wishes and hoped that he would soon be freed to see his daughter, little Leonorica.[61]

Although prisoners were sworn to secrecy about their own cases, and in fact enjoined from saying anything substantive to their cell mates, the Inquisition counted on them incriminating themselves to each other. The warden and his assistants prowled the corridors night and day, taking notes about the prisoners' chatter—notes that were inevitably introduced sometime during the protracted interrogations. During the long months between interrogation sessions, Antonio Díaz de Cáceres found solace in talking with his cellmates and the prisoners in adjoining cells. In this institutionally manipulated comfort zone, he talked unguardedly about his experiences and his beliefs, even though he knew that the Secret Prison was rife with spies. The inquisitors persisted in their certainty that Antonio Díaz de Cáceres's testimony was a tissue of lies, in part because his cell mates and the prisoners in neighboring cells reported the conversations they had with him about things pertaining to Judaism.

Because the inquisitors could not get Díaz de Cáceres to acknowledge that he was indeed a habitual Judaizer, on March 2, 1600, they voted to submit him to torture. In the torture chamber, faced with a session on the rack (*potro*), not only did he refuse to confess but he advised the inquisitors that "if I should say something, be it understood that I only confessed out of fear of further torture." As the ropes tightened around him, he continued to remain silent. After the first turn of the ratchet, silence; after the fifth, silence; even after the twelfth, his mouth continued shut. They now tightened the ropes around each of his arms in turn, and after twelve more turns of the ratchet he still refused to speak. As a last inducement they subjected him to waterboarding, putting a thin gauze cloth over his face, pouring a pitcher of water into his mouth to force the gauze into his esophagus, and then pulling it out. Seven jars are noted in the scribal record of the session, and though Díaz de Cáceres screamed that they were killing him, he would not confess to Judaizing. Finally they slacked the ropes and allowed him to rise to his feet and put on his clothes. Once more they urged him to tell the truth. In a low voice he replied, "Alas, woe is me, I have done so."[62]

In Martin Cohen's words, "since the application of torture was a kind of trial by ordeal, a prisoner's emergence from it without confession could theoretically be regarded as a demonstration of innocence."[63] Even so, the preponderance of evidence of Díaz's guilt meant that the Inquisition was unwilling to absolve him completely. On March 8, 1601, they voted that Díaz de Cáceres be assigned penance after abjuring of his sins *de vehementi* (with a strong suspicion of heresy) and paying a fine of one thousand gold ducats to the Inquisition for its extraordinary costs in having to imprison him for such a long time. The sentence was read out in the March 25 auto-de-fé, after which he was released with the requirement that he attend instructional sessions in Catholicism.[64] His daughter Leonorica, then age seven, received a light penance.[65]

At some point Díaz de Cáceres made his way back to Europe, where he joined his brother Henrique Dias de Milão's business in Lisbon.[66]

Tomás de Fonseca Castellanos[67]

Tomás de Fonseca Castellanos was a social animal, frequently inviting business associates and friends in Taxco to dine with him at his house. Almost from the start, they began to feel that Tomás might be a secret Jew, and in 1586 some of them began to report their suspicions to the Inquisition. Felipe Freire, the mine guard who was a close enough friend that he had sat frequently at Tomás's table, noted that he did not eat pork and seldom went to mass.[68] Mateo Ruiz, who worked for Jorge de Almeida, and Francisco de Cáceres, a merchant colleague in Taxco, also noted that Tomás never served pork at his table.[69] This sort of information, added to the data provided by Isabel de Carvajal and Julián de Castellanos upon their arrests, led the Inquisition on May 9, 1589, to order Tomás's arrest and seizure of his material possessions.[70]

In the Cárcel Secreta they placed Tomás in a cell adjacent to Fray Gaspar de Carvajal's. Through a crack in the wall, the two men consoled each other and wondered what was going to happen to Gaspar's sister Isabel and the rest of the Carvajal family.[71] Tomás's aversion to pork aside, it is clear that the inquisitors did not believe the evidence of his Judaizing sufficient to condemn him. In late spring 1589, the inquisitors voted to absolve Tomás of serious heresy but to make him appear in an auto-de-fé, fine him for his minor transgressions, and then release him and return his sequestered property. As was often the case, the bureaucratic wheels of the Real Fisco ground frustratingly slowly, and on December 11 Tomás respectfully petitioned the Holy Office to release what they had seized:

> I was sentenced in the *auto-de-fé* held in the Cathedral of this city, and in my sentence your lordships ordered that all my goods be given back to me and returned, in regard to which I request that you give me a written order of release so that I may pay the fine that you levied on me and justice may be done.[72]

Though there is no record of the return of his assets, Fonseca lodged no further petitions.

By mid-summer of 1590, Tomás was back in Taxco, thanking God for having released him from the Cárcel Secreta. Despite his obvious relief, he worried constantly about his financial interests. Like Almeida and Díaz de Cáceres, men whose livelihoods depended on their ability to manage cash flow and diverse financial commitments, he turned his attention to protecting his flexibility in the event that he was again arrested. On January 16, 1591, Tomás de Fonseca Castellanos went to the royal scribe Juan García Parra and, before two businessmen friends as witnesses, executed a general power of attorney to his uncle old Tomás de Fonseca.

For the next year and a half, Tomás communed with his Judaizing friends. If he was cautious about safeguarding his money, he was much less so about his personal safety. He shared with Gonzálo Pérez Ferro the joy of observing the Sabbath. In March, 1591, he went to Tlatelolco, where Luis de Carvajal was serving his penance, and celebrated the Passover with Luis's extended family.

By late July, young Tomás was back in prison. The power of attorney he had given to old Tomás proved useful when the Real Fisco attempted to seize Leonor de Carvajal's portion of the assets that Jorge de Almeida had forfeited when he fled to Europe. Old Tomás, petitioning on behalf of his young cousin Tomás, claimed that his cousin had a lien on Almeida's estate by virtue of loans to Almeida in 1586 and 1589 that remained unpaid.[73]

As before, young Tomás remained firm in protesting his commitment to Christianity, even though under torture he admitted to having observed some Jewish customs in years past. The inquisitors appear to have given him the benefit of doubt. In the auto-de-fé of December 8, 1591, Tomás abjured his sins de vehementi and was assigned a light penance, fined three hundred pesos, and again set free.[74]

This second brush with the Holy Office did not dissuade Tomás from continuing to Judaize with his friends. In 1592 he again celebrated the Passover in Tlatelolco with the Carvajals, this time in the company of Manuel de Lucena and Manuel Gómez Navarro.[75] In 1593 he purchased his hacienda de minas in Taxco.[76] In March he observed the Fast of Esther with Clara Enríquez, Justa Méndez, Manuel de Lucena, and his wife, Catalina.[77] A sense of calm seems to have settled over his life. Nonetheless, he continued to take precautions, beginning to shelter some of his assets by recording his purchase of slaves and mules under the name of his employee Tomás de Cardoso.[78]

Fueled by the expanded information in their files, on May 3, 1595, the Inquisition ordered Alonso Pérez Serrano to take two black slaves armed with swords to Tomás's hacienda in Taxco to arrest him as a relapsed heretic, a crime almost always punished by death. When Fonseca saw the men approaching, he jumped on a horse and galloped wildly down the mountain, but the two slaves rapidly overtook him. Pérez spent the next few days calming Fonseca's employees and taking the steps necessary to ensure that the hacienda's production of silver would not falter during Fonseca's absence.[79]

The first audience in this, his third arrest for Judaizing, came on June 22, 1595. In response to prosecutor Bohórquez's detailed charges, he acknowledged his two earlier incarcerations but insisted that both were the result not of his guilt but of poisonous denunciations by enemies:

> Manuel de Lucena, Manuel Gómez, Gómez's brother Sebastián Rodríguez, Justa Enríquez [he meant Justa Méndez], Manuel Rodríguez, and the wife of Manuel de Lucena [Catalina Enríquez] are all enemies because I have had differences and arguments with them with angry, hurtful words.

He reluctantly admitted that there had been no third-party witnesses to these disputes.[80]

What young Tomás probably did not know was that this time the prosecutor's case was based on the detailed reminiscences of twenty individuals, harvested over five years during their own procesos for Judaizing. These included statements from Francisca de Carvajal and four of her children: Luis, Isabel, Ana, and Leonor; from Manuel de Lucena and two of the Enríquez women: Lucena's wife, Catalina Enríquez, and Justa Méndez; and from many of Lucena's and Carvajal's circle of close friends. Their depositions describe Sabbaths and holidays spent with young Tomás, his attention to Jewish dietary regulations, his scorn for the sacraments of the church and the external trappings of Catholicism, his enthusiasm for stories from the Jewish Bible, his love of discussion of halachic precepts, his repertoire of prayers, and his yearning for the coming of the Jewish Messiah.

The most damning evidence was the packet of written Jewish prayers found on him when he was arrested. These he attempted to pass off as hand-copied notes on Psalms that he remembered having read in Latin years before. He said he kept them with him because he recited them daily. When the inquisitors reminded Tomás that he had previously testified that he did not understand Latin, his tangled attempt to explain the inconsistency convinced no one. Equally unconvincing was his claim that he ended the prayers merely with the word *gloria*, without invoking the Father, Son, and Holy Spirit, because he understood that *gloria* automatically included the three persons of the Trinity.[81]

In September, when the inquisitors reminded Tomás that during his second imprisonment, in 1591, he had confessed to many Judaizing activities, he protested that under torture he had said a lot of untrue things to keep from being tortured more. In the days following this interview, he reflecting on his recent ordeal and came to the conclusion that this strategy was not working. On October 7 he requested an audience and promised to come clean "in order to relieve my conscience, . . . even though it might result in harm to my person, my honor, my children[82] and the loss of my hacienda." He admitted to having Judaized in the late 1580s in Taxco and blamed Baltazar Rodríguez de Carvajal and Francisco de Cáceres (both by then absent from New Spain and thus unavailable for interview) for having led him astray. He steadfastly insisted that the Judaizing was in the past and that now he was wholly Christian. Then he suddenly fell on his knees, clasped his hands together as if in prayer, begged for mercy, and admitted that up until his 1591 incarceration, he had indeed practiced Judaism, believing that it was essential for the salvation of his soul, but that his jailhouse conversion to Christianity had been real.[83]

Over the next month, during intense grilling in which he was confronted with allegations of much more recent Judaizing, he tangled himself in a web of conflicting replies. Confronted with testimony from other prisoners that he had refused to eat prison food that contained pork, he protested that he had left the meat by the cell door not because it was pork but because he had already eaten his fill. As for all the Portuguese friends who regularly visited him in Taxco, he admitted that they had indeed Judaized in his presence, but he protested that he had resisted them as best he could and that he had in particular shied away from Luis de Carvajal.[84] Asked why he had lied to them for so long, he said he had been attempting to safeguard his children and preserve his property.

In audiences all through the winter and spring of 1595–1596, Tomás tried to explain himself. He blamed his self-incrimination on his fears, and he begged the Holy Office to deal with him mercifully. In July 1596, threat of torture improved his memory for details about the Taxco and Mexico City Judaizing communities, and in particular the Carvajal and Enríquez-Lucena families.

On September 13, 1596, the inquisitors and the tribunal of advisers voted to remand Tomás to the secular authorities for execution, but as his mine of knowledge about the Judaizing communities was still yielding useful nuggets of information, he was not included in the auto-de-fé of December 8. Instead, the inquisitors left Tomás in his cell, and for the next four years they intermittently called him to the audience chamber to answer further questions. Finally, on October 20, 1600, seeing that his vein of information had run dry and that he was no longer of any use to them, the tribunal resolved that the previously voted sentence be carried out at the next public auto-de-fé. On March 25, 1601, Tomás de Fonseca Castellanos was garroted and his body was consumed by flames.

Manuel de Lucena and Catalina Enríquez[85]

When the news of Isabel Rodríguez de Andrada's arrest reached Pachuca in May 1589, it provoked a panic among the friends gathered at the home of Manuel de Lucena and Catalina Enríquez. After a long night of frenzied activity and talk of impending arrests and precipitous flight, with dawn the first rush of fear began to fade. But over the next weeks, as one by one Isabel's Carvajal siblings and many of their Judaizing friends were arrested, the Lucenas threw themselves into contingency planning. In early summer, Lucena, increasingly worried about protecting the wealth he had accumulated, wrapped up all the silver in his possession and carried it in the dead of night to his friend Cristóbal Gómez to hide for him. But a few days later, when the dreaded knock at the door still had not come, Gómez returned the unopened packages of silver and shared with Lucena his dreams of escape:

> If God would only give me enough to go someplace where I could serve him without these scares, even if it was only just enough to pay my debts, I would go, even if I had to leave without a single *tomín*. If God has sustained us here, where we have offended him so greatly, surely he would do even more for us if we were to serve him.[86]

Lucena assured Gómez that he felt the same way. But, unlike Jorge de Almeida and Antonio Díaz de Cáceres, neither Gómez nor Lucena put their dreams of flight into action.

Instead, with the comforting routines of store and household, an aura of normalcy returned to the Lucena-Eriquez families. From autumn 1590 through 1593, Lucena continued to talk about Judaism with his friends. On the roads between the capital and Pachuca, Lucena discussed the Bible with traveling companions such as his father-in-law, Simón Paiba, Duarte Rodríguez, Antonio López, Jorge Váez, Manuel Gómez Navarro, and the pearl merchant Juan de Ayllón.[87] When Diego Enríquez was released from prison in 1590, he came to Lucena's store in Pachuca, and there the two men buoyed each other with religious conversation.[88] Lucena's Pachuca home continued to function as a salon, if not a full-fledged synagogue.[89] For Yom Kippur in 1590, a large group gathered at their house, despite the fact that by then several more members of the community had been taken to the Inquisition's Secret Prison.[90] Nearly every week, Lucena's friends and colleagues met at his home to celebrate the Sabbath with prayer and song and rejoicing.[91] When Beatriz and Catalina were in Mexico City, similar groups gathered at their home there. When Jorge Álvarez, Diego López Regalón,[92] Antonio López, and Fabián Granados joined the Enríquez family one evening, Lucena read Bible passages aloud and talked to them and Catalina's family about the prophets.[93] The Enríquez and Carvajal families gathered together for Passover in 1591 in Tlatelolco, where Luis de Carvajal was serving his penance.[94] When Luis completed his penance and was free to move about, he could frequently be found with Lucena in Pachuca. In 1593 Luis observed Passover there with the Enríquez-Lucena family, Justa Méndez, Manuel Gómez Navarro, and Francisco Váez. For Sukkot of 1591, Lucena took his wife to Álvaro de Carrión's ranch in Tilcuautla for an idyllic few days in the country.[95] The following year he and Sebastián Rodríguez tried hard, though unsuccessfully, to induce Carrión to be more consistent in his Judaizing.[96] In September 1594 Luis was again in Pachuca for Yom Kippur, but this time he did not stay with the Lucenas because Manuel told him that his presence would provoke too much negative comment about the family.[97]

This idyll ended in autumn 1594. On Saturday, October 29, the Inquisition's chief prosecutor, Dr. Martos de Bohórquez, judging that the twenty-three witnesses who had attested to Lucena's heretical statements and Judaizing activities were sufficient, signed the order for his arrest.[98] Shortly afterward, Lucena found himself in the Cárcel Secreta in Mexico City.[99] His wife and children remained at home in Pachuca.

On November 3, inquisitors took thirty-year-old Lucena upstairs to the audience chamber to face them for the first time. Lucena identified himself as a businessman with residence in Pachuca. He told inquisitors that his whole family was Portuguese and that most had been born in either Fundão or São Vicente da Beira, towns where some of his aunts and uncles, two of his five brothers, and his only sister were still living. He said that one of his uncles on his mother's side had gone to Peru, and his other three brothers had followed him there. One of these brothers, Antonio Váez, was a slaver; the other two, Gaspar and Baltazar de Lucena, were living in the Andean mining community of Potosí. He stated that he and his wife, Catalina Enríquez, had four living children: Clara, seven; Felipe, four; Simón, three; and Tomás, aged a year and a half. An unnamed daughter had died when she was about ten. He neglected to mention that Catalina was at that moment six months pregnant.

The inquisitors had three immediate tasks: to sequester Lucena's assets, to get the rest of Lucena's Mexican Judaizing family into jail, and to figure out what to do with the children.

Lucena knew that the Holy Office would move swiftly against his material possessions, so he persuaded his cell mate Luis Díaz to pen a letter to Lucena's business colleagues in Pachuca, instructing them to draw down his cash on hand by paying off as many of his outstanding debts as they could. They were to tell Gómez Pertierra, his business partner and manager of his branch store in Real del Monte, to continue processing silver ore, and to caution Pertierra to guard against thieves by never leaving Lucena's store unattended. Most of all, Lucena urged them to tell his "darling wife" not to come to the capital, even if the Inquisition should hold him there for two years, and to reassure "his little angels" that the blessings of God would cover and protect them. The letter was never sent. Luis Díaz, a sometimes Judaizing priest, had his own troubles with the Holy Office. Trying to gain favor by spying on the Judaizers, he turned the letter over to the Inquisition almost before the ink was dry.[100]

Nevertheless, somehow the word got to Pachuca, and Catalina and Lucena's friends took steps to safeguard as much as they could. Already by mid-November, Catalina had sent a packet of valuable items to the family friend Juan de Casal, then *mayordomo* of Agustín Guerrero's hacienda de minas in nearby Atotonilco, for safekeeping. Helping her hide the material were her brothers Pedro and Diego Enríquez; her mother, Beatriz Enríquez la Paiba; and her Chichimeca servant.[101]

In December Gómez Pertierra wrote to Mexico City that thieves had punched a hole in the wall of Lucena's store and made off with inventory worth two thousand pesos, including cash, silver, and jewels. Pertierra's letter made clear that he wanted to absolve himself of any culpability for the robbery, and even more so of guilt by association with the accused Judaizer and his friends.

> I have 1,600 pesos of Lucena's assets stored with Hernando de Castro, though 600 pesos are money he owes to Juan de Miranda.... Instruct me what to do. I do not want any suspicion to fall on me in this matter. Although it is true that I have associated myself with these people, it is because I was poor and in great need, and I did not understand or even suspect that they were bad Christians.

On December 21, Pertierra, who had not yet received an answer from the Holy Office, wrote again. "Lucena's wife wants to go to Mexico City and she wants me to go with her. I have no one to leave in charge of the store."[102]

Two days later the Holy Office dispatched Pedro de Vega, a royal scribe and state's attorney of the Real Audiencia, to Pachuca to look into the robbery and to seize anything of Lucena's that he could still lay his hands on. Vega interviewed Lucena's stock boy, Juan de la Serna, and Gómez Pertierra, who voiced his suspicion that the robbery had been staged in an attempt to spirit away and shelter some of Lucena's most valuable assets. Pertierra reported that Catalina Enríquez said she had heard the noise of the break-in but had been too frightened to open her door. He vowed that he himself had heard nothing. Vega did not formally conclude that the burglary had been a ruse, but he hinted that it was likely.[103]

The Inquisition next turned its attention to the other Judaizing members of the Lucena-Enriquez family. Late in December, inquisitors Alonso de Peralta and Bartolomé Lobo Guerrero tasked Pedro de Vega with bringing back from Pachuca Lucena's wife, Catalina Enríquez, very advanced in her pregnancy, and his mother-in-law, Beatriz Enríquez la Paiba. Vega in turn commissioned Alonso Pérez Serrano, an Inquisition familiar in Pachuca, to attend to the matter. Vega allotted Pérez Serrano eighty-seven pesos to cover trip expenses and instructed him to turn over any unspent portion to the prison's warden to help pay for the women's maintenance during their first year of confinement. Pérez Serrano hired a teamster named Redondo to transport the women in his mule cart. The transport fee, including meals and lodging for three days and a pair of gloves that Pérez Serrano bought for one of the women, came to twelve pesos and six tomines.[104] The women entered the Cárcel Secreta on December 29.

The Holy Office's remaining concern was to see that the family's young children were fostered out to a responsible guardian. Baby Tomás accompanied his mother to her prison cell, along with Catalina's Indian servant Juana to help take care of the child.[105] The older children's physical well-being was important, of course, but for the Inquisition it was more crucial that the children be raised in an environment free of any taint of Jewish beliefs or practices. Pedro de Vega selected as foster parents Juan López Tavera and his wife, Margarita Quijada, who were of impeccable Christian reputation and knew Lucena and his family.[106] Along with the three older children, Vega relegated to López Tavera's care four of Lucena's household servants, including a Chichimeca woman named Catalina who had been baby Tomás's wet nurse and who at the time of Catalina's arrest still had several months outstanding on her service obligation to the family.[107]

Vega arranged for several household items to accompany the children to the foster home. There were bedclothes: three linen sheets, one used and two brand new; three blankets, two Mexican and one Castilian; and two cambric pillowcases with green ribbons. He included a smattering of clothing as well: some old shirts of Catalina's and eight head scarves, some of them embroidered and some trimmed with lace. He also allotted one hundred pesos to cover the expense of food and clothing for the children and their servants for a year.

López Tavera soon complained that the sum was not enough. On July 1, 1595, he petitioned the Inquisition for more money, alleging that he had already spent the entire one hundred pesos. "The children are running around naked," he wrote, "because the few clothes their mother sent with them are all in tatters and they need shirts and a featherbed and two sheets because they are just innocent children." The Inquisition sent him another fifty pesos. Two months later, López Tavera petitioned again: "The one hundred fifty pesos has not even covered the cost of food; the children are naked, their skin is peeking out. I've bought them shoes and shirts but these are all worn out." The inquisitors disbursed another fifty pesos. On November 23 López Tavera came back to the well: "I've fed them and bought them clothes to keep them from going naked; it has been six months since I have had any clothing made for them; they need food and clothing; the girl is almost grown up and she needs a dress." They sent him another fifty pesos, and shortly afterward, not quite two years after they had placed the Lucena children in López Tavera's care, they removed them.[108] It is unclear what happened next to the two younger children, but the inquisitors sent Clara, the eldest, to live with her mother, Catalina Enríquez, in the Perpetual Prison in Mexico City.

The Cárcel Perpétua was less of a prison than a mandatory boarding house, where prisoners were assigned in small groups to cells in the men's or women's section. Penitents remanded to the Cárcel Perpétua were required to spend their nights in the prison, but during the day they were expected to go about their business to earn money for their upkeep. The penitents knew that they had to project scrupulous observance of Christian custom

> and avoid any hint of Judaizing because they were watched, both inside and outside the prison, by Inquisition officials and by fellow prisoners who worked for the Holy Office as informers.

Two years later, Clara was fostered out again, this time to Mateo de Santa Ana and his wife, Juana de Robles. In January 1603, during her own trial, seventeen-year-old Clara claimed that she had received no Christian instruction when she was living with her parents in Pachuca, nor from López Tavera or his wife, nor from Catalina Enríquez during their shared time in jail. She swore that it was the Santa Ana family that taught her that the Jewish beliefs she had absorbed from her mother ran contrary to Christianity. The Santa Anas' daughter Ana de Tuesta reported in her testimony one particularly shocking incident. She said that when Clara had observed Ana lifting her eyes to a household icon and praying "O Virgen María Santísima," Clara had chided her: "Señora Ana, she wasn't a virgin because she gave birth; she'd been fucked!"[109] Ana's father, in his testimony, said that her two teenage cousins had been just as scandalized as Ana was. He speculated that Clara must have learned those words from her parents. But as to Clara's own true beliefs, "only God knows what is in her heart." Ana de Tuesta added that she'd overheard Clara singing a scurrilous ditty that Clara claimed she had learned from her parents' friend Luis de Carvajal, the heretic who had been burned:

> Santa Barbola is in Heaven, turned into a star.
> God protect me from lightning and the tree of the Cross.
> Everybody say "Amen, Jesus."[110]

On November 8, 1594, five days after the initial audience in which Manuel de Lucena described his family and narrated for inquisitors his abbreviated life story, he was asked to speak fully and honestly about his Judaism. As was almost always the case in the trials of Judaizers in Mexico, initially he denied the allegations and was warned of the consequences to his body and soul of not making a complete confession. A week later the principal actors reprised their roles, and Lucena was returned to his cell with another warning. After several weeks in which he was left to meditate on his conscience and his fate, Lucena came to a decision about the strategy he would take in his defense: he would make a full confession. He had been a Jew, he had been proud of being a Jew, but now he wanted to be a Christian. On December 20, 1594, Lucena requested an audience.

> I have kept the Law of Moses for the past seven years.... Antonio López from Celorico, who went back to Spain four years ago . . . taught me the Law of Moses as I was coming and going on the road in his company from Mexico City to Pachuca.... He was well read in the Bible . . . and he taught me a great prayer that begins: "Adonai, open my lips so that they may proclaim your praise. Blessed are you, Adonai, our God and God of our fathers Abraham, Isaac, and Jacob."[111]

Over the next two years, Manuel de Lucena spoke expansively about his Jewish beliefs and practices. He also attempted to make clear that he now considered himself a Christian. Explaining his current view of Psalm 72 and certain verses in Isaiah dealing with last days, he said,

> Before I converted to our holy Catholic faith I misunderstood them, because I was blind, wandering in a fog without light; now that I have converted I understand them Catholically, and that God through his prophets wanted to say that because of the people of Israel's sins—the greatest of them being not having recognized his precious son Jesus Christ to be the true Messiah—that they would be scattered and wander afflicted and beaten down; and that little by little God would bring them knowledge of his precious son our redeemer Jesus Christ, and the Law of Grace.[112]

The inquisitors were interested in Lucena's current thinking but were even more interested in his wide circle of converso friends and colleagues, the majority of whom were Portuguese. In the course of his testimony, Lucena identified 118 individuals as being secret Jews.[113] He also tried, unconvincingly, to protect some of the people who were closest to him, as in this exchange:

"I held Luis de Carvajal and his mother and sisters to be good Christians, all of them converted to the Law of Christ."

"Why did you go visit Luis de Carvajal in Santiago if you think he such a good Christian, since you said you hate Christians so much, given the way you call them idolatrous dogs who are burning in Hell?"

"I used to say that. I befriended Luis de Carvajal not because he was a Christian but because he was poor; I had lots of poor Christians as friends."[114]

The person who caused Lucena the greatest concern was his wife, Catalina. When it was pointed out that his attempts at defending her were contradicted by the testimony of many witnesses, Lucena's only excuse was that love and the devil had directed his tongue to lie:

> I have tried to tell the truth, but for a long time the Devil deceived me and blinded me, holding up before me my love of flesh and blood, telling me that I would be doing wrong in speaking clearly about the person I love most in this life, who is my wife.[115]

When Lucena was not deliberately concealing details, he seemed to revel in his prodigious memory, describing the Judaizing statements and practices of himself and his family and friends in copious detail. Time and again he requested audiences with the Inquisitors to elaborate on the practices of the Judaizing communities of Pachuca and Mexico City. When inquisitors confronted Lucena with the statements of the witnesses against him, on the whole he corroborated their testimony. When, toward the end of his two-year incarceration, they read him the full, detailed Inquisition indictment against him, he had to admit that all of it was true.

Even though Lucena persisted in claiming that in prison God had granted him an understanding of the truth of Christianity and the rightness of the church's teachings, which had led to his sincere conversion to the law of Jesus Christ, he talked so enthusiastically and so knowingly about his life as a Jew that the inquisitors had a hard time believing his newfound Christian zeal. When on September 11, 1596, they pressed him on this point, Lucena answered by relating to them a prison debate he had recently had with Manuel Gómez Navarro, who had bragged how he was still clinging stubbornly to his Jewish beliefs. Lucena said he had advised Gómez Navarro that his best strategy would be to confess, ask the inquisitors for mercy, and request they assign someone to help him learn the law of Christ. The inquisitors were incredulous.

"You tried to convert him?"

"I said that I told him those things to see if he agreed with me, and to help him clarify what he was saying, because when people talk about things, it eases the pain that they have in their hearts."

"What pain do you have in your heart?"

"Seeing myself battling between two paths, one that is the Law of Jesus Christ and the other the Law of Moses, and knowing that I can only be saved in one of them."[116]

The inquisitors, further shocked by this revealing confession of doubt on the heels of so many months of assertion of certainty, challenged Lucena to state for them, in writing, the core issues that were still impeding his wholehearted acceptance of the law of Christ. Lucena jumped at the chance and shortly afterward handed them a numbered list of what for him were seven fundamental stumbling blocks:

Jews believe and the Bible says to believe in only one God, and the Christian God has three persons.
The Bible says that the law that God gave to Moses cannot be changed or added to, and the Christians have changed it.
The Bible promises that the Messiah will gather up the Jews and redeem them from captivity, but they are still dispersed and beleaguered. It says that the Messiah will impose one unified law, but the world is divided into many paths and sects. How, then, can Jesus be the Messiah?
Deuteronomy says that the people of Israel suffer when they draw away from the Law that God gave to Moses and worship idols, and that their suffering today comes from this.
God says to follow his law and promises that all blessings will flow from it; turning Christian will not cause their persecution to cease.
The Bible says that the Messiah will lead the scattered Jews to the Holy Land and rebuild Jerusalem, but none of that has happened.

> God says keep the seventh day as Sabbath and do not worship idols and many other things, but Christians do all those things differently.[117]

Unfortunately, the trial dossier does not include the inquisitors' point-by-point refutation of these concerns but merely reports that "they read their responses to him; and falling to his knees, he said that he was satisfied . . . and professed to live and die in the Law of Jesus Christ."[118]

On October 3, 1595, seven votes were cast, according to established procedure, by two Inquisitors—Peralta and Lobo Guerrero—and five honest and learned men. All seven agreed that Lucena must march in a penitential habit in an auto-de-fé and that all his property be confiscated. Three were of the opinion that he should serve ten years rowing in the king's galleys and spend the rest of his life in prison. Four voted that he be executed as an impenitent Judaizing heretic. In the auto-de-fé of December 8, 1596, the vote of the majority was carried out: Lucena was "garroted to death and his body burned in fire until it became ash so that no memory of him would be left."[119]

The first interrogation of Catalina Enríquez, Lucena's very pregnant wife, came on January 12, 1595, two weeks after she entered the prison. Catalina revealed her genealogy, narrated her capsule biography, and claimed that she was a good Christian of Old Christian stock who had been arrested only because of the malicious denunciation of Gómez Pertierra, whom she had criticized for selling too much on credit.[120] A month later Catalina went into her sixth labor, and the unusually intense pains led her to fear for her life. She called for help and a delegation of inquisitors rushed to her cell. Catalina told them that she wanted to make full confession both of her Judaizing and that of her husband and his friends. With that promise, and their fear for her life, the inquisitors voted that she be reconciled immediately to the church. After performing an abbreviated ceremony of reconciliation in her cell, they administered the sacraments to her and called for the midwife María de Valverde to be brought in. The baby, unnamed in the documents, was born on February 17.[121]

True to her word, over the next twenty-one months, Catalina talked expansively about the Judaizing activities of the Enríquez-Lucena family and their wide circle of friends in Pachuca and Mexico City. In the end she convinced her inquisitors of the sincerity of her Christian belief and practice. On

November 23, 1596, they voted that she be formally reconciled to the church in the upcoming auto-de-fé, after which she be remanded to the Cárcel Perpétua and given religious instruction.

December 9, one day after marching in the auto-de-fé at which her husband, Manuel de Lucena, was garroted and his body burned, Catalina was assigned her penance: to fast every Friday, to pray the rosary every Friday and Sunday, and to make confession and take communion on the three major annual festivals.

But the Inquisition was not through with her yet. During the early summer of 1597, as part of their ongoing campaign to seize the remnants of her deceased husband's assets, inquisitors quizzed her several times about the dowry she had brought to her marriage. It is hard to judge Catalina's emotional state during this difficult year, with all but her youngest children fostered out and memories of the auto-de-fé fresh in her mind. It seems that she found some consolation among the community of reconciled Judaizers living in the Cárcel Perpétua. Late in September 1597, the prison's warden, Diego de Espinosa, reported that Catalina had begun living openly with Domingo Cuello and that both he and the community of prisoners were scandalized at the couple's behavior, not only because of the widow's immodesty but because everyone knew that Cuello was married and had left a wife behind in Spain. The inquisitors ordered that Cuello be barred from entering Catalina's cell upon penalty of two hundred strokes with the lash.[122]

Catalina was still incarcerated in the Perpetual Prison when she died in 1601.[123] Of Catalina's surviving five children, of three—Felipe, Tomás, and the unnamed baby born in prison—nothing is known. The other two, Clara and Simón, left a thin paper trail.

Simón, who took for himself the surname Paredes, twice ran afoul of the Holy Office. In 1613 the Inquisition charged him with assuming privileges that the law denied to the children and grandchildren of convicted heretics: riding on horseback, carrying a sword, and wearing elegant, expensively accessorized clothing. On July 20 the Inquisition pronounced his sentence: "Henceforth you shall call yourself Lucena or Enríquez, which are your parents' surnames; and you shall not ride a horse, or carry any weapons, or wear gold, silver, pearls, silk, or fine cloth, under pain of a hundred lashes." By 1619 Simón had settled in Cuernavaca, working as a barber and surgeon, now adopting the name Simón Gómez and telling people that his wife, Francisca de Medina, whom none of the witnesses against him had ever actually met, was in Mexico City, or else in Puebla, or perhaps Cholula, or Tlaxcala. Witnesses described Simón as a thin-faced, long-nosed man with a yellowish complexion and a sparse reddish beard, who in his habits of dress favored blue stockings. In 1621 Simón, now twenty-nine years old, was arrested a second time and charged not with Judaizing but with the same offenses as before: wearing prohibited clothing and going about armed on horseback—essentially, with trying to mask the fact that he was the child of convicted Judaizers.

Paredes/Gómez/Lucena/Enríquez admitted his guilt but claimed that everybody violated those prohibitions, whereupon he named several offenders, including two of his relatives. "I have seen them wearing silk and fine cloth, carrying arms, and for that reason, and because I am married to an honorable women, I dared to do it too." Then he threw himself on the mercy of the court, which sentenced him as before and prohibited him from leaving Mexico City. The file ends with his pathetic plea to have that restriction lifted:

> I have this city for my prison, as you ordered, but I am very poor, and in need, and have no one to help me, nor any way of earning a living. Though I have sent for my wife and children, they are so poor that they cannot come, and my wife lies stricken from having just given birth and she has no one to turn to. . . . I humbly beg that I be permitted to go help my wife. I will bring her to this city and remain here until you order me otherwise.[124]

In 1629 María de Landeta,[125] a witness in a case concerning the fifth sibling, thought that Paredes/etc. might be living with his uncle Pedro Rodríguez in Las Amilpas.[126]

This fifth sibling was Clara Lucena. After the account of when young Clara scandalized her foster parents with her blasphemous tongue, her only other appearance in the documents records rumors of her death. Landeta testified that she had heard Clara's brother Simón say that he had heard from Clara's aunt Justa Méndez in Llerena, Spain, that Clara had died, and she added that her brother suspected that Justa had murdered Clara, perhaps by throwing her in a well, because she was fearful of Clara's Judaizing.[127]

With the exception of that single hint of Jewish practice, there is no record

Figure 15. Signature of Héctor de Fonseca. Used with permission of the Archivo General de la Nación, Mexico City.

of any of Manuel de Lucena and Catalina Enríquez's children carrying on their parents' traditions of Judaizing.

Héctor de Fonseca[128]

All through 1595 and early 1596, Francisca de Carvajal and her imprisoned children talked to inquisitors about Héctor de Fonseca's Judaizing activities. So too did Justa Méndez, Marco Antonio, Manuel de Lucena, Jorge Álvarez, and Sebastián Rodríguez. Héctor's file grew thick. On March 4, 1596, Pedro de Fonseca, the Inquisition notary, and Garci Rodríguez, a miner in Taxco who had been deputized by the Inquisition, went to Rodrigo Tirado Morlite's house in Taxco, where Héctor was talking with a group of friends, and arrested him "without any scandalous fuss, and sequestered his hacienda and possessions."[129] Héctor was forty-eight years old. His three younger brothers—Jorge de Almeida and Miguel and Francisco Hernández—had all fled the country. His Old Christian wife and their three children, the oldest of whom was seven, remained in Taxco.

After being left to stew in his cell for two months, early in May Héctor was called to the audience chamber to account for himself. Like most of his contemporary unfortunates, at first he swore that he was a believing, practicing Christian, and he denied ever having been a Jew or having practiced any Jewish customs. When confronted with the specifics of witness testimony, he attempted to discredit the reports by claiming that the witnesses were his enemies and undoubtedly were lying. He included on his tachas list Antonio Díaz de Cáceres, Justa Méndez,[130] and all the Carvajals, adducing another list of miners and their employees who could corroborate that they had been feuding. When pressed, he also admitted that he had since smoothed things over with the Carvajals and had gone back to visiting them and eating with them at their home. In between interrogation sessions, back in his cell, he and his cell mate Sebastián Rodríguez entertained each other by teaching each other all the Jewish prayers they could remember.[131] After eleven months of audiences, and finally realizing that his protestations of innocence would never be believed, in late February 1597 Héctor requested to meet with his interrogators. His revised strategy was to acknowledge the Judaizing acts while portraying himself as a poor doubting sinner, a Christian at heart, who had been led astray by others.

On his knees and with many tears, taking the cross from the table and kissing it, he said that he had requested this audience to speak the truth and to reveal his sins, adding that since he had felt no shame in committing them, he had no right to feel shame in confessing them.[132]

The inquisitors pressed him about why he had not confessed previously.

He said that he had not confessed because he had daughters, and it was out of concern for his daughters' and his wife's honor, and the infamy that would attach to them. He thought his sins were hidden and not of the visible sort that should be reported. He promised in his heart that he would denounce himself to the Holy Office once he had found husbands for them.[133]

Héctor then recounted how fourteen years earlier, the silversmith Luis Díaz had spoken to him about the Law of Moses, and how from that point on he had lived in confusion about which was the better law, and which would save his soul, observing first one law and then the other, and sometimes bits of both of them simultaneously. He also blamed several of the Carvajals, Antonio de Morales, Francisco Jorge, and Sebastián Rodríguez for proselytizing to him. However, Héctor was not adept at lying, and in his struggle to distance himself from responsibility he often confused names, dates, and events. The inquisitors noted every discrepancy and hammered him about his inconsistencies.

In August 1597, a year and a half after his arrest, the syphilis that had been gradually eroding Héctor's body erupted into virulent sores on his face and elsewhere. In an effort to save his life, the Inquisition transferred him to the Hospital de las Bubas, the syphilitics' hospital, ordering the supervising physician to prevent Héctor from speaking to anyone besides the medical staff and Inquisition officials.[134] Two weeks later Héctor was back in his cell, and there he sat for the next eight months. High on his list of worries was his hacienda de minas with its six mine shafts and its processing plant. On May 4, 1598, Héctor requested an audience. He said that he'd been in jail a long time, and he was aware that if a mine was not being worked, someone else could rightfully claim it. "I beg you to order [my employees] to keep digging," he pleaded, "because the mines are valuable and I don't want anyone else to take them. . . . I don't want them to be sold on the cheap to settle my debts."[135]

There is no record of whether anyone complied with this request. What is clear is that Héctor's most pressing concern was not his wife and children, the sickness in his body, or the disposition of his immortal soul. Like so many of the Judaizers in the mining towns, what kept him awake nights was the precarious condition of his financial well-being. On September 22, he again requested an audience, this time to declare and assert his ownership of five shares in Pedro de Prado's rich Margarita Mine.[136]

In between audiences with the inquisitors, Héctor spent much of 1599 in conversation with fellow converso prisoners in the Secret Prison. In the intimacy of their shared misfortune, they were enveloped by a sense of camaraderie; they joked, complained, and shared their scorn for Christians and their hatred of the Inquisition. The Inquisition-placed informants reported their most incriminating conversations as close to verbatim as they were able.

> Manuel Tavares said . . . that the inquisitor don Alonso [de Peralta] had died after six days in a seizure, and that *o Demó* had taken him, which all the prisoners laughed at . . . and in particular Héctor de Fonseca who said that all of them came to a bad end. . . . I asked Manuel Tavares what did it mean that when the inquisitor don Alonso died the *Demó* had taken him, and he said that *o Demó* in the Portuguese language means the Devil, which made everybody laugh.[137]

Hector's illness came back worse than before, and in October 1599 he was again remanded to the Hospital de las Bubas, where he remained all through the next year, while additional testimony from further witnesses piled up against him. When inquisitors asked him to comment on these new charges, he replied that "with my illness, my head and my memory have grown weak, and I beg mercy as a faithful Christian for what I cannot remember."[138] When confronted specifically with reports about his role in the marriage muddle with Mariana de Carvajal so many years previous, both his lucidity and his anger returned.

> May I be burned if I lie about this. By God, the witness is lying, because in Taxco I fled from the Carvajals as I would from devils, because they had quarreled with my wife Juana López, so we did not talk to each other. ... [As to Mariana,] may the heavens rain justice! I was eager for doña Mariana, Luis de Carvajal's sister, not so that I could marry her, because I was already married, but to have sex with her. That is why Antonio Díaz de Cáceres and Jorge de Almeida came after me with a knife. ... If I've already confessed that I used to keep the Law of Moses, why would I lie about this?[139]

On November 21, 1600, Héctor de Fonseca was sentenced to life imprisonment in the Cárcel Perpétua with confiscation of all his property. The sentencing document notes that he would have been condemned to death were it not for his age and infirmities. He was reconciled formally with the church in the auto-de-fé of March 25, 1601, and sent back to his cell. For the next three years he never missed a Friday night dinner with his two best friends in prison, Antonio Méndez and Ruy Díaz Nieto, who was so fussy about the ritual purity of his food that he would eat only meals prepared by Isabel and Violante Rodríguez or Héctor, who would cook for him there in the prison.[140]

Old Tomás de Fonseca of Tlalpujahua[141]

When Julián de Castellanos was arrested in April 1590, he gave inquisitors a long list of conversos in Mexico City who were secret Jews.[142] Among those he denounced was his half brother old Tomás de Fonseca, with whom he said

Destruction and Survival 279

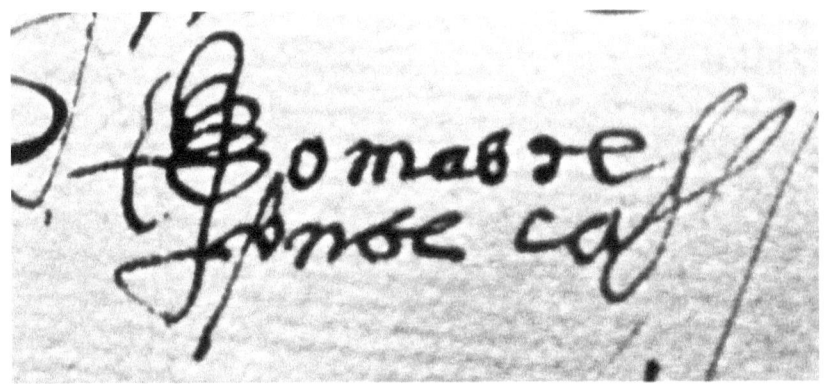

Figure 16. Signature of old Tomás de Fonseca. Used with permission of the Archivo General de la Nación, Mexico City.

he had shared many religious confidences and practices. That was enough to set the inquisitorial wheels in motion.

On July 3, 1590, Matías González, an Inquisition familiar, accompanied by Tlalpujahua's alcalde de minas and the Inquisition bailiff Pedro de Villegas, arrested old Tomás and seized his hacienda de minas. The Inquisition's first priority, as always, was to make certain that there be no interruption in the hacienda's production of silver, and for that it needed to designate an interim supervisor. González recommended that either of Tomás's sons, Lope or Teodosio, both in their early twenties, would do, as long as he worked in tandem with Jerónimo Pérez, who, as the estate's mayordomo, was already familiar with every aspect of the operation. The younger of the two boys, Lope de Fonseca, who had already been working on the hacienda for some years, got the job. Diego López Tavaltero was named formal overseer to look out for the Inquisition's financial interests. The arresting officer sold ten of the hacienda's mules to cover the costs of taking Tomás to jail. This arrangement did not please Tlalpujahua's alcalde de minas, who, fearing that the loss would negatively affect production, swore that he would not issue any mercury to the mine until he received guarantees that the interim administration would make no changes to the hacienda's proven work protocols.[143]

In late July 1590, Julián de Castellanos recanted his testimony. The Inquisition suspended its case against him and released the people Julián had identified as Judaizers.[144] From old Tomás's sequestered assets, the Holy Office deducted seventeen pesos for the expenses of his arrest, transportation, and lodging en route to prison; five pesos, paid to the prison's warden for administrative overhead; and forty-six reales (5.75 pesos) for the cost of Tomás's food for the three weeks he had been in jail. The proceeds from the sale of the mules seem to have been forgotten. On July 20 the remaining pesos were returned to the now free man.[145]

Old Tomás was ebullient. No sooner did he leave the Cárcel Perpétua than he ran to Luis de Carvajal's lodgings and, in the company of Luis and his mother and his sisters Mariana and Leonor, danced and sang a Spanish version of the Hebrew hymn "Mi k'mochah":

Who is strong and powerful? Who can do good deeds or ill?
Who? Do you want to know who? Adonai, who is powerful.[146]

Then, old Tomás de Fonseca, whom friends were now speaking of as the "old man with the long beard,"[147] returned to Tlalpujahua to resume his mining activities with the help of Lope and Jerónimo Pérez. He also began to travel more often to Mexico City. Old Tomás could often be found on Calle San Agustín in the store of his friend Cristóbal Gómez, a fervent crypto-Jew who was close to most of the prominent Judaizing merchants and miners of his day.[148] In Gómez's store, in Antonio Díaz Márquez's store, in the Tlatelolco house where the Carvajals were serving out their penance, and in Lucena's Mexico City residence, old Tomás shared the joy of participating in communal Jewish life. He visited his nephews Miguel Hernández and Jorge de Almeida when they were in hiding behind the Tlatelolco Indian market. Tomás, by now in his seventies, was several decades older than most of the others, and they respected him for his age, his knowledge of Latin, and his ability to his recount Bible stories.[149]

When the arrests began, old Tomás's incarcerated friends related to the Inquisition what they knew about his Judaizing activities. On April 4, 1596, the Inquisition rearrested old Tomás in Tlalpujahua and again sold some of his mules for expenses. Despite his ill health, he was transported in chains to the Cárcel Secreta in Mexico City.[150] Old Tomás seemed to be as much infuriated as frightened. As he complained to Manuel de Lucena in a prison conversation, "these Inquisition dogs have destroyed me by selling off for a pittance the mules I need to make a living in my mine."[151]

Again they turned over administration of his hacienda de minas to Lope. Fifteen-year-old Gabriel, Tomás's youngest boy, was now assisting his brother. Tomás's oldest son, Teodosio, was rumored to have just returned from a long absence in China. His two daughters, Beatriz and Ana, both in their early twenties, were still living with their mother, Ana Jiménez, in Mexico City.[152]

On May 6, 1596, during his first interrogation, old Tomás told inquisitors that enemies in Tlalpujahua had denounced him out of spite, since "miners are a grudge-bearing, cantankerous lot."[153] After a month of his refusing to say anything more substantive, they read him the charges against him: that he believed the Messiah had not come; that he did not believe in what the church holds to be true; that he Judaized with his many friends; that he believed that God would reward them in this life and the next; and that he gave material assistance and comfort to Judaizers who were hiding from the Inquisition. In repeated audiences, Tomás denied every charge.

In March 1597 the inquisitors read Tomás a transcript of all the witness testimony against him. Again Tomás remained obstinate, claiming that he was and had always been an observant Christian and that his denouncers—by then he had surmised most of their identities—were all enemies whose words could not be trusted.

He remained in prison. Over the next three years, as the purge of the Mexican Judaizers continued, new incidents of Judaizing involving old Tomás de Fonseca came to light, leading to new charges and new denials. During much of these long, boring, uncomfortable years, old Tomás shared his cell with Manuel Tavares, a Judaizer then in his early thirties, and Thomas Day, a young British Protestant. In due course the inquisitors learned how the two Judaizers were fascinated by Day's descriptions of so-called Lutheranism, with which Fonseca and Tavares found they had much in common, particularly their scorn for what they considered the Catholics' idolatrous worship of images. By mid-December 1600, Tomás, now approaching his eightieth birthday, made one last plea of innocence: "My feet are in the grave and I am concerned to save my soul; what [the witnesses] say about me is a great wickedness. . . . I beg you to absolve me and set me free."[154]

On December 20 the votes were cast and recorded: Tomás de Fonseca was found guilty and ordered to be reconciled with the church, penalized with the confiscation of all his property, and confined in the Cárcel Perpétua forever. On March 25, 1601, old Tomás, still defiant but forced to accept the inevitable, abjured his sins in a public auto-de-fé. He was returned briefly to jail and then, gravely ill, was transferred to the Convalescent Hospital. On February 6, 1602, notary Pedro de Fonseca was called to certify Tomás's death and supervise his burial in a niche in the wall of the Church of San Hipólito, one yard to the left of the doorway.[155]

As was so often the case, disputes over the property confiscated by the Inquisition lived on long after the principals. On March 22, 1606, Antonio de Castro Lobato brought suit to recover eighty-seven pesos and four tomines owed to him by Tomás de Fonseca of Tlalpujahua, noting that if his estate should be unable to pay, then the estate of old Tomás's guarantor, young Tomás de Fonseca Castellanos (who had been executed 1601), was responsible for payment. Castro's bookkeeper, the slave Juan Antonio, produced for the Holy Office the relevant account book and a promissory note that increased the sum that old Tomás owed to Castro and to Martín de Jaso to 259 pesos. The suit alleged that since the Inquisition had confiscated the property of both the debtor and the guarantor, the Inquisition itself was now liable for the debt. After review, García de Carvajal, the Inquisition attorney in charge, ruled that since both Fonsecas had been convicted of heresy, the Inquisition's claims trumped all others. He added that there was nothing left in either estate, the resources of both men having been exhausted to pay for their incarceration.[156]

Survivors

The purge of the 1590s culminated in the great auto-de-fé of 1596. During the next few years the Inquisition brought to resolution the cases of the Judaizers who remained incarcerated. With the community of overtly Judaizing Portuguese conversos and their friends virtually eliminated or neutralized, senior officials of the Inquisition and the viceroyalty seem to have felt that the problem of Mexico's community of Judaizers had been effectively addressed. In 1598 Spain had a new king, Felipe III, and he and his counselors were initially less aggressive in their pursuit of Judaizing New Christians. During the first six years of the seventeenth century, the Mexican Inquisition began only one new case against a Judaizer. In January 1602, inquisitors arrested Clara Enríquez, the teenage daughter of Catalina Enríquez and

Manuel de Lucena, whom they accused of having been taught to practice Judaism as a child by her mother in the Inquisition's Secret Prison and having continued to Judaize after she was taken from her mother and fostered out to an Old Christian family.[157]

During these same years, the Inquisition brought another two dozen cases against reconciled Judaizers who had violated the provisions of sentences that prohibited them from riding a horse, carrying a sword, or dressing in silk. It also listened to a handful of accusations against persons who had been observed removing the sinews from legs of lamb before roasting them, but it decided not to pursue any of the matters further.

Meanwhile, in Spain, a large group of wealthy Portuguese New Christians were lobbying to have the pope and the king declare a general pardon for Portuguese conversos who had been accused or convicted of Judaizing. And they backed their lobbying efforts with cash. Already in April 1601, in exchange for two hundred thousand *cruzados*, Felipe III had agreed to permit them to sell their property in Spain and to leave the country. During the following two years, intense negotiations were conducted in Rome and Valladolid—briefly at that time capital of Spain—for a more comprehensive pardon.[158]

Negotiations for a general pardon resumed early in 1604, and a *real cédula* (royal memorandum) ordered all further Inquisition activity regarding Judaizing conversos to be put on hold. On August 23 Pope Clement VIII signed a *breve*, and the Spanish Inquisition Suprema reluctantly ordered all tribunals to comply with its stipulations. Cases in progress were to be suspended; no new cases were to begin; sequestered property not yet entered in the Royal Treasury was to be returned; no one would be required to wear a sambenito; and the rights to ride a horse, dress in silk, and carry a weapon were to be restored. With regard to New Spain, however, persons who wished to avail themselves of the pardon would have to leave the country immediately.

The Mexican Inquisition delayed publication of these rules until shortly before the fleet was scheduled to depart for Spain. Eighteen converso prisoners in the Perpetual Prison petitioned the Holy Office to delay the sailing until they could get themselves to Veracruz. Among the eighteen were Marco Antonio; Diego and Ruy Díaz Nieto; Justa Méndez's mother, Clara Enríquez; Jorge Fernández; Antonio López; Ana López; Isabel Machado; Costanza, Duarte, and Isabel Rodríguez; and Héctor de Fonseca. By the end of the summer of 1604, Héctor was on his way back to Spain.[159]

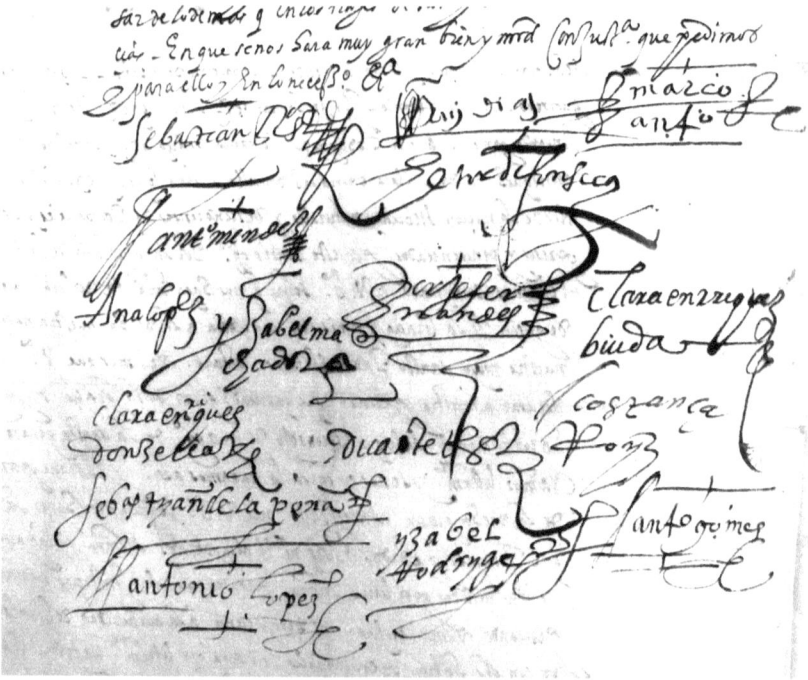

Figure 17. Signatures on a petition (AGN 279-8, 103v). Used with permission of the Archivo General de la Nación, Mexico City.

But before the promulgation of the pardon, back when it was still only an increasingly widely known rumor, a subtle change came over the Cárcel Perpétua. Rules seemed more relaxed. There was vigilance, but reports of infractions seemed likely not to be acted on. In this environment, the incarcerated survivors of the great purge of Judaizers that had culminated in the 1596 auto-de-fé were able to sustain a clandestine semblance of Jewish community life.

Although prisoners were forbidden from talking with each other about their cases or Inquisition procedures, they always did, even though they knew that some of their cell mates were Inquisition plants and that informers prowled the corridors at night to record whispered conversations. One of these informers was Juan Antonio de Oria.[160] In the summer of 1599 he related how Manuel Tavares, housed in an adjoining cell, used to cry out at the top of his lungs, asking for information about his father. Oria talked regularly with Manuel Álvarez, sometimes in Spanish and sometimes in Náhuatl, and with Álvarez's son Jorge, who was sharing a cell with a Flemish Lutheran named Adrián Suster.[161] When news of the sudden death of an inquisitor in Havana was passed around the cells, the conversos all laughed, Oria reported, particularly Héctor de Fonseca, who said he hoped that all inquisitors ended that way.[162]

Manuel Gil de la Guarda was a particularly enthusiastic stool pigeon. In 1603 he reported how the loosened conditions in the Cárcel Perpétua had permitted the Judaizing community to conduct an active social and religious life. When he reported that Ruy Díaz Nieto and Héctor de Fonseca were behaving suspiciously, the inquisitors told him to go back and gather up solid evidence, which for the next six months he did. In early autumn he requested an audience to deliver his reports report, but the Inquisitors put him off. Wait until after Yom Kippur and Sukkot, they instructed him, and tell us what they do. Gil's report was filled with revealing anecdotes. He said that his cell mate Ruy Díaz Nieto regularly took his meals with Antonio Méndez, Duarte Rodríguez, and Héctor de Fonseca. The four men observed the Sabbath together in one or another of their cells, carrying their food back and forth. They would observe Jewish fast days together, often with Sebastián Rodríguez and Sebastián de la Peña joining the group. Gil peppered his denunciations with tidbits such as how Díaz Nieto suffered from hemorrhoids and was particularly fond of eating raisins, cheese, and quince paste.[163]

On September 21, 1603, Sebastián Rodríguez hosted a large—and in Manuel Gil's opinion ostentatiously expensive—party, to which he invited the whole Portuguese Judaizing community resident in the prison. Sukkot, the Jewish harvest festival, is celebrated by building little booths outdoors, decorating the booths with ripe fruits and vegetables, and feasting there for three days with one's friends in thanks for the divine bounty. The men drew their tables out into the prison courtyard under the open sky. They decorated the pillars of the corridor with willow branches and leaves that Rodríguez had purchased and arranged to be carried to the prison by four Indians. Three of Rodríguez's invitees—Ruy Díaz Nieto, Héctor de Fonseca, and Antonio Díaz Márquez—turned down the invitation because, Gil de la Guarda speculated, they insisted on eating only food that was prepared to kosher standards, and "everyone else in the Cárcel Perpétua . . . eats salt pork and is not concerned about it." While Ruy Díaz Nieto sat in his cell praying, Héctor de Fonseca and Antonio Díaz Márquez decorated the corridor in front of their cell with branches and strewed the floor with twigs.

The non-Judaizing invitees to the Sukkot gala were the prison's warden, Diego de Espinosa; his wife; the Inquisition's registrar of sequestered property, Pedro de Fonseca; and his cousin Captain Esteban de Lemos. The host's cover story was that the party was to honor Captain Lemos, whom the viceroy had recently promoted to command rank. To reinforce this fiction, Rodríguez invited three of Lemos's command rank colleagues as well.[164]

The banquet itself was prepared in the kitchen of Sebastián Rodríguez's house, around the corner from the Cárcel Perpétua on Calle Santo Domingo. The cooks, under Sebastián's direction, were his wife, Costanza Rodríguez; Ana López; her daughter Leonor Díaz; and Sebastián de la Peña's wife, Isabel Rodríguez. The women slaughtered chickens in the kitchen, scattering ashes over the blood and then sweeping it up, plucking the feathers, and washing the carcasses thoroughly before roasting them. The women carried the roasts to their rooms in the Cárcel Perpétua to ready them for presenting the following day, when they were augmented with sweet pastries, meat pies, and white pudding that Sebastián de la Peña had contracted to be brought from outside. Strangely, the meal also included fried bacon, which the conversos would not have eaten except for the presence of the Christian guests. After they had all dined, they were joined by Justa Méndez and Juan López, one of Isabel Rodríguez's sons. Antonio López and his sister Ana Váez sang a selection of songs, after which everyone danced to tunes played by a musician from Puebla hired by Rodríguez. There was so much food left over that Sebastián Rodríguez had it taken the next day from his prison quarters back to those of his wife, Costanza Rodríguez, for her to share with conversas in the women's section of the prison.[165]

By then most of the miners—old Tomás de Fonseca, Jorge de Almeida, Antonio Díaz de Cáceres, young Tomás de Fonseca Castellanos, and Manuel de Lucena—were gone, some of them from Mexico, others from the world of the living. This thinly disguised Sukkot party in the Perpetual Prison appears to have been the last communal event celebrated by the remnants of Mexico's sixteenth-century Judaizing community.

Chapter 16

Some Conclusions

> [Díaz Nieto] said that in Madrid he knew Juan Rodríguez de Silva, a Portuguese, ... who had been in the Jewish quarter in Salonica ... and knew a little Hebrew ... and he was staying in Jorge de Almeida's house ... on the Correo Mayor. ... Juan Rodríguez de Silva had been in Ferrara, too. ... My father [Ruy Díaz Nieto] knew Jorge de Almeida because he had been in his house in Ferrara ... and he advised him to come [to Mexico] because it is such a rich land.
> —DIEGO DÍAZ NIETO, JANUARY 1601[1]

> Antonio Machado was very cautious about his daughters, and if one of them was with him when I came in [to talk about Jewish things], he sent her out of the room. ... Catalina Enríquez told me that Machado said he had never dared to teach his daughters about the Law of Moses ... except for the oldest one, Isabel. ... Pelayo Álvarez's daughters were lost because he had not taught them the Law of Moses ... on account of they had too many outside friends.
> —MANUEL DE LUCENA, APRIL 1591, 1596[2]

THE THREE EXTENDED families we have traced in *Living in Silverado* help us understand why and how so many Spanish-Portuguese converso families migrated to Mexico late in the sixteenth century. We have noted the range of Jewish knowledge and practices that these New Christian clans brought with them and how they accommodated their sense of Jewishness with their lives as Christians in the mining towns of central Mexico. Although these three family clans maintained ties with the central hub of colonial life in Mexico City, and some maintained dual residences in the mining towns and the capital, their relative isolation much of the time in small, peripheral communities affected how they sustained and transmitted their Jewishness. We have also explored the daily life of the members of these three clans in the pioneer Mexican mining world and seen the wide variety of ways in which silver was the economic lifeblood of these Portuguese-Spanish crypto-Jews.

In the stories of the conversos in these mining towns, several points are useful in considering the lives and fortunes of other relatively isolated groups of crypto-Jews in the worldwide Sephardic Diaspora.

The Character of the Players

Forty-two years ago a hiking companion, an organist friar in a monastery in the Spanish Pyrenees, told me (I don't know if in seriousness or in jest): "You Americans are different from us Europeans. It's genetic selection. You descend from the people who had the strength and the courage to get out and make new lives for themselves. We descend from the people who didn't." Some sociological research has corroborated that people who choose to emigrate tend to have a greater commitment to work, achievement, and power than does the general population.[3] Whether or not there is any truth to these hypotheses, they point to a character trait shared by most of the Portuguese conversos who in the late sixteenth century chose to make their living in the Mexican mining communities. They were, on the whole, an adventurous lot: self-assured, energetic, committed to their passions, ambitious, and willing to take risks.

Consider briefly the founding immigrants profiled in this book. Gabriel de Castellanos, the young Portuguese widower with three children, ran off with another man's pregnant wife and took her and the children to Mexico City, where he abandoned them to go dig for silver in the Ayoteco hills.

The four sons of the Portuguese bureaucrat Antonio Fernández de Almeida—Héctor de Fonseca, Jorge de Almeida, and Francisco and Miguel Hernández—were all decisive young men. They all fled the Portuguese Inquisition—Héctor directly to the silver mines of Mexico; the others to the New World by way of a stint in Ferrara. Jorge de Almeida, most successful of the brothers, became friends with Antonio Díaz de Cáceres, likewise a risk taker. Despite their ignorance of the world of mining, in the late 1580s the two men each bought a working hacienda de minas in Taxco. Their choice of the Carvajal sisters as wives was also a gamble, for the girls were conscientious and fervent Judaizers, while both men shied away from Jewish practice to protect their public personae as faithful Christians. As it turned out, they erred in trusting their ability to curb their wives' Judaizing behavior.

Manuel de Lucena was only thirteen when his parents sent him from Fundão to work in Sevilla, and only fourteen when his employer sent him to Mexico to assist in his brother Simón Paiba's store. Even as a teenager, Lucena's talents and passions stood out. In Mexico he married Paiba's daughter Catalina Enríquez, with whom he was deeply in love. He loved music, too, and was accomplished on the clavichord and the vihuela. He was widely read, and, despite his youth, Lucena's contemporaries considered him one of the sages of the community. He was good with numbers, was ambitious, and had a superb business sense. Not long after marrying, he struck off on his own to build a business Pachuca, a burgeoning mining town. He was not yet twenty years old.

All these men were strong-minded and not averse to taking risks. As we have seen, they put a high value on their sense of Jewishness and an equal or sometimes greater value on their economic ambitions and their need for sexual companionship, even when these conflicted with their Jewish identities. Many of the conversas who accompanied them as wives or consorts were likewise strong women who were fervent about what they held to be their Jewish obligations. This was true of Manuel de Lucena's wife, Catalina Enríquez, who remained close to her Jewishly observant parents while she was living in Pachuca, maintained the Enríquez-Paiba-Lucena household as a center of Judaizing activity even in her husband's absence, and, while she was prisoner in the Inquisition's Secret Prison, introduced her young daughter Clara Enríquez, who was incarcerated with her, to Judaizing practices. Similarly strong in their Jewish commitment were the two young Carvajal sisters, although the older of them, Antonio Díaz de Cáceres's wife, Catalina, who remained steadfast in her Judaizing despite her husband's attempt to stifle her activity, was brighter, more competent, and more willing to take initiatives than was Jorge de Almeida's wife, Leonor.

Branching Points

These men and women, like almost all the Spanish-Portuguese converso immigrants to Mexico in the sixteenth century, brought with them a powerful sense of Jewish identity that was the inheritance of the choices their immediate ancestors had made at the crucial decision points of their lives. Each of these branching points involved a choice between remaining in place and living with the risks of known but potentially worsening threats, or emigrating and braving the challenges of a new environment. Complicating the decision was that each of their own ancestors had lived simultaneously in multiple cultures, which infused their multiple senses of identity.[4] They grew up in the secular culture of their particular geographic location. They acquired the mores and practices of the culture of their professions. And they participated in the religious culture of their Jewish or Judaizing converso communities.[5] Because their professional identities were for the most part portable, the question of whether or not to emigrate—taken in its broadest sense of leaving one cultural milieu to take up residence in another—tended to focus on choice of place and choice of religion. Each decision required their ancestors to weigh carefully the relative values of those two cultures in their lives.

The first of the branching points for their Spanish ancestors was the 1492 so-called Alhambra Decree, which demanded that Jews choose between remaining in Spain or remaining Jewish. For the ancestors of most of the people discussed in *Living in Silverado*, Jewish identity came first: they left Spain and, when forcibly converted four years later in Portugal, chose to continue to Judaize clandestinely. In the 1560s and 1570s, in the face of intensifying activity by the Portuguese Inquisition, their children and grandchildren likewise had to choose between leaving Portugal and staying put, as well as whether to hold fast to their religious culture or adopt the beliefs and practices of the Christian majority. Those who elected religious assimilation even as they remained within their physical homes were emigrating from the crypto-Jewish community in which they had been raised to resettle in the culture of the Christian majority.

Those who opted to leave Portugal in the 1560s and 1570s had to choose where to go. They could seek out one of the European, Turkish, or North African havens that were relatively relaxed in allowing them to revert to

Judaism, or at least to put their religious commitment into semi-open practice without risking mortal consequences. Or they could go to Spain, or one of the Iberian overseas colonies, where the cultural ambience was familiar and where, at that moment, the Inquisition was not quite as menacing as in Portugal. A few, like Jorge de Almeida and two of his brothers, chose the first option, moving to the openly Jewish communities of Italy. Later, spurred by a change in circumstances or a change of heart, they returned to the Iberian Peninsula and then to the New World.

At no time did any of these people leave evidence that their reason for going to America was to find a greater degree of religious freedom. Neither did anyone express surprise at the fact that in Mexico, as in Spain and Portugal, they would be subject to scrutiny by the Inquisition. Opting to go to Mexico while remaining clandestine Jews in effect struck a balance between their religious and their secular cultures. While Jewish identity remained important to them, so too did the familiar ambience of the Iberian way of life, a familiarity sweetened by the economic opportunities open to them in the Americas. As we have seen, both the habits of behavior of most of these men and their occasional direct expressions regarding motivation suggest that their economic well-being was at least as important to them as their commitment to Jewish identity.

Sustaining Jewish Identity

The majority of the hundred or so known Judaizing Portuguese immigrants to Mexico in the last third of the sixteenth century clustered in Mexico City.[6] Although the concept of minyan, the quorum of ten adult males required for certain acts of communal Jewish ritual, does not seem to have been part of the repertoire of knowledge brought to America by the immigrants,[7] those who settled in Mexico City, or who shuttled to and from the city to peddle their wares to the growing market towns of the Mexico's central plateau, constituted an informal, amorphous, ever-changing minyan. Many knew each other personally from when they had been neighbors in the market cities and feeder villages of the Raya de Portugal. Many of them were, in fact, interrelated. Those whose sense of Jewish identity impelled them to some measure of Judaizing practice might gather at one of their Mexico City

292   CHAPTER 16

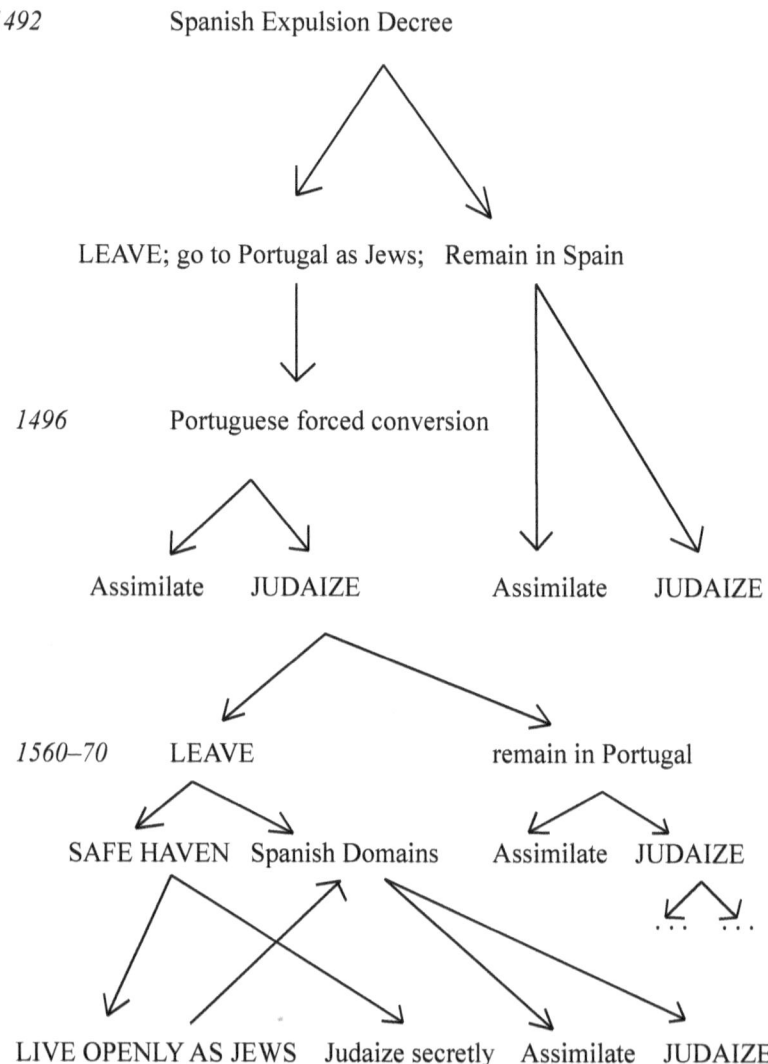

homes to observe the Sabbath, the feast of Passover or Sukkot, or the fast of Yom Kippur or Esther. In guarded moments they might pray together, relate snippets of knowledge or biblical stories to one another, or share a joke about the credulity of their Old Christian neighbors. Even though they had immigrated to Mexico, and numerous aspects of their surroundings were new to them, in many ways both the secular and the religious cultures in which they participated were familiar ones. Their business ventures were circumscribed by rules and institutions structured largely like those they had known at home.[8] Their religious lives were sustained by the relationships and practices of Mexico City's informal minyan just as they had been by the informal minyanim in their native Portuguese villages and their sojourn in Sevilla.[9]

Compared with the loosely cohesive Judaizing conversos of Mexico City, the crypto-Jews who are the subject of this book spent large portions of their lives in relative isolation. Old Tomás de Fonseca was apparently the only converso living anywhere near Tlalpujahua. The family of Manuel de Lucena; his wife, Catalina Enríquez; and sometimes her mother and brothers, constituted the resident converso community of Pachuca. In Taxco, Héctor de Fonseca, his cousin Tomás de Fonseca Castellanos, and for a few years Héctor's brother Jorge de Almeida and Jorge's friend Antonio Díaz de Cáceres might together have had the mass to function as the nucleus of a community of Judaizers, but it did not work out that way. The four men did not like each other very much, their personalities grated, and they had very different views about how, or even whether, to put their Jewish identity into practice.[10]

How, then, did these people sustain their sense of Jewish identity? One way was by solitary study. The most isolated of the miners, old Tomás de Fonseca, had in his house in Tlalpujahua an extensive library, larger even than Luis de Carvajal's collection.[11] His twelve books included two of the most popular reads among his contemporary Judaizers, Fray Luis de Granada's *Symbol of Faith* (*Símbolo de la fe*, 1582) and Fray Juan de Dueñas's *Mirror of Consolation* (*Espejo de consolación*, 1549).[12] Christian apologetics such as these were easily and licitly accessible. Judaizers read them for their treatment of prophecies, and especially for their inclusion of many direct citations in Spanish from the Hebrew Scriptures.[13] Old Tomás was particularly fond of these two books and frequently cited from them to Judaizing friends and acquaintances.[14] Manuel de Lucena, too, according to his wife, was fond of studying these books, sometimes reading portions aloud when they had company: "From *Symbol* he read [to his friends] about the creation of the world, and from the *Mirror* he read about the plagues in Egypt, the stories of Judith and of Queen Esther, and lots of other stories from the Old Testament."[15] Lucena induced at least two of his employees to buy their own copy of *Symbol of Faith*, which he claimed was full of delightful things.[16] Likewise, it was his ability to cite from *Mirror of Consolation* that led young Tomás de Fonseca Castellanos's friends to consider him an expert in Jewish matters.[17] Jorge de Almeida shared readings from *Symbol of Faith* with old Tomás de Fonseca in 1587,[18] and when Almeida was in hiding near Tlatelolco before departing for Spain in 1590, Luis de Carvajal brought him a copy of the book because, he said, of its "close citing of texts and discussion of aspects of the Law that God gave to Moses."[19]

On the other hand, there is no evidence that Héctor de Fonseca read much beyond the Bible. It was the Bible, he told inquisitors, that during his crisis of conscience in 1584 had left him confused whether Jesus was or was not the Messiah.[20] And we know nothing at all about Antonio Díaz de Cáceres's reading habits.

A second strategy for sustaining Jewish identity was to come together socially—in groups sometimes large but generally quite small—to talk of Jewish things or engage in Judaizing practices. Often the Judaizers residing in a mining town would host travelers in their homes, in effect constituting a mini-minyan. We have seen how Manuel de Lucena and Catalina Enríquez turned their Pachuca home into a meeting place for businessmen traveling from Mexico City to the northern mining towns, as well as for local Judaizers like Lucena's converso employees and the Tilcuautla goat farmer Álvaro de Carrión. On the Sabbath or the principal Jewish festivals, visitors to the Lucena household could be certain of a meal that met Jewish dietary standards, stimulating conversation about religious themes and texts, communal prayer, and good music. Tomás de Fonseca Castellanos's home and store in Taxco functioned the same way. Jorge de Almeida's Cantarranas hacienda likewise hosted visiting Judaizers, but generally only when one or more of the Carvajal siblings was in residence. This was not the case with old Tomás de Fonseca's home in Tlalpujahua, both because old Tomás did not have the gregarious personality of Lucena or young Tomás de Fonseca and because Tlalpujahua was too far off the beaten track to draw many visitors.

The open roads that connected Mexico City with the mining and market towns were another locus for sustaining Jewish identity. The spacious landscapes of the Mexican interior insulated travelers from the spying eyes and eavesdropping ears that were a constant threat in the cities, where one was never safe from scrutiny from neighbors, colleagues, or servants. The Inquisition procesos of the late 1500s document scores of instances when two or more Judaizer travelers shared their knowledge, exchanged confidences, shored up one another's faltering faith, and prayed or sang together. In many ways, the road functioned as their synagogue.

These sorts of comings together tended to be serendipitous, but other gatherings were deliberately convened. The active Judaizers in the mining towns made an effort to mark the major Jewish festivals with a community of residents and invited visitors. This generally required travel, either to the host home in the mining town or to the capital. The most important events were Yom Kippur, the Fast of Esther/Purim, Passover, and Sukkot. When possible, people also tended to group for the Sabbath and to a lesser extent for the midweek fasts. People from each extended family clan tended to congregate with each other, but, as can be seen in appendix 2, the crossover was considerable, as was the magnetism of these festival or Sabbath gatherings for people not associated with any of the family clans.

The Transmission of Jewish Identity

A central dilemma of Judaism, as with any minority culture living in the midst of a seductive or coercive majority culture, is how (or sometimes whether) to transmit that culture to the next generation. The authors of Deuteronomy, in their preface to the enumeration of the laws that govern the people of Israel, expressed this obligation to transmit in the clearest of terms: "These words ... shall be upon your heart; and you shall teach them diligently to your children, talking of them when you are sitting in your house, and when you are walking by the way, and when you lie down, and when you rise."[21]

Most people belong simultaneously to two families: that of their parents and previous generations of ancestors, of which they are the end product; and the family of which, with a spouse or partner, they are the progenitors. If the attitudes, values, and patterns of behavior of the ancestral family carry over into the forward-evolving family, the heritage has been transmitted.[22] As we have seen throughout this book, the transmission of Jewish identity and practice *to* the conversos who made their living in the Mexican mining towns in the last third of the sixteenth century was remarkably consistent. These people were almost all the grandchildren or great grandchildren of Jews who had personally been converted to Christianity, the exception being old Tomás de Fonseca, whose parents had converted. The immediate ancestors of these people had all been endogamous; that is, none had married Old Christians.[23] They had clearly been aware, as Jaime Contreras put it, that endogamy ensured faith and preserved the entity of lineage.[24]

However, as Christopher Jensen reminds us, "belonging to an identifiable cultural group is no guarantee of being in possession of a particular set of cultural ideas." This is true because transmitters "pass on their cultures continuously and in difficult-to-quantify forms," and transmittees tend to be selective in choosing from among the vast array of possible values and behaviors those that they will espouse and perform.[25] This is true whether the transmission is vertical (from one's grandparents and parents), horizontal (from one's peers and the members of one's immediate social or professional milieu), or oblique (from the broader environments—political, economic, and religious—and the institutions in which one's life is immersed). As we have seen, the choices made consciously or unconsciously by the conversos profiled in this book resulted in the transmission of their Jewish identity and practice to the *next* generation being notably spotty.

The descendants of Gabriel de Castellanos are a case in point. Gabriel had four children with his conversa wife Felipa de Fonseca in Portugal: Lope, Guiomar, Isabel, and Tomás. Lope opted out of Judaism early and became a cleric. While Guiomar de Fonseca was a knowledgeable Judaizer, her first marriage, to the Old Christian Antonio Pérez Herrero, produced three children, none of whom have left evidence of having Judaized. Her oldest child, Juan Pérez de Herrero, did not marry. Her two daughters, Felipa and Isabel de Fonseca, each married and had children; two of Isabel's children joined Catholic religious orders. Guiomar's second marriage, to the observant Judaizer Cosme de Pereira, produced no children.

Isabel de Fonseca's first two children (with her converso first cousin, whom she could not marry) were Francisca, who probably Judaized, and Tomás de Fonseca Castellanos, who definitely did. Isabel's later marriage to the Old Christian Tomás Méndez produced another son, Diego Méndez, who was taken to Mexico by his father and apparently did not Judaize.

Gabriel and Felipa's third child, Tomás de Fonseca, never married. Old Tomás did, however, sire five children: Teodosio, with an Indian woman in Ayoteco, and Beatriz, Lope, Ana, and Gabriel, with an Old Christian woman named Ana Jiménez during his visits from Tlalpujahua to Mexico City. All five children took the surname Fonseca, but there is no evidence that any of them absorbed any sense of their father's strong Jewish identity.

Julián de Castellanos, whom Gabriel claimed as his fourth child, was born to Blanca Rodríguez, the presumably Old Christian woman he had brought to Mexico with him. In his youth Julián sired two children, Florian and Juliana de Castellanos, with an unnamed woman or women. In later life he married the Old Christian Francisca Zarfate de Vargas, with whom he had four children: Francisco, Graviel, Gerónimo, and Felipa. None of these six children is known to have Judaized.

Gabriel's grandson young Tomás de Fonseca Castellanos, who was Isabel's son and old Tomás de Fonseca's nephew, never married, but between 1572 and 1581 he had three children: Francisco, María, and Álvaro. Tomás never identified the mother or mothers, but in his testimony he acknowledged the children. He never seems to have lived with the children or taken responsibility for them. All three received the surname Fonseca but apparently none of their father's sense of Jewish identity.

The second family, the Almeida-Fonsecas, produced four sons: Héctor, Jorge, Miguel, and Francisco, who adopted a variety of surnames. Héctor de Fonseca acknowledged having had a daughter as a young man, but named neither the daughter nor the mother in the documents, and nothing is known of either. His marriage to the Old Christian Juana López de la Torre in Taxco produced three children: Francisco Núñez, and María and Antonia de la Zarza. Beyond their birth, there is no further record of the first two. The third, Antonia, who later went by the name Antonia Rivera (possibly to escape the stigma of her father's having been penanced by the Inquisition), married a foreigner named Diego de Oliver. In 1640 in Taxco one of this couple's Indian servants reported that her masters had beaten a processional crucifix in their home. The four witnesses called by the Inquisition commissioner in Taxco were unanimous in their opinion of the family. "They meet their Christian obligations and do not dig into other people's lives." "They are good Christian people." "They are honorable people and good Christians." In his report the commissioner concluded: "I consider them good Christians and they have raised their children admirably."[26]

Jorge de Almeida married Leonor Andrada de Carvajal in 1587, and during the three years they lived together sporadically they produced no children.

The third son, Miguel Hernández, never married. The fourth, Francisco Hernández, had a son with an Old Christian woman in Spain, neither of whom is named in the documents. When Francisco returned to Spain in 1590 with his brother Jorge de Almeida, he collected the son and went to Italy, where he married an openly Jewish woman.[27]

Before his marriage, Almeida's colleague Antonio Díaz de Cáceres had a daughter, Agustina de Quiñones, with a mestiza woman. Neither Agustina, nor the four children Agustina later had with her two husbands, left evidence of having Judaized. With his wife, Catalina Carvajal y de la Cueva, Díaz de Cáceres had one daughter, Leonor, who was tried twice for having Judaized as a young woman with her mother. Leonor married an Old Christian named Núñez, and neither he nor their four children was ever said to identify as a Jew.

Simón Paiba and Beatriz Enríquez la Paiba were staunch Judaizers who made passing their Jewish identity to their three children a high priority. Their sons Pedro and Diego Enríquez, both active Judaizers, never married and did not have children. Their daughter Catalina Enríquez and her husband, Manuel de Lucena, had five: an unnamed daughter who died before she was ten; Clara, Felipe, and Tomás Enríquez; and Simón, who was known as Simón Gómez, Simón de Paredes, and Simón Lucena. Clara Enríquez, tried by the Inquisition in 1602 at age fourteen or fifteen, explained that although she had absorbed much Jewish culture from her mother during the two years she shared a prison cell with her, she was a faithful and observant Christian. Despite her protestation, she was penanced in April 1603 and sentenced to four years of Christian instruction.[28] Simón de Paredes, a barber and surgeon who lived in Cuernavaca, was charged with taking privileges that the law denied to the children and grandchildren of convicted heretics: riding on horseback, carrying a sword, and wearing elegant, expensively accessorized clothing. On July 20 the Inquisition pronounced his sentence: "Henceforth you shall call yourself Lucena or Enríquez, which are your parents' surnames; and you shall not ride a horse, or carry any weapons, or wear gold, silver, pearls, silk, or fine cloth, under pain of a hundred lashes."[29] The other two siblings do not seem to have run afoul of the Inquisition.

For these people the tally of transmission to their children of some aspect of Jewishness is as follows:

PROGENY OF CONVERSOS LIVING IN THE MINING TOWNS
 Children out of wedlock with non-conversos: N = 12
  Number of those known to have had some Jewish identity: N = 0
 Children with Old Christian spouses: N = 12
  Number of those known to have had some Jewish identity: N = 1
 Children out of wedlock with conversos: N = 2
  Number of those known to have had some Jewish identity: N = 2
 Children with converso spouses: N = 5
  Number of those known to have had some Jewish identity: N = 3

Among the converso men in the Mexican mining communities, this prevalence of exogamy and of having children out of wedlock appears to run counter to commonly asserted prevailing trends among conversos in general, and conversos in the Americas in particular.[30] Idiosyncrasies of character aside, one reason for this pattern of nontransmission of Jewish identity and practice among this group of conversos has to do with their choosing to live apart from the nucleus of the Judaizing community in Mexico City. This relative isolation, and the scarcity of available marriage partners, helps explain their proclivity to form sexual unions with Old Christians, both in and out of marriage.[31]

It also suggests that while this particular group of Judaizing converso men retained a strong sense of Jewish identity, their commitment to the primacy of the Shema's injunction to transmit Jewish identity to the next generation had weakened to the point of extinction. Many of the children born to the men in these mining towns, especially those born out of wedlock, lived with their mothers, apart from their fathers, throughout their formative years and had little exposure to Judaizing practices or ideas.[32] The household rhythms of Judaizing that centered on food preparation, cleaning for the Sabbath, lighting candles, and the rituals of prayer associated with these tasks that were commonly in the hands of women were absent from these children's lives.[33] When the parents did cohabit—Guiomar de Fonseca with her first husband, Antonio Pérez Herrero, or Héctor de Fonseca with his wife, Juana López de la Torre—fear of the Old Christian spouse kept the converso spouse from introducing the children to Jewish ideas and practices.[34] As sociologists have consistently pointed out, intergenerational cultural continuity, understood as the vertical transmission of attitudes, values, and patterns of behavior, is most reliably achieved through intensive shared family experience. Particularly important, in Linda A. Bennett's words, are the celebrations that "denote the family's perceived identification with a wider ethnic, cultural, or religious community."[35]

In deciding not to initiate their children into the beliefs and practices of Judaism in the family, and not to include them in their sporadic forays into the culture of crypto-Judaism as practiced by the large informal minyan of Spanish-Portuguese Judaizers that clustered in Mexico City, these men effectively relegated themselves to be the last of their line to Judaize.

APPENDIX 1

Origins and Arrivals

Name	Town of Origin in Portugal or Spain (*indicates places in Spain)	Date of Birth	Date to Mexico	Residence in Mexico	Profession/Status
Almeida, Jorge de (husband of Leonor Andrada de Carvajal)	Almeida	± 1550	± 1582	Mexico City, Taxco	businessman, miner
Álvarez, Jorge (husband of Ana Váez)	Fundão	1564–1566	1588	Mexico City	merchant
Álvarez, Manuel (brother of Simón Paiba; husband of Leonor Rodríguez)	Fundão	1540	1582	Mexico City	merchant
Álvarez, Pelayo (second cousin of Jorge de Almeida)	Freixo de Espada-à-Cinta	1526	by 1584	Mexico City, Taxco	merchant
Antonio, Marco (brother of Manuel Gómez de Casteloblanco)	Covilhã? Casteloblanco?	1563	± 1581	Mexico City, Taxco (also Guatemala, Peru)	street merchant
Carrión, Álvaro de	Cervera del Río Pisuerga*	1551	1580	Tilcuautla, Pachuca	shoemaker, goat rancher
Carvajal y de la Cueva, Catalina (wife of Antonio Díaz de Cáceres)	Benavente*	1564	1580	Mexico City, Taxco	housewife
Carvajal y de la Cueva, Luis (governor)	Mogadouro				

APPENDIX 1

Name	Town of Origin in Portugal or Spain (*indicates places in Spain)	Date of Birth	Date to Mexico	Residence in Mexico	Profession/ Status
Lemogodorio		1539	1564, 1580	various	soldier, captain, governor
Carvajal, Ana de León (wife of Cristóbal Miguel)	Medina del Campo*	1579	1580	Mexico City	child
Carvajal, Baltazar Rodríguez de	Benavente*	1562	1580	Mexico City, various	merchant
Carvajal, Francisca Núñez de (wife of Francisco Rodríguez de Matos)	Lemogodorio	1540	1580	various	housewife
Carvajal, Isabel Rodríguez de	Benavente*	1559	1580	various	housewife
Carvajal, Leonor Andrada de (wife of Jorge de Almeida)	Benavente*	1574	1580	Mexico City, Taxco	housewife
Carvajal, Luis	Benavente*	1566	1580	various	merchant
Carvajal, Mariana Núñez de	Benavente*	1571	1580	Mexico City	housewife
Carvajal, Miguel Rodríguez de	Benavente*	1572	1580	Various	merchant
Castellanos, Gabriel de	Freixo de Espada-á-Cinta	1490	1534	Mexico City, Ayoteco	teacher, miner
Castellanos, Julián de (son of Gabriel de Castellanos)	Jarandilla*	± 1530	1534	Mexico City	jeweler, obrajero (cloth factory owner)
Correa, Gaspar	Lisbon	?	by 1592	Mexico City	merchant
Cuello, Domingo (husband of Inés López)	Almofala (Lamego)	1558?	1594?	Mexico City, Pachuca, Michoacán	merchant
Díaz de Cáceres, Antonio (husband of Catalina Carvajal y de la Cueva)	Santa Comba Dao (Viseu)	± 1540	1572	Mexico City, Taxco, various (also China)	businessman, miner
Díaz Márquez, Antonio (husband of Francisca Rodríguez)	Alvalade (Lisboa)	by 1546	± 1563	Mexico City, Sombrerete	storekeeper, tailor

Origins and Arrivals 303

Name	Town of Origin in Portugal or Spain (*indicates places in Spain)	Date of Birth	Date to Mexico	Residence in Mexico	Profession/ Status
Díaz Nieto, Diego (son of Ruy Díaz Nieto)	Oporto	1573–1574	by 1591	Texcoco (also Italy)	businessman
Díaz Nieto, Rodrigo (father of Diego Díaz Nieto)	Oporto	1529	by 1591	Texcoco (also Italy)	businessman
Díaz, Leonor (sister of Manuel Gómez Navarro)	Sevilla*	1567–1568	by 1589	Mexico City	seamstress
Díaz, Luis	Portugal	± 1547	1586?	Mexico City, Taxco	cleric, miner
Enríquez la Paiba, Beatriz (wife of Simón Paiba)	Fundão	?	1581	Mexico City, Pachuca	housewife
Enríquez Pedro (son of Beatriz Enríquez; d. before 1595)	Sevilla*	1570 or 1573?	1581	Atotonilco, various	cloth merchant, soldier, tavern keeper
Enríquez, Catalina (daughter of Beatriz Enríquez)	Sevilla?*	1565	1580	Mexico City, Pachuca	housewife
Enríquez, Clara (sister of Beatriz Enríquez)	Fundão	1540–1545	1580	Mexico City	housewife
Enríquez, Diego (son of Beatriz Enríquez)	Sevilla?*	± 1574	after 1582	Mexico City, Acapulco (also Guatemala)	businessman, soldier
Enríquez, Gabriel (son of Clara Enríquez)	Fundão	1560	by 1591	Guadalajara	muleteer
Fonseca Castellanos, Tomás de (son of Isabel de Fonseca)	Viseu	± 1548	1562	Taxco	storekeeper, miner
Fonseca, Antonio	Oporto	± 1575	after 1593	Mexico City	merchant
Fonseca, Felipa de (d. 1591; wife of A. Pérez Herrero and G. de Enciso)	Mexico City	± 1556	± 1556	Taxco	housewife

APPENDIX 1

Name	Town of Origin in Portugal or Spain (*indicates places in Spain)	Date of Birth	Date to Mexico	Residence in Mexico	Profession/ Status
Fonseca, Francisco de (son of T. F. Castellanos)	Mexico City	1572	born Mexico City	Veracruz (also China)	businessman
Fonseca, Guiomar de (daughter of Gabriel de Castellanos)	Freixo de Espada-á-Cinta?	before 1516	1534	Mexico City	housewife
Fonseca, Héctor	Viseu	± 1548	± 1571	Taxco	miner
Fonseca, Isabel de (d. ± 1575; daughter of Gabriel de Castellanos)	Viseu?	before 1520	by ± 1575	Mexico City	housewife
Fonseca, Tomás (aka old Tomás)	Freixo de Espada-á-Cinta	± 1520	1534	Mexico City, Ayoteco, Pachuca, Tlalpujahua	miner
Francisco Belmonte, Manuel	Covilhã	± 1537	before 1582	Sultepec, Mexico City	merchant
Gerónimo, Miguel (aka M. G. de León?; husband of Catalina López)	?	?	before 1592	Pachuca	miner
Gil de la Guarda, Manuel (brother of Pedro Rodríguez Saz)	Guarda	± 1565	± 1592	Mexico (also Manila)	merchant
Gómez de Casteloblanco, Manuel (aka M. González)	Casteloblanco	1567	1588	Mexico City, Sultepec	merchant
Gómez Navarro, Manuel (son of Ana López)	San Martín de Trevejo*	1565	before 1589	Mexico City, Sichú	soldier, merchant
Gómez Silveira, Manuel (d. by 1595)	Morón de la Frontera*	?	before 1589	Mexico City	merchant
Gómez, Antonio (husband of Úrsula Bueno de Herrera)	Fundão	1571?	by 1597	Mexico City	merchant

Origins and Arrivals 305

Name	Town of Origin in Portugal or Spain (*indicates places in Spain)	Date of Birth	Date to Mexico	Residence in Mexico	Profession/ Status
Gómez, Cristóbal (cousin of Antonio López)	Fundão (Escarigo)	1554	by 1585	Mexico City	businessman
González, Álvaro	Fundão	1573	by 1587	Mexico City (also Peru)	merchant
González, Baltazar	Portugal	?	by 1584	Guachiapa (also China)	merchant
Hernández, Francisco (brother of Jorge de Almeida)	Viseu	± 1549	1582	Mexico City, Tonacatepec (also Peru)	merchant
Hernández, Isabel Clara (sister of Manuel Morales; wife of Francisco Hernández)	Seia?	?	1580	Mexico City	housewife
Hernández, Miguel (brother of Jorge de Almeida)	Viseu	± 1549	before 1586	Mexico City, Taxco	?, drunkard
Jorge, Francisco (cousin of Francisca N. de Carvajal; wife in Spain)	Salcedo	?	before 1588	Taxco	servant
Jorge, Manuel (son of Jorge Váez)	Casteloblanco	1568	by 1589	Mexico City	street vendor
López Regalón, Diego (aka Felipe López; husband of Ana López)	Casteloblanco	?	by 1589	Mexico City	merchant
López, Ana (wife of Diego López Regalón)	Fundão	± 1535	by 1589	Mexico City	housewife, street vendor
López, Antonio (son of Ana López)	Celorico	± 1561	± 1573	Pachuca, Mexico City, Puebla	singer in theater
López, Diego	São Vicente da Beira	1574	1580	Mexico City	street vendor, merchant
López, Felipa (daughter of Ana López; wife of Felipe Núñez)	Sevilla?*	?	by 1589	Mexico City (also Peru)	housewife

Name	Town of Origin in Portugal or Spain (*indicates places in Spain)	Date of Birth	Date to Mexico	Residence in Mexico	Profession/ Status
Lucena, Manuel de	São Vicente da Beira	1564	± 1577	Pachuca, Mexico City	storekeeper, miner
Luna, Bernardo	Lisboa	1568?	1591	Michoacán, various	Merchant, textile factory foreman
Machado, Antonio	Lisboa	by 1500	1580	Mexico City	tailor
Méndez, Antonio (husband of María de los Santos)	Teba (Málaga)*	1567	1582	Pachuca, Real del Monte	merchant
Méndez, Francisco (husband of Clara Enríquez; d. by 1595)	Alentejo	?	1582?	Mexico City	merchant
Méndez, Justa	Sevilla*	1575	1588	Mexico City, various	housewife
Morales, Antonio de (nephew of Manuel Morales)	Seia?	?	1580	Mexico City, San Luis Potosí	doctor
Morales, Manuel	Seia	1551	1580	Mexico City (also Venice)	doctor
Núñez, Duarte	Portugal	± 1556	before 1589	Mexico City	street vendor
Núñez, Felipe	Lisbon	± 1561	1580	Mexico City (also Peru)	tailor
Paiba, Simón (husband of Beatriz Enríquez; d. 1592)	Fundão	?	1576, 1581	Mexico City, Pachuca	merchant
Peña, Sebastián de la	São João de Pesqueira	1572	1592	Mexico City	traveling merchant
Pereira, Cosme (husband of Guiomar de Fonseca)	Portugal	?	1572	Mexico City (also Italy, Peru)	merchant, lawyer
Pereira, Nicolás	Portugal	?	1590	Mexico City	slaver
Pérez Ferro, Gonzalo	Vila Flor	1551–1552	1580	Mexico City	merchant
Pertierra, Gómez	Frejo, Asturias	± 1571	by 1594	Pachuca	storekeeper
Rodríguez de Herrera, Hernando	Fundão	1564	1588	Michoacán, Pachuca	merchant

Origins and Arrivals   307

Name	Town of Origin in Portugal or Spain (*indicates places in Spain)	Date of Birth	Date to Mexico	Residence in Mexico	Profession/ Status
Rodríguez de Ledesma, Francisco	Barrueco Pardo (Salamanca)	1556	1586	Mexico City, Tula	slaver, merchant, rancher
Rodríguez de Matos, Francisco (husband of Francisca de Carvajal)	Balderas (León)*	1536	1580	Pánuco	merchant
Rodríguez de Silva, Juan (cousin of Cristóbal Gómez; left wife in Salonica)	?	?	by 1590	Salonica, Mexico City	soap maker, businessman
Rodríguez Saz, Pedro (brother of Manuel Gil de la Guarda)	Fundão		by 1595	Mexico City	merchant
Rodríguez Silgueiro, Manuel	Fundão	1567	by 1589	Mexico City	street vendor
Rodríguez, Álvaro (aka A. R. Achocado)	Fundão	?	by 1583	Pachuca	ranch worker
Rodríguez, Andrés	Fundão	± 1565	1583	Texcoco	merchant, tavern keeper
Rodríguez, Antonio (son of Sebastián Rodríguez; drowned)	São Vicente da Beira	± 1878	1580	Mexico City	?
Rodríguez, Blanca (cousin of Justa Méndez; wife of Sebastián Rodríguez)	Sevilla*	1565	by 1589	Mexico City	housewife
Rodríguez, Costanza (wife of Sebastián Rodríguez)	Sevilla*	1565	1589	Mexico City	housewife
Rodríguez, Duarte (husband of Clara Rodríguez)	Covilhã	1570–1571	?	Mexico City, various	traveling merchant

308 APPENDIX 1

Name	Town of Origin in Portugal or Spain (*indicates places in Spain)	Date of Birth	Date to Mexico	Residence in Mexico	Profession/ Status
Rodríguez, Francisco (aka Francisco Ríos, Núñez; brother of Sebastián Rodríguez)	São Vicente da Beira	1575	1597	Mexico City	merchant, rancher
Rodríguez, Francisco (brother of Sebastián Rodríguez)	São Vicente da Beira	1575	1587	Mexico City	?
Rodríguez, Gonzalo	Portugal	± 1552	before 1586	Mexico City (also Cuba)	musician, soldier
Rodríguez, Hernán (aka H. R. de Herrera; left wife in Spain)	Fundão	?	1588	Pachuca, Peru	merchant
Rodríguez, Jorge (brother of Ana Váez and Costanza Rodríguez)	Sevilla*	1565?	by 1589	Mexico City Puebla (also China, Peru)	merchant
Rodríguez, Manuel	Fundão	1570	by 1594	Mexico City (also China)	merchant
Rodríguez, Pedro (brother of Antonio Rodríguez)	Fundão	?	by 1593	Mexico City (also Peru, China)	merchant
Rodríguez, Sebastián (husband of Blanca Rodríguez)	São Vicente da Beira	1570–1572	1588	Mexico City	merchant
Rodríguez, Simón (brother of Andrés Rodríguez)	Salzedas (Tarouca)	± 1578	before 1593	Mexico City, various (also China)	merchant
Tavares, Rodrigo (father of Manuel Tavares)	Covilhã	1533	1585	Pátzcuaro, Michoacán	merchant
Váez, Ana (wife of Jorge Álvarez)	Fundão	1566?	1594	Mexico City	housewife
Váez, Francisco (brother of Antonio Rodríguez)	São Vicente da Beira	?	by 1593	Pachuca, Puebla (also Guatemala, Japan)	merchant
Váez, Jorge (father of Manuel Jorge)	São Vicente da Beira	± 1535	by 1589	Pachuca	merchant, clerk

APPENDIX 2

Holiday Observances

Year-Event Number	82-1	83-1	83-2	84-1	86-1	86-2	87-1	87-2	87-3	87-4	88-1	88-2	88-3	88-4	88-5	89-1
Holiday: PM (Purim); PS (Passover); YK (Yom Kippur)	YK	PS	YK	YK	PM	PS	PM	PS	YK	YK	PM	PS	PM	YK	YK	PM
Place	M-A	M-B	M-A	M-C	M-A	M-A	M-A	M-A	M-D	P-E	P-E	T-F	M-C	P-E	M-H	M-I
Source	1,7	22	1	1	1	1			23		1,7	16	7	1,10	1,14	8

TAXCO–MEXICO CITY NUCLEUS

	82-1	83-1	83-2	84-1	86-1	86-2	87-1	87-2	87-3	87-4	88-1	88-2	88-3	88-4	88-5	89-1
Almeida, Jorge de (husband of Leonor Carvajal)		✓														
Carvajal, Ana de León														✓		
Carvajal y de la Cueva, Catalina (wife of Antonio Díaz de Cáceres)												✓		✓		
Carvajal, Baltazar Rodríguez de										✓	✓			✓		
Carvajal, Francisca Núñez de												✓				
Carvajal, Isabel Rodríguez de Andrada												✓				
Carvajal, Leonor Andrada de (wife of Jorge de Almeida)												✓				

Holiday Observances

ID			
94-3	YK	M-O	1
94-2	YK	M-C	1, 10
94-1	PS	P-K	1, 6
93-5	YK	M-M	1
93-4	YK	MN	1, 9
93-3	PS	P-E	6
93-2	PS	M-N	1, 9, 19
93-1	PM	P-E	1, 7
92-5	YK	M-N	9
92-4	PS	M-N	1, 7, 9
92-2	PS	M-K	12
92-1	PM	M-C,M	1, 2, 5
91-2	YK	M-L	1, 7
91-1	YK	M-K	7
90-2	PS	M-K	1, 7
90-1	YK	P-E	1, 9
89-5	YK	M-A	1, 7, 9,
89-4	YK	T-J	13
89-3a	PS	M-C	1

APPENDIX 2

Year-Event Number	82-1	83-1	83-2	84-1	86-1	86-2	87-1	87-2	87-3	87-4	88-1	88-2	88-3	88-4	88-5	89-1
Holiday: PM (Purim); PS (Passover); YK (Yom Kippur)	YK	PS	YK	YK	PM	PS	PM	PS	YK	YK	PM	PS	PM	YK	YK	PM
Place	M-A	M-B	M-A	M-C	M-A	M-A	M-A	M-A	M-D	P-E	P-E	T-F	M-C	P-E	M-H	M-I
Source	1,7	22	1	1	1	1	1		23		1,7	16	7	1,10	1,14	8
Carvajal y de la Cueval, Luis de		✓								✓	✓		✓			
Carvajal, Mariana Núñez de											✓			✓		
Carvajal, Miguel Rodríguez de										✓						
Castellanos, Julián de	✓															
Díaz de Cáceres, Antonio (husband of Catalina Carvajal)	✓															
Fonseca Castellanos, Tomás de (young Tomás)																
Fonseca, Felipa de (mother of Tomás de Fonseca Castellanos)	✓															
Fonseca, Francisco de (son of T. Castellanos)																
Fonseca, Héctor de (brother of Jorge de Almeida)	✓															
Fonseca, Tomás de (old Tomás)																
Hernández, Francisco (brother of Jorge de Almeida)																
Hernández, Miguel (brother of Jorge Almeida)	✓															

Holiday Observances   313

94-3	94-2	94-1	93-5	93-4	93-3	93-2	93-1	92-5	92-4	92-2	92-1	91-2	91-1	91-1	90-2	90-1	89-5	89-4	89-3a	89-3
YK	YK	PS	YK	YK	PS	PS	PM	YK	PS	PS	PM	YK	YK	PS	YK	YK	YK	YK	PS	PS
M-O	M-C	P-K	M-M	MN	P-E	M-N	P-E	M-N	M-N	M-K	M-C.M	M-L	M-K	M-K	P-E	M-A	M-A	T-J	M-C	M-B
1	1,10	1,6	1	1,9	6	1,9,19	1,7	9	1,7,9	12	1,2,5	1,7	7	1,7	1,9	1,7,9,	1,3,4	13	1	12
					✓			✓		✓	✓	✓	✓	✓				✓	✓	
										✓			✓	✓						
											✓									
																	✓			
									✓	✓	✓								✓	
																			✓	
												✓							✓	

APPENDIX 2

Year-Event Number	82-1	83-1	83-2	84-1	86-1	86-2	87-1	87-2	87-3	87-4	88-1	88-2	88-3	88-4	88-5	89-1
Holiday: PM (Purim); PS (Passover); YK (Yom Kippur)	YK	PS	YK	YK	PM	PS	PM	PS	YK	YK	PM	PS	PM	YK	YK	PM
Place	M-A	M-B	M-A	M-C	M-A	M-A	M-A	M-A	M-D	P-E	P-E	T-F	M-C	P-E	M-H	M-I
Source	1,7	22	1	1	1	1	1	1	23		1,7	16	7	1,10	1,14	8

PACHUCA–MEXICO CITY NUCLEUS

	82-1	83-1	83-2	84-1	86-1	86-2	87-1	87-2	87-3	87-4	88-1	88-2	88-3	88-4	88-5	89-1
Álvarez, Manuel (brother of Simón Paiba)		✓														
Enríquez la Paiba, Beatriz (wife of Simón Paiba)	✓			✓			✓				✓			✓		
Enríquez, Catalina (daughter of Beatriz, wife of Lucena)	✓		✓	✓	✓		✓	✓			✓			✓	✓	
Enríquez, Clara (sister of Beatriz; widow of Francisco Méndez)						✓						✓	✓			
Enríquez, Costanza (niece of Clara Enríquez)																
Enríquez, Diego (son of Beatriz)	✓		✓	✓							✓			✓		
Enríquez, Gabriel (son of Clara Enríquez)																
Enríquez, Pedro (son of Beatriz)	✓		✓	✓							✓			✓		
López, Felipa (daughter of Clara Enríquez)																
Lucena, Manuel de (husband of Catalina Enríquez)	✓		✓	✓	✓		✓	✓		✓	✓			✓	✓	
Méndez, Justa (daughter of Clara Enríquez)												✓	✓	✓		
Méndez, Francisco (husband of Clara Enríquez)																

	94-3	94-2	94-1	93-5	93-4	93-3	93-2	93-1	92-5	92-4	92-2	92-1	91-2	91-1	91-1	90-2	90-1	89-5	89-4	89-3a
	YK	YK	PS	YK	YK	PS	PS	PM	YK	PS	PS	PM	YK	YK	PS	YK	YK	YK	YK	PS
	M-O	M-C	P-K	M-M	MN	P-E	M-N	P-E	M-N	M-N	M-K	M-C,M	M-L	M-K	M-K	P-E	M-A	M-A	T-J	M-C
	1	1,10	1,6	—	1,9	6	1,9,19	1,7	9	1,7,9	12	1,2,5	1,7	7	1,7	1,9	1,7,9,	1,3,4	13	1
								✓									✓			
	✓		✓		✓		✓			✓						✓	✓			✓
	✓	✓	✓	✓	✓	✓	✓	✓	✓	✓		✓	✓		✓	✓	✓	✓	✓	✓
			✓	✓	✓	✓		✓	✓	✓	✓	✓		✓		✓	✓		✓	
				✓	✓											✓				
		✓	✓	✓			✓									✓				?
				✓					✓		✓									✓
				✓			✓									✓				
					✓		✓			✓										
	✓	✓	✓	✓	✓	✓	✓	✓		✓	✓	✓		✓	✓	✓	✓			✓
	✓	✓	✓	✓	✓	✓	✓	✓	✓	✓	✓	✓	✓				✓			✓
												✓								

APPENDIX 2

Year-Event Number	82-1	83-1	83-2	84-1	86-1	86-2	87-1	87-2	87-3	87-4	88-1	88-2	88-3	88-4	88-5	89-1
Holiday: PM (Purim); PS (Passover); YK (Yom Kippur)	YK	PS	YK	YK	PM	PS	PM	PS	YK	YK	PM	PS	PM	YK	YK	PM
Place	M-A	M-B	M-A	M-C	M-A	M-A	M-A	M-A	M-D	P-E	P-E	T-F	M-C	P-E	M-H	M-I
Source	1,7	22	1		1	1	1		23		1,7	16	7	1,10	1,14	8
Paiba, Simón (husband of Beatriz Enríquez)	✓		✓	✓	✓		✓	✓			✓					
Rodríguez, Diego (brother of Catalina Enríquez)																
Rodríguez, Jorge (brother of Ana Váez and Costanza Rodríguez)	✓		✓		✓		✓				✓					
Váez, Ana (wife of Jorge Álvarez)																

OTHERS

	82-1	83-1	83-2	84-1	86-1	86-2	87-1	87-2	87-3	87-4	88-1	88-2	88-3	88-4	88-5	89-1
Álvarez, Jorge (husband of Ana Váez)																✓
Ángeles, María de los (wife of Antonio Méndez)																
Antonio, Marco (brother of Manuel Gómez de Casteloblanco)							✓									
Correa, Antonio																
Correa, Gaspar																
Díaz, Leonor (sister of Manuel Gómez Navarro)														✓	✓	
Fernández Cardoso, Manuel																
Franca, María (wife of Antonio Méndez)																
Francisco Belmonte, Manuel	✓		✓			✓			✓				✓			
Gerónimo, Miguel (husband of Catalina López)																

Holiday Observances

	89-2	89-3a	89-4	89-5	90-1	90-2	91-1	91-1	91-2	92-1	92-2	92-4	92-5	93-1	93-2	93-3	93-4	93-5	94-1	94-2	94-3
	PS	PS	YK	YK	YK	YK	PS	YK	YK	PM	PS	PS	YK	PM	PS	PS	YK	YK	PS	YK	YK
	M-R	M-C	T-J	M-A	M-A	P-E	M-K	M-K	M-L	M-C.M	M-K	M-N	M-N	P-E	M-N	P-E	MN	M-M	P-K	M-C	M-O
	12	1	13	1,3,4	1,7,9,	1,9	1,7	7	1,7	1,2,5	12	1,7,9	9	1,7	1,9,19	6	1,9	1	1,6	1,10	1
		✓		✓																	
						✓															
		✓										✓									
	✓	✓		✓			✓			✓							✓				
										✓											
	✓																				
												✓									
✓		✓	✓	✓	✓		✓		✓		✓				✓						
												✓			✓					✓	
						✓		✓		✓		✓									
				✓	✓																
										✓		✓									

318   APPENDIX 2

Year-Event Number	82-1	83-1	83-2	84-1	86-1	86-2	87-1	87-2	87-3	87-4	88-1	88-2	88-3	88-4	88-5	89-1
Holiday: PM (Purim); PS (Passover); YK (Yom Kippur)	YK	PS	YK	YK	PM	PS	PM	PS	YK	YK	PM	PS	PM	YK	YK	PM
Place	M-A	M-B	M-A	M-C	M-A	M-A	M-A	M-A	M-D	P-E	P-E	T-F	M-C	P-E	M-H	M-I
Source	1,7	22	1	1	1	1	1		23		1,7	16	7	1,10	1,14	8
Gómez de Casteloblanco, Manuel (aka M. González)																
Gómez Navarro, Manuel (son of Ana López)														✓		
Gómez Silveira, Manuel																✓
Gómez, Cristóbal (cousin of Antonio López)																
González, Álvaro	✓		✓				✓									
González, Baltazar	✓		✓													
Jorge, Francisco (cousin of Francisca N. de Carvajal)															✓	
Jorge, Manuel													✓			
López, Ana (wife of Felipe Núñez)													✓	✓		
López, Antonio (son of Ana López)										✓	✓		✓			
López, Catalina (wife of Miguel Gerónimo)													✓			
López, Felipa (daughter of Ana López)													✓			
López, Leonor (daughter of Ana López)																
Machado, Antonio								✓								
Machado Isabel (daughter of Antonio Machado)								✓								

Holiday Observances

94-3	94-2	94-1	93-5	93-4	93-3	93-2	93-1	92-5	92-4	92-2	92-1	91-2	91-1	91-i	90-2	90-1	89-5	89-4	89-3a
YK	YK	PS	YK	YK	PS	PS	PM	YK	PS	PS	PM	YK	YK	PS	YK	YK	YK	YK	PS
M-O	M-C	P-K	M-M	MN	P-E	M-N	P-E	M-N	M-N	M-K	M-C,M	M-L	M-K	M-K	P-E	M-A	M-A	T-J	M-C
1	1,10	1,6	1	1,9	6	1,9,19	1,7	9	1,7,9	12	1,2,5	1,7	7	1,7	1,9	1,7,9	1,3,4	13	1
																	✓		
✓	✓						✓									✓			
																	✓		
																✓	✓		
					✓		✓			✓			✓	✓		✓	✓		
					✓		✓										✓		
							✓			✓	✓								
					✓		✓						✓			✓	✓		
																✓	✓		

APPENDIX 2

Year-Event Number	82-1	83-1	83-2	84-1	86-1	86-2	87-1	87-2	87-3	87-4	88-1	88-2	88-3	88-4	88-5	89-1
Holiday: PM (Purim); PS (Passover); YK (Yom Kippur)	YK	PS	YK	YK	PM	PS	PM	PS	YK	YK	PM	PS	PM	YK	YK	PM
Place	M-A	M-B	M-A	M-C	M-A	M-A	M-A	M-A	M-D	P-E	P-E	T-F	M-C	P-E	M-H	M-I
Source	1,7	22	1	1	1	1	1		33		1,7	16	7	1,10	1,14	8
Méndez, Antonio (husband of María de los Ángeles)																
Méndez, Francisco (brother of Antonio Méndez)																
Morales, Antonio de														✓		
Núñez, Duarte																
Núñez, Felipe (husband of Ana López)															✓	
Peña, Sebastián de la										✓						
Pereira, Nicolás																
Rodríguez de Silva, Juan (cousin of Cristóbal Gómez)																
Rodríguez Navarro, Manuel																
Rodríguez Noro, Pedro																
Rodríguez Saz, Pedro (nephew of Ana Váez)		✓														
Rodríguez Silgueiro, Manuel																
Rodríguez, Álvaro	✓		✓													
Rodríguez, Andrés																
Rodríguez, Antonio																
Rodríguez, Blanca (cousin of Justa Méndez)														✓		

Holiday Observances

	89-3a	89-4	89-5	90-1	90-2	91-1	91-2	92-1	92-2	92-4	92-5	93-1	93-2	93-3	93-4	93-5	94-1	94-2	94-3
	PS	YK	YK	YK	YK	PS	YK	PM	PS	PS	YK	PM	PS	PS	YK	YK	PS	YK	YK
	M-C	T-J	M-A	M-A	P-E	M-K	M-L	M-C,M	M-K	M-N	M-N	P-E	M-N	P-E	MN	M-M	P-K	M-C	M-O
	1	13	1,3,4	1,7,9,	1,9	1,7	1,7	1,2,5	12	1,7,9	9	1,7	1,9,19	6	1,9	–	1,6	1,10	1
						✓		✓				✓							
				✓			✓												
																			✓
										✓		✓		✓					
	✓			✓			✓						✓						
					✓			✓	✓	✓		✓							
	✓																		
				✓	✓	✓			✓	✓			✓		✓		✓		
	✓				✓								✓		✓				
																			✓

APPENDIX 2

Year-Event Number	82-1	83-1	83-2	84-1	86-1	86-2	87-1	87-2	87-3	87-4	88-1	88-2	88-3	88-4	88-5	89-1
Holiday: PM (Purim); PS (Passover); YK (Yom Kippur)	YK	PS	YK	YK	PM	PS	PM	PS	YK	YK	PM	PS	PM	YK	YK	PM
Place	M-A	M-B	M-A	M-C	M-A	M-A	M-A	M-A	M-D	P-E	P-E	T-F	M-C	P-E	M-H	M-I
Source	1,7	22	1	1	1	1	1		23		1,7	16	7	1,10	1,14	8
Rodríguez, Costanza (wife of Sebastián Rodríguez)														✓		
Rodríguez, Duarte (husband of Clara Rodríguez)																
Rodríguez, Enrique (brother of Simón Rodríguez)																
Rodríguez, Gonzalo	✓															
Rodríguez, Hernán																
Rodríguez (de Ledesma), Francisco (husband of Leonor Díaz)																
Rodríguez, Pedro (brother of Antonio and Francisco Rodríguez)							✓									
Rodríguez, Sebastián (husband of Blanca Rodríguez)												✓				
Rodríguez, Simón (brother of Andrés Rodríguez)																
Váez, Francisco (nephew of Jorge Váez)																

Holiday Observances

94-3	94-2	94-1	93-5	93-4	93-3	93-2	93-1	92-5	92-4	92-2	92-1	91-2	91-1	90-2	90-1	89-5	89-4	89-3a	89-3	89-?
YK	YK	PS	YK	YK	PS	PS	PM	YK	PS	PS	PM	YK	YK	YK	YK	YK	YK	YK	PS	PS
M-O	M-C	P-K	M-M	MN	P-E	M-N	P-E	M-N	M-N	M-K	M-C,M	M-L	M-K	M-K	P-E	M-A	M-A	T-J	M-C	M-B
1	1,10	1,6	1	1,9	6	1,9,19	1,7	9	1,7,9	12	1,2,5	1,7	7	1,7	1,9	1,3,4	1,3,4	13	1	12
✓						✓			✓							✓	✓			
	✓		✓	✓		✓	✓			✓	✓					✓	✓	✓		
				✓	✓															
												✓				✓	✓			
		✓	✓	✓		✓		✓			✓			✓	✓	✓	✓	✓		
✓				✓										✓						
															✓	✓	✓		✓	
																				✓
					✓	✓									✓	✓	✓	✓	✓	✓

Sources: Manuscript and Informant

1. Bancroft, Lucena, 19, 88v, 89, 97r, 99, 135, 151r, 153, 172, 185r, 194v, 198, 203r, 221, 225r, 226v, 234r, 237, 263r, 343r, 349v, 437v, 445r, 450r, 460, 466r, 467, 511, 524, 563r, 564v, 570v, 653
2. AGN 17-3, Justa Mendez: 12r
3. AGN 127-2, Francisco Rodríguez Herrera: 224r
4. AGN 149-2, Francisco Rodríguez Herrera: 18r
5. AGN 150-1, Jorge de Almeida: 10v
6. AGN 152-3 Francisco Váez: 244
7. AGN 152-4, Catalina Enriquez: 33v, 35, 129v, 130v, 199r, 242, 289, 329v
8. AGN 153-1, Jorge Álvarez: 153, 175
9. AGN 153-7, Clara Enríquez: 18v, 29, 68, 69r, 120r, 181, 184, 262v
10. AGN 153-9, Beatriz Enríquez la Paiba: 44v, 45v, 51r, 53, 61v, 848
11. AGN 153-10, Juan Rodríguez de Silva: 6r
12. AGN 154-1 Justa Méndez: 4, 15r, 28r, 152, 197, 204v, 437
13. AGN 156-4, Tomás de Fonseca Castellanos: 93r, 262v
14. AGN 159-1, Antonio Díaz de Cáceres: 34v
15. AGN 160-12, Diego López Regalón: 6v
16. AGN 1488-2, Catalina León de la Cueva Carvajal: 37v, 55r
17. AGN 1489-1, Luis de Carvajal: 129r, 351r
18. AGN 1490-2 Antonio López: 55r
19. AGN 1492-2, Francisco Rodríguez de Ledesma: 15r, 47
20. AGN 1492-3, Antonio Méndez: 15r, 23r, 67v
21. AGN 1493-1, Jorge Álvarez: 11v
22. AGN 1529-1, Julián de Castellanos: 45r
23. AGN 1529-3, Isabel Machado: 33r, 96r

Locations

M-A: Mexico City home of Simón Paiba and Beatriz Enríquez la Paiba
M-B: Mexico City apartments of Jorge Almeida
M-C: Mexico City apartments of Manuel de Lucena and Catalina Enríquez
M-D: Mexico City apartments of Manuel Machado
P-E: Pachuca home of Manuel de Lucena and Catalina Enríquez
T-F: Taxco Cantarranas hacienda of Jorge de Almeida
M-G: Mexico City home of Antonio Machado
M-H: Mexico City apartments of Antonio Díaz de Cáceres
M-I: Mexico City apartments of Manuel Gómez Silveira
T-J: Taxco home of Tomás de Fonseca Castellanos
M-K: Mexico City home of Francisca Rodríguez de Carvajal in Tlatelolco
M-L: Mexico City home of Felipa López
M-M: Mexico City home of Francisca Rodríguez de Carvajal
M-N: Mexico City home of Clara Enríquez
M-O: Mexico City home of Sebastián Rodríguez

APPENDIX 3
Enríquez-Lucena Holiday Attendees

People Attending Purim, Passover, or Yom Kippur with Manuel de Lucena and Catalina Enríquez (*indicates a relation of the Lucena-Enríquez-Paiba family)

NAME	BIRTHPLACE IN PORTUGAL	BIRTHPLACE IN SPAIN	ATTENDED IN MEXICO CITY N = 15 events	ATTENDED IN PACHUCA N = 8 events
Almeida, Jorge de	Almeida		1	
Álvarez, Jorge	Fundão		4	2
Álvarez, Manuel	Fundão		4	
Ángeles, María de los			4	
Carvajal y de la Cueva, Catalina		Benavente	4	1
Carvajal y de la Cueval, Luis de		Benavente	4	2
Carvajal, Baltazar Rodríguez de		Benavente	1	2
Carvajal, Francisca Núñez de		Benavente		
Carvajal, Isabel Rodríguez de Andrada		Benavente	4	
Carvajal, Leonor Andrada de		Benavente	2	
Carvajal, Mariana Núñez de		Benavente	1	
Carvajal, Miguel Rodríguez de		Benavente		1
Correa, Antonio	unknown		1	
Díaz de Cáceres, Antonio	Santa Comba Dao		2	
Díaz, Leonor		Sevilla	6	4

APPENDIX 3

People Attending Purim, Passover, or Yom Kippur with Manuel de Lucena and Catalina Enríquez (*indicates a relation of the Lucena-Enríquez-Paiba family)

NAME	BIRTHPLACE IN PORTUGAL	BIRTHPLACE IN SPAIN	ATTENDED IN MEXICO CITY	ATTENDED IN PACHUCA
Enríquez la Paiba, Beatriz*	Fundão		9	4
Enríquez, Catalina*		Sevilla?	14	4
Enríquez, Clara*	Fundão		10	3
Enríquez, Diego*		Sevilla	7	4
Enríquez, Gabriel*	Fundão		14	
Enríquez, Pedro*		Sevilla	6	2
Fernández Cardoso, Manuel	Lisboa		1	
Fonseca Castellanos, Tomás de	Viseu		2	
Franca, María			3	
Francisco Belmonte, Manuel	Covilhã		4	4
Gerónimo, Miguel	unidentified		2	
Gómez de Casteloblanco, Manuel	Castelo Branco		1	
Gómez Navarro, Manuel*		San Martín de Trevejo	14	1
Gómez Silveira, Manuel		Morón de la Frontera	1	
González, Álvaro	Fundão		2	
González, Baltazar	unidentified		2	
Jorge, Manuel	Castelo Branco		3	
López, Ana	Fundão		6	2
López, Antonio	Celorico		3	3
López, Catalina			3	1
López, Felipa*		Sevilla	5	
López, Leonor	Fundão?		2	
Lucena, Manuel de*	São Vicente da Beira		15	6
Méndez, Antonio	Teba		14	
Méndez, Francisco*	Botán		1	
Méndez, Justa*		Sevilla	9	5
Núñez, Felipe	Lisboa		1	1
Paiba, Simón*	Fundão		8	3
Peña, Sebastián de la				2

Enríquez-Lucena Holiday Attendees

People Attending Purim, Passover, or Yom Kippur with Manuel de Lucena and Catalina Enríquez
(*indicates a relation of the Lucena-Enríquez-Paiba family)

NAME	BIRTHPLACE IN PORTUGAL	BIRTHPLACE IN SPAIN	ATTENDED IN MEXICO CITY	ATTENDED IN PACHUCA
Pereira, Nicolás			5	
Rodríguez, Álvaro	unidentified		2	
Rodríguez, Andrés	Fundão		3	
Rodríguez, Blanca		Sevilla	1	
Rodríguez, Costanza		Sevilla	4	1
Rodríguez, Diego*		Sevilla	1	
Rodríguez, Domingo		Sevilla	4	3
Rodríguez, Duarte*	Covilhã		7	
Rodríguez, Hernán	Fundão		3	
Rodríguez, Pedro	Fundão		3	
Rodríguez, Simón	Salzedas		1	
Rodríguez (de Ledesma), Francisco		Barrueco Pardo	5	2
Rodríguez de Silva, Juan			3	
Rodríguez Saz, Pedro	Fundão		2	
Rodríguez Silgueiro, Manuel	Fundão		5	2
Rodríguez, Gonzalo	unidentified		1	
Rodríguez, Jorge	São Vicente da Beira		4	5
Rodríguez, Sebastián	São Vicente da Beira		2	2
Váez, Ana	Fundão		1	
Váez, Francisco	São Vicente da Beira		5	1
Totals				
65 people attended at least one holiday	38 from Portugal	22 from Spain	5 from other birthplaces or unknown birthplaces	
	15 from Fundão	10 from Sevilla		
	4 from São Vicente da Beira	8 from Benavente		
	2 from Covilhã			
	17 from other places in Portugal	4 from other places in Spain		

NOTES

Note to Book Epigraph: "Una vez estando pesando una poca de plata, meneándose el peso, dijo Francisco Váez criado suyo: ¡Cómo baila este peso! Y el dicho Manuel de Lucena respondió, Si así supiera bailar Dios." Reported by Gómez Pertierra, Friday, December 2, 1594 (AGN 152–54, 326r).

Introduction

1. Díaz del Castillo, *Historia*, chap. 105. Translation mine.
2. See appendix 1, "Origins and Arrivals."
3. Pulido Serrano, "Plural Identities," 132.
4. An example in the broad spectrum is how the range of conversos' Judaizing beliefs and practices narrowed over time, while over the same period they assimilated and incorporated many aspects of Christian thought and practice (explored in Gitlitz, *Secrecy and Deceit*). An example of narrower focus is the dependence of the inquisitors on Jewish culinary customs as a tool to identify conversos' retention of Jewish identity (Gitlitz and Davidson, *A Drizzle of Honey*).
5. This pattern, highlighted first by Robert Ricard in *Pour une étude* in 1939, has been noted by many subsequent scholars. For a detailed treatment of this migration, see chapter 8.
6. Recopilación 2: libro 4, título 19, ley 1, cited in Cubillo Moreno, Dominios, 120. Translation mine.
7. In these magmatic eruptions of the Tertiary period, the silver bonded with sulfur, arsenic, or antimony in compounds such as argentite (silver sulfide), freibergite (silver and copper antimony-arsenic sulfide), and proustite-pyrargirite (silver antimony-arsenic sulfide). They tended to be found in andesitic or balsatic bodies that were often laced with quartz, pyrite (iron sulfide), calcite (calcium carbonate), and rhodonite (manganese silicate). In some areas, such as

around Taxco, the silver had compounded with lead in metamorphic rocks such as slate and schist. For negrillos, see Brading and Cross, "Colonial," 547; Castillo Martos, *Bartolomé*, 91–92; West, "Early," 123. The colorados generally contained argentite, cerargyrite (native silver with silver chloride), and cerussite (lead carbonate) (West, "Early," 126).

8. Information about first-generation professional miners or metallurgists in Mexico is thin. We know that two employees of the Fugger family, Martin Verger and Christoph Keiser, made the voyage in 1536, bringing with them some mining machinery (Sánchez Flores, "Technology," 139). The German metallurgist Johann Engel was working in Sultepec by 1536 (Wagner, "Early," 58). Ida Altman, who studied extant notarial records of immigrants from 1536 to 1538, found only four people identified as miners ("Spanish," 423).
9. See discussion in chapter 2.
10. As Miriam Bodian points out, "The interrogations, formulated as indirect speech in the third person and often paraphrased, are not strictly verbatim transcripts. But they are *close* to verbatim" (*Dying*, xii).

Chapter 1

1. Archivo General de la Nación Inquisición (61) 158-3, title page. Subsequent references to Mexico's Archivo General de la Nación Inquisition archive will use the short form: AGN volume–expediente, folio, as in note 3, below.
2. Casa de Contratación 5536, libro 3, fol. 1(1). The documents give Lorenzo's surname indiscriminately as Castellano or Castellanos. Blanca's surname may indicate merely that she was Lorenzo's wife.
3. AGN 158-3, 75v.
4. Other Jewish centers in Galicia were Allariz, Orense, Monforte, Pontevedra, Rivadavia, and Rivadeo. Richard Gottheil and Meyer Kayserling, "Galicia, Spain" (*Jewish Encyclopedia*, 2002–2011, www.jewishencyclopedia.com/articles/6474-galicia-spain [accessed July 25, 2016]).
5. Francisco Enriquez's star rose when he married into the prestigious Ulloa family, lords of the great castles of Toro and Mota del Marqués and financial advisers to Fernando and Isabel. In 1521 Francisco distinguished himself at the Battle of Villalar in the Comunero Rebellion and was rewarded in 1533 by being named the first Marqués of Alcañices. Francisco's fourth son, Diego, would serve as bishop of Coria, in the Spanish province of Cáceres, from 1550 to 1565. In 1568 King Felipe II would name Francisco's third son, Martín Enríquez de Almansa, viceroy of New Spain, and in 1580 Martín would become viceroy of Peru (Wikipedia, "Francisco Enríquez de Almansa," Wikipedia, https://es.wikipedia.org/wiki/Francisco_Enr%C3%ADquez_de_Almansa [accessed July 25, 2016]). Today the five villages, located in the

provinces of Zamora and Valladolid, have a combined population of fewer than five thousand.

6. Lorenzo's grandson Julián de Castellanos, whose 1590 testimony in Mexico provides glimpses of these events that took place almost one hundred years earlier, said that his father "was one of the Jews expelled from Spain by the Catholic Monarchs." He should have said his grandfather Lorenzo, for he indicates elsewhere that his father was born in Portugal shortly after the expulsion (AGN 1529-1, 21v).

7. Tomás de Fonseca's half brother Julián recalled hearing that his grandfather Lorenzo had served the king of Portugal, and he took pride in his status: "He served King Manoel, because although he was a Jew, he was not one of the lower class ones but one of the honored" (AGN 1529-1, 13r).

8. Mea, "Inquisição portuguesa," 231. Eugenio Hoyo considers that in the early sixteenth century, the conversos all along the Raya de Portugal "lived in a permanent coming-and-going between Spain and Portugal" (Hoyo, *Historia*, 202-3; translation mine).

9. AGN 127-1, 40v; AGN 1529-1, 22r. Contemporary documents refer to him alternately as Gabriel and Graviel.

10. Freixo de Espada-à-Cinta, with twenty-one hundred inhabitants, bills itself as the village with the largest number of Manueline-style window frames in all of Portugal. It also touts a Manueline church, an octagonal tower that is all that remains of its frequently fought-over castle, and the spectacular landscape of which the village forms a part.

11. AGN 158-3, 58r.

12. For example, Juan de Salcedo, a New Christian living in Soria said, "The year that their highnesses ordered the Jews to leave Castilla, one day during the festival of unleavened bread . . . I was at the home of Isaac the Portuguese, teaching his son to read Hebrew (*meldar*)." Testimony to the Inquisition in Aranda, March 10, 1502 (Carrete Parrondo, *Fontes*, 155); translation mine.

13. AGN 1529-1, 50r, 60v.

14. In his testimony in 1590, old Tomás de Fonseca was unsure which of the two cities his grandmother was from (AGN 158-3, 67v, 220v). His half brother Julián thought it was Porto, although the marriage took place in Viseu (AGN 1529-1, 1v, 19v). Tomás said that his maternal grandfather, Lope de Fonseca, who had worked as a butcher in the household of King Manoel, may have been born in Portugal. He claimed not to know his maternal grandmother's name (AGN 158-3, 220v). For Porto, see Paulo, "Commune"; Moreno, "Judeus." For Viseo, see Monteiro, *Judeus*.

15. These towns, including Belmonte, Castelo de Vide, Guarda, Lamego, Penamacor, and Trancoso, today jointly promote tourism via the Rede de Judiarias de Portugal.

16. AGN 159-4, 275v; AGN 1529-3, 31v; Cohen, *Martyr*, 100; Uchmany, *Vida*, 55, 106.

17. AGN 158-3, 220v.
18. AGN 158-3, 220v, 222v; AGN 1529-1 passim.
19. AGN 158-3, 213v; AGN 1529-1, 68r.
20. AGN 158-3, 68v, 78r, 222v.
21. AGN 158-3, 222r.

Chapter 2

1. AGN 152-2, 10v.
2. AGI ES.41091.AGI/11//PASAJEROS,L.1,E.4870. Pasajeros, October 9, 1534. PDF of document accessible at Archivo General de Indias (AGI), Contratación 5536.L.3, F.1(1). Julián de Castellanos's belief that the Portuguese king's influence helped Gabriel secure a berth among the thirty may have an element of truth in it, even though it was Gabriel's father who had served King Manoel I and by 1534 the king had been dead for thirteen years (AGN 1529-1, 13r).
3. Boyd-Bowman, "Emigración," 176–77.
4. Sicroff, *Controverses*; Jacobs, "Legal"; Lira Montt, "Estatuto."
5. These instructions are found in the *Collección of documentos inéditos del Archivo de Indias*, cited in Lewin, "Struggle," 217, 220. These restrictions were codified in the Nuevas Leyes de Indias (New Laws of the Indies) in 1542 and reiterated in later editions and revisions through the next century and a half.
6. For techniques for evading immigration regulations, see Jacobs, "Legal."
7. AGN 1529-1, 13r.
8. *Recopilación de las leyes* (1680): libro 9, título 28, ley 21, cited in Pérez-Mallaína Bueno, *Spain's Men*, 130.
9. The Castellanos family arrived in Mexico City in early 1535 (AGN 158-3, 69r).
10. Sixteenth-century shipping records suggest that the average duration of the 7,820-kilometer voyage from Sanlúcar de Barrameda to New Spain was ninety-one days (Chaunu et al., *Séville*, 6:1, 178).
11. AGN 158-3, 69r.
12. In August 1534, the cargo of a boat that Gallego piloted was registered in Sevilla. In October Gallego was named in the document that gave Gabriel Castellanos permission to sail. In May 1535, Gallego registered 195 pesos, seven tomines, and six *granos* worth of gold and silver that he had brought to his wife, Juana Pérez, from Cuba in the nao *Santa Catalina*, whose master was Juan de la Puebla (Pacheco et al., *Colección*, 7:337, 478). In partnership with Rodrigo Álvarez, Gallego brought two gold objects from Mexico in 1536 (AGI 23.82.1, Justicia 1152). In 1537 Gallego transported several canvas-wrapped *fardos* of goods for Fernando Pérez Jarada of Sevilla (AGI 13.47.29, Justicia 724). A Blas Gallego also piloted the 110-ton nao *San Juan* to New Spain (Chaunu et al., *Séville*, 2:242).

13. There is documentary evidence for various shipmasters named Andrés and Juan García from this period. An Andrés García Cancino was active as master from at least 1501 to 1516–1517, when he commanded the caravel *La Concepción* (Mira Caballos, *Nicolás*, 178; Otte Sander, *Sevilla*, 136. A Juan García, resident of Cádiz, was master of the nao *La Tiscareña* in 1519 (Otte, *Sevilla y sus mercaderes*, 104). Another, resident of Palos de Moguer, mastered a ship to Peru in 1533 (Izquierdo Labrado, "Emigración," 294).
14. AGN 158-3, 69r.
15. AGI, Indiferente General 2673, cited by Pérez-Mallaína, *Spain's Men*, 130. For conditions on board, see also Rodríguez Lorenzo, "Mar."
16. AGI, Contratación 3251, cited by Pérez-Mallaína, *Spain's Men*, 132.
17. "San Niculás, quiera guarder nuestra quilla, nuestra tilla, nuestra puente, nuestra jarcia, que de fuera pende y dentro cae; aqueste viaje y otros muchos mejorados ... con mar bonanza y largo viento, y buen viaje y salvamento, recemos la oración del Pater noster y la Ave María" (Fernández del Castillo, *Libros*, 369, 392).
18. Pérez-Mallaína, *Spain's Men*, 158–62. See also Fernández del Castillo, *Libros*; Leonard, *Books*; González Sánchez, "Libro."
19. Pérez-Mallaína, *Spain's Men*, 162.
20. By the end of the sixteenth century, perhaps earlier, port officials had marked the rocks and banks with flags (Vázquez de Espinosa, *Compendio*, cited in Felix, *Urban*, 112).
21. By 1580 civic and commercial building on both the island and the mainland city had taken on an air of permanence, with sturdy walls of planks or brick and roofs of tiles imported from Spain or manufactured locally. The fullest contemporary portrayal is by the *alcalde mayor* Álvaro Patiño in his 1580 *Descripción de la ciudad de la Veracruz y su comarca* (Ramírez Cabañas, *Ciudad*, 38). See also Pérez-Mallaína, *Spain's Men*, 10–11.
22. Trens, *Historia*, 102, 106. Six tomines equaled one real; eight reals equaled one peso.
23. López de Velasco, *Geografía y descripción universal de las Indias* (1571–1574), cited in Ramírez Cabañas, *Ciudad*, 9. "The Spaniards who live in this city all depend on the fleets that dock in this port; for the only occupation of the people in this city is to receive the goods brought to these lands from Spain, and to service the fleets and ships that come here" (Álvaro Patiño, *Descripción de la Ciudad de la Veracruz y su Comarca* [1580], cited in Ramírez Cabañas *Ciudad*, 35; translation mine).
24. Hernán Cortés, *Ordenanzas sobre ventas* (1524), cited in Butzer, "Roadside Inn," 3. The complete text of these ordinances appears in Trens, *Historia*, 101–102.
25. Roughly four hundred kilometers separate Veracruz and Mexico City. Ross Hassig estimated that in the seventeenth century, a loaded wagon could travel about twenty kilometers per day (Hassig, *Comercio*), 231.

Chapter 3

1. AGN 158-3, 59r.
2. A 1554 report described Calle Tacuba as wide, straight, and level. "The whole street is paved with stones to prevent its becoming muddy and filthy in the rainy season. Through its middle water flows in an open canal, which adds to its beauty and its usefulness to the people" (Cervantes de Salazar, *Life*, 38–39).
3. AGN 127-1, 40v. Notarial documents of October 30, 1536, identify Gabriel de Castellanos as a "master of showing young people how to read" and place his school on the Calle Tacuba (Millares Carlo and Mantecón, *Índice*, 2:docs. 2015-16). In 1590 Melchor López Castellanos (apparently not related) testified that as a child, he learned his letters in Gabriel's school (AGN 1529-1, 94r).
4. At 450 *maravedís*, the peso de oro de minas was worth 90 percent of a *peso de oro castellano* (Riva Palacio, *México*, 158).
5. AGN 158-3, 79r. Dr. Blas de Bustamante, from Tordehumos in Valladolid, came to Mexico in 1528 or 1529. Probably on the strength of his wife's nobility—Leonor de Bobadilla she was daughter of the Count of Gomera—Bustamante was assigned tribute from several haciendas in the province of Veracruz. In Mexico City he taught Latin to the sons of the privileged and moderately well-to-do. In the early 1550s, he and six colleagues founded the University of Mexico City (Carreño, "Maestro," 10). Cervantes de Salazar notes in 1554 that Bustamante's university classes were always thronged, adding that he teaches "with earnestness as well as diligence . . . he interprets the authors carefully, solves the difficulties, and subtly notes the more important points. He is well versed in dialectics and philosophy. . . . Because he has taught the Mexican youth for twenty-six years, there is scarcely anyone lecturing or teaching who has not been his student" (Cervantes de Salazar, *Life*, 29). In 1596 Tomás testified that he had also heard canon law from *provisor* Aldana (AGN 158-3, 78r).
6. Bancroft, Lucena, 304r, 485r. See also AGN 158-3, 243r, 262r.
7. AGN 158-3, 109r, 262rv. The five parts of *Espejo de consolación de tristes* were published in Burgos between 1540 and 1560.
8. AGN 97-9-3, 76r. Matías González, an Inquisition familiar, compiled the inventory.
9. AGN 1529-1, 49v–63r.
10. AGN 1529-1, 102r.
11. AGN 1529-1, 42v.
12. AGN 1529-1, 103r.
13. AGN 1529-1, 17v, 28v, 49v, 51v, etc.
14. AGN 1529-1, 56v. See Gitlitz, *Secrecy*, 321.
15. AGN 1529-1, 52r, 53r, 104v.
16. The starting date most commonly observed by Mexican crypto-Jews was the evening of Holy Thursday.

17. AGN 1529-1, 26v-27.
18. "In my house they taught and required another Jewish rite, which was that on Christmas Eve and the Eve of Saint John the Baptist, that occurred at six month intervals, one could not drink water by itself because in honor of those nights waters changed into blood. And by putting a little wine into the glasses of water that we drank on those nights, the blood would not understand; so on those nights we did not drink water alone but only watered wine; they said it was a Jewish rite that the Jews knew about and performed" (AGN 1529-1, 52v-53r). José Faur has documented this custom among Portuguese conversos (*In the Shadow*, 125).
19. AGN 1529-1, 50r. Either Julián was lying about not knowing the language was Hebrew or he did not get as good a Hebrew education as Tomás.
20. Pedro López, who came to Mexico to help his widowed sister, graduated in medicine from the Universidad de México in 1553. He is known for having founded the city's leprosy hospital, San Lázaro, in 1572, and in 1582 he founded the Hospital de Nuestra Señora de los Desamparados, near the present site of San Juan de Dios, for mestizos and blacks. The Inquisition queried him in 1570 about the accusation that he beat a crucifix, but the case was never brought to conclusion and did not hamper his activism in social causes or his integration into the highest levels of colonial society (AGN 72-11). He died in 1597.
21. AGN 1529-1, 13r.
22. AGN 158-3, 76v, 222r; AGN 1529-1, 28v. The children were Juan Pérez de Fonseca, Felipa de Fonseca, and Isabel de Fonseca (AGN 158-3, 76v).
23. AGN 150-1, 32r; AGN 1529-1, 14r and throughout. Julián ingenuously tried to claim in 1590 that he had acquired his detailed knowledge of Jewish practice not from his family but from listening to the condemnations read aloud at autos-de-fé in Mexico over the previous forty years (AGN 158-3, 217v-218r).
24. AGN 1529-1, 17v, 28v, 52rv.
25. AGN 1529-1, 53rv.
26. Overviews of converso presence in New Spain during this period can be found in Greenleaf, *Zumárraga*; Liebman, *Jews in New Spain*; Uchmany, "Participation"; and Uchmany, "Judíos."
27. There does not appear to be any connection between Gabriel de Castellanos and Diego de Castellanos, a gold miner in Oaxaca who is mentioned in two April 5, 1527, notarial documents. In them, his employer, Alonso González of Mexico City, authorizes Lorenzo Juárez, also of Mexico City, to take charge of Diego de Castellanos's mining equipment, thirty-five slaves, herd of pigs, and all the gold he had thus far extracted from his mine (Millares Carlo and Mantecón, *Indice*, 1:docs. 477, 478).
28. AGN 1529-1, 87r.
29. AGN 1529-1, 98v.

30. AGN 1529-1, 94rv.
31. AGN 1529-1, 99v.

Chapter 4

1. AGN 158-3, 69v, 79r.
2. Soto Oliver, *Minería*, 11.
3. Grinberg, *Señores*, 24. Some surviving Purhépecha trench mines are as long as 12 meters and more than 6 meters deep.
4. These methods were often illustrated by Native American artists in early colonial codices such as the *Lienzo de Jucatacato*, the *Mapa Tlotzin*, and the *Mendoza*, *Azoyu*, *Florentine*, and *Xolotl* codices. See Boone, *Stories*.
5. Estrada Carrión, *Zacualpan*, 43-46. By the end of the classic period, with the decline of Teotihuacan and the rise of Tajín and the Maya, these techniques had spread to the coastal nations of the Gulf and the Pacific, the Yucatan Guatemalan highlands, and the diverse peoples of the Mexican highlands. Pérez Rosales, *Minería*, 26-29.
6. Pérez Sáenz, "Minería," 59; Altman, "Spanish," 422, 423n37.
7. In the first division of conquered lands in 1521, the six thousand Indians around Chiautla were assigned in encomienda to Diego de Ordaz, who had served in Cuba from 1511 and had come to Mexico with Cortés in 1519 (Nettel Ross, *Testigos*, 280; Himmerich y Valencia, *Encomenderos*, 152). Although there is no record of Ordaz having mined in Chiautla, he did know something of minerals. While the army was provisioning in Tlaxcala, prior to the assault on Tenochtitlán, Cortés sent Ordaz with a number of Tlaxcaltecans to the top of the Popocatépetl volcano to gather sulfur for the manufacture of gunpowder (Díaz del Castillo, *Historia*, chap. 9). Shortly thereafter, the encomienda passed to Alonso de Grado (d. 1527), who had served Cortés for a time as administrator of Villa Rica and was wed to doña Isabel (born Tecuichpoch Ixcaxochitzin), the young widow of the Mexica chieftain Cuauhtémoc (Cortés Espinoza, *Inventario*, 13). When the encomienda's next owner, Diego Becerra de Mendoza, was accused of having had a heretic grandfather and was assassinated in 1533, the encomienda reverted to the crown, which administered it at first as a *corregimiento* and from 1540 as an *alcaldía mayor*, with Pedro Ladrón de Guevara as chief administrator (Gerhard, *Geografía*, 110; cited in Cortés Espinoza, *Inventario*, 11-12). Ladrón de Guevara was succeeded in 1546 by Juan Juárez (Hanke and Rodríguez, *Virreyes*, 1:110-20).
8. Christian instruction had come to Ayoteco with a mission of Augustinian friars. By 1531 the friars had ceded parish duties to a new village church. Today this small city in the Mixteca Baja region of the state of Puebla, sixty kilometers south of Izúcar de Matamoros, is called Chiautla de Tapia.
9. The sale was recorded on October 30, 1536: "Master Cristóbal de Benavente,

resident of Tunuxtitán [Mexico City], sells to Gabriel de Castellanos, a schoolmaster who teaches young people to read, . . . a parcel on the Calle del Árbol, bordering the buildings of Juan de Valencia and others of Antonio de la Cadena that used to belong de Juan Tirado, for twenty-five pesos of *oro de minas*" (Millares Carlo and Mantecón, *Indice*, 2:2015).

10. AGN 158-3, 79r.
11. Hirschberg, "Alternative," 258.
12. Agricola, *De re metallica*, 212. *De re metallica*, first published in 1556, was the most important mining text circulating in the New World in the sixteenth century (Young, "Black," 110). It deals more with mining techniques and equipment than minerals per se.
13. Lang, *Monopolio*, 37. A late sixteenth-century description of the Zacatecas mining district highlights this devastation: "When they were discovered, these gullies were covered with trees and brush, which are all gone, now that the mines have been developed, so that the only vegetation that has remained are some small wild palms. For that reason firewood is very expensive in this city, as it has to be brought from eight or ten leagues away in wagons" (Mota y Escobar, *Descripción*, 139–40). See also Studnicki-Gizbert et al.
14. Deeper tunnels were hard to dig, hard to shore up, hard to light, and hard to drain, and although their European contemporaries were beginning to solve these problems, their innovations were not yet in general use in Mexico.
15. By the mid-1530s, stores in the mining camp stores were supplied by wholesalers who bought from local producers. Clergymen, who by order of their bishop were paid in produce by their parishioners, might also sell these foodstuffs to wholesalers. For example, in 1536 the clergyman Antón de Carmona sold to Diego de Logroño twelve hundred bushels of corn, one hundred bushels of beans, and one hundred bushels of chiles for delivery to the Real de Sultepec; he sold another portion of his tithes to Pero Núñez for delivery to Zumpango, Taxco, and Amatepec (Millares Carlo and Mantecón, *Indice*, 2:docs. 1815 and 1890).
16. On the Mixtón war, see López-Portillo y Weber, *Rebelión*. There appear to be no records of the part that Gabriel de Castellanos played in the campaign, which suggests that it was in no way significant.
17. Icaza, *Diccionario*, 2:90, no. 715.
18. AGN 158-3, 69r, 79r.
19. AGN 158-3, 222v.

Chapter 5

1. Fernández del Castillo, *Libros* 47:231, cited in Probert, "Bartolomé," 96.
2. The dates of Fonseca's residence in Pachuca are problematic. The first strike in Pachuca occurred in 1552. In 1596 Fonseca testified that "In 1550 I . . . went to

the newly discovered mines of Pachuca; in Pachuca I was one of the first discoverers, and I resided there for a year and a half; from there in 1558 I went to the newly discovered mines of Tlalpujahua" (AGN 158-3, 223rv).
3. Agricola *De re metallica*, 170.
4. Cubillo Moreno, *Dominios*, 85.
5. Mecham, "*Real de Minas*," 45-46.
6. Lavrin, "Search," 41.
7. Hoberman, *Mexico's Merchant*, 93.
8. See, for example, the instructions given by Viceroy Mendoza in 1550 to his successor, Luis de Velasco (*Colección de documentos inéditos* 6:484-515, cited in Cubillo Moreno, *Dominios*, 87). A miners' petition to lower the price at which the government sold mercury to the miners justified their request, saying, "The preservation of the Indies depends on [the miners]; and if they should be lacking, all commerce will disappear" (*Colección de documentos Inéditos* 6:183, cited in Cubillo Moreno, *Dominios*, 163; translation mine).
9. Moreno de los Arcos, "Instituciones," 69.
10. Brading and Cross, "Colonial," 549. In October 1580, miners in Pachuca petitioned the alcalde mayor to name two miners to figure out how to drain the mines (AGN 051 General de Parte 2-1029).
11. Hoberman, *Mexico's Merchant*, 73.
12. The inquisitors Alonso de Peralta and Gonzalo Martos de Bohórquez, who presided over the Tomás de Fonseca case, were both accused of involvement in the mining business (Alberro, *Inquisición*, 42).
13. Bakewell, "Notes," 187.
14. Hoberman calculates that Mexico's 25 million Native inhabitants in 1519 had shrunk to 1.5 million by 1643 (*Mexico's Merchant*, 6).
15. Bakewell, "Notes," 171.
16. Castillo Martos, *Bartolomé*, 73-74. For an early detailed description of the patio process, see Egleston, "Patio"; Rapp, *Archaeominerology*, 242. My thanks to Fernando Palero for technical information on this subject.
17. A metallurgist named Álvaro López, for example, had found in the early 1520s that nitrous acid could be used to separate some gold and silver. Sánchez Flores, "Technology," 139.
18. Probert, *Medina*, 101-3.
19. Barrera-Osorio, *Experiencing*, 69.
20. Young, "Black," 115.
21. Barrera-Osorio, *Experiencing*, 65-72; Brading and Cross, "Colonial," 552; Castillo Martos, *Bartolomé*; Probert, "Bartolomé"; Young, "Black," 115.
22. Burnes Ortiz, *Minería*, 44-45; Sánchez Flores. "Technology"; Castillo Martos, *Bartolomé*, 109.
23. The first part of the translation of this document is from Probert, *Bartolomé*, 96; the rest is mine.
24. Though patents were known in antiquity, the first modern patent for intellectual property was granted in 1474 in the Venetian Republic to protect certain

innovations in the glassmaking industry. The modern system of granting limited-term monopolies for inventions became systematized in mid-sixteenth-century Florence, France, and England (Stanford Encyclopedia of Philosophy, "Intellectual Property," SEP, September 22, 2014, http://plato.stanford.edu/entries/intellectual-property [accessed February 8, 2015]).

25. The largest number were in the vicinity of Temascaltepec (thirty mines), Guanajuato (twenty-nine), Taxco (twenty-seven), and Pachuca (seventeen) (Castillo Martos, *Bartolomé*, 116–17). Unfortunately, the patent did not cover Nueva Vizcaya or Nueva Galica, the site of many important mines, such as those in Zacatecas, where the patio process quickly took hold without Medina's receiving so much as a maravedí (Probert, *Bartolomé*, 116).
26. Barrera-Osorio, "Experiencing," 70–71.
27. Veitia Linaje, *Norte de la contratación de las Indias Occidentales*, book 1, chap. 4, no. 3, cited in Lang, *Monopolio*, 43.
28. Hernández et al., "Almadén."
29. Thirty forced laborers, culled from the chains of galley slaves, were allocated to the mines in 1566; the number was increased to forty in 1583 (Hernández et al., "Almadén").
30. "All the veins of silver, gold, and lead, and any other metal found in our dominions belong to us [the king]" (*Alfonso XI, Ordenamiento Real*, book 4, tit. 1, law 7, cited in González, "Panorama," 792; translation mine).
31. Wagner, "Early," 51.
32. Tandeter, "Mining," 319.
33. Pérez Sáenz, "Minería," 115.
34. Cubillo Moreno, *Dominios*, 248–49.
35. Hoberman, *Mexico's Merchant*, 81.
36. Flynn and Giráldez, "Born." For lively discussions of the massive trade in smuggled silver and its effect on the economies of Spain, Mexico, Peru, the Philippines, and China, see Mann, *1943*, chap. 4; Bonialian, *China*, 36–39; del Valle Pavón, "Mercaderes," 213–40.
37. Flynn et al., *European*, 434–37.
38. Rodrigo de Albornoz to Carlos V, March 1, 1533, cited in Studnicki-Gizbert, "From Agents," 52.
39. Garner, "Long-Term," 903–4.
40. Burnes Ortiz, *Minería*, 34–35.
41. Burnes Ortiz, *Minería*, 38.

Chapter 6

1. AGN 158-3, 69v.
2. Herrejón Pereda, *Tlalpujahua*, 38.
3. AGN Tierras (110) 91-1, 34v.
4. A map drawn in 1575 indicates the holdings of twelve miners by name,

including Tomás de Fonseca (AGN Instituciones Coloniales, "Ingenio de agua"). A census taken in the viceroyalty in 1570 recorded the population of Tlalpujahua to be forty Europeans and 120 slaves. Although this census recorded the Indian populations of many other mining towns, it made no mention of Indians in Tlalpujahua ("Censos," 53, cited in Wagner, "Early," 68). A 1597 survey on the labor force in Mexico's major mining communities reported that working in the Tlalpujahua mines were nineteen miners, four slaves, and 250 Indians, of whom 137 were assigned in repartimiento; the others were free laborers (Palmer, *Slaves*, 80).

5. AGI, ES.41091.AGI/23.10.1105//MEXICO,1090,L.7,F.320R-320V 1574-12-23 Madrid.
6. León Alanis, "Evangelización."
7. Agricola, *De re metallica*, 128.
8. Miners seldom were allotted as much mercury as they thought they needed, so pleas for more were common. Although no azogue petition by Tomás de Fonseca appears to have survived, the AGN preserves one from 1591 by Tomás's nephew Héctor de Fonseca in Taxco. Héctor requested ten quintales of azogue, arguing that the royal treasury would suffer if his hacienda de beneficiar had to shut down. He was allotted four quintales, despite the fact that Taxco's alcalde de minas, Martín de Salinas, had supported his request for an increase (AGN General de Parte [51] 4-304, 87v).
9. AGN Real Fisco (97) 6-5, 267r.
10. AGN Real Fisco (97) 6-5, 310r.
11. AGN Mercedes (072) 10, 100v.
12. AGN Tierras (110) 91-1, 17v-19. See below for the lawsuits that delayed the building of this structure.
13. Agricola, *De re metallica*, 109.
14. Mota y Escobar, *Descripción*, 144.
15. AGN Real Fisco (97) 6-8, 257-330; AGN Real Fisco (97) 9-3, 73r-81r.
16. Fonseca's library of books on religious topics that the Inquisition inventoried in 1596 includes many that, judging from their publication dates, Tomás purchased late in life.
17. Agricola, *De re metallica*, 247.
18. Even Bartolomé de Medina, the developer of the patio process, in 1579 found himself embroiled in a water rights dispute in Pachuca (AGN Tierras [110] 2809-28, 12, cited in Cubillo Moreno, "Actividad," 130).
19. Often attributed, apocryphally, to Mark Twain (Quote Investigator, "Whiskey Is for Drinking; Water Is for Fighting Over," Quote Investigator, June 3, 2013, http://quoteinvestigator.com/2013/06/03/whiskey-water/ [accessed July 7 2014]).
20. The first Spanish owner of Ramírez's land appears to have been Luis de Armengol. Sometime during the 1560s, Tomás's neighbor Rodrigo de Quesada bought the parcel, which was adjacent to another of his holdings, and soon after that sold it to Bartolomé Rodríguez. When he died, his widow, María de los Reyes,

sold the property to Luis Ramírez. Ramírez's widow, Inés de Malaber, managed the property for her two small children, Cristobal and Antonio (AGN Mercedes [072] 10, 100v–101r).

21. In 1590 this same Bustamante was serving as alcalde de minas in Pachuca ("Informaciones: Agustín de Bustamante," AGI Mexico 219, N. 11).
22. AGN Tierras (110) 91-1, 1r–12v.
23. He is either affirming his contribution to the government policy of encouraging population growth, which unmarried Fonseca was not, or else implying that Fonseca was perhaps living in sin.
24. AGN Tierras (110) 91-1, 17v–20v.
25. AGN Real Fisco (97) 6–8, 259v, 263r.
26. AGN Real Fisco (97) 6–5: 260r. A quintal equaled approximately one hundred pounds.
27. AGN 158-3, 69v, 79v.
28. Young, *Chocolate*, chaps. 1, 2; Prinz, *On the Chocolate*, chap. 7.
29. In 1513 Hernando de Oviedo y Valdez, who went to America as a member of Pedrarias Dávila's expedition, reported that he bought a slave for one hundred cocoa beans (Coe and Coe, *True*, 99–101, 176–77).
30. Lee, "Cochineal," 451.
31. Berdan and Anawalt, *Codex Mendoza*, fol. 43r.
32. Cervantes de Salazar, *Life*, 105, 144; López de Gómara, *Historia*, 34.
33. Instrucción a Don Martín Enríquez, vissorrey de la Nueva España, June 7, 1568 (AGN Audiencia de México, 1089, Libro CS, cited in Lee, "Cochineal," 458–60).
34. Both of these men were well-known to Tomás de Fonseca in other contexts. Both were New Christians descended from Jews, and Simón Rodríguez, from Salceda (near Vigo in Galicia), was one of the more active Judaizers in New Spain in the early 1590s. Rodríguez owned a store on the *zócalo* in Mexico City, loaned money to other businessmen (who thought him stingy), and invested in the China trade. A religious colleague of many Mexico City Judaizers and a one-time friend of Manuel de Lucena and Luis de Carvajal, Rodríguez married an Old Christian named Bernardina Castellanos, repudiated Judaism, and was soon known as an exemplary Christian, leading Lucena to call him a dog (AGN 154-1, 175r). He was arrested in 1596, penanced in an auto-de-fé in 1601, and in 1606 petitioned the Inquisition to be allowed to return to Spain (AGN 153-1, 144r; AGN 163-3, 106v; AGN 279-8, 100r–112r; AGN, *Libro primero*, 184; Uchmany, *Vida*, 84, 104). The other well-known cochineal exporters were Diego Serrano, Diego Anzúrez, the *alférez mayor* of Puebla, Luis de Mancilla, Juan Martínez Gallegos, Álvaro de Cáceres, Diego Cortés, Hernando de Castro, and Pedro Díez de Aguillar (Lee, "Cochineal," 460–61).
35. Tepaxco is probably Tapaxco, a village in the northwestern part of the state of Mexico, not far from Tlalpujahua (AGN Indiferente 5568-039, 1rv).
36. Powell, "Presidios"; Rees, "Origins."

Chapter 7

1. AGN 158-3, 59r.
2. AGN 1529-1, 19v; AGN 127-1, 43v.
3. AGN 127-1, 40v; AGN 1529-1, 1r.
4. So recalled her son Tomás in 1596 (AGN 156-4, 185v).
5. AGN 156-4, 181r, 186r.
6. AGN 156-4, 208r, 209r, 211r.
7. AGN 156-4, 181v. In his testimony, old Tomás does not mention Álvaro de Fonseca, only Isabel's husband Tomás Méndez (AGN 158-3, 67v).
8. AGN 1529-1, 103r.
9. AGN 127-1, 43v.
10. Julián de Castellanos said young Tomás had recounted this shared fast to him but did not say whether it occurred in Tlalpujahua or Mexico City. The date suggests Tlalpujahua (AGN 1529-1, 19v).
11. AGN 156-4, 210v-211r; AGN 158-3, 76r. Young Tomás called Méndez "dissolute" (*un hombre perdido*). In 1617 Tomás's half brother Diego, who was then living in Tlaxcala, was tried for Judaizing (University of California Berkeley, Bancroft Archive MSS 67/140, box 1:70).
12. The date of Pérez Herrero's death is unrecorded (AGN 1529-1, 8v).
13. Both Pereira and Guiomar de Fonseca were deceased by 1590; both were buried in the New Church of Santo Domingo in a niche on the left side of the aisle that Guiomar's first husband, Antonio Pérez Herrero, had purchased. AGN 1529-1, 2r, 8v, 29rv.
14. The sole surviving piece attributed to Orona is a gilt silver chalice in London's Victoria and Albert Museum.
15. AGN 1529-1, 2v-3r, 82v, 83v, 92v, 102r-103v.
16. Julián described his factory as an *obrajillo* and an *obrajuelo* and himself as an *obrajero pobre*, living from *unos telares*; his cousin young Tomás de Fonseca said that Julián was a weaver (AGN 127-1,42r; AGN 150-1, 32r; AGN 158-3, 58r; AGN 1529-1, 86r, 92v). For obrajes, see Greenleaf, "Obraje"; Castillo Sandoval, "Obraje"; Salvucci, *Textiles*; Miño Grijalba, "Obraje."
17. His taking them to mass was mentioned by Blas de Bustamante, Luis Alonso de Mercado, Leonor de Fisco, and her daughter Ana de Vera (AGN 1529-1, 83v, 86rv, 92v, 93r).
18. His poverty was confirmed by his neighbor, the druggist Hernán Gómez Rubio (AGN 1529-1, 98v).
19. AGN 158-3, 76r; AGN 1529-1, 2r.
20. AGN 158-3, 213v.
21. AGN 158-3, 220v, 222v.
22. AGN 158-3, 212r.
23. AGN 158-3, 212r.

24. So said young Tomás de Fonseca Castellanos (AGN 156-4, 186r). Julián Castellanos also gave the date of his death as 1570 (AGN 158-3, 212r). Nevertheless, a 1573 Inquisition investigation into personal libraries used the present tense in recording that a Gabriel de Castellanos "tiene un *Cancionero General y Epístolas y Evangelios* y cuatro o cinco pares de *Horas*" (Fernández del Castillo, *Libros*, 490). In his 1596 testimony, Tomás probably erred when he recalled the death date as 1575 or 1576 (AGN 158-3, 220v).
25. AGN 158-3, 220v.
26. AGN 158-3, 223r.
27. AGN 156-4, 259v; AGN 158-3, 223r.
28. AGN 1529-1, 2r.

Chapter 8

1. An early version of this chapter appeared as "The Where of the Mexican Conversos" in the *Journal of Spanish, Portuguese, and Italian Crypto Jews*.
2. AGN 153-9, 18rv.
3. AGN 333-1, 3rv.
4. For broad views of Portuguese converso immigration to the Americas, see Böhm, "'Portugueses'"; Uchmany, "Participation"; Israel, *Diasporas*, chap. 3. In Mexico's Inquisition files from the 1530s, a handful of people are designated as Portuguese, and some are tagged as being descended from converts or suspected of being Judaizers. These include, for the years 1537–1539: Manuel Borrullo, suspected (AGN 22-9) and Francisco Millán, suspected (AGN 30-8); 1539: Beatriz Gómez, absolved (AGN 30-9 bis) and her husband, Álvaro Mateos, absolved (AGN 30-9). In none of these procesos do the data suggest sophisticated knowledge or Judaizing practice, or the existence of a community of Judaizers.
5. See, for example, Cantera Burgos, "Judíos."
6. AGN 158-3, 67r.
7. Cohen, *Martyr*, 28–29. The surname Carvajal was not per se indicative of converso origin. The AGN index references at least thirty-six other persons named Carvajal in Mexico in the sixteenth century—six of them clergy—who do not appear to be related to this family. Insofar as other surnames used by this Carvajal family, the AGN likewise references at least nineteen unrelated Andradas; the surnames Cueva, León, and Núñez are too numerous to tally.
8. Mea, *Inquisição de Coimbra*, 225–40.
9. Mea, "Inquisição portuguesa," 231.
10. García, *Inquisição*. Sampaio's family seems to have had status in the region: in 1530, Fernã Vaz de Sampayo was mayor of two neighboring towns, Freixo de Espada-à-Cinta and Torre de Moncorvo (Freire, "Povoação," 256).

11. Bancroft, Lucena, 213r.
12. Antonio Enríquez told Mexican inquisitors in 1594 that his parents, Violante and Manuel Rodríguez, who were related to Manuel de Lucena by marriage, had fled to the Spanish city of Cáceres from their native village of Fundão to escape the Inquisition (AGN 152-2, 24r).
13. Graizbord, *Souls*, 21.
14. There are many Mexican examples from the 1590s:

    "We will go far away where we are not always watching ourselves over our own shoulders (meaning that he would go to a judiaria)," Antonio Gómez to Manuel Tavares, 1598 (AGN 163-3, 143v).

    "They all want to go to Salonica, ... this one says his wife is there, that one says he didn't go because he doesn't have enough money," Antonio López de Morales to Catalina Enríquez, 1596 (AGN 152-4, 371r).

    "I want to go to Italy, to some Jewish quarter, and live with Jews and marry a Jew, and observe their law," to which Luna replied, "Me, too," Manuel Tavares to Bernardo de Luna, 1598 (AGN 164-3, 34v).

    "You see these fields, these cattle? They are all cursed by the Lord because they belong to Christians. Very shortly I am planning to go to a land where I can freely keep the Law of Moses," Manuel de Lucena according to Jorge Álvarez, 1591 (AGN 153-1, 157r).

    "I am determined not to remain in this land, and with whatever I have, be it little or much, to go to Spain from where I can take my wife and children to good lands where they will come to well and truly know the Lord," Manuel de Lucena, according to Diego Enríquez, 1594 (AGN 153-9, 86v).

    "I told him I planned to go to some land where I could observe the Lord's law without the oppression that the Christians subject us to, and I would do it as soon as I had amassed enough money," Manuel de Lucena, 1596 (Bancroft, Lucena, 581r). See also Gitlitz, *Secrecy*, 602-5.
15. Temkin, *Luis de Carvajal*, 192-98.
16. Liebman, *Jews in New Spain*, 145.
17. All the 1580 arrivals except these last two came with the Carvajal group.
18. Bancroft, Lucena, 586r.
19. See Huerga, "Judíos."
20. Hordes, *To the End*, 80-81. Álvaro Huerga terms the Díaz Nietos and other confesos who resided for a time in Ferrara an "ítalo-hispano-lusa" hybrid (Huerga, "Judíos," 117).
21. Uchmany, *Vida*, 274.
22. Escobar Quevedo, *Inquisición*, 368; Liebman, *Jews in New Spain*, 47.
23. The magnetic attraction of economic opportunity in the Indies was highlighted by Jonathan Israel, who noted how in the early seventeenth century, the "economic opportunities for Jews in such safe, or relatively safe, areas as France, Italy, or Brazil, were very limited as compared with the opportunities in

Spanish-speaking lands, and that the lure of silver-producing, textile-importing colonies with a weak native bourgeoisie was a powerful one" (*Race*, 129–30). This analysis concords with that of scholars like Uchmany ("Participation," 192) and Alberro ("Crypto-Jews," 174).

24. Twenty-four-year-old Fernando Rodríguez de Herrera, of Fundão, came to Mexico in 1588. His wife and daughter, left behind in Spain, never joined him. He worked as a small-time tratante, buying and selling in Pachuca, Atotonilco, Texcoco, and Michoacán, where he was arrested for Judaizing in 1589 when he was observed slaughtering a chicken in the Jewish fashion. He was described at his arrest as a tall man with a long, sunburned nose, wearing tattered clothes, a green hat, and a blue cape (AGN 127-2, 220r–224v). Reconciled with the church in 1593 and released, he interacted with many of the Portuguese Judaizers in central Mexico until his second arrest and trial in 1596 (AGN 149-2; AGN 233-28). This time he was held for five years. After being tortured, he confessed to having secretly practiced Judaism, and he informed about many of his fellow Judaizers. He died in prison in 1601 (AGN 271-1, 12v; Uchmany, *Vida*, 146–47).
25. Bancroft, Lucena, 484r.
26. For lyrical descriptions of this "colorful and dynamic metropolis," see Montoto de Sedas, *Sevilla*; Pike, "Seville"; and Castillo Martos, *Bartolomé*. On Sevilla's role in transatlantic trade, see Pike, *Linajudos*, 67–73.
27. McCann and Acs, "Globalization," 25.
28. AGN 153-9, 7r; AGN 152-4, 316v. See Escobar Quevedo, *Inquisición*, 70–73.
29. AGN 252-3, 67r.
30. AGN 156-3, 31r.
31. In addition to the aforementioned: Álvaro González (AGN 1492-1, 58r), Francisco Manuel (AGN 155-1, 16r), Duarte Rodríguez (AGN 161-1, 15r; AGN 152-4, 243r), Pedro Rodríguez (AGN 159-5, 56v), and Violante Rodríguez (AGN 153-1, 94v). For Portuguese crypto-Jews in Sevilla during this period, see also Aguado de los Reyes, "Apogeo," and Pike, *Linajudos*.
32. AGN 154-1, 4r; his 1598 proceso: 1493-1; AGI/16419//PASAJEROS, L.7, E.2251; 16403.15.2136//INDIFERENTE,2066,N.2; Cohen, *Martyr*, 191.
33. Bancroft, Lucena, 585v.
34. AGN 152-4, 67v.
35. Liebman, *Jews in New Spain*, 146.
36. AGN 153-7, 68rv; Bancroft, Lucena, 16v, 88r.
37. The title page of a Spanish or Mexican Inquisition proceso often records the subject's country of origin. Later, at the first interrogation, the accused *judaizante* was instructed to narrate the basic story of his or her life (*el discurso de su vida*). Almost always these *discursos* began with the phrase, "I was born in a town called Thus-and-So."
38. Demographic data derived mainly from the records of the Coimbra Inquisition, which exercised jurisdiction over the northeast, make this patently clear:

of the 4,047 individuals prosecuted for Judaizing in Portugal between 1541 and 1755, 3,708 (91 percent) were from Trás-os-Montes (Sousa, "Silk," 4–5).
39. This concentration was first highlighted by Ricard, "Pour une étude." See also Liebman, *Jews in New Spain*, 185; Cohen, *Martyr*, 38.
40. Those claiming to have been born in Sevilla with Portuguese parents were Leonor Díaz, Catalina Enríquez, Diego Enríquez, Pedro Enríquez, Antonio López de Morales, Justa Méndez, Costanza Rodríguez, and Jorge Rodríguez.
41. Of the 204 victims whose country of birth Stanley Hordes was able to track, 37 percent were born in Spain, 40 percent were born in Portugal, and only 23 percent were born in the Americas. When Hordes looked at the victims' parents, taking the study back one generation, nearly 71 percent of their fathers and 51 percent of their mothers were born in Portugal. Taking it back another generation, 73 percent of their grandfathers and 57 percent of their grandmothers were born in Portugal. These data suggest that about a third of the Portuguese men left Portugal as bachelors and subsequently found wives in Spain (Hordes, "Crypto-Jewish," 40–41).
42. Jonathan Israel takes this argument a step further: "This overwhelming preponderance of Portuguese among the Judaizers sentenced in Mexico demonstrates that in general there was no correlation in New Spain . . . between New Christians . . . and crypto-Jews, or Jews. . . . It may be safely assumed, though it can never be proved, that there were many more Spanish New Christians than Portuguese in Mexico, but that the Spanish New Christians had forsaken the old faith to a much greater extent" (*Race*, 126). His assumptions echo those of Martin Cohen: "By any reasonable judgment, the number of Judaizers revealed by the Inquisition records and other reliable sources represents only a fraction of the total number of New Christians. Yet, while one might well assume the existence of numerous other Judaizers among the New Christians, the documents fail to support any contention that the majority or near totality of the New Christians were crypto-Jews" ("Some Misconceptions," 280).
43. A noun akin to the terms *chicano* or *nuyorican* would have been useful to indicate this fusion, but it never emerged.
44. AGN 164-7, 81r.
45. "I have dealt with many people in this land, both Portuguese and Castilian" (AGN 159-5, 46r). "I have always dealt with the Portuguese and Castilians around here." (AGN 164-7, 6r).
46. "Who are these Jews you are talking about?" inquisitors asked Manuel Tavares in 1596. Tavares replied: "The New Christians from my land, because I have always held all of them to be Jews, though I have not observed them Judaizing" (AGN 163-3, 141r).
47. AGN 1492-2, 159r.
48. AGN 163-3, 138r.
49. AGN 158-3, 79v.

50. AGN 152-4, 228r.
51. AGN 163-3, 116v, 126v.
52. AGN 152-3, 273r.
53. AGN 163-3, 116v.
54. *Adonay, a que fes o ceu a ha terra, líbranos de tanta guerra pues que somos os teuos* (AGN 402-2, 506rv).
55. AGN 1492-1, 59v.
56. AGN 1529-1, 10rv.
57. AGN 163-3, 94v.
58. AGN 1489-1, 347r.
59. AGN 164-7, 67v.
60. AGN 161-2, 8v.
61. AGN 163-3, 115v.
62. Noted by Ricard ("Pour une étude," 521).
63. AGN 1492-1, 12v; also reported in AGN 163-3, 96v. When Juan Antonio de Oria wondered why Manuel Tavares said that when the inquisitor Alonso de Peralta died, "*o demó* had taken him," Tavares explained to him, "because *o demó* in Portuguese means 'the Devil'" (AGN 163-3, 44v).
64. AGN 1529-3, 24v, 51r.
65. AGN 17-3, 69r.
66. "They were speaking Portuguese and I did not understand them." (AGN 161-6, 48r, 52rv).
67. AGN 163-3, 54r.
68. Castro, *Structure*, 607.
69. AGN 156-4, 219v.
70. Young Tomás de Fonseca and his employee Marco Antonio "trimmed the fat from their meat and ate strangled fowl as the Portuguese do" (AGN 156-4, 248r).
71. Marco Antonio wrote to Fonseca from Guatemala that when Lope Rodríguez came to visit, Fonseca should treat him well and could trust him, "because he was of the Portuguese Nation, meaning that he was Jewish, so he could be trusted" (AGN 156-4, 267v).
72. AGN 1529-1, 10rv.
73. Bancroft, Lucena, 26r. Gómez Navarro, from San Martín de Trevejos on the Spanish side of the border with Portugal, was the brother of Justa Méndez and Domingo Gómez. Though he had little formal education, he was widely read and knew much of the Bible by heart. After serving as a soldier in Colombia and Guatemala, he operated a store in the real de Sichú. In the auto-de-fé of 1596, he was sentenced to confiscation of all property and six years in the galleys, followed by life imprisonment in Sevilla (AGN 151-6; AGN Real Fisco (97) 4-4; AGN Real Fisco (97) 4-17; AGN Indiferente General 4383-009, Escobar Quevedo, *Inquisición*, 378; Liebman, *Jews in New Spain*, 175).

Chapter 9

1. AGN 154-1, 189r.
2. AGN 151-6, 167v. The song appears to have been a favorite (Bancroft, Lucena, 20r, 29r, 177r, 439r).
3. Liebman, "Hernando Alonso," 291-96. Martin Cohen (*Martyr*, 286n24) and Schulamith C. Halevy ("Blood") argue that he was not Jewish. Alonso was from Niebla, in Huelva near the Portuguese border.
4. Conway, "Hernando."
5. Uchmany, "Participation," 191.
6. AGN 2-2; Warren and Warren, *Gonzalo Gómez*.
7. During his interrogation, he tried to stave off a session of torture by denouncing as Judaizers a dozen of his acquaintances—the majority also from Jerez—but most of his allegations were considered spurious (AGN 30-8; Greenleaf, "Francisco Millán").
8. AGN 125-7.
9. Greenleaf, *Zumárraga*, 90-8. Accusations of Judaizing during the years 1537-1539 against the Portuguese Manuel Borullo, the Sevillian clog maker Juan Ruiz, Diego Machuca from the Duero region (AGN 22-9), Juan Cercado from Ocaña, and Antón de Heredia from Toledo (AGN 40-3D,E) were likewise not deemed worth pursuing.
10. A movement of Gnostic origin, deemed heretical by the church, that asserted perfectibility of the human soul in this life and the irrelevance of external forms of worship. See Sánchez-Barbudo, *Algunos*; Márquez Villanueva, *Alumbrados*; Huerga, *Historia*.
11. Liebman, *Jews in New Spain*, 42-43; Roth and Salomon, *History*.
12. Testimony from 1590, later unconvincingly recanted (AGN 1529-1, 19v).
13. AGN 156-4, 74r. Eva Uchmany notes that the custom of porging was so widespread among Judaizing conversos that "it was the first and last Jewish rite detected by the Inquisition in Spanish America" ("Participation," 193). See Gitlitz, *Secrecy*, 533-42.
14. AGN 1490-2.
15. AGN 158-3, 95v.
16. He was executed in 1579 for having Judaized for twenty years and for not revealing the names of other Judaizers (AGN 56-9; Lea, *Inquisition*, 208; Cohen, *Martyr*, 60). Another was Juan Ruiz Ortiz from Sevilla, an attorney in Tlaxcala, who was circumcised and in 1579 was suspected of Judaizing (AGN 59-3). Beatriz González and Isabel Ocampo, both from Llerena and residents in Veracruz, were descended from penanced Judaizers; the 1581 investigation into their activities was inconclusive (AGN 90-38). Accusations in 1585 against Luis Mener, a Franciscan friar, were deemed trivial (AGN 126-7).
17. The eight were Governor Luis de Carvajal y la Cueva; the governor's sister

Francisca; her children Luis, Leonor, Gaspar, Isabel, and Mariana; and Gonzalo Pérez Fero, a cousin of the Carvajals. The other two 1589 procesos targeted Julián de Castellanos and Hernán Rodríguez de Herrera, two Portuguese merchants.

18. Manuel de Lucena: "I hold him to be a Jew . . . because he communicates with the Carvajals and is their friend; and I once I saw him visiting Luis de Carvajal's mother and sisters" (AGN 156-4, 23r). Manuel Gil de la Guarda: "No man of honor could deal with the Carvajals; I hold them to be base people" (AGN 160-1, 106r). Francisco Rodríguez: "also because I saw him dealing routinely with Luis de Carvajal's people" (AGN 1491-2, 37v).

19. The most comprehensive and accurate study to date is Cohen, *Martyr*. See also Toro, *Familia*; Liebman, *Enlightened*; Perelis, "Marrano"; Temkin, *Luis de Carvajal*.

20. Hoyo, *Historia*, 108.

21. Related to Governor Carvajal y de la Cueva by blood or by marriage were Francisca Rodríguez de Carvajal (his sister); her husband, Francisco Rodríguez de Matos, and eight of their nine children; Catalina de León Carvajal (his cousin) and her husband, Gonzalo Pérez Ferro; Felipe Núñez (his wife's brother); Francisca Núñez Viciosa (his wife's half sister) and her husband, Alonso del Águila; Jorge and Diego de León (her brothers); and Ginebra Márquez de León (her sister).

22. AGN 154-3, 3v-5r. See also AGI ES.41091.AGI/11//PASAJEROS,L.6,E.3586 and AGI ES.41091.AGI/11//PASAJEROS,L.6,E.3633.

23. Gitlitz, "Anusim."

24. AGN 126-12, 4v.

25. Gonzalo Pérez Ferro, testifying in December 1589 about his arrival in New Spain, says that the governor's party landed in Tampico and went to the Villa de Pánuco (AGN 126-11, 160v, December 5), went to Isabel de Carvajal's home in the Puerto de Pánuco (AGN 126-11, 169r, December 9), landed in Tampico de Pánuco, and lived for a year and a half in separate houses in Tampico y Pánuco (AGN 126-11, 172v, January 4, 1590).

26. Lucena's wife, Catalina Enríquez, who clerked in and often managed Lucena's store, was an exception. Among the women who reported that they derived their living from their needle and their needlework between 1595 and 1597 were Isabel, Francisca, and Leonor de Carvajal and Justa Méndez (AGN 159-1, 14r, 20v; AGN 156-4, 76r; AGN 156-1, 14r). Antonio Machado's daughters took in mending to help support their ailing father (AGN 1491-3, 30v).

27. Texts are given in Cohen, *Martyr*, 78-79, 307. It is Martin Cohen's view that despite Morales's reputation, his "knowledge of Judaism was extremely limited" and that what he did purport to know was "all acquired second hand and all distorted" (*Martyr*, 308n29). In 1584 Morales, unhappy in America, returned to Europe, where he was reputedly sighted in Pisa, Venice, and Salonica. In

1590, when two of the Carvajal children went back to Spain, fleeing the Mexican Inquisition, they lodged with him for a time in Sevilla.
28. AGN 1529-3, 7r, 9v; Cohen, *Martyr*, 131.
29. Cohen, *Martyr*, 131.
30. AGN 156-4, 125v, 246r.
31. Gonzalo Pérez Ferro, born in 1581 in Vilaflor in the bishopric of Braga, came to Mexico with Governor Carvajal in 1580 with his wife, Catalina de León, who was a cousin of the Carvajals. The families were close: Pérez Ferro revealed his Judaism to young Luis back in Medina del Campo; he soldiered with Governor Carvajal in Nuevo León; he attended Francisco Rodríguez de Matos, Luis's father, in his last illness; he was present at the wedding of Jorge de Almeida and Antonio Díaz de Cáceres to the Carvajal sisters. In Mexico he described himself as a poor businessman. He and his wife were reconciled in the 1590 auto-de-fé; arrested a second time, he was reconciled in 1601. Catalina de León perished in the 1596 auto-de-fé (AGN 126, 11; AGN 156-4, 135r, 400r; AGN 251A, 431r; AGN 1492-2, 86r; Cohen, *Martyr*; Uchmany, *Vida*).
32. The brothers Domingo and Jorge Rodríguez, siblings of Costanza Rodríguez and Ana Váez, were born in Sevilla in the mid-1560s. Coming to Mexico with Governor Carvajal, they became traveling merchants in the Puebla region. Active Judaizers, they were close friends of Manuel de Lucena and Luis de Carvajal. When the first arrests began in 1589, they fled the country, taking passage to Manila on Antonio Díaz de Cáceres's ship. They were arrested, brought back to Mexico, and tried as Judaizers. Domingo refused to confess, was tortured, and not long after died in jail of his injuries. His bones were burned in the 1596 auto-de-fé. Jorge was tried a second time and in the 1601 auto was sentenced to two hundred lashes and ten years of service in the galleys, followed by prison. He later petitioned to be released from the galleys. AGN 150-5: 272r-301; AGN 163-3, 108r; AGN 214-13; AGN Indiferente 6596-124; Escobar Quevedo, *Inquisición*, 394; Temkin, *Carvajal*, 197; Uchmany, *Vida*.
33. AGN 1529-3, 11r; AGN 1491-3, 8v, 101r. Fabián Granados, a tall, ruddy-complexioned man from Lamego, owned a store selling Mexican blankets and cacao beans in Mexico City's tianguis de San Juan and the Portal de Tejada. Granados's close friends included Manuel de Lucena, Manuel Gómez Silveira, Cosme Pereira, and Luis de Carvajal. He fled Mexico prior to 1596 and his effigy was burned in the auto-de-fé of that year (AGN 153-1, 170r; AGN 155-1, 51v; AGN 1529-1, 7rv). Juan Rodríguez, prior to marrying a woman named Bernardina, lived in a soap factory near the Hospital de Indios. He also fled to Spain before the Inquisition could seize him and was sentenced in 1600 to be burned in effigy (AGN 1491-3, 8v; AGN 1529-3, 11v; AGN, *Libro primero*, 258).
34. AGN 1491-1, 43r.
35. Bancroft, Lucena, 238r; AGN 161-1, 14v. Born and raised in Covilhã and well educated in Judaism, Franciso Belmonte had the reputation among his

contemporaries in Mexico as a "Seneca in the Law of Moses." He owned a general store in the mining community of Sultepec, high in the mountains west of Taxco. In the great auto-de-fé of 1596, he was penanced and remanded to the Perpetual Prison, and his property was confiscated (Chuchiak, *Inquisition*, 156).

36. Testimony in 1598 (AGN 163-3, 134r).
37. AGN 127-3, 348r.
38. AGN 127-3, 350v.
39. Bancroft, Lucena, 164r.
40. Bancroft, Lucena, 322v-23r.
41. Luis de Carvajal under torture, February 10, 1596 (AGN 156-4, 54r; AGN 1489-1, 358r). Ironically, in this case it was Luis de Carvajal—not an outsider—who brought Tomás's outburst to the attention of the Inquisition.
42. Judaizers were well aware of the increased risk in groups of more than two. As Luis de Carvajal said to Manuel Gómez Navarro, "You don't have to worry about it; as long as there is no more than a single witness you have nothing to fear" (AGN 1489-1, 224v). For an analysis of the psychological dynamics of a triad, see Gilman, "Case."
43. The denunciation came from Francisco Belmonte (Bancroft, Lucena, 238r). The location of San Bartolomé is unclear; within a day's ride from Pachuca are San Bartolo de los Tepates (Hidalgo), San Bartolomé del Monte (Tlaxcala), and San Bartolo Actoban (México).
44. AGN 153-9, 71r.
45. AGN 1489-1, 176r.
46. Bancroft, Lucena, 374r.
47. Bancroft, Lucena, 446r; González Obregón and Gómez, *Procesos*, 231.
48. Bancroft, Lucena, 31v.
49. Bancroft, Lucena, 445v.
50. Antonio Rodríguez, Sebastián Rodríguez's brother, an active Judaizer who was fond of playing the guitar, drowned at age eighteen; his effigy was burned in the auto-de-fé of 1596 (AGN 154-4: 50v; AGN 156-3, 29v; Bancroft, Lucena, 514v).
51. Bancroft, Lucena, 134r.
52. Bancroft, Lucena, 286v, 360r, 376r; AGN 151-5, 47v; AGN 1490-2, 6r, 69v.
53. Bancroft, Lucena, 37v, 423r; AGN 152-4, 327r.
54. AGN 1489-1, 354r.
55. AGN 153-9, 84r.
56. AGN 156-4, 64v.
57. AGN 163-3, 35r.
58. Gitlitz, "Expulsion."
59. Bancroft, Lucena, 59v.
60. Bancroft, Lucena, 459v.
61. AGN 163-3, 91v, 94v.
62. Bancroft, Lucena, 484r.

63. Bancroft, Lucena, 566r.
64. AGN 153-1, 157r.
65. AGN 159-1, 26r, 43v.
66. AGN 150-1, 52v.
67. AGN 156-2, 47r.
68. 1595 Luis de Carvajal reported to inquisitors that he observed the "the fast they call in Hebrew Quipur, which means Day of Pardon" (AGN 1489-1, 169r).
69. Manuel de Lucena reported, and Catalina Enríquez confirmed, that fear of being observed moved both Luis de Carvajal and Álvaro de Carrión to celebrate the Ayuno Grande (Great Fast) alone, either in the countryside or in an Indian village (AGN 1529-4, 16r; Bancroft, Lucena, 90v).
70. While the Enríquez family believed that Passover began on the fourteenth day after the new moon in March, in practice they celebrated it on Holy Thursday (Bancroft, Lucena, 292r).
71. AGN 126-11, 140v; AGN 153-1, 155r; AGN 153-9, 53v; AGN 1491-3, 24v, 101v; AGN 1529-1, 50v.
72. Shavuoth: Leonor de Carvajal (Bancroft, Lucena, 172v). Sukkot: Luis de Carvajal (AGN 127-3, 349v), Leonor de Carvajal (AGN 1489-1, 126v), Manuel de Lucena (Bancroft, Lucena, 341r), and Manuel Gil de la Guarda (AGN 276-14, 412r).
73. In 1595 Luis de Carvajal testified that as a child in Benavente he had learned about the festival of the "rebuilding of the Temple, called 'of the lights'" (AGN 1491-3, 24v). In 1629 Diego Pérez de Albuquerque, who had been raised in the French city of Rouen, mentioned Hanucah and Rosanah to his Mexican inquisitors (AGN 348-5, 528r).

Chapter 10

1. AGN 158-1, 61r.
2. AGN 127-1, 1r.
3. AGN 150-1, 3r.
4. AGN 127-3, 346r.
5. García, *Mineros*, 123; Cortés, "Cuarta carta."
6. This is the most commonly held date; 1532 is given by West ("Early," 119, 123).
7. AGN 158-3, 232v.
8. Both cases date from the 1560s. Toro, *Judíos*, 3, 131, 143, cited in Enciso Contreras, *Taxco*, 71.
9. Craig and West, *Quest*, 130.
10. Enciso Contreras, *Taxco*, 22, citing the 1581 account of Pedro Ledesma, alcalde mayor of the Taxco mines and *corregidor* of the Indian towns of Taxco and Tenango.

11. Enciso Contreras, *Taxco*, 39. By 1590 the Taxco reales were in decline, with sixty-one miners divided among forty-seven *haciendas de minas*. The workforce had shrunk to 266 slaves, 406 repartimiento Indians, and 834 free Indian laborers (naboríos). See also Zavala, *Servicio*, 322–23.
12. Almeida's other two brothers were Miguel and Francisco Hernández (or Fernández). On the wide variety of surnames among siblings, see Gitlitz, "Anusim."
13. She is not to be confused with Felipa de Fonseca, the wife of Gabriel de Castellanos and mother of Jorge de Almeida, Héctor de Fonseca, and Miguel and Francisco Hernández.
14. AGN 127-1, 42r; AGN 156-4, 92v. Despite the Inquisition's general concerns with fornication and with tracing the networks of people with whom the Judaizers regularly associated, it appears to have expressed no curiosity about the identities of the sexual partners of either old Tomás or young Tomás de Fonseca.
15. AGN 156-4, 156r.
16. AGN 127-1, 1, 43v; AGN 156-4, 137r, 156r. Sometimes Tomás even combined the two professions, as when he purchased a quantity of salt for use in his amalgamation patio and then sold what he did not need to a miner in Izúcar (AGN 156-4, 250v).
17. AGN 156-4, 4r–5r.
18. This tally was noted by Alonso Gómez de Castañeda, the Inquisition's agent in Taxco, who had been charged with taking stock of all of Tomás de Fonseca's assets, including moneys owed to him and his accounts receivable, and making inquiry, as appropriate, to ensure that nothing of value was omitted from the count. He took testimony from a Pedro Muñiz to the effect that to protect his assets, Fonseca had listed a black slave and twenty or thirty mules as belonging to Tomás Cardoso (AGN 156-4, 7r, 11rv).
19. AGN 156-4, 170v, 174v.
20. AGN 156-4, 14v.
21. Young Tomás and his son Francisco referred to Cardoso as Tomás's cousin (AGN 156-4, 170v, 174v), while Luis de Carvajal and the Inquisition familiar in Taxco spoke of him as a nephew (AGN 153-9, 107r; AGN 156-4, 4v, 5r). On other occasions, for Luis de Carvajal and Sebastián de la Peña he was merely a "relative" and a "good Christian" (AGN 152-4, 96v; AGN 155-4, 108v; AGN 156-4, 53r, 65v, 336r).
22. AGN 156-4, 11v.
23. AGN 251A, 534r, 713r. Felipe de Palacios was the winning bidder in the 1591 public auction of Jorge de Almeida's Cantarranas hacienda.
24. Testimony of Luis de Carvajal, who calls him *fulano* (somebody) Rodríguez, transcribed in AGN 156-4, 65v. He may be the Juan Rodríguez whom young Tomás offered as a character witness in 1589 (AGN 127-1, 65v).

25. AGN 156-4, 14v.
26. AGN 156-4, 4v.
27. Pedro Muñiz, testifying in September 1595 to what Lorenzo Núñez had told him (AGN 156-4, 11v).
28. AGN 156-4, 267v.
29. AGN 1491-1, 59r.
30. AGN 156-4, 247r.
31. AGN 156-4, 92v-93r.
32. AGN 127-1, 167r.
33. AGN 127-1, 158r.
34. AGN 127-1, 143r.
35. AGN 127-1, 67v.
36. AGN 127-1, 46r; 156-4, 54v.
37. AGN 156-4, 172v.
38. Domínguez was born in the Portuguese village of Viana da Camiña in 1551 (AGN 127-1, 195v, 198v).
39. AGN 127-1, 133r, 158r.
40. AGN 127-1, 64r.
41. AGN 127-1, 32v, 64v, 67r, 71r. Fonseca did not comment on the ironic religious implications of the pig reference. Mateo Ruiz confirmed Freire's animus.
42. AGN 127-1, 64v, 65v, 67r; AGN 158-1, 82v.
43. AGN 127-1, 71v.
44. AGN 127-1, 65v, 71v.
45. AGN 29-1; AGN 43-1. Palacios is too young to have been the Felipe Napolitano listed among the many Italian soldiers who accompanied Cortés in the conquest (JGBL, "400 años").
46. AGN Indiferente Virreinal 72-028 (1586); 6956-053 (1600); AGN Indios, 6-647 (1592); AGN Tierras 2974-94 (1587); AGN 2965-121 (1594); AGN 2944-277 (1600); AGN 2941-92 (1600); AGN 2970-86 (1606); AGN Indiferente Criminal 2448-019 (1610). Hueyxtaca is probably Huixtac, Guerrero, southwest of Taxco.
47. AGN 127-1, 71v.
48. AGN 127-1, 67r, 68v, 72r, 139v, 143r, 167r.
49. After his first appointment as a royal scribe in 1550 (AGN Reales Cédulas D1-28, 37, 44), Tapia served in 1583 as alcalde mayor in Tenayuca (Mexico) (AGN Indiferente Indios 2-1010) and in 1584 in Taxco (AGN Hacienda 008-2486-161). In later years he owned land in Cuautinchán (Puebla), Cuautitlán (Mexico), Amozoc (Tlaxcala), Papantla (Veracruz), and many other towns (AGN 127-1, 68v; AGN Hacienda 008-2485-161; AGN Indios 2-93, 2-1010, 4-217; AGN Tierras 0037-69-6; AGN Jesuitas 064-1-14-113; AGN Reales Cédulas D1-28).
50. Saballos, born in the Spanish city of Zafra in 1564, had a store in Taxco (AGN 127-1, 68r).

51. Mercado, a bachelor who lived next door to the Hospital de Nuestra Señora in Mexico City, in 1599 served as a magistrate in Tlapa (southeast Guerrero) (AGN 127-1, 68r; AGN General de Parte 51-5-173).
52. This may have been the royal cosmographer Francisco Domínguez de Ocampo, one of the observers of the lunar eclipse of 1584 in Mexico (Velázquez Fernández, "Instrumentación," 114, 119).
53. In the early 1600s, Mena owned an orchard in Chapultepec and, for a time, served as alcalde mayor in Tabasco. He was an irreverent, outspoken man whose tongue sometimes got him in trouble with the Holy Office and whose sloppy bookkeeping and weakness for corruption was likewise noted (AGN 269-2; AGN 368-28; AGN Indiferente Real Fisco 4883-77; AGN 4601-2; AGN Indiferente Indios 5496-102; AGN Tierras 2976-1).
54. In 1587 Pereira also acted as guarantor for twenty-two *quintales* of mercury allotted to Jorge de Almeida, as did Héctor de Fonseca (AGN 251A, 286r, 483v).
55. See Gitlitz, "Anusim."
56. González Obregón and Gómez, *Procesos*, 314.
57. Héctor de Fonseca offered this version of his biography, with enough corroborative detail to make it credible, in his testimony to the Mexican Inquisition in 1596. Eva Uchmany believes that Héctor's story was fiction and that none of the family crossed to Mexico until 1580, after several years of residence in Italy, principally in Ferrara and Venice, where there is good evidence that Héctor's three brothers spent much of the 1570s (*Vida*, 52).
58. AGN 158-1, 63r; Garza Martínez and Pérez Zevallos, *Real y minas*, 17. Old Tomás may have been in Mexico City caring for his ailing father.
59. The exact relationship is murky. Most likely the maternal grandmother of both Héctor and young Tomás was María de Fonseca, of Viseu (AGN 158-1, 62r).
60. Luna, "Juliantla."
61. AGN General de Parte (51) 4-304, 87v.
62. AGN 158-1, 104v-105r. That is, Héctor's five stakes constituted half ownership of the mine.
63. AGN 127-1, 66r, 67r.
64. For the Spanish-Portuguese Jewish community in Ferrara, see Di Leone Leoni, *Nazione*.
65. AGN 157-1, 159-2. The principal study of their lives is Uchmany, *Vida*. See also Cohen, *Martyr*, 196; Escobar Quevedo, *Inquisición*, 273; Israel, *Diásporas* 112-13.
66. AGN 159-4, 376v. In 1601 Díaz Nieto described Hernández as fat-faced, dark-bearded, ugly, and in his thirties (Uchmany, *Vida*, 176).
67. AGN 159-4, 270r-276r.
68. They arrived sometime between 1580 and 1582, when Almeida purchased property in Taxco, putting into question Uchmany's claim that from 1578 to 1580, Almeida was partner with Antonio Díaz de Cáceres in a mining venture between Taxco and Tenango (*Vida*, 57). In her cited source for the datum (AGN

Real Fisco de la Inquisición 3-1, 8), I have found no mention of this partnership.
69. AGN 159-4, 376r.
70. AGN 251A, 265v, 428r. In the 1590 inventory of Almeida's possessions, her estimated value was 150 pesos.
71. García, *Mineros*, 129; Zavala, *Asientos*, 183. See also Pérez Rosales, *Minería*, chap. 1. Cortés gave nearby properties to his two other sons, Jesús and the other Martín, who called their mine La Campaña.
72. Espino Hernández, *Historia*. Leonor was related to Antonio de Mendoza, viceroy of Mexico from 1535 to 1550. Pedro Ruiz de Alarcón's son Juan, after moving back to Spain definitively in 1611, became one of Madrid's illustrious Golden Age playwrights.
73. Census of 1569 (Enciso Contreras, *Taxco*, 39).
74. AGN 251A, 302v. Diego de Nava was one of the first miners in Taxco to purchase a license to Bartolomé de Medina's patio process (Pérez Rosales, *Minería*, 40).
75. Espino Hernández, *Historia*.
76. The purchase price was thirty-six thousand pesos (AGN 251A, 302r-306v).
77. AGN 251A, 305r. Another guarantor was Vicente Pereira, whom Tomás de Fonseca Castellanos listed among the character witnesses in his 1589 proceso (AGN 127-1, 65v).
78. Louisa Hoberman's classic study, *Merchant Elite*, provides a concise description of the role of the tratante, whom she terms a Mexico City wholesaler:

> At the apex of the credit pyramid stood the Mexico City wholesalers, at the base, a wide variety of agents, ranging from the well-known example of the *alcalde mayor* to local retailers, priests, assayers, and muleteers. Through partial ownership, employee and debtor relationships, which might be complemented by *compadrazgo* or other social ties, merchants cultivated connections with suppliers in the capital and provinces. . . . Credit, backed by silver, was what made the Hispanicized economy work (*Merchant Elite*, 72, 92).

79. AGN 159-1, 57rv; AGN 251a, 352r.
80. AGN 150-1, 46r-52v.
81. AGN 251A.
82. The inventories list by name the following tools: *adazones, almadanetas, barretas de fierro, cedazos de cernir metales, cucharas, cunas garabatos de juntar plata, lapas con sus clavos, picos, y sierras de aserrar* (AGN 251A, 532r-535r).
83. AGN 150-1, 47v; AGN 251A, 282v passim.
84. Leonor reported that the family took care to mask their Judaizing from the black servants. The sisters reported that on Passover the family ate tortillas

instead of making matzo out of fear of being seen by the maids (AGN 126–13, 344v, 352v; AGN 1488-2, 37rv).
85. AGN 251A, 285v, 302v.
86. AGN 150-1, 46r.
87. AGN Real Fisco 3-1, 3r.
88. AGN 150-1, 46v.
89. AGN 150-1, 52v.
90. AGN 251A.
91. Tellingly, though Díaz de Cáceres detailed all his paternal relatives in relating his genealogy to the Inquisition in 1596, he claimed not to know the identity of his mother's parents or any of her siblings (AGN 159-1, 161v). Díaz's brother Henrique Dias de Milão was a tratante in Lisbon (ANTT, Tribunal do Santo Ofício, Inquisição de Lisboa, proc. 3338, fols. 4, 25v, 44, cited by Sousa, *Jewish Diaspora*, 30). The most detailed study of Díaz's life is Cohen, "Díaz de Cáceres."
92. AGN 159-1, 163v. Francisco I de Portugal, Count of Vimoso, was a bastard son of Alfonso de Portugal, bishop of Évora, and third cousin to King Manoel I. The infante Duarte, Duke of Guimarães, was the sixth son of Manoel I.
93. Possibly Captain-General Vasco de Acuña, who is known for his later explorations off the coast of India (Cuesta Domingo, *Alonso de Santa Cruz*, 2:218). Martin Cohen gives his name as Gaspar de Cunha (*Martyr*, 113). García Álvarez de Toledo, a first cousin of Fernando Álvarez de Toledo, the Duke of Alba, was King Philip II's captain-general of the Mediterranean fleet during the naval war against the Turks in the 1560s. Francisco Barreto led a Portuguese expedition to Mozambique in 1568–1569 and later was appointed viceroy of Portuguese India.
94. See AGI ES-AGI-41091-UD-1863031 to ES-AGI-41091-UD-92891 for his lawsuit that year against the Audiencia de la Contratación over his permit to engage in trade with the Indies.
95. AGN 159-1, 87r.
96. AGN Real Fisco (97) 3-1, 3r; AGN 251A, 429v.
97. The partnership, which invested in merchant ships and their cargoes, lasted fourteen years. In the early 1580s, Cobos worked for Jorge de Almeida in Taxco; in 1582 he was serving as alcalde de minas in Sonsonete. When Almeida fled Mexico in 1590, Cobos accompanied him to Veracruz and Havana, from where Cobos returned alone to Campeche. He amassed sufficient capital by 1594 to be part owner of the merchant ship *San Pedro*. He died no later than 1597 (AGN 150-1, 46rv; AGN 159-1, 235v; AGN 251A, 429v; AGN Real Fisco [97] 3-1, 3r; AGN Tierras [110] 3252, 2–4).
98. AGN Real Fisco (97) 3-1, 4r–5r.
99. AGN Real Fisco (97) 3-1, 3v; AGN Tierras (110) 2974-238. Díaz subsequently sued to have the hacienda returned to him; in 1594 Piedra and his two partners still owed Díaz seven or eight thousand pesos.

Chapter 11

1. AGN 156-4, 170v.
2. According to Díaz de Cáceres's friend Antonio de los Cobos, the two men "wanted to marry them, though they were poor and without dowry, in order to improve circumstances for the two maidens" (AGN 251A, 430r).
3. Mariana de Carvajal confirmed that had the four spouses not been Judaizers, the marriage would not have been acceptable to any of the parties (AGN 159-1, 35r).
4. AGN 126-13, 322v.
5. González Obregón and Gómez, *Procesos*, 15–17; see also pages 8, 41, 50, 66, 420; AGN 150-1, 52v.
6. AGN 154-1, 194v.
7. AGN 150-1, 34r; AGN 1529-1, 45r. The house was owned by Juan Rodríguez Sánchez.
8. According to Antonio de los Cobos, the following year Almeida bought a second Chichemeca named María from Diego López de Luis (AGN 251A, 430r).
9. AGN 150-1, 34r–36r; AGN 1529-1, 45rv.
10. Cohen, "Antonio Díaz de Cáceres."
11. For what Jonathan Israel calls the "network connecting Ferrara to the viceroyalty of Mexico," and Jorge de Almeida's role in it, see *Diasporas*, chap. 3.
12. Glick, "Converso and Marrano Ethnicity," 74.
13. Cohen, *Martyr*, 175. Ana, testifying in 1600, said that Díaz de Cáceres occasionally did observe the Sabbath (Cohen, *Martyr*, 316n65).
14. AGN 159-1, 34v. See appendix 2, "Holiday Observances."
15. AGN 126-13, 325v.
16. AGN 126-13, 356v; AGN 1488-2, 87rv.
17. AGN 126-13, 353v, 356r.
18. AGN 1489-1, 376rv. Testimony of February 14, 1596. Carvajal was describing a later period, but the observations about character seem consistent with Díaz's earlier life as well.
19. AGN 159-1, 36v.
20. 1 Esdras 9:7–13. Many Mexican Judaizers thought of themselves as living in captivity. Diego Enríquez, 1595: "As we were in captivity among the Christians, it was better not to do those ceremonies, which would offend God less than if we did them wrong" (AGN 153-9, 90v). Francisco Díaz heard Luis and Isabel de Carvajal say, in 1590, "May God free us from our captivity" (AGN 150-1, 47r). Tomás de Fonseca Castellanos said that Luis de Carvajal thought "this is a captivity, because in this land we suffer great deprivation and are stigmatized with *sambenitos*" (AGN 158-4, 68r). Beatriz Núñez used to pray, "May God free the Jews from the captivity where they are in the power of Old Christians who have a different ancestry than they do" (AGN 1488-2, 35r).

21. Héctor, his neighbors, and many of his friends knew her as Juana López de la Torre (AGN 158-1, 8r, 62r; AGN 251A 377r), while to Luis de Carvajal and Miguel Hernández she was Juana Núñez de la Torre (AGN 158-2, 130v). For details of this marriage, see below.
22. AGN 158-1, 64r, 95r.
23. AGN 158-1, 86v, 97rv.
24. AGN 158-1, 95v, 109v, 111r.
25. Cohen, *Martyr*, 125.
26. AGN 159-1, 15r.
27. AGN 127-3, 346r; AGN 1489-1, 339v.
28. AGN 127-3, 346r
29. AGN 126-13, 334v. Leonor, with her customary naivete, said that it was because they had run out of flour (AGN 352v).
30. Eugenio del Hoyo characterizes Almeida as "a cruel and heartless man," adding gratuitously that "cruelty and hardness of character is common among the crypto-Jews we are studying" (*Historia*, 215).
31. Bancroft, Lucena, 583r.
32. AGN 150-1, 23v; AGN 153-1, 159r, 170v; AGN 153-9, 78r; AGN 158-4, 411v; AGN 251A, 430r; AGN 1491-3, 8rv; AGN Real Fisco (97) 3-1; AGN, *Libro primero*, 258. A Cristóbal Gómez from the Portuguese village of Almeida was denounced as a Judaizer to the Coimbra Inquisition around 1579 (Mea, *Sentenças*, 239).
33. AGN 150-1, 47r, 50v-53v.
34. AGN 150-1, 47rv, 53v.
35. AGN 150-1, 46v.
36. AGN 150-1, 46v.
37. AGN 150-1, 46v-47r.
38. AGN 150-1, 47v-48r.
39. "'Mirad que salamotio me han dado'—y no sabe a fe que quiere dicir salamotio—y despues de esto colgo al dicho Cristo a los pies de su cama y echaba sobre ella; ventoseaba y decia al Cristo, 'Tomad y bebed'" (AGN 158-1, 8r). Luis noted that this was not the only time Miguel Hernández amused his friends by parodying the mass. Once in Mexico City, in the presence of Luis, his brother Baltazar, and Marco Antonio, he draped a saddle pad over his head like a chasuble, elevated a clay cup like a chalice, drank, and wiped his fingers as the priests do.
40. AGN 158-1, 8r; AGN 158-2, 131r.
41. González Obregón and Gómez, *Procesos*, 314-15.
42. For Francisco Díaz, AGN 150-1, 46r; AGN 158-2, 131r; González Obregón and Gómez, *Procesos*, 315. For Mateo Ruiz, AGN 158-1, 65r, 82v; González Obregón and Gómez, *Procesos*, 350. For Francisco Jorge, AGN 150-1, 7r; AGN 158-2, 131r; AGN 159-1, 34v; AGN, *Libro primero*, 182; Uchmany, *Vida*, 87.
43. AGN 150-1, 50r-51v.
44. Hebrew Union College, Transcripts, 29-30.

45. AGN 159-1, 187v, 188v, 269v.
46. The first incident, narrated by Díaz de Cáceres himself in 1597, in an attempt to discredit testimony against him by the Carvajals, was witnessed by Leonor's brother Fray Gaspar de Carvajal; Almeida's brother Héctor de Fonseca and their cousin Tomás de Fonseca Castellanos; Diego Marcos de Andrada; Jorge de León; Gonzalo Pérez Ferro' Pérez's wife, Catalina de León; and Catalina's sister Ginebra. The latter incident was witnessed by a number of neighbors (AGN 159-1, 187rv, 195r). While in what Susan Socolow calls "the moral economy of marriage" of the time, men were considered to have the right to use "moderate physical punishment to secure obedience" from the women for whom they were responsible, Díaz de Cáceres's behavior toward the Carvajal women clearly exceeded normal bounds (*Women*, 67).
47. AGN 126-13, 325v.
48. AGN 150-1 27v.
49. Mariana confirmed this emnity (AGN 1488-2, 37v, 78v)
50. See appendix 1, "Origins and Arrivals."
51. In 1596 he told inquisitors that he still remembered a few Psalms in Spanish, or perhaps Portuguese, from his childhood (AGN 158-1, 90r).
52. Marco Antonio termed him "super observant" (*observantísimo*) of the Law of Moses (AGN 161-2, 14v).
53. AGN 150-1, 34rv; AGN 1529-1, 45r. Dinner rather than seder; the fact that the family hid from Julián de Castellanos that they were celebrating the holiday suggests that no rituals were performed.
54. AGN 158-1, 42r.
55. AGN 158-1, 84r-89r.
56. AGN 158-1, 49v
57. AGN 158-1, 85v.
58. "Since Héctor de Fonseca knows Latin and is well-read, he cited me some authorities of the Old Testament like the prophet Daniel when they put him in the oven in Babylonia with the three children; and I answered him with passages of Scripture" (AGN 158-1, 8r).
59. AGN 154-1, 194v-195r; AGN 1490-3, 212v.
60. Liebman, *Jews in New Spain*, 154; Uchmany, *Vida*, 82; Warshawsky, "Justa Méndez," 35-43; Wachtel, *Faith*, 69-70, 76, 81.
61. AGN 158-1, 86r-87v. The texts of a number of these songs are preserved in the trial dossier of Leonor de Carvajal (Hamilton, "Poesía").
62. AGN 1489-1, 339r; AGN 1490-3, 213r.
63. AGN 156-4, 27r, 63v, 112v; AGN 158-1, 27v, 28r; AGN 1489-1, 403v. Héctor acknowledged the rift, saying that he rarely talked with Luis de Carvajal in Taxco because Luis lodged at his cousin Tomás de Fonseca's house (AGN 158-1, 83v).
64. AGN 158-1, 92v.

65. AGN 158-1, 32v.
66. AGN 1529-1, 21r.
67. AGN 1489-1, 421rv.
68. AGN 158-1, 21v; González Obregón and González, *Procesos*, 409.
69. AGN 158-1, 11r, 18r.
70. Her name is given alternately as Juana López de la Torre and Juana Núñez de la Torre (AGN 158-1, 62r; AGN 251A, 377r).
71. Bancroft, Lucena, 243v.
72. AGN 153-9, 22v; AGN 158-3, 9r.
73. AGN 158-4, 90v; AGN 1489-1, 362r; González Obregón and Gómez, *Procesos*, 320-21.
74. AGN 156-4, 52v; AGN 158-4, 67rv; González Obregón and Gómez, *Procesos* 320; Liebman, *Jews in New Spain*, 263; Cohen, *Martyr*, 228.
75. AGN 1492-2, 48r; Bancroft, Lucena, 546r. Antonio Méndez, a Portuguese from Teba, owned a store on the outskirts of Mexico City on the road to Pachuca. He married María de los Ángeles (AGN 1490-2, 20v; AGN 1493-1, 57r, 121r).
76. AGN 163-3, 137r. Antonio Gómez alleges this in the context of listing Antonio Fernández as his enemy.
77. AGN 163-3, 131v. Rodríguez, born in 1546 in São Vicente da Beira to an Old Christian father and a Jewish mother, was a pastry chef and sometimes dealer in cacao. Jorge Váez was his brother; his wife was Juana de Luján. Accused of Judaizing, in 1596 he abjured *de levi* and was fined four hundred pesos (AGN 156-2, 4r, 10r; AGN 163-3, 104v; AGN 223-36, 427r; AGN 1492-1, 60v; Uchmany, *Vida*, 81; Chuchiak, *Inquisition*, 169).
78. AGN 1529-4, 13v, 34v; Bancroft, Lucena, 116v. In 1604, with Carrión now deceased, Juana successfully sued the Real Fisco for return of her marriage portion (*dote y arras*), which they had sequestered from him (AGN Real Fisco [97] 8-12).
79. Pelayo Álvarez married an Old Christian and had two daughters, Ana and Felipa. Catalina Enríquez said that when the girls were young, Pelayo put them to board with Antonio Machado and that by 1596 both were married and living in Mexico City. Álvarez blew hot and cold about Judaism. He was well-read and knowledgeable, but as he told Manuel de Lucena, who criticized him for eating pork, he preferred not to practice. Even so, he asked Lucena to teach his girls the basics of Judaizing, because their grandmother had been one of the greatest Judaizers ever born. Though sometimes he grew weepy when Lucena talked to him about Judaism, he did not share many of his friends' scorn for Christian beliefs and practices. "The world is a garden of different kinds of trees," he told Lucena around 1584, "some like the Christians keep the law of a dead man, and the Jews keep and believe the law of a living God." AGN 152-4, 260v; AGN 159-4, 275v; AGN 1529-3, 31v; González Obregón and Gómez, *Procesos*, 398-400; Bancroft, Lucena, 113v-114v, 121v, 465v.

80. AGN 163-3, 143v; AGN 164-3, 33r; AGN 1492-1, 40v.
81. Bancroft, Lucena, 332v. Either Lucena or the scribe mistakenly refers to him as Rodríguez.
82. According to Manuel de Lucena, who heard it from Antonio López (AGN 158-1, 52r).
83. AGN 158-1, 87r.
84. AGN 158-1, 111r.
85. AGN 158-1, 63r.
86. Martin Cohen, perhaps misreading Antonia for Antonio, says there were two boys and one girl (*Martyr*, 112). Héctor told inquisitors that his fear of not being able to find husbands for his daughters if his Judaizing were known is what kept him from reporting it to his confessors or admitting it during the early stages of his trial (AGN 158-1, 89v). In 1640 Antonia, calling herself Antonia Rivera, and her husband, Diego de Oliver, were investigated briefly by the Inquisition in Taxco (AGN 389-12A, 522r-526r).
87. AGN 251A, 377r-378v.
88. The dossier of this first trial is not extant, and we do not know the details or the date of his arrest. His presence in prison in November 1594 is attested to by Sebastián Rodríguez, who communicated with him from an adjacent cell (AGN 158-1, 25r).
89. AGN 1A-38. The document is a single folio bearing three page numbers (97r, 180r, and 189r) and erroneously dated 1570. The church would not grant a woman a divorce even for extreme mistreatment but would sometimes approve a separation agreement. Acceptable causes were "extreme physical or spiritual danger, including gross mistreatment, threat of murder, and wanton adultery, as well as forcing a wife into crime, paganism, or heresy" (Scopolow, *Women*, 68).
90. AGN 158-1, 81r.
91. AGN 158-1, title page, 101r-106r.
92. AGN 156-4, 181r.
93. AGN 156-4, 171r.
94. AGN 127-1, 50v, 133r, 211v, 212r.
95. AGN 156-4, 74r. Both Tomás's habitual avoidance of pork and his rationalization were noted by many witnesses (AGN 127-1, 32r, 34r, 46r; AGN 156-4, 38v, 48v, 165v). After he left Enciso's employ, Juan Álvarez peddled merchandise in Michoacán.
96. Old Tomás de Fonseca knew Tomás Méndez and did not like him; he evidently took no action in bringing Méndez and his estranged wife back together (AGN 156-4, 209r).
97. AGN 127-1, 43v; AGN 156-4, 186v, 209r-211r. Her son Diego, who sometimes called himself Diego Méndez de Fonseca, was living in Taxco in 1589 and in Jalapa in 1595. Julián de Castellanos was mistaken when he said that Isabel's second son was blind and had remained in Spain (AGN 156-4, 210v).

98. AGN 156-4, 54v, 159v.
99. AGN 156-4, 54r.
100. AGN 156-4, 160r. Many scholars have noted that for sixteenth-century crypto-Jews, the idea of personal salvation was—in Miriam Bodian's phrase—"a foundational concept in their religious consciousness." Also widespread was the belief "that the pope did not have special powers but was like any other bishop," an idea echoed in the Protestant Reformation rhetoric that was increasingly influential in the Iberian world (Bodian, *Dying*, 23, 25).
101. AGN 156-4, 54v–55r.
102. Francisco Rodríguez said in 1595 that Sebastián de la Peña was most of the time living in Taxco (AGN 156-3, 20r).
103. AGN 156-4, 170v–171v. Of Isabel's siblings, only Leonor Machado married. Leonor and her husband, the Taxco miner Gonzalo Rodríguez de Molina, had twelve children, one of whom, their son Gaspar (whose name may have been Gonzalo) Rodríguez, married the daughter of another Taxco miner named Castillo. The Inquisition arrested this Gonzalo Rodríguez in 1615 and charged him with wearing silk and riding a horse, both of which were activities forbidden to the children and grandchildren of those convicted of heresy (AGN 308-1, 2r). There is no record that any of Leonor's family having interacted religiously with the Judaizing community in Taxco (AGN 1529-3, 62rv).
104. Fonseca had once bought some *sinabafas* (finely woven undyed cotton cloth) from Lucena; he paid for them with a lame mule (AGN 156-4, 24v, 155v–156v).
105. Bodian notes how arguments such as these reflect a familiarity with Jewish and Christian polemical debates of the period (*Dying*, 13).
106. AGN 156-4, 23r–24v.
107. Duarte Rodríguez, from Fundão, where his mother was known as a saint in the Law of Moses, came to Mexico with Governor Carvajal in 1580. In Mexico City and Pachuca he often stayed with the Lucenas. His reputation among the Judaizing community was spotty; Clara Enríquez called him a crazy gossiping liar. Arrested and tried in 1596, he was remanded to the Cárcel Perpétua, where he remained until the General Pardon of 1604 (AGN 17-3, 6r; AGN 156-4, 88r; AGN 1492-3, 68v; AGN 1493-1, 115r; Bancroft, Lucena, 135v).
108. AGN 156-4, 92v–93v. Francisco Fonseca (born in 1572), a thin young man of dark complexion and beard, in the mid-1590s traveled to China as a trader. His close friend Marco Antonio once characterized him as a scamp (*bellaco*) (AGN 156-4, 127v; AGN 1491-1, 111v–112r).
109. AGN 1489-1, 360rv; AGN 155-4, 105v; AGN 156-4, 41r–42v, 46r. Sebastián de la Peña, from São Vicente da Beira, a thin, small man with a reddish beard and a thin, down-curved nose, was an itinerant merchant, selling small goods to the reales in Guanajuato, Celaya, and Michoacán and trading in cacao beans. For a while he was based in Taxco. Like so many of the converso merchants, when visiting Mexico City, he was accustomed to lodging with the Carvajal family. In the

1595 *procesos* he testified against many of the miners and the Carvajals. He was tried in 1598. After his reconciliation and release, he continued to run afoul of the Inquisition (AGN 155-4, 4r, 33v; AGN 156-3, 20r; AGN 167-3; AGN 279-8, 101rv).
110. AGN 127-1, 32rv.
111. AGN 127-1, 35v. This classic anti-Semitic stereotype, which is so prevalent in literature in Spain in the seventeenth century, appears rarely in testimony in Mexican trial dossiers of the 1590s.
112. AGN 127-1, 32v, 45v.
113. AGN 156-4, 63r, 89r, 93r, 244v.
114. AGN 127-1, 24r, 32r, 133r, 139v; AGN 156-4, 38v, 74r.
115. AGN 127-1, 26r; AGN 156-4, 48r.
116. AGN 156-4, Messiah 90v, 160rv, 181v, 204v; Salvation 31v, 90r, 160r.
117. AGN 127-1, 63r.
118. Tomás's phrasing recalls—with intended irony?—the Shema, the Jewish daily declaration of faith.
119. AGN 127-1, 79r.

Chapter 12

1. Bancroft, Lucena, 287r, 291r.
2. Bancroft, Lucena, 463r, 478r.
3. Bancroft, Lucena, 654v. In one of his last interrogation sessions, on December 8, 1596, Lucena reported that when he was about ten, he had seen some neighbors Judaizing in his village of Fundão (Bancroft, Lucena, 657v).
4. The previous year, Duarte's brother Simón had established a branch of the family business in Mexico City. Whether Simón's absence had left Duarte shorthanded, requiring him to bring in young Manuel de Lucena from Fundão to help out in the store, or whether Duarte's wife, Clara Rodríguez, was in some way related to Manuel's mother, Clara Rodríguez, in Fundão, so that Duarte was offering Manuel a job as a way of helping out his in-laws' family, is unclear (AGN 152-4, 243r).
5. Ricardo Escobar Quevedo noted how for the Portuguese crypto-Jews on the Calle Sierpe, "the cultural interaction during their residence in [Sevilla] permitted the reactivation of their collective practices and encouraged matrimonial alliances and fostered group solidarity" (*Inquisición* 70).
6. Bancroft, Lucena, 555v.
7. Ana was the daughter of Felipa Hernández, of Fundão, and Antonio Pérez, of Covilhã. Her son Antonio, who married a María Pérez, was reconciled by the Inquisition in 1601. Her other two children were reconciled by the Inquisition in Sevilla—Felipa López in 1600 and Cristóbal López, together with his wife, María Enríquez, at an unrecorded date (Escobar Quevedo, *Inquisición*, 355).

8. AGN 156-1, 24v; AGN 1492-3, 32v.
9. AGN 155-1, 16r.
10. Bancroft, Lucena, 558r.
11. Three of Manuel de Lucena's six siblings migrated to Perú: Gaspar and Baltazar de Lucena settled in Potosí, while a third sibling, Antonio Váez, imported slaves to the colony. Manuel's maternal uncle Antonio Rodríguez also went to Perú (Bancroft, Lucena, 56v, 282v).
12. López, a thin, light-complected, asthmatic man, spoke knowledgeably to Manuel about Manuel's mother back in São Vicente (Bancroft, Lucena, 477v–480r, 654v).
13. AGN 152-4, 256v.
14. He was eighteen; she was seventeen. He was well educated; she was illiterate (Bancroft, Lucena, 283v; AGN 152-4, 112v, 136r). "The lord inquisitor signed for her because the aforesaid Catalina Enríquez said that she does not know how to write" (AGN 153-9, 45r).
15. The description is by Pedro de Fonseca, who arrested him for the Inquisition on October 29, 1594 (Bancroft, Lucena, 2r). Of the sixty-three physical descriptions of people I have noted in Mexican Inquisition documents of the last quarter of the sixteenth century, only one is of a woman, Jorge de Almeida's cousin Blanca Lorenzo, the proprietress of an inn in Sevilla that catered to conversos. She was described as "more than forty-five years old, tall, neither fat nor thin, white faced, and ugly" (AGN 159-4, 376v).
16. The government attempted to control the distribution of alcohol to the mining reales both for fiscal reasons and because drunkenness was disruptive. In May 1580, the miners and residents of Pachuca petitioned "to prevent the Indians from drinking because their drunkenness keeps the mining haciendas from having enough people to do the work of processing silver" (AGN 051 General de Parte 2-745).
17. The girl's name is not given—only that she lived for ten years and died prior to 1594 after a lingering illness, without having been given last rites (Bancroft, Lucena, 44v, 308v).
18. Bancroft, Lucena, 234r, 522v. The others were Real del Monte, Real de Arriba (today called San Miguel Cerezo), and Real de Atotonilco el Chico (today Mineral del Chico).
19. AGN Real Fisco (97) 3-2, 249r.
20. Principally AGN Real Fisco (97) 3-2, 244r–334v. All references to Lucena's business and family possessions, the confiscations, and the logistics of the arrest are to this document unless otherwise noted.
21. AGN 217-5, 35r–36r. This is a list of Catalina Enríquez's property deposited with Margarita Quijada and Juan López Tavera, the couple who fostered Catalina's children after she was arrested.
22. Bancroft, Lucena, 13r.
23. AGN (97) 3-2, 245r.

24. The Lucenas had an estrado too, but it was given to Juan López Tavera when he and his wife agreed to foster the Lucena children during their parents' incarceration (AGN 217-5, 35r–36r). It had disappeared by the time their daughter Clara Enríquez's goods were inventoried in 1603 (AGN Real Fisco [97] 9-2).
25. Bancroft, Lucena, 90r, 207v, 222v, 547v .
26. Bancroft, Lucena, 111v, 351v. The modern closet for storage did not become popular until the nineteenth century, evolving from a small, enclosed private sitting or reading room adjacent to the bedroom in upper-class French houses. Vertical cabinets to store clothes, evolving from medieval armoires for storing weapons, likewise did not become popular until relatively modern times.
27. AGN Real Fisco (97) 3-2, 315r.
28. Bancroft, Lucena, 637r. The clock maker was possibly Juan Pérez, who received a license to come to New Spain in 1576 and lived in Mexico City near Santa Clara Church. Lucena subsequently had the clock's red satin case made into a chair seat (AGN 174-4, 80v; AGN 051 General del Parte 1-742).
29. Bancroft, Lucena, 49r.
30. A marco was approximately a half pound.
31. Bancroft, Lucena, 8r-9r.
32. Lucena bonded so deeply with Casal, whom he found to be intelligent and trustworthy, that, even though Casal was not a converso, Lucena felt comfortable discussing the Law of Moses with him (AGN 1489-1, 432–34). When the Inquisition jailed Lucena and his wife, Casal left Pachuca to become mayordomo of the mining hacienda of Agustín Guerrero de Luna in Atotonilco (AGN Indiferente, Minería 6655-04).
33. Bancroft, Lucena, 636v.
34. Anderson, *Hispanic*,165.
35. Also called *toquillas, tocadorcillas,* and *sobretocas.*
36. Bancroft, Lucena, 636v–637r.
37. The monastery of Tezontepec, built in 1554, lies a third of the way between Pachuca and Mexico City.
38. An arroba equals approximately twenty-five pounds.
39. AGN Real Fisco (97) 3-2, 249r.
40. *Mantas de conga* were mantles either from the Congo or produced in Mexico by slaves of Congolese origin. They could be worn as articles of clothing (Aguirre Beltrán, *Cuijla,* chap. 8, cited in Thornton, *Africa,* 234).
41. For a brief history of silk production in Mexico, see Grace, "460 Years."
42. AGN (97) 3-2, 251v.
43. AGN 156-2, 9r. Despite his antipathy to Judaizing, Jerónimo Rodríguez permitted Francisco Váez to hide with him in Puebla when Manuel de Lucena was arrested (AGN 223-36, 427r). He was tried in 1596, convicted *de vehementi* of Judaizing, and banished from Mexico for two years (Liebman, *Jews in New Spain,* 129).

44. AGN 152-3, 243r-250v; AGN 156-2, 16v; AGN 1491-1, 118v; Bancroft, Lucena, 29r passim. Váez fled Mexico for Guatemala early in 1596. His effigy was burned at the December 8 auto-de-fé in Mexico City. He later returned to Mexico, where his arrest was again ordered in September 1600 (AGN, *Libro primero*, 283). He is recorded in Japan in 1613 (AGN 293-21, 113r).
45. AGN Indiferente Judicial 2194-013, 1602. The date of Pertierra's death is not recorded. This document involves his mother, as his heir, suing his creditors. Asturias, a mountainous region on Spain's north coast that in the Middle Ages had never been part of Muslim Iberia, likewise had never attracted a significant Jewish population. This adds to the circumstantial evidence that Pertierra was an Old Christian.
46. AGN Real Fisco (97) 3-4, 342r. López Tavera had frequent business dealings with Lucena. His wife, Margarita Quijada, bought on credit in Lucena's store (AGN 217-5, 35r).
47. AGN (97) 3-2, 253r.
48. María del Pilar Martínez López-Cano, in her study of the investment culture in New Spain, notes that Mexico City shopkeepers often invested directly in mines in the second quarter of the sixteenth century but that such investment was less common in the last quarter ("Comerciantes").
49. For example, Gómez Pertierra told inquisitors that he was in possession of three thousand pesos worth of silver planchas, plus fifty or sixty marcos of rescate silver and thirty-eight silver pesos Lucena had given him to settle a debt with a neighbor (Bancroft, Lucena, 316r). Names for coins, their equivalencies, and their values relative to prices and wages varied widely from place to place and over time, leading to what Henry Charles Lea called a system characterized by "unutterable confusion" (*History*, 1:560-66).
50. Thus a twelve-hundred-peso loan to Juan de Casal: "I am lending to him in silver to be repaid in *reales*" (Bancroft, Lucena, 636v). Lucena's loan to Leonel de Cervantes, the alcalde de minas of Pachuca, of two hundred pesos and a gold chain to finance a fiesta in Pachuca had still not been repaid in 1594 (AGN 174-4, 80v).
51. Catalina's brother Diego Enríquez "entered the store with a little silver" (AGN 152-4, 72v).
52. Bancroft, Lucena, 37r; AGN 152-4, 326r.
53. AGN 152-4, 263r.
54. In January 1595, for example, Lucena owed Juan del Casal 748 pesos for 103 marks and 3.5 ounces of silver that he had bought from him (AGN Real Fisco [97] 5-1, 4r).
55. He bankrupted his father with his excesses (AGN 153-1, 123v-24v).
56. Miranda acted as agent for several miners; he may also have owned an ingenio, for he was sued over his right to the water he was using (no date given) (AGN Real Fisco [97] 3-2, 257r-258r; Bancroft, Lucena, 3r).

57. Hernando de Castro was a frequent litigant, bringing suit in the late 1590s against the miners Juan Bautista Lamadilla and Agustín Guerrero, and the heirs of Josef Bazán de Acosta, for moneys owed (AGN Bienes 14-132-18; AGN Indiferente General 1947-001, 2194-006). In 1596 he brought suit against old Tomás de Fonseca in Tlalpujahua, alleging that Fonseca owed him eighty-seven pesos and four reales (AGN Real Fisco [97] 8-11, 282r).
58. Angulo was also a frequent litigant; in 1601 he served as alcalde in Real del Monte (AGN 17-3, 107v; AGN Real Fisco [97] 3-2, 257r, 311r).
59. AGN Real Fisco (97) 3-2, 258v.
60. AGN Real Fisco (97) 3-2, 269r.
61. AGN 152-4, 176v.
62. Bancroft, Lucena, 287r, 291r.
63. Bancroft, Lucena, 9r-16.
64. Bancroft, Lucena, 3r, 9r-10v, 12r; AGN (97) 3-2, AGN (97) 3-3, AGN (97) 5-1; AGN Indiferente Virreinal 4883-078, 5145-061.
65. Bancroft, Lucena, 305r; AGN 156-4, 16r.
66. AGN Real Fisco (97) 3-2, 308r.

Chapter 13

1. AGN 152-4, 199r.
2. Simón's brother Duarte Rodríguez, who was Lucena's employer in Sevilla, wed Clara Rodríguez; they had one son, Manuel Álvarez. In 1588 Beatriz's widowed sister Clara Enríquez brought to Mexico her three children, Justa Méndez, Violante Váez (the mother of Domingo and Jorge Rodríguez), and Gabriel Enríquez (AGN 127-2, 225v-226r). Beatriz's brother Diego Rodríguez was father to Ana Váez, who, after a stay in Sevilla, where household servant Gómez Pertierra taught her to read, came to Mexico in 1594. There she married Jorge Álvarez (AGN 152-2, 62r).
3. López spoke knowledgeably to Manuel about Manuel's mother back in São Vicente (Bancroft, Lucena, 477v-480r, 654v).
4. Bancroft, Lucena, 2r.
5. The site of the Plaza del Volador, southeast of the Plaza de la Constitución, is occupied today by the Suprema Corte de Justicia de la Nación. Diego Enríquez, after serving as a soldier in Acapulco and Guatemala, became a traveling clothing merchant (AGN 252-3, 8v; AGN 152-4, 111v; AGN 153-1, 3r). Pedro Enríquez, who also soldiered for a while and sold clothing, became a tavern keeper in Atotonilco. In the auto-de-fé of December 8, 1596, Diego was executed; Pedro was reconciled to the church and sentenced to five years in the galleys (AGN 154-4, title page).
6. AGN 161-2, 5rv; AGN 1492-1, 58r, 61r. The Casas del Marqués were on the west side of the cathedral, where the Monte de Piedad now stands.

7. Bancroft, Lucena, 231r. When the arrests began, Álvaro Rodríguez fled Mexico. His effigy was burned in the auto-de-fé of 1601 (Escobar Quevedo, *Inquisición*, 393).
8. Today Huichapan, Hidalgo.
9. AGN 151-6, 42r; AGN 152-2, 5r; AGN 153-1, 6r; AGN 153-7, 60v. Baltazar González went to China in 1584 (Bancroft, Lucena, 231r).
10. AGN 159-5, 45v; González Obregón and Gómez, *Procesos*, 422.
11. AGN 152-4, 105rv; AGN 158-2, 131v; AGN 159-5, 51v.
12. AGN 214-13; Uchmany, *Vida*, 57, 104.
13. Fourteen years later some of these same people, including Lucena, found themselves back at San Hipólito, which had been designated as the Inquisition's execution ground. The site is today the northwest corner of Mexico City's Alameda Park.
14. AGN 152-4, 232rv, 373v. Witnesses differ on whether or not Catalina's brothers Pedro and Diego were present (Bancroft, Lucena, 231r-232v, 514v; AGN 152-4, 231v).
15. AGN 154-2, 372r; 161-1, 8r.
16. Rodríguez Saz was Ana Váez's nephew. He came to Mexico when the Inquisition arrested his wife and sister in Sevilla. In Mexico he made his living as a street peddler. He lived first in Ana López's house and then with Jorge Fernández. Tried in 1596 as a Judaizer, he was condemned to row in the galleys for four years (AGN 164-7, 48r; AGN 1489-1, 335, 353r; AGN 1492-3, 37r; Bancroft, Lucena, 585v).
17. AGN 152-4, 59r, 62rv, 372r-373v; AGN 159-5, 47r; AGN 161-1, 9r.
18. AGN 155-4, 4r.
19. See appendix 3, "Enríquez-Lucena Holiday Attendees."
20. Bancroft, Lucena, 119r. Gonzalo Rodríguez and Pedro Méndez both went back to Spain in the late 1580s to work for their rich uncle Enrique Méndez on Sevilla's Calle de la Sierpe.
21. The baker is not identified (AGN 152-4, 317r).
22. Bancroft, Lucena, 570v. The street was located near today's Calle Madero. Larios, who was deceased by 1602, owned property in Ixtapaluca, east of Mexico City, in 1562 (AGN Tierras [110] 0035-65-2), in the Llanos de Almería near Papantla in 1576 (AGN General de Parte [051] 1-767/1028), in Tlazazalca in northern Michoacán in 1580 (AGN General de Parte [051] 2-840), and in Tlalpujahua (AGN General de Parte [051] 6-208). About the time Lucena was renting from him he owned a cattle ranch in the northwest and a slaughterhouse and butcher shop in Texcoco (AGN Indios [058] 10-2-590). In 1596 Larios held the title of *chantre*, or keeper of the hymnals, in the Mexico City Cathedral (AGN Regio Patronato Indiano, Bienes Comunales [014] 132-37).
23. The two men later moved to some other part of New Spain. Beatriz recalled that the men all bathed together and put on clean clothes and that the next day they fasted because it was Yom Kippur (AGN 152-4, 237r). Domingo Rodríguez,

the son of Violante Váez, was at one time a suitor of Justa Méndez, Beatriz Enríquez's granddaughter. In 1592 he traveled to Manila (AGN 150-5, 272r; AGN 153-9, 22v).
24. Bancroft, Lucena, 361v, 477v, 592r; AGN 152-4, 369r; AGN 1492-3, 10r.
25. Bancroft, Lucena, 616r, 640r. At one time or another, Diego de León's renters included Clara Enríquez, Justa Méndez and her daughter Costanza Rodríguez, Ambrosio and Francisco Álvarez, and several members of the Morales family (AGN 152-4, 237r; AGN 154-1, 4r; AGN 161-2, 9v; AGN 1492-1, 6r).
26. Seymour Liebman interpreted the "the unusual degree of fasting" common among late sixteenth-century Mexican crypto-Jews as a kind of expiation for their sin of skimping on their Jewish observances while protecting themselves by observing many Catholic rites. So prevalent was the practice that it "almost became an end in itself, a virtue" (Liebman, "Jews," 99).
27. AGN 154-1, 211r; AGN 1492-3, 11r.
28. AGN 163-3, 116r.
29. AGN 1492-2, 40v-42r, 70v. Rodríguez Ledesma left a wife in Sevilla on the Calle de la Sierpe.
30. AGN 151-5, 49v-50v.
31. AGN 1493-1, 12v-13r. Sebastián Rodríguez reported a similar 1594 get-together at young Tomás de Fonseca's house in Taxco: "After we had eaten, the four of us went to [Fonseca's] bedroom to sleep.... Luis de Carvajal and I ... slept in one bed together. And in the same room Tomás de Fonseca [Castellanos] shared the other bed with Sebastián de la Peña. And when he lay down, Luis de Carvajal began to recite prayers of the Law of Moses ... and we all talked together about being Jews and keeping the Law of Moses.... In the morning Luis de Carvajal woke up and knelt down facing east to recite the morning prayers." (AGN 156-4, 42v, 306rv).
32. AGN 152-4, 260v-261r. In an earlier audience, Catalina said that they turned the sisters out because she and Manuel had so many guests staying with them that there was no room for them (Bancroft, Lucena, 113v). For a time the girls also stayed with the Machados (AGN 1491-3, 7v).
33. Yom Kippur in Mexico at their Mexico house (1586, 1589, 1590, 1593) and their house in Pachuca (1587, 1588); Passover at their Mexico house (1586, 1593) and their home in Pachuca (1588, 1594); the Fast of Esther in Mexico with the Enríquez-Paibas (1587), in Pachuca (1588), and at their own home in Mexico (1591).
34. AGN 153-9, 71r; Bancroft, Lucena, 460v.
35. Marcus, "Why study."
36. Díaz was his cell mate in December 1594 (AGN 153-9, 28v).
37. AGN 152-4, 334rv.
38. AGN 152-4, 48v. Catalina admitted to inquisitors that while she usually prepared the Sabbath meal on Friday afternoon, sometimes she left it until Saturday, following the custom of some of her relatives back in Spain.

39. AGN 152-4, 121r, 229r; Bancroft, Lucena, 86v. In the late sixteenth century, collars were detachable items.
40. AGN 152-4, 121v; Bancroft, Lucena, 51r, 87r, 186r.
41. AGN 152-4, 129v, 266r, 328r.
42. AGN 151-5, 49v. See also AGN 154-1, 189r–90r, 194v; AGN 156-4, 26v, 61v, 112v. While not part of the canonical Jewish Bible, the *Libro de la sabiduría* was popularly held to have been written by Solomon. It is considered by Catholics a deuterocanonical or secondary authority; Protestants include it among the apocrypha. It was widely known in the Middle Ages and remained popular through the colonial period.
43. AGN 156-4, 27rv.
44. Bancroft, Lucena, 42r, 120v, 355r, 626v.
45. Bancroft, Lucena, 286v. "Adonai, mis labios abrirás y mi boca anunciará tu loor. Bendito tú, Adonai, nuestro Dios y Dios de nuestros padres Abrahán, Isaac, y Jacob."
46. Bancroft, Lucena, 577v, 581v.
47. AGN 1489-1, 222rv; Bancroft, Lucena, 59r, 129v, 169v, 186r, 193v, 319v, 520r.
48. AGN 152-4,105r; AGN 158-2, 136rv.
49. AGN 161-1, 14v.
50. AGN 1493-3, 43v.
51. "Quitar de vicios de mujeres" (Bancroft, Lucena, 231rv).
52. Bancroft, Lucena, 292v.
53. Bancroft, Lucena, 176r.
54. AGN 153-9, 71r; AGN 152-4, 199r; AGN 1489-1, 207r; Bancroft, Lucena, 31v, 444r, 460v. Luis visited Lucena in Pachuca at least eight times (Cohen, *Martyr*, 128). In 1594, after Carvajal had completed his penance in Santiago Tlatelolco but was still required to wear his sambenito in public, Lucena asked him to lodge elsewhere because the neighbors were gossiping (Bancroft, Lucena, 116r).
55. Manuel de Lucena, Catalina Enríquez, Beatriz Enríquez la Paiba, and Clara and Diego Enríquez; Luis and Baltazar Carvajal; Ana, Antonio, and Felipa López; Leonor Díaz, Manuel Francisco Belmonte, Manuel Gómez Navarro, Manuel Jorge, Justa Méndez, Felipe Núñez, and Costanza Rodríguez (AGN 17-3, 21v; AGN 152-4, 33v; AGN 1492-3, 21v; Bancroft, Lucena, 124v, 129r, 185r).
56. In the first audience at his 1597 trial, Francisco Rodríguez told inquisitors that during the last few years he had appended Ledesma to his name "because there are so many men named Francisco Rodríguez" (AGN 1492-2, 82r). The Inquisiton documents from the 1590s that I have consulted record a minimum of fifteen men named Francisco Rodríguez in Mexico at that time.
57. Bancroft, Lucena, 171r–172r.
58. Bancroft, Lucena, 317v–319v.
59. Reported by Lucena's cell mate Luis Díaz in 1594 (AGN 174-4, 71v).
60. AGN 160-1, 120r. Bancroft, Lucena, 317v.

61. Bancroft, Lucena, 421v; see also 19r, 20r, 29r, 64v, 135r, 218r, and so on.
62. "Cantemos con alegria alabanzas al Señor; que todo que en él confía no le faltará su favor." Manuel de Lucena's congregation at Clara Enríquez's house that Yom Kippur of 1592 included Clara and her daughter Justa Méndez, Duarte Rodríguez, Manuel Rodríguez Suilguero, Francisco Váez, Gabriel Enríquez, and Beatriz Enríquez la Paiba (Bancroft, Lucena, 222v). Lucena was also in the habit of leading his Judaizing friends in song when they were traveling together. In 1593, near the Carpio Inn on the Mexico–Pachuca road, he sang in quartet with Sebastián Rodríguez, Manuel Gómez Navarro, and Diego Enríquez (Bancroft, Lucena, 445v).
63. Bancroft, Lucena, 68r.
64. Bancroft, Lucena, 134r.
65. AGN 154-1, 90v; AGN 1490-2, 15v.
66. Bancroft, Lucena, 137v.
67. Bancroft, Lucena, 29r, 56v, 198rv, 206r, 214v, 237v, 303v, 422v, 429rv; AGN 151-6, 45v; AGN 152-3, 243v; AGN 153-9, 28v, 30r; AGN 154-4, 47v; AGN 155-1, 19v; AGN 155-4, 23r; AGN 156-1, 32r; AGN 156-3, 19r; AGN 1492-1, 11v; AGN 1493-1, 43v-44r.
68. Bancroft, Lucena, 147v-149r.
69. AGN 1529-4, 20r.
70. AGN 1529-4, 39v.
71. Carrión's estancia was "one league from the Real de Tlaulilpa [the center of Pachuca], bordering on Tilcuautla, a little distant from the Camino Real [the Royal Highway] that goes to Octupan." The estancia of his father-in-law, Alonso (González), was two leagues from the mines on the wagon road, the Camino Real de las Carretas (Bancroft, Lucena, 581v).
72. AGN 1529-4, 12r-13r, 52r-59r.
73. AGN 152-4, 357r.
74. When they reached Carrión's estancia they looked up and saw a total eclipse of the moon (AGN 156-2, 39).
75. AGN 1529-4, 13r passim; Bancroft, Lucena, 116r, 577v.
76. AGN 1529-4, 16v. For recipes and the history of frutas del sartén, see Gitlitz and Davidson, *Drizzle*, 277-78.
77. AGN 1529-4, 37v.
78. AGN 152-3, 273r; AGN 1491-1, 118v.
79. AGN 152-3, 243r, 250v; Bancroft, Lucena, 124v, 303v.
80. AGN 152-3, 251r; Bancroft, Lucena, 347r.
81. AGN 152-3, 261r; Bancroft, Lucena, 38r, 42r.
82. In Sevilla, before coming to Mexico, Ana Váez learned to read from her household servant Gómez Depertierra (AGN 152-2, 63v).
83. Bancroft, Lucena, 42r.
84. AGN 151-6, 134r.

85. Known today as Xichú or San Luis de la Paz.
86. These events were reported by Lucena (Bancroft, Lucena, 56v, 293r) and confirmed by Gómez Navarro, who acknowledged Lucena as his sole teacher (AGN 151-6, 159v).
87. As related by Lucena (AGN 151-6, 46r-47r).
88. AGN 1489-1, 207rv.
89. Bancroft, Lucena, 35r, 42r, 422v-23r.
90. AGN 154-1, 4r. After a stint in the China trade, he purchased a mine in Sultepec (AGN Real Fisco [97] 7-8). In 1603-1604 he owned a store with Sebastián de la Peña (Uchmany, *Vida*, 141).
91. AGN 1529-4, 26v, 60r.
92. AGN 151-6, 167v; AGN 155-4, 23r; AGN 156-3, 20v. Manuel de Tavares reported hearing the Psalm sung by Antonio Gómez (AGN 163-3 139v). In 1603 Antonio Méndez was reported to have sung it in prison to Duarte Rodríguez and Ruy Díaz Nieto (AGN 271-1, 18r). In 1621 Jorge López sang to his companions the version of the Psalm from Lope de Vega's *Pastores de Belén* (AGN 333-1, 3v).
93. AGN 156-3, 19r; Bancroft, Lucena, 176r.
94. The Fast of Esther in Pachuca (1588, 1593); Yom Kippur (1589, 1590) and Passover (1592) in Mexico at the Enríquez house. See appendix 3, "Enríquez-Lucena Holiday Attendees."
95. AGN 17-3, 86r, 103r; AGN 1490-2, 20v, 55rv; AGN 1492-3, 47v, 65v, 69r, 86v. This event and the fact that the Gerónimo family was accepted without question by the converso community are the only evidence that they were Judaizing conversos, for the Inquisition does not seem to have engaged with the family. A Miguel Gerónimo is recorded in an undated document as having bought a mining hacienda, complete with refining machinery and mercury, from an Andrés Martín de Bustos (AGN Indiferente Virreinal, Caja 3917, Exp 010).
96. AGN 160-1, 74r-76v. His name is variously recorded in Portuguese (Guarda) and Spanish (la Guardia).
97. Identified as a converso by Ricardo Escobar Quevedo ("Criptojudíos," 68).
98. AGN 160-1, 15rv.
99. Bancroft, Lucena, 577r, 580v.
100. AGN 1491-2, 12v. In Ferrara the two had lived as Jacob and Isaac Nieto.
101. AGN 1491-2, 17v, 24v, 29r; Bancroft, Lucena, 210v.
102. Bancroft, Lucena, 211r. When Cuello came to Mexico late in 1594, he roomed with Manuel Álvarez and with the Carvajals. He worked briefly as a traveling merchant and in early 1596 owned a cattle and horse ranch at Tzintzinoco in Michoacán. He was tried in 1596 for Judaizing and remanded to the Cárcel Perpétua (AGN 1491-2; AGN 1493-1, 97r).
103. Casal was also known as Juan de las Casas and sometimes as Juan de Casar (Bancroft, Lucena, 121v). Casal was still working for Guerrero in 1600 (AGN Indiferente Minería Caja 6655, Exp 041).

104. The book cost twenty pesos, according to both Catalina Enríquez and Luis de Carvajal (AGN 152-4, 259v-260r).
105. AGN 152-4, 259v; AGN 1489-1, 450r; Bancroft, Lucena, 627r-628v.
106. Reported by Antonio Méndez (AGN 1492-3, 103r). Another Old Christian at the event was Antonio Méndez's wife, María Franca (aka María de los Ángeles). Miguel Gerónimo attended as well. Those two, accompanied by Antonio Méndez, went out to the street to march in the procession (AGN 1490-2, 55r).
107. Bancroft, Lucena, 137rv.
108. AGN 1489-1, 451r.
109. Bancroft, Lucena, 512r, 630r, 636rv.
110. In Mexico City, Duarte Rodríguez often spent evenings at the Carvajal house with Manuel Rodríguez Silguero and Justa Méndez, listening to Luis de Carvajal reading and preaching (AGN 154-1, 196v). When Luis was serving his penance in Tlatelolco, Duarte visited him there, often in the company of Manuel Gómez Navarro and Tomás de Fonseca Castellanos (AGN156-4, 89r).
111. AGN 151-6, 195r; Bancroft, Lucena, 205r, 211r, 464v, 511v.
112. AGN 156-4, 90v, 170v.
113. Manuel Tavares called him a "reckless [*atronado*; also irresponsible, hotheaded] Portuguese young man" (AGN 163-3, 109v). To Jorge Álvarez he was "a crazy man, a fool [*loco, mentecado*], a man known for not being able to tell the truth" (AGN 1493-1, 98r). Domingo Cuello thought him "a long-winded gossip [*palabrero y hablador*]" and a "crazy liar [*loco mentiroso*]" (AGN 1493-1, 115r; Bancroft, Lucena, 135v).
114. AGN 1492-2, 18r; AGN 1493-1, 6r, 65v; Bancroft, Lucena, 206r.
115. AGN 1493-1, 6r.
116. AGN 1492-2, 46v, 57v; AGN 1493-1, 44r.
117. See appendix 3, "Enríquez-Lucena Holiday Attendees."
118. AGN 17-3, 6r-8v; AGN 1491-1, 55r; AGN 1491-2, 17r-20r; AGN 1492-3, 6v-8r; AGN 1493-1, 4r.
119. Bancroft, Lucena, 26r, 92v, 95v, 172r.
120. See appendix 3, "Enríquez-Lucena Holiday Attendees."

Chapter 14

1. AGN 158-3, 70r-71v.
2. One was Simón Rodríguez, who had a store in Mexico City next to the Casas del Marqués and traveled widely throughout Mexico in his business. He reported that on one visit to Tlalpujahua, in 1595, he fell off his horse and was laid up for well over a month, but he does not mention seeing old Tomás there (AGN 153-7, 5r). Another was Manuel Gómez Navarro, who observed a Jewish fast in the real, again without meeting Fonseca (Bancroft, Lucena, 577v, 581v).

Pelayo Álvarez, who like old Tomás had been born in Freixo de Espada-à-Cinta and was only five years younger than old Tomás, was a third who in Tlalpujahua did not meet with old Tomás (AGN 1529-3, 31v). In his biographical statement, Héctor de Fonseca mentions having passed through Tlalpujahua about 1572, but he does not mention seeing his uncle (AGN 158-1, 63r). In his own testimony old Tomás never mentions any of these visits.

3. In May 1590 Julián de Castellanos, never good with dates, said his father had died in 1572 (AGN 1529-1, 24v), 1573 (17v), and 1577 (14r). Two months later he stated that Gabriel had died in 1570 (AGN 158-3, 212r). He also said that Blanca had predeceased Gabriel by a year (AGN 1529-1, 17v) and that both Gabriel and Blanca had been buried in the Hospital de Nuestra Señora (AGN 1529-1, 84v).
4. AGN 158-3, 67v-68r.
5. AGN 1491-1, 124r.
6. AGN 158-1, 10v.
7. AGN 158-3, 96v-97r.
8. "lo mal que había hecho en haberse apartado de ella y pasado a la Ley de Moisén por enseñanza de unos mozos rapazes, quedando confuso de que a un hombre viejo como él le hubiesen engañado" (AGN 158-3, 98r).
9. AGN 158-3, 97r.
10. AGN 158-3, 100v; AGN 158-4, 128v. In Carvajal's recollection, Julián de Castellanos also witnessed this conversation (AGN 156-4, 56v).
11. González Obregón and Gómez, *Procesos*, 313; AGN 158-1, 10v. Carvajal added that López was by then (1595) in Salonica and Gómez was in Peru or Cartagena. Manuel de Lucena also recalled seeing old Tomás in Gómez's store a couple of times (AGN 158-3, 9v).
12. AGN 156-4, 16v.
13. AGN 1491-1, 123rv.
14. He is thus unlikely to have been Luis de Carvajal. He is equally unlikely to have been the other Luis associated with young Tomás in Taxco, Dr. Luis de Villanueva, a neighbor of twelve years whom young Tomás listed as someone who could testify that he prayed Christian prayers (AGN 127-1, 68r, 167r, 201r).
15. AGN 156-4, 93r.
16. AGN 1491-1, 123rv.
17. AGN 158-3, 105r, 107r.
18. AGN 158-3, 108r. In reporting this conversation, old Tomás said that he had contributed the story of King Nebuchadnezzar's bronze idol (Daniel 3), which he had read about in *Mirror of Consolation*.
19. AGN 158-3, 110r.
20. AGN 158-3, 113v.
21. Cohen, *Martyr*, 192.
22. AGN 251A, 296r, 376r.

Chapter 15

1. AGN 163-3, 113rv. Luna, born in the Raya de Portugal around 1547, was a small man with a long red beard that was beginning to go white. He dreamed of going to India, where he could live his Judaism openly.
2. Núñez, born in 1561, was uncle to Manuel Gómez de Casteloblanco. He wed Diego López Regalón's daughter Felipa López. He was fond of playing the guitar. In 1589 he was a character witness for Governor Carvajal. Núñez left Mexico for Peru in 1593 with his wife and children (Cohen, *Martyr*, 142; AGN 153-9, 57v, 75r, 97r; AGN 160-1, 17r; AGN 163-3, 108r; Bancroft, Lucena, 22r).
3. The definitive treatment of these arrests is Cohen, *Martyr*, 144-48.
4. Also present were Simón Paiba; his wife, Beatriz Enríquez la Paiba; their sons Diego and Pedro; Antonio and Miguel López; and Domingo, Jorge, and Sebastián Rodríguez (AGN 152-4, 199r; AGN 153-9, 71r; AGN 1489-1, 351r, 389r; Bancroft, Lucena, 460v, 467r, 469v, 525r).
5. AGN 152-4, 238v.
6. Bancroft, Lucena, 569v.
7. Antonio López, who was born in Celorico in Portugal and came to Mexico as a young man, was a close friend of Lucena. Of these six, only López fled before the Inquisition could arrest him. He was burned in effigy in the Mexican auto-de-fé of 1596 (AGN 1490-1, 15v; AGN 1492-2, 82v).
8. AGN 152-4, 238r.
9. AGN 150-1, 23v.
10. AGN 1488-2, 84v; Cohen, *Martyr*, 146.
11. Cohen, *Martyr*, 146.
12. González Obregón and Gómez, *Procesos*, 51; Cohen, *Martyr*, 144.
13. González Obregón and Gómez, *Procesos*, 20.
14. Cohen, *Martyr*, 146, 148. Luis's signature is from AGN 251A, 577r.
15. AGN 126-13, 299v; AGN 1488-2, 62r. Cohen (*Martyr*, 171) gives the dates of December 4 for Catalina and Leonor and December 12 for Mariana. Leonor's signature is from AGN 560-1, 15v.
16. Even though none of the documents that detail the events of this period mention Jorge de Almeida's emotional reaction to his wife's incarceration, letters that he wrote from Madrid in 1595 make clear that, despite his much-chronicled gruff and sometimes violent character, he both loved and respected his wife (Cohen, *Martyr*, 225).
17. Cohen, *Martyr*, 197. Tlatelolco today is part of Mexico City's central historic district. Its Plaza de las Tres Culturas was site of the October 2, 1968, massacre of students and civilians by the police and military.
18. AGN, *Libro primero*, fol. 144.
19. AGN 150-1, 13r.
20. AGN 158-3, 18r.

21. AGN 150-1, 21v.
22. AGN 251A, 262r. When Díaz could not come up with his fare for the voyage to Spain, Almeida left him in Havana, from where Díaz eventually found passage to Peru.
23. AGN 150-1, 23r. Galicia may be an error for Cádiz.
24. In Mexican documents of this period, it is common for speakers to particularize which of the at minimum twelve men in Mexico named Francisco Rodríguez they are talking about.
25. Luis de Carvajal, in his testimony about Almeida's intentions, makes this explicit (AGN 150-1, 25r).
26. The signed letter, in Almeida's hand, is in his dossier in AGN 150-1, 23rv.
27. AGN 150-1, 25r.
28. AGN 159-4, 274rv; Israel, *Diasporas*, 112.
29. Díaz's Asian expedition is discussed later in this chapter. Jonathan Israel's brief biography of the extraordinary Díaz Nieto family (*Diasporas*, 112-16) is based on the work of Liebman (*Jews in New Spain* 173, 191-93) and Uchmany (*Vida*, 45, 57, 172, 193, and "Judío italiano," 55-60).
30. AGN 159-1, 270r.
31. Cohen, *Martyr*, 221. AHN Inquisición, Correspondencia de México, book 1049, fol. 4, cited in García-Molina Riquelme, "Utilización." The document adds: "after this I note that the said Luis de Carvajal relapsed, so we arrested him."
32. Cohen, *Martyr*, 192.
33. AGN 251A, 533r, 576r, 713r; AGN 254A-12, 507r; AGN Indiferente Virreinal 4383-007, 1r.
34. The several hundred folios of AGN 251A are devoted to these attempts.
35. See, for example, Antonio de los Cobos's 1593 suit to recover some 1,045 pesos that Almeida still owed him (AGN 159-1, 79r). According to Martín de Salinas, the alcalde mayor of the Taxco mines, Almeida still owed an outstanding debt of 6,535 pesos. In addition he owed Tomás de Fonseca Castellanos 5,070 pesos and owed 1,094 pesos to Francisco de Castro (AGN 251A, 281r, 295r).
36. AGN 251A, 294r.
37. AGN 251A, 578rv.
38. García-Molina Riquelme, *Hogueras*, 217-18; Hebrew Union College, Transcripts, 63-93. Eva Uchmany, without documenting the source of the datum, writes that soon after the 1596 auto in which Luis de Carvajal and several other Judaizers were executed or jailed, Almeida "went back to Italy and years later embarked for the East Indies." Uchmany, "Participation," 194.
39. AGN 159-1, 72r.
40. AGN 159-1, 79r.
41. Cohen, *Martyr*, 171; AGN Real Fisco (97) 3-1; AGN 1488-2, 32r.
42. AGN Real Fisco (97) 3-1, 3r, 4r. Díaz de Cáceres put up an eighth of the money; Ibáñez an eighth. Cobos's quarter was made up of cash, some casks of wine, an

emerald cross, and a black slave named Francisco. The most comprehensive study of this voyage remains Martin Cohen's "Antonio Díaz de Cáceres," 175–79.
43. Uchmany, *Vida*, 57.
44. Cohen, *Martyr*, 176.
45. Sousa, *Jewish Diaspora*, 31, without citing a source. Sousa notes that ecclesiastical authorities in Macao must have been unaware that he was a converso, let alone sought by the Inquisition in Mexico.
46. In both bulk and value, silk and porcelain were the principal goods traded by the Chinese for American silver. The main entrepôt was Manila's foreign merchant enclave of Parián (Mann, *1493*, 196–99), so it is likely that Díaz de Cáceres acquired the porcelain there.
47. AGN Indiferente Virreinal 0707-071, 1rv.
48. AGN 159-1, 73r.
49. In 1594 he was fined by Mexico's Cónsules de la Universidad de los Mercaderes for certain infractions of the business code (AGN Hacienda [008] 1291-41).
50. AGN 560-1, 11r. Agustina may have been conceived prior to Díaz's marriage. When she grew up, she married a barber in Mexico City.
51. Ana Machado, in prison in 1601, said he felt certain that Díaz de Cáceres loved Catalina (AGN 1529-3, 138r).
52. AGN 150-1, 35v; AGN 1529-1, 45v.
53. AGN 159-1, 35r.
54. Luis de Carvajal (AGN 159-1, 6r); Francisca de Carvajal (AGN 20v); Mariana Núñez de Carvajal (AGN 39v, 57r; AGN 1490-3, 207v, 209r); Diego Díaz Nieto (AGN 159-4, 270v); Manuel Rodríguez (AGN 156-1, 54v).
55. AGN 159-1, 36v-40r, 65v. Díaz de Cáceres confirmed this last point in presenting his defense (AGN 159-1, 178v).
56. AGN 159-1, 46v-47r.
57. AGN Real Fisco (97) 3-1, 8r. Márquez de Andrada, second cousin to the Carvajal siblings, sailed to New Spain with Governor Carvajal in 1580. When the first round of Carvajal arrests occurred in 1589, he took care of the youngest daughter, Anica, while her siblings and their mother were in prison (AGN 251A, 431v; Cohen, *Martyr*, 62). Uchmany believes that he may have partnered with Jorge de Almeida in the mining business (*Vida*, 5).
58. AGN, *Libro primero*, 184; AGN 159-1, 1r.
59. AGN 159-1, 171r, 178v, 199v, 236r, 268v.
60. Meyo, a Flemish Protestant vat maker from Hedo, was arrested in 1598 in Havana and in 1599 was a cell mate of Rodrigo Tavares (AGN 165-1; AGN 1492-1, 50v).
61. AGN 163-3, 57r, 62r, 64r, 205v; AGN 1529-3, 135r.
62. AGN 159-1, 278r-281r.

63. Cohen, "Antonio Díaz de Cáceres," 103.
64. Cohen, *Martyr*, 101, 112, 186, 262–64; Cohen, "Antonio Díaz de Cáceres," 103; Uchmany, *Vida*, 102.
65. AGN 560-1, 11v. Eventually Leonor married a Portuguese teamster named Lope Núñez, who died in 1649. In 1652 she testified to the Inquisition that she did not know if her father was still alive or, if he was, what he might be doing.
66. ANTT, Tribunal do Santo Ofício, Inquisição de Lisboa, proc. 3338, fols. 4, 25v, 44 (cited by Sousa, *Jewish Diaspora*, 30).
67. Tomás de Fonseca Castellanos's signature is from AGN 156-4, 192r.
68. AGN 127-1, 24r–25r. See Freire's testimony in chapter 11.
69. AGN 127-1, 32v. See their testimony in chapter 11.
70. The dossier of Fonseca's first trial has not survived, although portions of his testimony survive in other procesos.
71. AGN 150-1, 31r.
72. AGN 127-1, 7r.
73. AGN 251A, 294r–296v.
74. AGN 156-4, 118r, 135v, 141r, 159r.
75. AGN 156-4, 130rv.
76. AGN 156-4, 156r.
77. AGN 1492-2, 21r, 91v.
78. AGN 156-4, 11r. Pedro Muñiz, a resident of the capital, testifying in September 1595, speculated that Fonseca might have been hoping that Cardoso would marry the daughter whom Cardoso had left pregnant.
79. AGN 156-4, 3r–5r.
80. AGN 156-4, 154v.
81. AGN 156-4, 143r. See chapter 10 for the description of the hacienda and its operation provided in Pérez's written reports.
82. Tomás, who never married, claimed to have sired three children: Francisco de Fonseca in 1572, María de Fonseca in 1578 or 1579, and Álvaro in 1581; he never identified the mother. Nothing more is known about María or Álvaro (AGN 127-1, 42r). Francisco, whom Marco Antonio termed a rogue (bellaco), entered the China trade (AGN 156-4, 92v; 1491-1, 111v, 112r).
83. AGN 156-4, 171v–172r.
84. AGN 156-4, 159rv, 163v, 167r, 171r.
85. Manuel de Lucena's signature is from AGN 156-4, 155v.
86. Bancroft, Lucena, 583r. In September 1596, Lucena reported having voiced this sentiment almost verbatim to Antonio López de Morales some years previous (AGN 152-4, 371r).
87. Ayllón, a Portuguese silversmith from Beja, came to Mexico in 1591 with pearls he had brought from Cartagena and the Margarita Islands. In Mexico, for a time he sought the hand of Justa Méndez. At Catalina Enríquez's house in Mexico City in 1592, Luis de Carvajal gave Ayllón handwritten copies of some

Psalms to take with him back to Spain (Bancroft, Lucena, 357v, 358v, 559r–560v; AGN 151-5, 47v; AGN 156-2, 43v; AGN 1493-1, 15v).
88. Bancroft, Lucena, 366v.
89. In addition to family members, a typical group in 1590 included Manuel Gómez, Antonio López, Sebastián Nieto, and Antonio Núñez (AGN 152-4, 158r; AGN 1493-1, 15r).
90. AGN 152-4, 128r–129r, 150v; AGN 153-7, 10v; AGN 153-9, 61v; AGN 153-10, 6r; Bancroft, Lucena, 221r–222v.
91. Cohen, *Martyr*, 207.
92. Diego López Regalón, a street vendor born in Fundão, was a close friend of Manuel de Lucena and Manuel Tavares. He and his wife, Ana López, were parents of the Antonio López who played the guitar and sang at the theater. López Regalón died prior to 1594 and was tried posthumously for Judaizing; his effigy was burned in 1601 in Lima (AGN 151-5, 47v; AGN 153-1, 133rv; AGN 160-12; AGN 164-7, 66v).
93. AGN 152-4, 129v; Bancroft, Lucena, 115r.
94. Bancroft, Lucena, 541r; AGN 152-4, 35v; AGN 1492-3, 23r.
95. Bancroft, Lucena, 341r; AGN 152-4, 357.
96. Bancroft, Lucena, 577v.
97. AGN 152-4, 133r.
98. Martin Cohen considers that it was Domingo Gómez Navarro's denunciation of his brother Miguel in late September that began the chain of events that resulted in Lucena's arrest (*Martyr*, 205).
99. Bancroft, Lucena, 2r, 282r.
100. Bancroft, Lucena, 287r–291r.
101. The Inquisition was not able to trace these sheltered goods until 1602, when Lucena's daughter Clara Enríquez revealed them in the course of her own trial. The goods are described in detail in the relation of their seizure. They were auctioned between 1602 and 1604 despite Marco Antonio's assertion of rights to some of the material (AGN Real Fisco [97] 9-2, 12r–71v, especially 16r–17v).
102. Bancroft, Lucena, 3rv, 8r. Castro owned a hacienda de minas in Pachuca and was successful enough to be able to lend money to other miners. Miranda worked for both Castro and Lucena in *rescate de plata*, the buying and selling of refined silver (AGN Real Fisco 97-3-2, 257r). For Miranda's involvement in a water rights suit, see AGN Tierras 110-761-1741-4.
103. Bancroft, Lucena, 8r–9r.
104. AGN Real Fisco 97-3-2, 332r.
105. AGN 152-4, 133r, 154v; AGN Real Fisco (97) 3-2, 252v. Martínez López, *Genealogical*, 178.
106. Juan López Tavera knew Lucena well enough, according to Luis Díaz, that when López Tavera saw how much time Luis de Carvajal was spending at Lucena's house, he warned Lucena that friendship with Carvajal was dangerous (Bancroft, Lucena, 68r).

107. AGN 97-3-2, 252v, 307r, 315r. The number of servants is given variously as two and four.
108. AGN 1493-3, 20v.
109. "Señora Ana no fue virgen porque parió, y fue jodida" (AGN 1493-3, 7v).
110. "Santa Barbola está en el cielo, está hecha estrella, Dios me libre de la centella y del árbol de la cruz, todos digan amén Jesús" (AGN 1493-3, 11v). The reference is to Saint Barbara, who was believed to protect against lightning.
111. Bancroft, Lucena, 286rv.
112. April 12, 1595 (Bancroft, Lucena, 354v–55r).
113. Their names are listed on the prefatory, unnumbered folios of Lucena's trial document in the Bancroft Archive, together with an indication of the folio numbers on which the condemning allegations are found, thus constituting an efficient tool for inquisitors preparing indictments against other members of the Mexican Judaizing community. Luis de Carvajal was arrested on February 1, 1595, largely on the basis of information provided by Lucena. Carvajal, in turn, provided much information about Lucena (Cohen, *Martyr*, 226, 233).
114. Bancroft, Lucena, 302r–303r, 337v.
115. April 2, 1595 (Bancroft, Lucena, 340v). A few days later Lucena repeated how he did not want to cause problems "for the person he loves more than his soul" (AGN 152-4, 356v).
116. Bancroft, Lucena, 531v–532r.
117. These affirmations are central to crypto-Jewish beliefs and were expressed frequently in Inquisition testimony on both sides of the Atlantic. See Gitlitz, *Secrecy*, 101–7, 115–17, 146–47, 162, and 317–18.
118. Bancroft, Lucena, 572v–575r.
119. Bancroft, Lucena, 666r. Accompanying Lucena to the stake were Lucena's mother-in-law, Beatriz Enríquez la Paiba; his brother-in-law Diego Enríquez; Manuel Díaz; Francisca de Carvajal; and four of her children (Luis de Carvajal; the widowed Isabel Rodríguez de Andrada; Antonio Díaz de Cáceres's wife, Catalina León de la Cueva y Carvajal; and Jorge de Almeida's wife Leonor Andrada de Carvajal). Ten others, either absent or previously deceased, were burned in effigy. Reconciled to the church and sentenced to the galleys were Manuel Gómez Navarro and Lucena's brother-in-law Pedro Enríquez. Sentenced to prison were Manuel Díaz's wife (also named Catalina Enríquez), Diego Díaz Nieto, Clara Enríquez and her daughter Justa Méndez, and Lucena's wife, Catalina.
120. AGN 152-4, 113r.
121. AGN 152-4, 136r. Years later the date was erroneously recorded as January 17 (AGN 152-4, 296v; Uchmany, *Vida*, 84).
122. AGN 1491-2, 82v; AGN 1493-1, 96r.
123. Uchmany, *Vida*, 108.
124. AGN Indiferente Virreinal 5574-054, 1r–49r.

125. Landeta was the wife of Texcoco's head bailiff, Gaspar de Contreras.
126. In 1613 the Mexican Inquisition found this Pedro Rodríguez guilty of activities prohibited to the children of reconciled heretics and banished him from Mexico for ten years, a portion of which Rodríguez spent doing business in China (AGN 366-27, 339r). Seven other men named Pedro Rodríguez are mentioned in Inquisition documents of this period.
127. AGN 366-27, 339r.
128. Héctor de Fonseca's signature is from AGN 279-8, 100r.
129. AGN 158-1, 4r.
130. "Justa Méndez is my enemy because I tried to break up her plans to marry a Somebody Cardoso, which made her hate me and threaten me that her relative Pedro Enríquez was going to make me pay for it" (AGN 158-1, 87r).
131. AGN 158-1, 75v.
132. AGN 158-1, 84r.
133. AGN 158-1, 89v.
134. AGN 158-1, 101r-102r. Bishop Juan de Zumárraga founded the Hospital del Amor de Dios (aka Hospital de las Bubas) and the Hospital de Santos Cosme y Damián in 1540. See Micheli-Serra, "Médicos" 257-63.
135. AGN 158-1, 104r.
136. AGN 158-1, 104v.
137. AGN 163-3, 44rv.
138. AGN 158-1, 106v.
139. AGN 158-1, 111r.
140. AGN 271-1, 15v. The sisters Isabel and Violante Rodríguez, from Salceda, who came to Mexico in 1594, were active in the Judaizing community of the late 1590s (AGN 152-2, 38r, 56v; AGN 159-5, 44v; AGN 276-14, 432v).
141. AGN Real Fisco (97) 8-11, 298r.
142. AGN, *Libro primero*, 144.
143. Correspondence from the arresting officer and Tlalpujahua's vicar, Hernán Vázquez (AGN 158-3, 51r-56r, 67r).
144. AGN 150-1, 21v; AGN 158-3, 73r; Cohen, *Martyr*, 192.
145. AGN 158-3, 57v, 74v.
146. "¿Quien es fuerte y poderoso? ¿Quién puede hacer mal o bien? ¿Quién? Quereis saber quién? Adonai que es poderoso" (Exodus 15:11), as reported by young Tomás de Fonseca (AGN 156-4, 16v).
147. AGN 164-7, 74v, as per Manuel Tavares.
148. AGN 1491-3, 8r. Gómez did business with Antonio Díaz de Cáceres and Jorge de Almeida (AGN 150-1, 23v); he attended their weddings with Luis de Carvajal (González Obregón and Gómez, *Procesos*, 18) and Manuel de Lucena (AGN 251A, 430v). He talked Judaism with Antonio Machado and Luis de Carvajal and other members of Luis's family (AGN 1491-3, 8r). As one of the more knowledgeable members of the Mexico City community in Jewish matters, he

helped educate Antonio Díaz Márquez (AGN 158-4, 127v, 411v), Ana López (AGN 155-2, 85r, 96r), and Marco Antonio (AGN 1491-1, 119v). When the Mexico City Judaizer trials heated up after 1594, Gómez fled and was reported in both Guatemala and Peru (AGN 158-3, 16r; González Obregón and Gómez, *Procesos*, 310).

149. Luis de Carvajal in February 1596 (AGN 158-3, 16v-19r; AGN 163-3, 166v).
150. AGN Real Fisco (97) 9-3.
151. AGN 158-3, 12r.
152. AGN 158-3, 75r-77r.
153. "Los hombres mineros tienen pasiones y pesadumbres con muchos" (AGN 158-3, 232v).
154. AGN 158-3, 119r-120r.
155. AGN 158-3, 284r. This church, at the northwest corner of the Alameda, has suffered numerous modifications over the centuries. No trace of the grave remains today.
156. AGN Real Fisco (97) 8-11, 280v-317t. In 1588-1589, Jaso was alcalde de minas in Guanajuato (AGN Real Hacienda, Archivo Histórico de Hacienda, 008-1292-31, 61-268). Castro Lobato had various business interests in Tlalpujahua (AGN Gobierno Virreinal, General de Parte 051-5-936, 197v; AGN 051-5-922, 193).
157. AGN 1493-3. As previously noted, after a year's interrogation, Clara publically abjured in an auto-de-fé and was remanded to the Convento de Jesús María in Mexico City to be instructed in the Catholic faith.
158. Uchmany, *Vida*, 166-69, 174-5; Domínguez Ortiz. *Judeoconversos*, 63; Uchmany, "Simón Váez," 127.
159. Uchmany, *Vida*, 175-76.
160. Oria, born in 1534, worked in Mexico City's Casa de la Moneda, the royal mint. He was imprisoned for having expressed doubts about Jesus's resurrection (AGN 163-3, 43r).
161. Suster was tried in 1598 (AGN 164-6).
162. AGN 163-3, 44rv.
163. *Membrillo* (AGN 276-14, 412v-413v, 421r, 422r, 425r, 428r).
164. Eva Uchmany notes that the viceroy awarded Lemos the sash of *alférez* (lieutenant) and that he never attained the rank of captain. Since the prisoners knew that Lemos was a spy, she speculates that Sebastián Rodríguez organized the party principally to win his favor (*Vida*, 155).
165. AGN 271-1, 10r-11v; AGN 276-14, 430v-432r.

Chapter 16

1. AGN 159-4, 275r.
2. AGN 1491-3, 10r, 31r-32r; Bancroft, Lucena, 611v.

3. For example, Boneva and Frieze, "Concept," and Freeze et al., "Psychological." John J. Ray underscores the perception of immigrants as people with higher drive, ambition, and independence ("Traits").
4. Juan Ignacio Pulido Serrano notes the dangers inherent in analyzing Portuguese-Spanish conversos according to either the "singularist" theory of identity, which holds that "every individual has a primary and principal affiliation uniting him to a single, specific group," or the "communitarian" theory, which alleges that "every individual belongs to a specific community which endows the individual with a singular, complete identity." As was noted in the introduction, he reminds us that "everyone may, and actually does, have plural affiliations to diverse groups or communities, and thus has at one and the same time multiple identities" ("Plural Identities," 130–31).
5. Gans, "Symbolic Ethnicity," 2.
6. See appendix 1, "Origins and Arrivals."
7. The *Jewish Encyclopedia* notes that the prescription of the quorum of ten for certain ritual practices first appears in the Mishnah (Megillah iv. 3). Norman Roth notes a reference to the custom of minyan in Spain as early as the seventh century (*Jews, Visigoths*, 15) and notes that in medieval Spain, under certain circumstances even boys under the age of thirteen could be counted for the minyan (*Daily Life*, 56). I have found no overt references to minyanim in sixteenth-century Mexican documents.
8. See the discussions throughout Israel, *Race*, and Israel, *Diasporas*.
9. For studies of sixteenth-century Sevilla as an economic powerhouse and of the influx of Portuguese conversos, see Aguado de los Reyes, "Apogeo"; Barrios, *Tribunal*; Fernández Chaves-Rafael et al., "Penetración"; Gil Fernández, *Conversos*; Pike, *Aristocrats* and *Linajudos*.
10. Boneva and Frieze ("Concept") and Frieze et al. ("Psychological") also found that immigrants tend to have a lower affiliation motivation and commitment to family centrality than does the nonimmigrant population.
11. Luis de Carvajal's library of eight books included three Jewish Bibles, one Christian Bible, and Granada's *Símbolo de la fe*, the *Guia de Pecadores, y Diálogos del Amor de Dios* (AGN 1489-1, 168v).
12. Gabriel de Castellanos was fond of *Mirror of Consolation*, and Old Tomás's copy may have belonged to him (AGN 1529-1, 50v). Escobar Quevedo (*Inquisición*, 290), citing Charles Amiel ("Quintanar"), notes that forty editions of *Mirror of Consolation* were published between 1540 and 1591
13. Manuel Gil de la Guardia, testifying in prison in 1598, said that his friend Fernán Gil Lerino had told him not to read saints' lives but only "the miracles that God performed for the Jews that he would find in the *Mirror of Consolation*, which was not a prohibited book, so no one would punish him even if they saw him reading it" (AGN 160-1, 109v).
14. AGN 158-3, 108r.

15. Bancroft, Lucena, 18v, 42r, 117r, 120v–121v, 615v, 632v; AGN 1529-4, 18v.
16. Francisco Váez (AGN 151-6, 161r) and Juan del Casal (AGN 1489-1, 450r; Bancroft, Lucena 120v, 354v, 626v).
17. AGN 156-4, 54r; AGN 1489-1, 458r.
18. AGN 158-2, 132v.
19. AGN 1489-1, 340v.
20. The major source of his confusion were the prophecies in the book of Edras (AGN 158-1, 42r, 74r, 86r).
21. Deut. 6:6–7; Deut. 11:19–20. In the daily liturgy these words are part of the Shema, a central prayer of Judaism and one of the few Hebrew prayers cited explicitly in Mexican Inquisition testimonies of the late sixteenth century (Luis de Carvajal, AGN 1489-1, 367v; Antonio Machado, AGN 1491-3, 116r, AGN 1529-3, 23v; Manuel Gómez Navarro, Bancroft, Lucena, 577v, 646v).
22. Bennett et al., "Family Identity," 214.
23. Pulido Serrano challenges the traditional arguments that "Endogamous marriage . . . gave families protection and guaranteed the continuity of Judaism through the ages thanks to the intimacy of the family redoubt, the chief site of cultural reproduction," arguing that to date "there are no studies sufficiently broad in scope to justify the use of this premise as a general explanation of New Christians' behavior." He prefers the term *homogamous*, noting, "'Endogamy' means marriage between people of common descent, that is, between members of the same family. By extension, historians have interpreted common decent not in a strict familial sense, but also in religious or ethnic terms. . . . What was really taking place is what today's sociologists call 'homogamy,' namely, marriage between equals in any of a variety of possible senses such as geographical origin, occupation, culture, or socio-economic status" ("Plural Identities," 141–42).
24. Contreras, "Family," 135.
25. These remarks appear in Jensen's online review of Ute Schönpflug's *Cultural Transmission* (Christopher Jensen, "What Do We Know about Cultural Transmission," christopherjensen.com, 2016, http://www.christopherxjjensen.com/2016/01/29/what-do-we-know-about-cultural-transmission [accessed December 26, 2018]).
26. The witnesses were Manuel Sánchez Delgado, Antonio de Montúfar, Isabel Bravo, and Ana de Pineda (AGN 389-12a, 522r–526r).
27. According to what Antonio López told Manuel de Lucena (Bancroft, Lucena, 332v).
28. María Landeta, the wife of Texcoco's head bailiff, Gaspar de Contreras, testified in 1629 that she had heard Clara's brother Simón say that he had heard from Clara's aunt Justa Méndez in Llerena, Spain, that Clara had died, and she added that her brother suspected that Justa had murdered Clara, perhaps by throwing her in a well, because she was fearful of Clara's Judaizing (AGN 366-27, 339r).

29. AGN Indiferente Virreinal 5574-054, 1r-49r. In 1621 Simón, age twenty-nine, was arrested a second time and charged, not with Judaizing but with the same offenses as before: wearing prohibited clothing and going about armed on horseback. He admitted his guilt, but he claimed that everybody violated those prohibitions, whereupon he named several offenders, including two of his relatives. "I have seen them wearing silk and fine cloth, carrying arms, and for that reason, and because I am married to an honorable women, I dared to do it too." Then he threw himself on the mercy of the court, which sentenced him as before and prohibited him from leaving Mexico City. In 1629 a witness in another case thought that Simón might be living in Las Amilpas with his uncle Pedro Rodríguez, who in 1613 had himself been found guilty of carrying a sword and riding a horse, both activities prohibited to the children of reconciled heretics, and banished from Mexico for ten years, a portion of which Rodríguez spent doing business in China (AGN 366-27, 339r).
30. Gitlitz, *Secrecy*, 245-51. Stanley Hordes found that in seventeenth-century Mexico, 75 percent of converso men married and that 96 percent of their marriages were endogamic ("Crypto-Jewish," 118; *To the End*, 46; "Inquisition," 210). Noting the conversos' proclivity to endogamy is a commonplace among historians. See Caro Baroja, *Judíos*, 1:395-402; Liebman, *New Spain*, 75; Star-LeBeau *Shadow*, 98; Wachtel, *Faith*, 242, 248. For questions about the validity of this thesis, see Pulido Serrano, "Prácticas."
31. Jacob Rader Marcus noted a similar phenomenon among nineteenth-century Jewish immigrants to the United States. "In larger towns, the rate of intermarriage was not inconsequential, but in the villages and hamlets the Jewish shopkeeper nearly always took a Christian wife." ("Why Study").
32. Bengtson et al., in a study of more than 350 modern interfaith families, found that in Judaism, a strong maternal bond plays the greater role in transmission of Jewish culture to the couple's children (*Families*, 113-30).
33. For Judaizing conversa women as transmitters of religious culture, see Melammed, *Heretics*, 42-49; Jacobs, "Women," 59; Gitlitz, *Secrecy*, 228.
34. Antonio Díaz Márquez, who had two children with his Old Christian wife, Francisca Rodríguez, told Luis de Carvajal that "if I could, I would take my son to a Jewish community somewhere to get him away from the influence of his old-Christian mother" (González Obregón and Gómez, Procesos, 320; AGN 1489-1, 16r).
35. See, for example, Bennett et al., "Family," 211-14, 216.

BIBLIOGRAPHY

AGN Instituciones Coloniales, "Ingenio de agua de Hernando Toledo en términos de las minas de Tlalpuxahua," 1575. Colecciones 280: Mapas, Planos, e Ilustraciones.
Agricola, Georg. *De re metallica*. Basel, 1556, 1621. *See also* Young, "Black."
Aguado de los Reyes, Jesús. "El apogeo de los judíos portugueses en la Sevilla americanista." *Cadernos de estudos sefarditas* 5 (2005): 135–57.
Aguirre Beltrán, Gonzalo. *Cuijla: Esbozo etnográfico de un pueblo negro*. Mexico City: Fondo de Cultura Económica, 1958.
Alberro, Solange. "Crypto-Jews and the Mexican Holy Office in the Seventeenth Century." In *The Jews and the Expansion of Europe to the West, 1400–1800*, edited by Paolo Bernardini and Norman Fiering, pp. 172–85. New York: Berghahn Books, 2001.
———. *Inquisición y sociedad en Mexico, 1571–1700*. Mexico City: Fondo de Cultura Económica, 1988.
Alfonso XI. *Ordenamiento real*. 1386. *See* González, "Panorama."
Altman, Ida. "Spanish Society in Mexico City after the Conquest." *Hispanic American Historical Review* (1991): 413–45.
American Jewish Historical Society. Spanish transcript of the proceso against Justa Méndez, 1595. Series II: Procesos Transcriptions and Translations, 1572–1656. Box 7, folder 1: Mendez, Donzella, Justa.
Amiel, Charles. "Les cent voix de Quintanar. Le modèle castillan du marranisme (II)." *Revue de l'histoire des religions* (2001): 487–577.
Anderson, Ruth Matilda. *Hispanic Costume, 1480–1530*. New York: Hispanic Society of America, 1979.
Antúnez Echegaray, Francisco. *Monografía histórica y minera sobre el distrito de Guanajuato*. Mexico City: Consejo de Recursos Naturales no Renovables, 1964.
Archivo General de la Nación (AGN). *Libro primero de votos de la Inquisición de México, 1573–1600*. Mexico City: Imprenta Universitaria, 1949.
Azevedo Mea. *See* Mea.

Bakewell, Peter John. "Notes on the Mexican Silver Mining Industry in the 1590s." In *Mines of Silver and Gold in the Americas*, edited by Peter John Bakewell, pp. 171–98. London: Variorum, 1997.

Bancroft Library. Diego Méndez. Banc mss 72/57m. Box 1, item 8: 1619, Tlaxcala. Mexican Inquisition original documents organized by collection and Bancroft manuscript classification. University of California, Berkeley.

———. Leonor de Carvajal. Banc mss 96/95m. Vol. 3: 1595, Mexico City. Mexican Inquisition original documents organized by collection and Bancroft manuscript classification. University of California, Berkeley.

———. Manuel de Lucena. Banc mss 96/95m. Vol. 2: 1594, Mexico City. Mexican Inquisition original documents organized by collection and Bancroft manuscript classification. University of California, Berkeley.

Barrera-Osorio, Antonio. *Experiencing Nature: The Spanish American Empire and the Early Scientific Revolution*. Austin: University of Texas Press, 2010.

Barrios, Manuel. *El Tribunal de la Inquisición en Andalucía*. Seville: Castillejo, 1991.

Bengtson, Vern L., Norella M. Putney, and Susan Harris, *Families and Faith: How Religion Is Passed Down across Generations*. Oxford: Oxford University Press, 2013.

Bennett, Linda A., Steven J. Wolin, and Katharine J. McAvity. "Family Identity, Ritual, and Myth: A Cultural Perspective on Life Cycle Transitions." In *Family Transitions: Continuity and Change over the Life Cycle*, edited by Celia Jaes Falicov, pp. 211–34. New York: Guilford Press, 1988.

Berdan, Frances, and Patricia Rieff Anawalt, eds. *The Essential Codex Mendoza*. Berkeley: University of California Press, 1997.

Bodian, Miriam. *Dying in the Law of Moses: Crypto-Jewish Martyrdom in the Iberian World*. Bloomington: Indiana University Press, 2007.

Böhm, Günter. "Los 'Portugueses' en el Nuevo Mundo." *Cuaderno judaico* 23 (1998): 41–65.

Boneva, Bonka S., and Irene Hanson Frieze. "Toward a Concept of a Migrant Personality." *Journal of Social Issues* 57 no. 3 (2001): 477–91.

Bonialian, Mariano. *China en la América colonial: Bienes, mercados, comercio, y cultura del consumo desde México hasta Buenos Aires*. Buenos Aires: Biblos-Instituto Mora, 2014.

Boone, Elizabeth Hill. *Stories in Red and Black: Pictorial Histories of the Aztecs and Mixtecs*. Austin: University of Texas Press, 2010.

Boyd-Bowman, Peter. "La emigración peninsular a América: 1520 a 1539." *Historia mexicana* (1963): 165–92.

Brading, David A., and Harry E. Cross. "Colonial Silver Mining: Mexico and Peru." *Hispanic American Historical Review* 52, no. 4 (1972): 545–79.

Burnes Ortiz, Arturo. *La minería en la historia económica de Zacatecas (1546–1876)*. Zacatecas: Departamento Editorial, UAZ, 1987.

Butzer, Elisabeth K. "The Roadside Inn or 'Venta': Origins and Early Development in

New Spain." *Yearbook, Conference of Latin Americanist Geographers* 23 (1997): 1–15.

Cantera Burgos, Francisco. "Los judíos expulsados de San Martín de Valdeiglesias." In *Actas del primer simposio de estudios sefardíes*, edited by Iacobo M. Hassan, pp. 23–32. Madrid: Consejo Superior de Investigaciones Científicas, 1970.

Caro Baroja, Julio. *Los judíos en la España moderna y contemporánea*. 3 vols. Madrid: Ediciones Arión, 1961.

Carreño, Alberto María. "Un maestro de maestros en el siglo XVI. Discurso de recepción del señor académico don Alberto María Carreño leído en la sesión del 2 de octubre de 1936." Mexico City: Academia Mexicana de la Historia correspondiente de la Real de Madrid, 1936.

Carrete Parrondo, Carlos. *Fontes iudaeorum Regni Castellae (1486–1502)*. Vol. 2, *El Tribunal de la Inquisición en el Obispado de Soria*. Salamanca: Universidad Pontificia de Salamanca, 1985.

Casas, Bartolomé de las. *Historia de las Indias*. 1561. See Pérez Sáenz, "Minería."

Castillo Martos, Manuel. *Bartolomé de Medina y el siglo XVI*. Santander: Universidad de Cantabria, 2006.

Castillo Sandoval, Roberto. "El obraje, embrión de la fábrica." *Nueva antropología; Revista de ciencias sociales* 8, no. 29 (1986): 125–34.

Castro, Américo. *The Structure of Spanish History*. Translated by Edmund L. King. Princeton, NJ: Princeton University Press, 1954.

"Censos de la población del Virreinato de Nueva España en el siglo XVI." *Boletín del Centro de estudios americanistas de Sevilla de Indias* 6, no. 23–24 (1919): 51–53. See Wagner, "Early."

Cervantes de Salazar, Francisco. *Life in the Imperial and Loyal City of Mexico in New Spain, and the Royal and Pontifical University of Mexico [. . .]*. Translated by Minnie Lee Barrett Shepard. Westport, CT: Greenwood Press, 1970.

———. *México en 1554*. Mexico City: Universidad Nacional Autónoma, 1939.

Chaunu, Huguette, Pierre Chaunu, and Lucien Febvre. *Séville et l'Atlantique (1504–1650)*. Paris: Colin, 1955–1959.

Chuchiak IV, John F., ed. and trans. *The Inquisition in New Spain, 1536–1820: A Documentary History*. Baltimore: Johns Hopkins University Press, 2012.

Coe, Sophie D., and Michael D. Coe. *The True History of Chocolate*. 3rd ed. London: Thames and Hudson, 2013.

Cohen, Martin A. "Antonio Díaz de Cáceres: Marrano Adventurer in Colonial Mexico." *American Jewish Historical Quarterly* 60, no. 2 (1970): 169–84.

———. *The Martyr: The Story of a Secret Jew and the Mexican Inquisition in the Sixteenth Century*. Philadelphia: Jewish Publication Society of America, 1973.

———. "Some Misconceptions about the Crypto-Jews in Colonial Mexico." *American Jewish Historical Quarterly* 61, no. 4 (1972): 277–93.

Contreras, Jaime. "Family and Patronage: The Judeo-Converso Minority in Spain." In *Cultural Encounters: The Impact of the Inquisition in Spain and the New*

World, edited by Mary Elizabeth Perry and Anne J. Cruz, pp. 127–45. Los Angeles: University of California Press, 1991.

Conway, George R. G. "Hernando Alonso: A Jewish Conquistador with Cortés in Mexico." *Publications of the American Jewish Historical Society* 31 (1928): 9–31.

Cortés, Hernán. "Cuarta carta de relación." 500 años de México en documentos. http://www.biblioteca.tv/artman2/publish/1524_274/Cuarta_Carta_de_Relaci_n_de_Hern_n_Cort_s_454.shtml (accessed August 1, 2016).

———. *Ordenanzas sobre ventas*. 1524. See Butzer, "Roadside Inn"; Trens, *Historia*.

Cortés Espinoza, Rogelio. *Inventario del Archivo Parroquial de San Agustín Obispo, Chiautla, Puebla*. Mexico City: Apoyo al Desarrollo de Archivos y Bibliotecas de México, 2008.

Craig, Alan K., and Robert C. West, eds. *In Quest of Mineral Wealth: Aboriginal and Colonial Mining and Metallurgy in Spanish America*. Baton Rouge: University of Louisiana Press, 1995.

Cubillo Moreno, Gilda. "La actividad productiva minera en la región de Pachuca, en el contexto colonial del siglo XVI." In *Memoria del primer congreso interno de investigación, 13–15 junio de 1984*, compiled by Jesús Monjarás-Ruiz, pp. 33–57. Mexico City: Departamento de Etnohistoria, INAH, 1985.

———. *Los dominios de la plata: El precio del auge, el peso del poder: empresarios y trabajadores en las minas de Pachuca y Zimapán, 1552–1620*. Mexico City: Instituto Nacional de Antropología e Historia, 1991.

Cuesta Domingo, Mariano, ed. *Alonso de Santa Cruz y su obra cosmográfica*. 2 vols. Madrid: Consejo Superior de Investigaciones Científicas, 1983.

De Grinberg. *See* Grinberg.

del Valle Pavón, Guillermina. "Los mercaderes de México y la transgresión de los límites al comercio Pacífico en Nueva España, 1550–1620." *Revista de Historia Económica, La Economía en tiempos del Quijote*, 23, número extraordinario (2005): 213–40.

di Leone Leoni, Aron. *La nazione ebraica spagnola e portoghese di Ferrara (1492–1559): I suoi rapporti col governo ducale e la popolaziones locale et i suoi legami con le Nazioni Portoghesi di Ancona Pesaro e Venezia*. 2 vols. Florence: Leo S. Olschki, 2011.

Díaz del Castillo, Bernal. *Historia verdadera de la conquista de la Nueva España*. Circa 1570. Mexico City: Porrúa, 1962.

Domínguez Ortiz, Antonio. *Los judeoconversos en España y América*. Madrid: ISTMO, 1971.

Egleston, Thomas. I. "The Patio and Cazo Process of Amalgamating Silver Ores." *Annals of the New York Academy of Sciences* 3, no. 1 (1883): 1–66.

Enciso Contreras, José. *Taxco en el siglo XVI: Sociedad y normatividad en un real de minas novohispano*. Vol. 4, Zacatecas. Zacatecas: Ayuntamiento de Zacatecas, 1999.

Escobar Quevedo, Ricardo. "Los criptojudíos de Cartagena de Indias: Un eslabón en la diáspora conversa (1635–1649)." *Anuario colombiano de historia social y de la cultura* 29 (2002): 45–71.

———. *Inquisición y judaizantes en América española (siglos XVI–XVII)*. Rosario, Argentina: Universidad del Rosario, 2008.
Espino Hernández, Rodrigo. *Historia de la Hacienda El Chorrillo*. Mexico City: Universidad Autónoma de México, 1917.
Estrada Carrión, Raúl. *Zacualpan, primer real de minas: Ensayo histórico sobre Zacualpan de Cohuixco y el Real de Minas de Zacualpan*. Mexico City: Universidad Autónoma del Estado de México, 1995.
Faur, José. *In the Shadow of History: Jews and Conversos at the Dawn of Modernity*. Albany: SUNY Press, 2012.
Felix, Jay. *Urban Communities in Early Spanish America, 1493–1700: Translation of Original Texts*. Lewiston, NY: Edwin Mellen Press, 2002.
Fernández Chaves-Rafael, Manuel Fernando, and Rafael María Pérez García. "La penetración económica portuguesa en la Sevilla del siglo XVI." *Espacio, tiempo y forma*. Seria IV, *Historia Moderna* 25 (2012): 119–222.
Fernández del Castillo, Francisco. *Libros y libreros en el siglo XVI; Selección de documentos y paleografía*. Mexico City: Fondo de Cultura Económica, 1982.
Flynn, Dennis O., and Arturo Giráldez. "Born with a 'Silver Spoon': The Origin of World Trade in 1571." *Journal of World History* 6, no. 2 (1995): 201–21.
Flynn, Dennis O., Arturo Giráldez, and James Sobrado, eds. *European Entry into the Pacific: Spain and the Acapulco-Manila Galleons*. Aldershot, UK: Ashgate Variorum, 2001.
Freire, Anselmo Braamcamp. "Povoação de Trás os Montes no XVI século." *Archivo historic portuguez* 7, no. 7 (July 1909): 241–90.
Frieze, Irene Hanson, Bonka S. Boneva, Nataša Šarlija, Jasna Horvat, Anuška Ferligoj, Tina Kogovšek, Jolanta Miluska, Ludmila Popova, Janna Korobanova, Nadejda Sukhareva, Ludmila Erokhina, and Eva Jarošová. "Psychological Differences in Stayers and Leavers: Emigration Desires in Central and Eastern European University Students." *European Psychologist* 9, no. 1 (2004): 15–23.
Gans, Herbert J. "Symbolic Ethnicity: The Future of Ethnic Groups and Cultures in America." *Ethnic and Racial Studies* 2, no. 1 (1979): 1–20.
García, María Antonieta. *Inquisição e independência, um motim no Fundão-1580*. Coimbra, Portugal: Alma Azul, 2007.
García, Trinidad. *Los mineros mexicanos: colección de artículos sobre tradiciones y narraciones mineras, descubrimiento de las minas más notables, fundación de las poblaciones minerales más importantes y particularmente sobre la crisis producida por la baja de la plata [. . .]*. Mexico City: Porrúa, 1970.
García-Molina Riquelme, Antonio M. *Las hogueras de la Inquisición en México*. Mexico City: Universidad Nacional Autónoma de México, Instituto de Investigaciones Jurídicas, Instituto de Investigaciones Jurídicas, 2016. https://biblio.juridicas.unam.mx/bjv/detalle-libro/4235-las-hogueras-de-la-inquisicion-en-mexico (accessed December 19, 2017).
———. "Utilización extemporánea de sambenitos en el distrito del Tribunal de la Inquisición de México." *Anuario mexicano de historia del derecho* 22 (2010):

407–24. www.juridicas.unam.mx/publica/rev/hisder/cont/22/otr/otr23.htm (accessed July 25, 2016).

Garner, Richard L. "Long-Term Silver Mining Trends in Spanish America: A Comparative Analysis of Peru and Mexico." *American Historical Review* 93, no. 4 (1988): 898–935.

Garza Martínez, Valentina, and Juan Manuel Pérez Zevallos. *El real y minas de San Gregorio de Mazapil, 1568–1700*. Mazapil, Zacatecas: Instituto Zacatecano de Cultura Ramón López Velarde, 2004.

Gerhard, Peter. *Geografía histórica de la Nueva España, 1519–1821*. Translated by Stella Mastrangelo. Mexico City: Universidad Nacional Autónoma de México, Instituto de Investigaciones Históricas, 1986.

Gil Fernández, Juan. *Los conversos y la Inquisición sevillana*. Sevilla: Universidad de Sevilla, 2000–2003.

Gilman, Stephen. "The Case of Álvaro de Montalbán." *Modern Language Notes* 78, no. 2 (March 1963): 113–25.

Gitlitz, David M. "Anusim Surnames: Myth and Reality." *Journal of Spanish, Portuguese, and Italian Crypto-Jews* 2 (Spring 2010): 21–36.

———. "The Expulsion Decree and the Alleged Profanations of Christian Ritual." In *Judíos. Sefarditas. Conversos: La expulsión de 1492 y sus consecuencias*, edited by Angel Alcalá, pp. 150–69. Valladolid, Yucatan: Ambito, 1995.

———. *Secrecy and Deceit: The Religion of the Crypto-Jews*. Philadelphia: Jewish Publication Society, 1996.

———. "The Where of the Mexican Conversos," *Journal of Spanish, Portuguese, and Italian Crypto Jews* 5 (2013): 6–20.

Gitlitz, David, and Linda Kay Davidson. *A Drizzle of Honey: The Life and Recipes of Spain's Secret Jews*. New York: Macmillan, 2000.

Glick, Thomas F. "Converso and Marrano Ethnicity." In *Crisis and Creativity in the Sephardic World, 1391–1648*, edited by Benjamin R. Gampel, pp. 59–76. New York: Columbia University Press, 1997.

González, María del Refugio. "Panorama de la legislación minera en la historia de México." *Jurídica; Anuario del Departamento de derecho de la Universidad Iberoamericana* 12 (1980): 791–811.

González Obregón, Luis, and Rodolfo Gómez, eds. *Procesos de Luis de Carvajal (El Mozo)*. Mexico City: Secretaría de Gobernación 1935.

González Sánchez, Carlos Alberto. "El libro en la carrera de Indias: Registro de ida de navíos." *Archivo hispalense: Revista histórica, literaria y artística*, 2nd ser., 72, no. 220 (1989): 93–104.

Grace, Leslie. "460 Years of Silk in Oaxaca, Mexico." Presented at the Textile Society of America Ninth Biennial Symposium, October 7–9, 2004, Oakland, California. Digital Commons@University of Nebraska-Lincoln. http://digitalcommons.unl.edu/tsaconf/482/ (accessed July 25, 2015).

Graizbord, David L. *Souls in Dispute: Converso Identities in Iberia and the Jewish Diaspora, 1580–1700*. Philadelphia: University of Pennsylvania Press, 2011.

Greenleaf, Richard E. "Francisco Millán before the Mexican Inquisition: 1538–1539." *The Americas* 21, no. 2 (1964): 184–95.
———. "The Obraje in the Late Mexican Colony" *The Americas* 23, no. 3 (1967): 227–50.
———. *Zumárraga and the Mexican Inquisition, 1536–1543*. Washington, DC: Academy of American Franciscan History, 1961.
Grinberg, Dora M. K. de. *Los señores del metal: Minería y metalurgia en Mesoamérica*. Mexico City: Consejo nacional para la cultura y las artes, Dirección General de Publicaciones, 1990.
Halevy, Schulamith C. "Blood in the Church: The Inquisition against Hernando Alonso." *Hispania Judaica Bulletin* 8 (2011): 39–56.
Hamilton, Michelle M. "La poesía de Leonor de Carvajal y la tradición de los criptojudíos en Nueva España." *Sefarad* 60, no. 1 (2000): 75–93.
Hanke, Lewis Ulysses, and Celso Rodríguez. *Los virreyes españoles en América durante el gobierno de la casa de Austria*. 5 vols. Madrid: Atlas, 1976–1978.
Hassig, Ross. *Comercio, tributo y transportes: La economía política del valle de México en el siglo XVII*. Translated by Juan José Utrilla. Mexico City: Alianza Editorial, 1990.
Hebrew Union College, Small Collections. Transcripts of the proceedings against Jorge de Almeida and Ana de Carvajal before the Inquisition, Mexico City, 1590–1609.
Hernández, A., M. Jébrak, P. Higueras, R. Oyarzun, D. Morata, and J. Munhá. "The Almadén Mercury Mining District, Spain." *Mineralium Deposita* 34, no. 5–6 (1999): 539–48.
Herrejón Pereda, Carlos. *Tlalpujahua. Monografías municipales del Edo. de Michoacán*. Mexico City: Gobierno del Estado de Michoacán, 1980.
Himmerich y Valencia, Robert. *The Encomenderos of New Spain, 1521–1555*. Austin: University of Texas Press, 1991.
Hirschberg, Julia. "An Alternative to *Encomienda*: Puebla's Indios de Servicio, 1531–45." *Journal of Latin American Studies* 11, no. 2 (1979): 241–64.
Hoberman, Louisa Schell. *Mexico's Merchant Elite, 1590–1660: Silver, State, and Society*. Durham, NC: Duke University Press, 1991.
Hordes, Stanley Mark. "The Crypto-Jewish Community of New Spain, 1620–1649: A Collective Biography." PhD dissertation, Tulane University, 1980.
———. "The Inquisition and the Crypto-Jewish Community in Colonial New Spain and New Mexico." In *Cultural Encounters: The Impact of the Inquisition in Spain and the New World*, edited by Mary Elizabeth Perry and Anne J. Cruz, pp. 207–17. Berkeley: University of California Press, 1991.
———. *To the End of the Earth: A History of the Crypto-Jews of New Mexico*. New York: Columbia University Press, 2005.
Hoyo, Eugenio del. *Historia del Nuevo Reino de León (1577–1723)*. Monterrey: Fondo Editorial de Nuevo León, 2005.
Huerga, Álvaro. *Historia de los Alumbrados: Los Alumbrados de Hispanoamérica*

(1570–1630). Madrid: Seminario Cisneros, Fundación Universitaria Española, 1986.

———. "Judíos de Ferrara en la Inquisición de México." *Annuario del'Istituto storico italiano l'etá moderna e contemporanea* 35–36 (1985): 117–65.

Icaza, Francisco A. de. *Diccionario autobiográfico de conquistadores y pobladores de Nueva España: Sacado de los textos originales*. 2 vols. 1923. Guadalajara: E. A. Levy, 1969.

Israel, Jonathan Irvine. *Diasporas within a Diaspora: Jews, Crypto-Jews, and the World of Maritime Empires (1540–1740)*. Boston: Brill, 2002.

———. *Race, Class and Politics in Colonial Mexico, 1610–1670*. London: Oxford University Press, 1975.

Izquierdo Labrado, Julio. "La emigración palerma a América." *Huelva en su historia* 1 (1986): 285–301.

Jacobs, Auke Pieter. "Legal and Illegal Emigration from Seville." In *To Make America: European Emigration in the Early Modern Period*, edited by Ida Altman and James Horn, 59–84. Berkeley: University of California Press, 1991.

Jacobs, Janet Liebman. "Women, Ritual and Secrecy: The Creation of Crypto-Jewish Culture." *Journal for the Scientific Study of Religion* 35, no. 2 (1996): 97–108.

JBGL. "400 años de inmigración española a Méxcio." Exploramex. http://exploramex.com/?p=648 (accessed April 4, 2013).

Lang, M. F. *El monopolio estatal del mercurio en el México colonial (1550–1710)*. Mexico City: Fondo de Cultura Económica, 1977.

Lavrin, Asunción. "In Search of the Colonial Woman in Mexico: The Seventeenth and Eighteenth Centuries." In *Latin American Women: Historical Perspectives*, edited by Asunción Lavrin, pp. 23–59. Westport, CT: Greenwood Press, 1978.

Lea, Henry Charles. *A History of the Inquisition of Spain*. 3 vols. New York: Macmillan, 1907.

———. *The Inquisition in the Spanish Dependencies*. 1922. Eugene, OR: Wipf and Stock Publishers, 2003.

Ledesma, Pedro de. "Relación de minas de Taxco." 1581. *See* Enciso Contreras.

Lee, Raymond L. "Cochineal Production and Trade in New Spain to 1600." *The Americas* 4, no. 4 (1948): 449–73.

León Alanís, Ricardo. "Evangelización, congregación de pueblos y administración eclesiástica en la región minera de Tlalpujahua-Tlacotepec (siglos XVI–XVIII)." Tlacotepec. http://tlacotepecmich.info/files/Download/evangelizacion.pdf (accessed July 7, 2014).

Leonard, Irving Albert. *Books of the Brave: Being an Account of Books and of Men in the Spanish Conquest and Settlement of the Sixteenth-Century New World*. Cambridge, MA: Harvard University Press, 1949.

Lewin, Boleslao. "The Struggle against Jewish Immigration into Latin America in Colonial Times." *YIVO Annual of Jewish Social Science* 7 (1952): 212–28.

Libro primero de votos. *See* Archivo General de la Nación.

Liebman, Seymour B. *The Enlightened: The Writing of Luis de Carvajal el Mozo.* Coral Gables: University of Miami Press, 1967.

———. "Hernando Alonso: The First Jew on the North-American Continent." *Journal of Inter-American Studies* 5, no. 2 (1963): 291–96.

———. "The Jews as an Ethnic Group in the Americas during the Sixteenth and Seventeenth Centuries." In *Community, Self, and Identity*, edited by Bhabagrahi Misra and James Preston, pp. 95–114. The Hague: Mouton, 1978.

———. *The Jews in New Spain: Faith, Flame, and the Inquisition.* Coral Gables: University of Miami Press, 1970.

Lira Montt, Luis. "El estatuto de limpieza de sangre en el derecho indiano." In *XI Congreso del Instituto internacional de historia del derecho indiano: Buenos Aires, 4 al 9 de septiembre de 1995: Actas y estudios*, 4: 31–48. Buenos Aires: Instituto de Investigaciones de Historia del Derecho, 1997.

López de Gómara, Francisco. *Historia de México, con el descubrimiento de la Nueva España.* 1554. Caracas: Biblioteca Ayacucho, 1979.

López de Velasco, Juan. *Geografía y descripción universal de las Indias.* 1571–1574. See Ramírez-Cabañas, *Vera Cruz.*

López-Portillo y Weber, José. *La rebelión de Nueva Galicia.* Mexico City: Colección Peña Colorada, 1975.

Luna, Francisco. "Juliantla: Emprenden rescate de la "Tierra de Judíos" en Guerrero." Enlace judío. http://www.enlacejudio.com/2013/01/10/juliantla-emprenden-rescate-de-la-tierra-de-judios-en-guerrero/ (accessed March 17, 2013).

Mann, Charles C. *1493.* New York: Vintage, 2011.

Marcus, Jacob Rader. "Why Study American Jewish History." Excerpt from *United States Jewry, 1776–1985.* Detroit: Wayne State University Press, 1986, posted on Jacob Rader Marcus Center of the American Jewish Archive. http://americanjewisharchives.org/exhibits/gv/print/scholar-03.html (accessed December 14, 2016).

Márquez Villanueva, Antonio. *Los alumbrados: Orígenes y filosofía, 1525–1559.* Madrid: Taurus: 1972.

Martínez López, María Elena. *Genealogical Fictions: Limpieza de Sangre, Religion, and Gender in Colonial Mexico.* Stanford, CA: Stanford University Press, 2008.

Martinez López-Cano, María del Pilar. "Los comerciantes de la Ciudad de México en el siglo XVI. Hipótesis para su estudio." In *Caminos y mercados de México*, edited by Janet Long Towell and Amalia Attolini Lecón, pp. 551–72. Mexico City: Universidad Nacional Autónoma de México, Instituto de Investigaciones Históricas, Instituto Nacional de Antropología e Historia, 2009. http://www.historicas.unam.mx/publicaciones/publicadigital/libros/caminosymercados/cm027.pdf (accessed July 25, 2014).

McCann, Philip, and Zoltan J. Acs. "Globalization: Countries, Cities and Multinationals." *Regional Studies* 45, no. 1 (2011): 17–32.

Mea, Elvira Cunha de Azevedo. *A Inquisição de Coimbra no século XVI: A instituição, os homens e a sociedade*. Porto: Fundação Eng. António de Almeida, 1997.

———. "A Inquisição portuguesa, agente de emigração para Espanha." In *Inquisición y conversos: conferencias pronunciadas en el III Curso de Cultura Hispano-Judía y Sefardí . . . Toledo, 1993*, edited by Ana María López Álvarez, pp. 225–40. Ciudad Real, Spain: Asociación de Amigos del Museo Sefardí; Caja de Castilla-La Mancha, 1994.

———. *Sentenças da Inquisiçao de Coimbra em Metropolitanos de D. Frei Bartolomeu dos Mártires 1567–1582*. Porto: Arquivo Histórico Dominicano Português, 1982.

Mecham, J. Lloyd. "The *Real de Minas* as a Political Institution: A Study of a Frontier Institution in Spanish Colonial America." *Hispanic American Historical Review* 7, no. 1 (1927): 45–83.

Melammed, Renée Levine. *Heretics or Daughters of Israel? The Crypto-Jewish Women of Castile*. New York: Oxford University Press, 2002.

Micheli-Serra, Alfredo de. "Médicos y medicina en la nueva España del siglo XVI." *Gaceta médica de México* 137, no. 3 (2001): 257–63.

Millares Carlo, Agustín, and J. I. Mantecón. *Índice y extractos de los Protocolos del Archivo de Notarías de México, DF*. 2 vols. Mexico City: El Colegio de México, 1945–1946.

Miño Grijalba, Manuel. "El obraje colonial." *Revista europea de estudios latinoamericanos y del Caribe* 47 (1989): 3–19.

Mira Caballos, Esteban. *Nicolás de Ovando y los orígenes del sistema colonial español, 1502–1509*. Santo Domingo: Patronato de la Ciudad Colonial de Santo Domingo, 2000.

Monteiro, Isabel. *Os judeus na região de Viseu: A história, a cultura, os lugares*. Viseu, Portugal: Região de Turismo Dão Lafões, 1997.

Montoto de Sedas, Santiago. *Sevilla en el imperio (siglo XVI)*. Seville: Viuda de C. García, 1937.

Montt. *See* Lira Montt.

Moreno, Humberto Baquero. "Os Judeus na Cidade do Porto nos Séculos XIV e XV." *Revista de ciências históricas* 8 (1993): 55–64.

Moreno de los Arcos, Roberto. "Las instituciones de la industria minera novohispana." In *La minería en México*, edited by Miguel León Portilla, Jorge Gurria Lacroix, Enrique Madero Bracho, and Roberto Moreno, pp. 68–164. Mexico City: Universidad Nacional Autónoma de México, 1978.

Mota y Escobar, Alonso de la. *Descripción geográfica de los reinos de Nueva Galicia, Nueva Vizcaya y Nuevo León*. 2nd ed. Mexico City: Robredo, 1940.

Nettel Ross, Margarita. *Los testigos hablan: La conquista de Colima y sus informantes*. Colima: UCOL, 2007.

Nuevas leyes de Indias. 1542. *See Recopilación*.

Otte, Enrique. *Sevilla y sus mercaderes a fines de la Edad Media*. Edited by

Antonio-Miguel Bernal and Antonio Collantes de Terán. Seville: Vicerrectorado de Relaciones Institucionales y Extensión Cultural Fundación El Monte, 1996.

Otte Sander, Enrique. *Sevilla, siglo XVI: Materiales para su historia económica.* Seville: Junta de Andalucía, 2008.

Pacheco, Joaquín Francisco, Francisco de Cárdenas, Luis Torres de Mendoza, and Luis Torres de Mendoza, eds. *Colección de documentos inéditos, relativos al descubrimiento, conquista y organización de las antiguas posesiones españoles de América y Oceanía, sacados de los archivos del reino, y muy especialmente del de Indias. Competentemente autorizada.* 25 vols. Madrid: Ministerio de Ultramar, 1864–1884.

Palmer, Colin A. *Slaves of the White God: Blacks in Mexico, 1570–1650.* Cambridge, MA: Harvard University Press, 1976.

Patiño, Álvaro. *Descripción de la ciudad de la Veracruz y su comarca.* 1580. See Ramírez Cabañas.

Paulo, Amilcar. "La commune juive de Porto au Moyen Age." In *Proceedings of the Sixth World Congress of Jewish Studies, Held at the Hebrew University of Jerusalem, 13–19 August, 1973,* pp. 61–70. Jerusalem: World Union of Jewish Studies, 1975.

Perelis, Ronnie. "Marrano Autobiography in Its Transatlantic Context: Exile, Exploration and Spiritual Discovery." PhD dissertation, New York University, 2006.

Pérez-Mallaína Bueno, Pablo Emilio. *Spain's Men of the Sea: Daily Life on the Indies Fleets in the Sixteenth Century.* Translated by Carla Rahn Phillips. Baltimore: Johns Hopkins University Press, 1998.

Pérez Rosales, Laura. *Minería y sociedad en Taxco durante el siglo XVIII.* Mexico City: Universidad Iberoamericana, 1996.

Pérez Sáenz de Urturi, Juan Eusebio. "La minería colonial americana bajo la dominación española." *Boletín Millares Carlo* 7, no. 8 (1985): 53–120.

Perry, Mary Elizabeth, and Anne J. Cruz. *Cultural Encounters: The Impact of the Inquisition in Spain and the New World.* Berkeley: University of California Press, 1991.

Pike, Ruth. *Aristocrats and Traders: Sevillian Society in the Sixteenth Century.* Ithaca: Cornell University Press, 1972.

———. *Linajudos and Conversos in Seville: Greed and Prejudice in Sixteenth- and Seventeenth-Century Spain.* New York: Peter Lang, 2000.

———. "Seville in the Sixteenth Century." *Hispanic American Historical Review* 41, no. 1 (1961): 1–30.

Powell, Philip Wayne. "Presidios and Towns on the Silver Frontier of New Spain, 1550–1580." *Hispanic American Historical Review* 24, no. 2 (1944): 179–200.

Prinz, Deborah R. *On the Chocolate Trail: A Delicious Adventure Connecting Jews, Religions, History, Travel, Rituals and Recipes to the Magic of Cacao.* Woodstock, VT: Jewish Lights Publishing, 2013.

Probert, Alan. "Bartolomé de Medina: The Patio Process and the Sixteenth Century Silver Crisis." *Journal of the West* 8 (1969): 90–124.

Pulido Serrano, Juan Ignacio. "Plural Identities: The Portuguese New Christians." *Jewish History* 25, no. 2 (2011): 129–51.

——. "Prácticas matrimoniales de los portugueses en Madrid durante el siglo XVII." In *Territorios distantes, comportamientos similares: Familias, redes y reproducción social en la Monarquía Hispánica (siglos XIV–XIX)*, edited by Sebastián Molina Piche and Antonio Irigoyen López, pp. 171–94. Murcia: Universidad de Murcia, 2009.

Ramírez Cabañas, Joaquín. *La ciudad de Vera Cruz en el siglo XVI*. Mexico City: Colegio de México, 1943.

Rapp, George. *Archaeomineralogy*. New York: Springer, 2009.

Ray, John J. "The Traits of Immigrants: A Case Study of the Sydney Parsees." *Journal of Comparative Family Studies* 17, no. 1 (1986): 127–30.

Recopilación de leyes de los Reinos de las Indias. 1680. Madrid: Ediciones Cultura Hispánica, 1973. See Pérez-Mallaína Bueno, *Spain's Men*.

Rees, Peter W. "Origins of Colonial Transportation in Mexico." *Geographical Review* 65, no. 3 (1975): 323–34.

Ricard, Robert. "Pour une étude du judaïsme portugais au Méxique pendant la période coloniale." *Revue d'histoire moderne* 14 (1939): 516–24.

Riva Palacio, Vicente. *México a través de los siglos*. Vol. 2, *El Virreynato*. Mexico City: Cumbre, 1977.

Rodríguez Lorenzo, Sergio M. "El mar se mueve: la experiencia del viaje transatlántico entre los pasajeros de la carrera de Indias (siglos XVI y XVII)." *Communication and Culture Online*, 2013. https://www.academia.edu/5150185/El_mar_se_mueve_la_experiencia_del_viaje_trasatl%C3%A1ntico_entre_los_pasajeros_de_la_carrera_de_Indias_siglos_XVI_y_XVII_ (accessed, November 12, 2018).

Roth, Cecil, and Herman P. Salomon. *A History of the Marranos*. New York: Meridian Books, 1959.

Roth, Norman. *Conversos, Inquisition, and the Expulsion of the Jews from Spain*. Madison: University of Wisconsin Press, 2002.

——. *Daily Life of Jews in the Middle Ages*. Westport, CT: Greenwood, 2005.

——. *Jews, Visigoths, and Muslims in Medieval Spain: Cooperation and Conflict*. Leiden: Brill, 1994.

Salvucci, Richard J. *Textiles and Capitalism in Mexico: An Economic History of the Obrajes, 1539–1840*. Princeton, NJ: Princeton University Press, 1987.

Sánchez-Barbudo, Angela. *Algunos aspectos de la vida religiosa en la España del siglo XVI: Los alumbrados de Toledo*. Madison: University of Wisconsin Press, 1953.

Sánchez Flores, Ramón. "Technology of Mining in Colonial Mexico: Installations, Tools, Artifacts and Machines Used in the Patio Process, Sixteenth to Eighteenth Centuries." In *In Quest of Mineral Wealth: Aboriginal and Colonial*

Mining and Metallurgy in Spanish America, edited by Alan K. Craig and Robert C. West, pp. 137–53. Baton Rouge: University of Louisiana Press, 1995.
Sicroff, Albert A. *Les controverses des statuts de "pureté de sang" en Espagne du xv au xvii siècle.* Paris: Didier, 1960.
Socolow, Susan Migden. *The Women of Colonial Latin America.* Cambridge: Cambridge University Press, 2000.
Soto Oliver, Nicolás. *La minería: El distrito minero Pachuca-Real del Monte a través de la historia.* Pachuca de Soto, Mexico City: Gobierno del Estado de Hidalgo, Coordinación de Turismo, Cultura y Recreación, 1982.
Sousa, Fernando de. "The Silk Industry in Trás-Os-Montes during the Ancient Regime." *e-Journal of Portuguese History* 3, no. 2 (Winter 2005): 1–14. https://www.brown.edu/Departments/Portuguese_Brazilian_Studies/ejph/ (accessed July 15, 2016).
Sousa, Lúcio de. *The Jewish Diaspora and the Perez Family Case in China, Japan, the Philippines, and the Americas (16th Century).* Macau: Fundação Macau/Centro Científico e Cultural de Macau, I.P., 2015.
Starr-LeBeau, Gretchen D. *In the Shadow of the Virgin: Inquisitors, Friars, and Conversos in Guadalupe, Spain.* Princeton, NJ: Princeton University Press, 2003.
Studnicki-Gizbert, Daviken. "From Agents to Consulado: Commercial Networks in Colonial Mexico, 1520–1590 and Beyond." *Anuario de estudios americanos* 57, no. 1 (2000): 41–68.
Studnicki-Gizbert, Daviken, and David Schecter. "The Environmental Dynamics of a Colonial Fuel-Rush: Mining and Deforestation in New Spain, 1522–1810." *Environmental History* 15, no. 1 (2010): 94–119.
Tandeter, Enrique. "The Mining Industry." In *The Cambridge Economic History of Latin America*, vol. 1, edited by Victor Bulmer-Thomas, John H. Coatsworth, and Roberto Cortes-Conde, pp. 315–56. Cambridge: Cambridge University Press, 2006.
Temkin, Samuel. *Luis de Carvajal: The Origins of Nuevo Reino de León.* Santa Fe, NM: Sunstone Press, 2011.
Thornton, John. *Africa and Africans in the Making of the Atlantic World, 1400–1800.* Cambridge: Cambridge University Press, 1998.
Toro, Alfonso. *La familia Carvajal: Estudio histórico sobre los judíos y la Inquisición de la Nueva España en el siglo XVI, basado en documentos originales y en su mayor parte inéditos, que se conservan en el Archivo General de la Nación de la ciudad de México.* Mexico City: Patria, 1977.
———. *Los judíos en la Nueva España: Documentos del siglo XVI, correspondientes al ramo de Inquisición.* Mexico City: Archivo General de la Nación, 1932.
Trens, Manuel B. *Historia de Veracruz.* Vol. 2, *La dominición española, 1519–1809.* Jalapa, Veracuz: Jalapa-Enríquez, 1947.
Twain, Mark. "Whiskey Is for Drinking; Water Is for Fighting Over." Quote Investigator. quoteinvestigator.com/2013/06/03/whiskey-water/ (accessed July 7, 2014).

Uchmany, Eva Alexandra. "Un judío italiano ante la Inquisición de la Nueva España." In *Jews and Conversos: Studies in Society and the Inquisition; Proceedings of the Eighth World Congress of Jewish Studies*, edited by Yosef Kaplan, pp. 55–60. Jerusalem: Magnes Press, 1982.

———. "Los judíos y la Inquisición." In *Inquisición novohispana*, vol. 1, edited by Noemi Quezada, Martha Eugenia Rodríguez, and Marcela Suárez, pp. 73–100. Mexico City: Universidad Nacional Autónoma de México, Instituto de Investigaciones Antropológicas, 2000.

———. "The Participation of New Christians and Crypto-Jews in the Conquest, Colonization, and Trade of Spanish America, 1521–1660." In *The Jews and the Expansion of Europe to the West 1400–1660*, edited by Paolo Bernardini and Norman Fiering, pp. 186–202. New York: Berghahn Books, 2001.

———. "Simón Váez Sevilla." In *Michael: On the History of the Jews in the Diaspora*, edited by Lloyd P. Gartner, pp. 126–61. Tel Aviv: Diaspora Research Institute, 1983.

———. *La vida entre el judaísmo y el cristianismo en la Nueva España, 1580–1606*. Mexico City: Fondo de Cultura Economica, 1992.

Vázquez de Espinosa, Antonio. *Compendio y descripción de las Indias Occidentales*. Circa 1620. See Felix, *Urban*.

Veitia Linaje, Joseph de. *Norte de la contratación de las Indias Occidentales*. Seville: Iuan Francisco de Blas, 1672. See Lang, *Monopolio*.

Velázquez Fernández, Héctor. "Instrumentación, ciencia y epistemología: La relevancia de la observación novohispánica del eclipse lunar de 1584." *En-claves del pensamiento* 2, no. 4 (December 2008): 113–30. http://www.redalyc.org/articulo.oa?id=141112787007 (accessed November 12, 2018).

Wachtel, Nathan. *The Faith of Remembrance: Marrano Labyrinths*. Philadelphia: University of Pennsylvania Press, 2013.

Wagner, Henry R. "Early Silver Mining in New Spain." *Revista de historia de América* 14 (1942): 49–71.

Warshawsky, Matthew. "Justa Méndez's Half Century of Resistance to the Inquisition of Colonial Mexico." *HaLapid: Journal of the Society for Crypto-Judaic Studies* 27–28, no. 3–4: 35–43.

Warren, J. Benedict, and Patricia S. Warren. *Gonzalo Gómez, primer poblador español de Guayangereo (Morelia): Proceso inquisitorial*. Translated by Álvaro Ochoa S. 2nd ed. Morelia, Michoacán: Firmax, 1991.

West, Robert C. "Early Silver Mining in New Spain, 1531–1555." In *In Quest of Mineral Wealth: Aboriginal and Colonial Mining and Metallurgy in Spanish America*, edited by Alan K. Craig and Robert C. West, pp. 119–35. Baton Rouge: University of Louisiana Press, 1995.

Young, Allen M. *The Chocolate Tree: A Natural History of Cacao*. Washington, DC: Smithsonian Institution Press, 1994.

Young, O. E. J. "Black Legends and Silver Mountains: Spanish Mining in Colonial

Latin America Reconsidered." In *In Quest of Mineral Wealth: Aboriginal and Colonial Mining and Metallurgy in Spanish America*, edited by Alan K. Craig and Robert C. West, pp. 109–17. Baton Rouge: University of Louisiana Press, 1994.

Zavala, Silvio Arturo. *Asientos de la gobernación de la Nueva España*. Mexico City: Archivo General de la Nación, 1982.

——. *El servicio personal de los indios de la Nueva España*. Vol. 1, 1521–1550. Mexico City: Colegio de México, Centro de Estudios Históricos/Colegio Nacional, 1984.

INDEX

Acapulco (Mex., Gro.), 223, 250, 252–53, 368n5
A Coruña (Spain, A Co.), 9
Acuña, Gascón de, 150, 357n93
Águila, Alonso del, 89, 349n21
Aguilar, María de, 217
Albornoz, Bernardino de, 57
Alcalde de minas, 38, 55–56, 64, 147
Alcalde mayor, 48
Alcañices (Spain, Zam.), 9
Alchemy, 50
Alfaro, Juan, 203
Alfonso, Domingo de, 136
Almadén (Spain, C.R.), 49, 53–54
Almeida, Jorge de, 6, 58, 94, 106, 108, 113, 122, 125, 131, 135, 138, 141–49, 151, 153, 156–70, 188, 227, 232, 235, 239–48, 250, 354, 278, 280, 287–88, 291, 293–94, 298; hacienda de, 128, 144–49, 158, 246
Almeida, Leonor de, 138, 188
Almeida (Port., Guar.), 78, 96, 138, 141
Almofala (Port., Vis.), 143
Alonso de Mercado, Luis, 31, 136, 355n41
Alonso, Hernando, 103
Alvalade (Port., Lis.), 302
Alvarado, Pedro de, 39
Álvarez, Ambrosio, 370n25
Álvarez, Ana, 210
Álvarez, Antonio, 90
Álvarez Castellanos, Pelayo, 11, 143
Álvarez de Castellanos, Lorenzo, 11
Álvarez de Merón, Luis, 82
Álvarez de Toledo, García, 357n93
Álvarez, Felipa, 210
Álvarez, Jorge, 98, 101, 120–21, 177, 201, 206–10, 222, 225–27, 238, 263, 275, 344n14
Álvarez, Juan, 177, 362n95
Álvarez, Manuel, 90, 94, 98, 186, 207–8, 227, 285, 368n2, 373n102
Álvarez, Pelayo, 12, 143, 175, 210, 287, 301, 361, 375, 361n79
Amatepec (Mex., Gro.), 35
Andrada de Carvajal, Leonor de. *See* Carvajal, Leonor
Ángeles, María de los, 222, 361n75
Angulo, Gonzalo de, 201–2
Antequera. *See* Oaxaca
Antequera (Spain, Mal.), 121
Antonio, Marco, 115, 132, 169, 179–80, 230, 233, 275, 283

Antúnez, Simón, 94
Anzúrez, Diego, 341n34
Apóstoles, María de los, 151
Arenas López, Ana, 106, 286
Armengol, Luis, 340n20
Arriarte, Juan de, 203
Asturias (Spain), 199
Atotonilco (Mex., Hgo.), 218, 224, 265
Atotonilco el Chico. *See* Mineral del Chico
auto-de-fé, 88, 104, 163, 166, 171, 174, 186, 217, 232, 239, 241, 247, 252, 254–55, 258–62, 272–73, 278, 282, 335n23, 350nn31–32, 367n44, 368n5, 369n7, 376n7, 381n119
Ávila, Gaspar de, 62
Ávila, Hernando de, 167
Ávila Quiñónez, Pedro de, 62
Ayllón, Juan de, 263, 379n87
Ayoteco (Mex., Pue.), 33–41, 71, 77, 297, 336n8
Azevedo, Elvira, 87
azogue. *See* mercury
azoguero. *See* patio master
Azores, 243

Baeza, Juan de, 104
Báez. *See* Váez
Barreto, Francisco, 150, 357n93
Barrueco Pardo (Spain, Sa.), 97
Bazán, Jorge Acosta, 92
Becerra de Mendoza, Diego, 336n7
Beira (Port.), 87, 95, 185
Beja (Port. Be.), 378n87
Belmonte (Port., C.B.), 331n15
Benavente (Spain, Zam.), 97, 110, 166
Bennett, Linda A., 300
Bernal, Isabel, 82
Bible, 27, 67, 80, 100–101, 119–20, 178, 212–13, 219, 223, 233–34, 261, 263, 271, 294, 343n24. *See also* books
Bohórquez. *See* Martos de Bohórquez

Bonilla, Diego de, 136, 183
Book of Wisdom, 213
books, 20–21, 27, 67, 80, 115, 118–19, 134, 163–64, 167, 209, 217, 229, 233, 242, 293, 340n16. *See also* Bible; *Book of Wisdom*; *Mirror of Consolation*
Bordeaux, 92, 121
Borullo, Manuel, 348n9
Bragança (Port. Br.), 217
Braga (Port. Br.), 96
branching points, 290–92
Bufa, Cerro de la. *See* Zacatecas
Buitrago, Luis de, 136
Buitrón, Juan Bautista, 22
Bustamante, Agustín de, 69, 334n5, 341n21, 342n17
Bustamante, Blas de, 26

Cabra, Juan de, 126
cacao, 64, 71–72, 194, 199, 351n33, 361n77, 363n109
Cáceres, Francisco de, 135–36, 181–82, 184, 258, 261
Cádiz (Spain, Ca.), 151, 333, 377
calendar of festivals, 122, 352n70. *See also* Judaizing
Camixtla. *See* Juliantla; Taxco
Campeche (Mex., Camp.), blankets from, 155, 191, 197
Canary Islands, 18, 243
Cantarranas. *See* Almeida, Jorge, hacienda de; Taxco
Cape Verde, 108, 244
Caponeta (Mex., Dur.), 120
captivity, living in, 160, 164, 358n20
Caracas. *See* Venezuela
Cárcel perpétua, 267–68, 273, 278, 281, 285, 286, 363n107
Cárcel secreta, 241, 253, 256, 264, 266, 277, 280
Cardoso, Fernando, 245
Cardoso, Tomás, 130–32, 260, 379n78

Carlos V. *See* Charles V
Carmona, Antón de, 337n15
Carpio. *See* Venta del Carpio
Carrión, Álvaro de, 105, 174–75, 217–19, 226, 264, 294
Cartagena de Indias (Colombia), 90, 209, 222
Carvajal, Ana (de León), 89, 108, 110, 125, 158, 160, 256–57
Carvajal, Baltazar (Rodríguez) de, 94, 108, 110, 113, 115, 117, 119–20, 133, 146, 154–55, 159, 161, 165, 178–79, 205–7, 210, 214–15, 226, 230–32, 238, 240–41, 243, 261
Carvajal, Catalina (de León; de la Cueva), 89, 108, 110, 152–53, 158, 167–68, 241, 249–50, 298; dowry of, 154, 252–55
Carvajal, Francisca (Rodríguez) de, 89, 108–12, 153–54, 160–61, 170, 215, 237, 239–41, 244, 250, 254, 261, 275
Carvajal, García de, 282
Carvajal, Gaspar de, 86, 108, 110, 112, 154, 238, 240, 243–44, 258
Carvajal, Isabel (Rodríguez) de, 89, 107–8, 110, 112, 147, 165, 176, 237–39, 241, 250
Carvajal, Leonor (Andrada) de, 89, 108, 110, 138, 146, 153–55, 158, 160–61, 167, 172, 188, 215, 227, 239, 241, 243–44, 246, 253–54, 280, 289; dowry of, 154, 217, 235, 246–47, 249, 252, 259
Carvajal, Luis de (the younger), 6, 86, 89, 100, 103, 107–8, 110, 112–13, 115–20, 133, 146, 153, 155, 160, 171, 178–80, 205, 210, 214–16, 218, 221, 226, 230, 232–33, 240, 242, 248, 264, 268, 270, 280, 293
Carvajal, Mariana (Núñez; Rodríguez de Matos) de, 89, 108, 110, 125, 146, 155–56, 158–62, 167, 170, 238–39, 241, 254–56, 278, 280

Carvajal, Miguel (Rodríguez) de, 89, 108, 159–60, 163, 205, 243
Carvajal y de la Cueva, Luis de (governor), 74, 89, 108–9, 111–12, 116–17, 139, 153, 238, 240
Casa de Contratación, 14, 17, 248
Casal (*also* Casas, Casar), Juan del, 193, 200, 224–25, 265, 366n32
Casas, Felipe de las, 251
Casta, 102; defined, 101
Castellanos, Bernardina, 341n34
Castellanos, Diego de, 335n27
Castellanos, Felipa, 83
Castellanos, Florián de, 82, 297
Castellanos, Francisco, 83
Castellanos, Gabriel de, 6, 10, 25–31, 33, 35–41, 77, 106, 229, 288, 296, 343n24
Castellanos, Gerónimo, 83
Castellanos, Graviel, 83
Castellanos, Juliana de, 82, 234, 297
Castellanos, Julián de, 11–12, 25–31, 77, 80–83, 99, 102, 106, 115, 156, 169, 172, 175, 230, 242, 278–79, 297, 331n6, 375n3
Castellanos, Lorenzo de, 9
Castelobranco (Port. C.B.), 96, 130, 220
Castelo da Vide (Port. Por.), 331n15
Castiglione (*Book of the Courtier*), 20
Castilla, Luis de, 144
Castro, Américo, 101
Castro, Francisco, 127
Castro, Hernando de, 201–2, 206, 265, 341n34, 368n57
Castro Lobato, Antonio, 282
Catemona, Diego de, 74
Catholic Monarchs. *See* Fernando and Isabel
Celorico (Port. Guar.), 96, 119, 269
Cepeda, Baltazar de, 131
Cercado, Juan, 348n9
Cerón, Martín, 137

Cerro de la Bufa. *See* Zacateas
Cervantes de Salazar, Francisco, 73, 334n2
Cervantes, Leonel, 367n50
Cervera del Río Pisuerga (Spain, Pa.), 97, 217
Cevallos, Fortunio, 203
Chalchihuites (Mexico, Zac.), 44, 74
charity, 115. *See also* Judaizing
Charles V, 4, 16, 53
Chávez, Juan de, 83
Chiautla (Mex., Pue.), 37–38, 336n7,8
Chichimecas, 62, 144, 198, 265–66; Chichimeca War, 38–40, 48, 220
Chihuahua (Mex., Chi.), 45
children, 10, 12, 14, 26, 104–5, 177, 295; born out of marriage, 82–83, 129, 177, 230, 254, 296–97; fostering of by Inquisition, 266–68; keeping knowledge of parent's religion from, 30, 79, 81, 175, 299
China, 58, 149, 190, 214, 251–52, 281, 341n34, 382n126, 386n29; goods from, 149, 190, 194–95, 197, 199, 253, 378n46
chocolate, 72, 194. *See also* cacao
Chontal Indians, 125
Chorrillos. *See* Cantarranas
Christian prayers, avoidance of, 78, 181–83, 210. *See also* Judaizing
Christian, project self as, 27, 31, 157–58, 172, 182–83. *See also* Judaizing
Citola, Dionisio de, 207
Clement VIII, Pope, 283
clothing, 82, 114, 128, 149, 174, 194–97, 203
cloth, yard goods, 73, 114, 128, 155, 195, 197
Cobos, Antonio de los, 149, 151, 164, 250, 253, 357n97, 377n42
cochineal, 41, 64, 71, 73–74
Cohen, Martin, 257
Coimbra (Port. Co.), 135, 164–66

Colima (Mex., Col.), 38, 44
colorados, defined, 5
Columbus, Christopher, 1
confiscation, 140, 146, 149, 241, 247, 272, 278, 281–82
Contreras, Gaspar de, 382n125, 385n28
Contreras, Jaime, 296
conversion, 1, 11, 86–87
conversos, difficult to characterize, 104–5, 290–92. *See also* Judaizers
Correa, Gaspar, 122
Cortés, Diego, 341n34
Cortés, Hernán, 1, 23, 35, 72, 111, 125–26, 141, 356n71
Cortiços (Port. Bra.), 86
Coruña. *See* A Coruña
Covilhã (Port., C.B.), 87–88, 95–96, 99, 186, 206, 209, 213, 225, 350n35, 364n7
Crato (Port., Por.), 170
credit, 58–59, 82, 144, 146, 200, 203–4, 243–44, 247, 272, 356n78. *See also* mining, financing
criollos, defined, 14
crypto-Judaizing. *See* Judaizing
Cuautla (Mex., Mor.), 33, 35
Cuba, 136, 243–45
Cuello, Domingo, 143, 223–24, 226, 273
Cuello, Simón, 226
Cuernavaca (Mex., Mor.), 125, 128, 273, 298
Cueva y Carvajal, Catalina de. *See* Carvajal, Catalina de
Cunha, Gaspar de. *See* Acuña, Gaspar de
Cuzcatlán (Mex., Ver.), 116
cyanide, 53

Day, Thomas, 27, 234, 281
death customs, 28. *See also* Judaizing
demographics, 14, 48, 95, 128, 145, 339–40n4, 345n38, 346n41, 353n11

Dias de Milão, Henrique, 258, 357n91
Díaz de Cáceres, Antonio, 58, 107–8, 122, 125, 137, 144–45, 149–62, 164, 166–67, 172, 227, 239–40, 244–46, 249–59, 276, 278, 289, 293–94, 298, 357n91
Díaz de Sotomayor, Pedro, 82
Díaz, Francisco, 122, 146, 149, 151, 163–66, 243
Díaz, Leonor, 226, 286, 298, 346n40
Díaz, Luis, 85, 106, 113, 115, 118, 168–70, 192, 212, 216, 232, 264–65, 276
Díaz, Manuel, 13, 90, 393n119
Díaz Márquez, Antonio, 173–74, 232–33, 255, 280, 285–86, 382–83n148
Díaz Nieto, Diego, 99, 142–43, 224, 245, 283, 287
Díaz Nieto, Ruy (Rodrigo), 92, 142–43, 224, 245, 278, 283, 285
dietary customs, 29, 104, 106, 120, 157, 163, 175, 177, 181, 199, 210, 217–18, 221, 233, 255, 283, 329n4, 345n24, 347n70. *See also* Judaizing
Díez de Aguillar, Pedro, 341n34
diezmo (king's tenth). *See* silver, taxed
Domínguez de Ocampo, Francisco, 355n52
Domínguez, Francisco, 134, 136, 203
Duarte of Portugal (4th Duke of Guimarães), 150
Dueñas, Fray Juan de. *See also* books; *Mirror of Consolation*
Durango (Mex., Dur.), 55–56, 111

economy, 58–59, 74–75, 92, 113
Edict of Faith, 178
education: in mining, 5, 330n8; schools, 26. *See also* Judaizing, education in
emigrating: dreams of, 89, 100, 121, 160, 218, 263; reasons for, 5–6, 85, 121, 138, 161, 290–91, 344n12, 369n16
Encinas, Lorenzo, 64

Enciso, Gaspar de, 106, 129, 139, 177, 183
encomienda, 47; defined, 4. *See also* mining, labor force
endogamy and exogamy. *See* marriage
Engel, Johan, 330n8
Enríquez, Antonio, 344n12
Enríquez, Catalina (wife of Manuel de Lucena), 89, 100, 115, 185, 187–88, 192, 195,
Enríquez, Catalina (wife of Manuel Díaz), 381n119, 199, 202, 205, 208–9, 212–14, 217–18, 238, 260–68, 272–74, 287, 289, 294, 298, 346n40
Enríquez, Catarina, 186
Enríquez, Clara (mother of Justa Méndez, Violante Váez, and Gabriel Rodríguez), 89, 100, 168, 170, 215, 283
Enríquez, Clara (daughter of Manuel de Lucena), 211, 214, 264, 266, 273–75, 282, 289, 298
Enríquez, Diego, 99–100, 120, 187, 203, 205–7, 210, 214–17, 225–26, 238, 263, 265, 298, 344n14, 346n40, 368n5
Enríquez, Felipe, 273, 298
Enríquez, Francisco, 9
Enríquez la Paiba, Beatriz, 90, 100, 115, 173, 187, 205, 209–10, 214, 217, 226, 265–66, 298
Enríquez-Paiba family, 113. *See also* Enríquez la Paiba, Beatriz; Paiba, Simón; Lucena Manuel de
Enríquez, Pedro, 100, 187, 206–7, 214–15, 216–17, 265, 346n40, 368n5
Enríquez, Simón, 244, 264, 273, 298
Enríquez, Tomás, 264, 266, 273, 298
Enríquez Viso, Martín, 68–69
Escarigo (Port. Guar.), 96
Esdras, Book of, 120, 160, 170, 206–7. *See also* Bible
Espino, Alonso de, 63
Espinosa, Diego de, 273, 286

Esquimilpa. *See* Ixmiquilpan
Este family, 142
expulsion from Spain, 9, 290

fasting, 28–29, 82, 109, 122, 159, 167, 172, 180, 182, 205, 218. *See also* Judaizing
Felipe de Jesús, Fray. *See* Casas, Felipe de las
Fernández, Antonia, 13
Fernández, Antonio, 90
Fernández Cardozo, Manuel, 226
Fernández, Clara, 185
Fernández de Abreu, Héctor, 137
Fernández de Almeida, Antonio, 137–38, 156, 288
Fernández, Inés, 95
Fernández, Jorge, 98, 101, 283
Fernández, Miguel and Francisco. *See* Hernández
Fernández, Simón, 185
Fernando, King, 16
Fernando and Isabel, 4
Ferrara, 11, 91–92, 99, 142–44, 157, 245, 287–88. *See also* Italy
Ferro, Francisco, 186
Flanders, 142, 245
Flos sanctorum, 119, 215
Fondón. *See* Fundão
Fonseca, Álvaro de (lover of Isabel de Fonseca), 78–79
Fonseca, Álvaro de (son of Tomás de Fonseca Castellanos), 129, 297
Fonseca, Ana de, 83, 230, 281, 297
Fonseca, Beatriz, 83, 230, 281, 297
Fonseca Castellanos, Tomás de, 6, 12, 64, 77–78, 103, 106, 113, 115, 118, 125, 129–37, 145, 162, 172, 177–84, 204, 213, 215, 225, 227, 233, 235, 240, 246, 258–62, 282, 293–94, 296–97; general store of, 133–34, 203; hacienda of, 129–33

Fonseca, Felipa de (first wife of Gabriel de Castellanos), 11, 296
Fonseca, Felipa de (daughter of Guiomar de Fonseca), 106, 129, 132, 296
Fonseca, Felipa de (daughter of Julián de Castellanos), 297
Fonseca, Felipa de (wife of Antonio Fernández de Almeida), 138, 156, 169, 183, 188
Fonseca, Francisca de, 78–79
Fonseca, Francisco de, 79, 129, 132, 135, 180, 233, 297, 363n108
Fonseca, Gabriel, 83, 230, 280, 297
Fonseca, Gaspar, 85
Fonseca, Gerónimo, 297
Fonseca, Guiomar de, 11–12, 27–28, 30, 79, 81, 106, 296, 300, 342n13
Fonseca, Héctor de, 105–6, 120, 125, 131, 137–42, 144–45, 156, 160–61, 168–77, 188, 213, 215, 227, 244, 246, 275–78, 283–85, 288, 293–94, 297, 300; hacienda of, 139–40, 277
Fonseca, Isabel de (daughter of Felipa de Fonseca), 11–12, 78–79, 178
Fonseca, Isabel de (daughter of Guiomar de Fonseca), 296
Fonseca, Lope de (father of Gabriel de Fonseca wife Felipa de Fonseca), 12, 343n14
Fonseca, Lope de (son of Gabriel de Castellanos), 12, 79, 83, 230, 279–80, 296, 297
Fonseca, Lope Teodoro de (son of Tomás de Fonseca), 279–80
Fonseca, María de (grandmother of Héctor de Fonseca), 355n59
Fonseca, María de (daughter of Tomás de Fonseca Castellanos), 79, 129, 131, 297, 379n82
Fonseca, Pedro de, 275, 282, 286, 377n15
Fonseca, Teodosio, 41, 64, 83, 279–81, 297

Fonseca, Tomás de, 6, 9, 11–12, 19, 25, 33, 36, 41, 43–44, 52, 61–62, 64–72, 74–75, 77–83, 86, 98, 103, 105–7, 127, 150, 177, 229–35, 239, 246–47, 255, 278–82, 293–94, 296–97; hacienda, 64–71, 279, 293
foodstuffs, 74–75, 156, 180, 206, 209, 218, 233, 285–86, 337n15
Fraile, Antonio, 99, 102
Franca, María. *See* Ángeles, María de los
Francis Xavier, 251
Francisca (servant of Juan Núñez de León), 157
Francisco Belmonte, Manuel, 116, 118, 206–8, 211, 213–14, 216, 350n35, 351n43, 371n55
fraud, 146, 154, 246. *See also* dowry
Freire, Felipe, 135, 141, 181, 184, 270
Freixo de Espada-à-Cinta (Port. Bra.), 9–11, 86–87, 96, 331n10
Fresnillo (Mex., Zac.), 44
Fuggar family, 53
Fundão (Port. C.B.), 87–88, 93–96, 106, 117, 121, 163, 170, 185–87, 201, 206–7, 220, 222, 225, 344n12
furniture, 66–67, 190–91

Galarza, Pedro de, 137
Gallego, Blas, 15, 19, 332n12
García de Inclán, María, 203
García, Francisco, 203
García Parra, Juan, 141. 259
General Pardon of 1606, 142, 283–84, 363n107
Gerónimo de León, Miguel, 222, 225, 373n95, 374n106
Gil de la Guarda, Manuel (aka de la Guardia), 215–16, 222–23, 285, 349n18, 352n72, 384n13
Glick, Thomas F., 157
Goa, 252

gold: names for, 33; refining, 49
Gómez, Alonso, 15
Gómez, Antonio, 98, 101, 175, 256, 344n14, 361n76, 373n92
Gómez, Beatriz, 343n4
Gómez, Cristobal, 100, 103, 146, 163, 233, 244, 263, 280
Gómez de Castañeda, Alonso, 131, 353n18
Gómez de Casteloblanco, Manuel, 90, 93, 132, 208, 221, 227, 376n2
Gómez, Gonzalo, 104
Gómez, Manuel, 209
Gómez Navarro, Domingo, 220–21, 347n73, 380n98
Gómez Navarro, Manuel, 102–03, 118–19, 153, 162, 172, 179, 199, 203, 213–16, 219–22, 225–27, 260, 263–64, 270–71, 347n73, 351n42, 372n62, 373n86, 374n110, 381n119
Gómez Rubio, Hernán, 31, 342n18
Gómez Silveira, Antonio, 256
Gómez Silveira, Manuel, 101, 350n33
Gómez, Simón. *See* Enríquez, Simón
González, Alonso, 217
González, Álvaro, 186, 206–8, 345n31
González, Antonio, 137
González, Baltazar, 206–7, 214
González, Beatriz, 348n16
González de Casteloblanco, Manuel. *See* Gómez de Casteloblanco, Manuel
González, Juana, 174–75, 217, 219
González, Matías, 279
González, Toribio, 176
González y Bemerejo, Garci, 107
Grado, Alonso de, 336n7
Graizbord, David L., 88
Granada, Luis de, 119, 167. *See also* books; *Symbol of Faith*
Granados, Fabián, 115, 263, 350n33
Guachiapa. *See* Huichapan

410 INDEX

Guadalajara (Mex., Jal.), 56
Guadalcanal (Spain, Sev.), 50
Guadalupe (Mex., D.F.), 234
Guadiana (Mex. Dur.), 56, 120
Guanajuato (Mex., Gto.), 35, 56, 74, 211, 263n109
Guarda (Port. Guar.), 87, 95–96, 187, 222, 331n15
Guatemala, 81, 347n71, 367n44, 368n5, 383n148
Guerrero de Luna, Agustín, 224, 265, 366n32
Guinea, 86, 209
Guiral, Antonia, 204
Guzmán, Nuño de, 38

hacienda chapel, 147, 158, 163
haciendas de beneficio de metals, 7, 38, 51, 54. *See also* Almeida, Jorge de, hacienda de; Fonseca Castellanos, Tomás, hacienda de; Medina, Bartolomé de; refining ore
Hanuka, 352n73. *See also* Judaizing
Havana. *See* Cuba
Hawkins, John, 108
Hebrew, use of, 30, 115, 211, 213, 269, 280, 299, 371, 382, 385. *See also* Judaizing
Heredia, Antón de, 348n9
Hernández, Beatriz, 104
Hernández de Merlo, Diego, 131
Hernández, Diego, 64
Hernández, Felipa, 364n7
Hernández, Francisco, 109, 138, 142, 172, 175, 188, 275, 288, 291, 298
Hernández, Gaspar, 137
Hernández, Miguel, 106, 138, 142–43, 154, 156, 165–66, 169, 172, 188, 242, 245, 280, 288, 291
Hernández. *See* Fernández
Herrera, Gabriel, 93
Hispaniola, 16, 19, 243
Hoberman, Luisa Schell, 45–46

Hordes, Stanley, 97, 346n41, 386n30
House of Trade. *See* Casa de Contratación
housekeeping customs, 28, 113–14. *See also* Judaizing
Huancavelica (Peru), 54
Hueyxtaca (Mex., Gue.), 136, 354n46
Huichapan (Mex., Hgo.), 206, 225
Huixtac. *See* Hueyxtaca

Ibáñez, Francisco, 250, 377n42
identity: multiple and hybrid, 2–3, 93, 95, 98–102, 290–91, 384n4; sense of, 6, 30–31, 80, 105–6, 115, 212, 214, 289–90, 294–95; transmission of, 295–300
idolatry, 156, 159, 179, 209, 212, 221–22, 224, 234, 270, 271–72, 281
Idrija (Czech Republic), 54
images, Christian, 30, 116, 156, 181, 183, 191–92, 209, 212, 221–22, 234, 271–72, 281. *See also* idolatry
immigration regulations, 5, 14, 16, 143. *See also* purity of blood
India, 86, 88, 252
Indulto General. *See* General Pardon of 1606
ineligibility (*inhabilidad*), 171, 241, 273–74, 282, 298–99, 363n103, 382n126, 386n29
inns, 22–23
Inquisition: Cartagena de Índias, 90; Mexico, 90, 97, 107, 237, 245; Portugal, 85–87, 185; Real Fisco, 188–89, 201–2, 247, 259, 361n78; Spain, 85; *tachas* lists, 134–36, 151, 183–84, 256, 260, 276, 281; torture, 7, 91, 224, 238, 241, 257–59, 261–62, 345, 348, 350–51
inquisitors: methods of investigation, 7
intellectual property, 52
Irimbo, 64
Italy, 91, 121, 136, 142–43, 161, 175, 291,

298; goods from, 194, 196. *See also* Ferrara; Venice
Ixmiquilpan (Mex., Hgo.), 225

Jacinto Bazán, Jorge, 92, 368n57
Jalapa (Mex., Ver.), 23–24, 374n97
Japan, 251
Jarandilla de la Vera (Spain, Các.), 11–12, 15, 82–83, 97
Jaso Vejilios, Martín de, 282, 383n156
Jensen, Christopher, 296
Jerez (Spain, Cád,), 348n7
jewelry, 195, 198, 204
Jiménez, Ana, 83, 230, 281, 297
Jorge, Francisco, 86, 137, 166, 169–70, 276
Jorge, Manuel, 227
Juárez, Juan, 336n7
Juárez, Lorenzo, 335n27
Juárez Tavares, Fernán, 85
Judaizing, 87; basic tenets, 212; circumstances trump observance, 205, 210, 213, 255; education in, 105, 111, 114, 117, 131, 154, 168, 175, 182, 200, 218, 221, 269, 287; initiation into, 27, 185, 210; material rewards of, 85, 119, 219, 224, 280; reluctance to, 112, 119, 131, 157–58, 160, 162, 174, 200, 210, 220, 254. *See also* charity; Christian, project self as; Christian prayers, avoidance of; death customs; dietary customs; fasting; Hanuka; Hebrew, use of; housekeeping; images, avoidance of; life cycle events; Messiah, beliefs about; Passover; prayers; praying, method of; proselytizing; Psalms; Purim and fast of Esther; Rosh Hashana; Sabbath; salvation, ideas about; scorn toward Christian matters; secrecy, need for; Sukkot; Yom Kippur
Juliantla (Mex., Gro.), 139. *See also* Taxco

Keiser, Christoph, 330n8
kitchen equipment, 193–94

labor force, 48, 58, 64, 128, 147, 149. See also *naboríos*; slaves, slavery
Lamadilla, Juan Bautista, 368n57
Lamego (Port. Vis.), 96, 331n15, 350n33
Landeta, María de, 274, 385n28
Lang, M. F., 54
Larios, Ana de, 149
Larios, Diego Alonso, 208, 369n22
Las Amilpas, 274
Lemos, Esteban de, 286, 383n164
León Carvajal, Ana de. *See* Carvajal, Ana
León, Álvaro de, 86
León, Antonio de, 86
León Carvajal, Catalina, 349n21
León, Catalina de, 108, 115
León de la Cueva, Catalina. *See* Cueva y Carvajal, Catalina de
León, Diego de, 209, 349n21, 370n25
León, Duarte de, 86, 244
León, Jorge de, 86, 89, 159–60, 349n21, 360n46
León, Juan de, 31–32
Liebman, Seymour, 104–5
life cycle events, 105, 113. *See also* Judaizing
Lima. *See* Peru
limpieza de sangre. *See* Purity of Blood
Livorno, 92
Lisbon (Port. Lis.), 86, 94, 96, 114, 122, 142, 173, 222, 232, 237, 258, 357n91
Llerena (Spain, Ba.), 274, 348n16, 385n28
Lobo Guerrero, Bartolomé, 202, 255, 266, 272
Logroño, Diego de, 337
Lope de Vega. *See* Vega, Lope de
López, Ana, 93, 186, 225, 283, 286, 369n16, 383n148
López, Antonio, 107, 118–20, 163, 186, 205, 214–15, 232, 238, 263, 269, 283, 286, 376n7, 380n89,92

López Castellanos, Melchor, 31, 334n3
López, Catalina, 222
López, Cristóbal, 117, 364n7
López de Gómara, Francisco, 73
López de la Torre, Juana, 138, 166, 175–76, 188, 278, 297
López de Morales, Antonio, 344n14, 346n40, 379n86
López de Obregón, Juan, 141
López de Velasco, Juan, 22
López, Domingo, 187, 206
López, Felipa, 216, 394n7, 376n2
López, Gaspar, 141
López, Hernán, 226
López, Isabel (aka Isabel López Pérez), 13, 89, 90, 109
López, Jorge, 85, 373n92
López, Juan, 137, 286
López, Juana (first wife of Antonio Díaz de Cáceres), 150
López, Juana. *See* Lopez de la Torre, Juana
López, Leonor, 150
López, Manuel, 150
López, Pedro, 30, 335n20
López Regalón, Diego, 90, 93, 106, 186, 263, 376n2, 380n92
López Tavaltero, Diego, 279
López Tavera, Juan, 200, 266–68, 377n21, 378n24, 380n106
Lorenza, Blanca de, 9
Lorenzo, Blanca, 11–12, 143, 365n15
Lucena, Baltazar de, 264, 365n11
Lucena, Gaspar de, 264, 365n11
Lucena, Manuel de, vi, 6, 27, 85, 91–92, 100, 103, 113, 115, 117, 119–21, 172–73, 175, 179, 185, 205–27, 238, 262–72, 275, 287, 289, 293–94, 298, 344n14; employees of, 198–200; house in Pachuca, 189–96; store in Pachuca, 196–98
Lucena, Simón. *See* Gómez, Simón

Luján, Juana de, 361n77
Luna, Bernardo de, 120, 344n14, 376n1
Luna, Francisco, 139
Luna, Juan de, 237
Lutherans and Lutheranism, 101, 104, 229, 281, 285

Macao, 251, 376n45
Machado, Ana, 378n51
Machado, Antonio, 113–15, 118, 163, 168, 179, 225, 287, 361n79
Machado, Isabel, 114, 179, 256, 283, 287
Machado, Leonor, 114, 363n103
Machado, Manuel de, 113, 213
Machorro, Juan Bautista, 22
Machuca, Diego, 348n9
Madrid (Spain, Mad.), 92, 142–43, 245–46, 287
Malabar, Inés de, 341n20
Málaga (Spain, Ma.), 92
Malinalco (Mex., Mex.), 169
Mancilla, Luis de, 341n34
Manila. *See* Philippines
Manoel I, 10
Manuel, Francisco, 186
Maravatío (Mex., Mich.), 64, 68
Marcos de Andrada, Diego, 360n46
Marcus, Jacob, 210, 386n31
María (wife of Francisco Pérez), 132, 135
Marqués del Valle. *See* Cortés, Hernán
Márquez de Andrada, Diego, 89, 255, 378n57
Márquez de León, Ginebra, 89, 349n21
marriage: abandon Old Christian spouse, 175; ceremony, 154; cohabitation (defined as fornication), 15; divorce, 176–77; dowry, 154, 235, 246–49, 252, 272–73, 358; endogamy, 173–74, 296, 385n23; exogamy (mixed marriage or cohabitation), 78, 81, 210, 217, 222–23, 225, 296–99, 361n77; plural, 161, 248

Marseilles, 92
Martínez Carral, Juan, 69–71
Martínez Gallegos, Juan, 341n34
Martínez, Rodrigo, 126
Martos de Bohórquez, Gonzalo, 248, 260, 264, 338n12
Marván de Fontiveros, Luis, 242
Mateos, Álvaro, 343n4
Mayan Indians, 72
Mazapil (Mex., Zac.), 6, 44, 106, 108–9, 139, 211
Mazahua Indians, 62
Medina, Bartolomé de, 43, 50–53
Medina del Campo (Spain, Va.), 86, 97, 110
Medinilla, Pedro de, 242
Meléndez, Leonor, 98
Mena, Hernando de, 137, 355n53
Mendes, Damião, 87
Méndez, Antonio, 90, 98, 174, 222, 226, 278, 285, 361n75
Méndez de Fonseca, Diego, 178, 297, 362n97
Méndez, Enrique, 186, 369n20
Méndez, Francisco, 170
Méndez, Isabel, 101
Méndez, Justa, 102–3, 119–20, 155, 170–72, 174, 215–16, 223, 225, 227, 260–61, 264, 274–75, 286, 346n40, 349n26, 370n23,25, 372n62, 374n110, 391n87, 393n119
Méndez, Pedro, 208, 369n20
Méndez, Tomás, 78–79, 178, 297, 342n7, 362n96
Mendoza, Antonio de, 38, 46, 356n72
Mendoza, Leonor de, 144
Mener, Luis, 349n16
Mercado, Luis Alonso de, 31, 354n17
merced (formal grant), 65
mercury, 49–57, 130, 139, 147; regulation of, 53, 55–56, 279, 338n8
Mesa, Gaspar de, 99

Mesas, Balaguida de, 199
Messiah, beliefs about, 115, 118–19, 159, 165, 167, 180, 182, 207, 212, 217, 230, 234, 248, 255, 269, 271, 280. *See also* Judaizing
Mexico City, 25, 55, 150, 159, 291; Calle de la Inquisición, 208; Calle de la Puerta de los Carros de Santo Domingo; Calle de los Ángeles, 187, 206; Calle de los Ángeles, 187, 206; Calle Donceles, 208–9, 226; Calle San Agustín, 173, 231–32; Calle San Francisco, 208; Calle Santo Domingo, 286; Calle Tacuba, 25–26, 101, 143, 222, 334n2; Casa de la Moneda, 58; Casas del Marqués, 206; Chapultepec, 117; Church of San Hipólito, 206, 255, 282; Church of Santa Catalina, 208; Hospital del Amor de Dios (aka) las Bubas, 177, 277–78; Hospital, Convalescent, 282; Plaza del Volador, 187, 206; Zócalo, 230, 244
Meyo, Alberto de, 256, 378n60
Meza, Francisco, 126
Michoacán (Mex., Mich.), 34, 57, 75, 121
Millán, Francisco, 104
mills, 63; stamping, 49, 65, 67, 146–47
miner: definition of, 45
mining: copper, 34, 125; drainage, 46; financing, 45, 47, 141, 200; labor force, 47; nasty effects of, 37; native metal, 34; pre-Columbian, 34; mills, 47, 140; placer, 4, 34; regulations, 46, 140; tools, 38, 65–67, 147, 198; tunneling, 46, 337n14. *See also* prospecting; refining ore
Miranda, Juan de, 201–2, 265, 367n56
Mirror of Consolation, 27, 29, 67, 118, 165, 178, 200, 213, 217, 220–21, 224, 293–94, 334n7. *See also* books
Mixteca, 35, 41, 64, 72–74, 167, 197

Mogadouro (Port. Bra.), 86–87, 96
Molina, Luis Martín de, 137, 183
money, defined, 3
Monforte de Lemos (Spain, Lu.), 206
Montemayor, Jorge de
Montezuma, Pedro, 203
Morales, Andrés de, 89
Morales, Antonio de, 64, 163, 276
Morales, Bartolomé de, 89
Morales, Gonzalo de, 103–4
Morales, Isabel de (aka Isabel López Pérez), 115
Morales, Luisa de, 137
Morales, Manuel de, 89, 94, 99, 101, 109, 112–15, 168–69, 207, 211, 217, 254, 349n27
Moratilla, Eugenio de, 137
Morocco, 88, 142
Morón de la Frontera (Spain, Sev.), 97
motivation to come to America. *See* emigrating, reasons for
Muñiz, Pedro, 131, 353n18, 379n78
Muñoz, Juana de, 89
music, 103, 107, 119, 172, 191, 198, 204, 213, 216, 255, 286, 289, 372n62

naborίos (wageworkers), 48, 58, 146–47, 149, 202
nação, as synonym for Portuguese *converso*, 99, 102
Nájera (Spain, Lo.), 208
nao. See ships
Napolitano, Felipe. *See* Palacios, Felipe de
Nava, Diego and Catalina de la, 145, 356n74
Nava, Juan de, 89
Nebrija, Antonio de, 67. *See also* books
negrillos, defined, 5
New Laws of the Indies, 48
Nieto, Antonio, 99
Nieto, Sebastián, 99, 209, 226

Nueva Galicia, 38, 44, 339n25
Nueva Vizcaya, 44, 339n25
Nuevo León, 109
Núñez, Antonio, 209, 226, 380n89
Núñez, Beatriz, 358n20
Núñez de Carvajal, Francisca. *See* Carvajal, Francisca
Núñez de Carvajal, Mariana. *See* Carvajal, Mariana
Núñez de la Torre, Juana. *See* López de la Torre, Juana
Núñez de León, Juan, 137
Núñez, Felipe, 89, 222, 349n21, 371n55
Núñez, Felipe (Captain), 237
Núñez, Francisca (daughter of Justa Méndez), 171
Núñez, Francisco (aka Rodríguez; husband of Justa Méndez), 171
Núñez, Francisco (son of Héctor de Fonseca), 138, 176, 188, 297
Núñez, Inés, 142
Núñez, Isabel (daughter of Justa Méndez), 171
Núñez, Lorenzo, 354n27
Núñez, Pedro, 183
Núñez Viciosa, Francisca, 89, 171, 349n21

Oaxaca (Mex., Oax.), 243–44
obraje, 82, 342n16
Ocampo, Isabel, 348n16
Ocaña, Diego de, 104
Oliver, Diego de, 297, 362n86
Oliveira, Fulano, 13
Oñate, Cristóbal de, 38
Oporto (Port., Port.), 96, 142
Ordaz, Diego de, 336n7
Oria, Juan Antonio de, 284–85, 347n63
Orona, Domingo de, 81, 342n14
Osorio, Juan Bautista, 62
Otomí Indians, 64
Ovando, Nicolás de, 16

Pachuca (Mex., Hgo.), 43–44, 51, 113, 118–21, 155, 185, 187–205, 211–27, 238, 262–66, 289, 293–94, 314, 337n2, 338n10, 339n25
pack animals, 65
pacos, defined, 5
Paiba, Simón, 90, 107, 119, 187, 205, 209, 214–15, 263, 298
Palacios, Alonso de, 70
Palacios, Felipe de, 131, 135–36, 149, 246, 353n23
Palacios, Pedro, 250
Pánuco (Mex., Ver.), 111–12, 154, 224, 349n25
Paredes, Simón de. *See* Enríquez, Simón
Pareja, Alonso de, 252–53
Parral (Mex., Chih.), 45
Passover, 28–29, 101, 122, 156–58, 162, 167–69, 182, 222, 225–26, 240, 254, 259, 264, 293, 295, 352n70, 356n84. *See also* Judaizing
patio process, 51–52, 65, 147
Pátzcuaro (Mex., Mich.), 121
peddling, 26, 59, 94, 197–98, 225, 291, 369n16
Pedroche (Spain, Cór.), 199
Penamacor (Port., C.B.), 331n15
Peñarrieta, Domingo de, 203
Peña, Sebastián de la, 153, 179–81, 208, 216, 226, 285–86, 363n109, 370n31
pepenas. *See* silver, taxed
Peralta, Alonso de, 193, 202, 255, 272, 277, 338n12
Pereira, Cosme, 81, 102, 106, 296, 342n13, 355n54
Pereira, Elías, 203
Pereira, Nicolás, 226
Pérez, Alonso, 183
Pérez, Antonio, 364n7
Pérez de Herrero, Juan, 296
Pérez de Monterrey, Gaspar, 70
Pérez de Zamora, Alonso, 44

Pérez Ferro, Gonzalo, 89, 115, 122, 154, 256, 259, 349n21,25, 350n33
Pérez, Francisco, 132, 135
Pérez Herrero, Antonio, 30, 81, 106, 129, 296, 300, 342n13
Pérez, Jerónimo, 279–80
Pérez, Juan, 101, 366n28
Pérez-Mallaína, Pablo, 21
Pérez, María, 132, 135, 364n7
Pérez Roldán, Luis (son of Justa Méndez), 171
Pérez, Rodrigo, 209
Pérez Serrano, Alonso, 129, 131, 260, 266
Perote (Mex., Ver.), 24
Pertierra, Gómez, vi, 119, 185, 199–202, 219, 226, 265–66, 272, 367n45,49, 368n2, 372n82
Pertronila (servant of Tomás de Fonseca Castellanos), 137
Peru, 54, 81, 90, 146, 149, 151, 163, 166, 264
Philip II, 4, 53, 88
Philip III, 4, 282–83
Philippines, 223, 251, 350n32
Piedra, Pedro de la, 152
Pinero, Diego, 244
Pisa, 92, 110, 349n27
placer mining. *See* mining, placer
Porto. *See* Oporto
Portugal, 85–92
Portuguese, as synonym for converso, 98, 104
Portuguese language, 85–86, 99–102, 277, 347n63
Potosí (Peru), 264, 365
Potosí. *See* San Luis Potosí
Prado, Pedro de, 137, 141, 277
prayers, Christian, 20, 99, 159, 167, 182–83, 375n14
prayers, Jewish or Judaizing, 11, 29–30, 79, 99, 109, 112, 118, 147, 162–64, 167, 172, 176, 179, 182, 205, 207, 211,

prayers (continued)
213, 261, 263, 269, 276, 300, 370n31, 385n21. *See also* Hebrew, use of; Judaizing
praying, method of, 29, 164, 167, 180, 370n31. *See also* Judaizing
prison. *See* Cárcel secreta; *Cárcel perpétua*
procesos, defined, 7
processions, 101, 122, 181, 183, 222, 232, 374n106
proselytizing, 155, 164–66, 209, 216, 224, 230, 276. *See also* Judaizing
prospecting, 6, 35
Provincia de Sonsonate. *See* Sonsonate
Psalms, 25, 29, 82, 99, 109, 115, 118, 165, 172, 180, 182–83, 191, 209, 213, 215, 220, 222, 224, 231, 254, 256, 261, 269, 360n51, 373n92, 379n87. *See also* Judaizing
Puebla (Mex., Pue.), 13, 72–74, 107, 174, 199
Pulido Serrano, Juan Ignacio, 2
Purhépecha Indians. *See* Tarascans
purity of blood, 15–17, 41, 109

Querétaro, 171, 245
Quesada, Rodrigo de, 69–70, 340n20
Quichiapa (Mex., Hgo?), 203
Quijada, Margarita, 266–67, 367n46
Quiñones, Agustina de, 254, 298
quinto (king's fifth). *See* silver, taxed

Ramírez de Arellano, Antonio, 67–71
Ramírez de Arellano, Cristóbal, 67–71
Ramírez de Padrón, Cristóbal, 69–71
Ramírez, Luis, 340n20
Raya de Portugal, Raya de Castilla, 9–10, 85–86, 95, 97, 108–9, 138, 186, 291
Real de Arriba, 43. *See also* San Miguel del Cerezo
Real del Monte (Mex., Hgo.), 43–44, 119, 137, 199, 200

reales de minas, 45
Real Fisco. *See* Inquisition
Rebenes, Julián de, 141
refining ore: copper-sulfite flux (*magistral*), 51, 65, 139–40, 147; lead flux, 34, 38, 41, 50, 70, 198; methods, 34, 36, 49–53; processing plant, 38, 49, 130; salt, 147; water, importance of, 38, 63, 67. *See also* mercury
Reformation, Protestant, 363n100
repartimiento, 40, 48, 64, 128, 149, 340n4, 353n11
Reyes, María de los, 340n20
Ribas, Antonio de, 137
Riotinto (Spain, Hue.), 50
Rivera, Antonia. *See* Antonia Fonseca
roads, 23–24, 115–16, 120–21, 224, 263, 294–95
Robles, Juana de, 268
Rodríguez, Álvaro, 206–7, 214, 369n7
Rodríguez, Andrés, 186, 216
Rodríguez, Antonio, 90, 119, 351n50
Rodríguez, Bartolomé, 340n20
Rodríguez, Beatriz, 174
Rodríguez, Blanca, 11–12, 28, 40, 77, 79, 230
Rodríguez, Carlos, 99
Rodríguez, Catalina, 102, 227
Rodríguez, Clara, 185–86, 364n4, 368n2
Rodríguez, Costanza, 215, 227, 283, 286, 346n40
Rodríguez de Acevedo, Miguel, 206
Rodríguez de Andrada, Isabel. *See* Carvajal, Isabel de
Rodríguez de Carvajal, Baltazar. *See* Carvajal, Baltazar de
Rodríguez de Carvajal, Francisca. *See* Carvajal, Francisca de
Rodríguez de Herrera, Fernando, 92, 121, 345n24, 349n17
Rodríguez del Monte, Diego, 136
Rodríguez de Matos, Francisco, 88–89,

108, 100, 110, 112, 153, 163, 241, 248, 349n21, 350n31
Rodríguez de Matos, Mariana. *See* Núñez de Carvajal, Mariana
Rodríguez de Molina, Gonzalo, 122, 208, 363n103, 369n20
Rodríguez de Silva, Juan, 143, 245, 287
Rodríguez, Diego, 136–37, 368n2
Rodríguez, Domingo, 90, 208–9, 215, 217, 350n32, 368n2, 369–70n23
Rodríguez, Duarte, 88, 94, 102, 153, 162, 179–80, 186–87, 210, 216, 225–26, 233, 263, 283, 285, 345n31, 363n107, 368n2, 372n62, 373n92, 374n110
Rodríguez, Francisca, 174
Rodríguez, Francisco, 90, 93, 115, 179, 210, 216, 349n18
Rodríguez, Francisco (son of Simón Gómez), 244
Rodríguez, García, 184, 275
Rodríguez, Isabel, 13, 278, 283, 231n119
Rodríguez, Isabel (wife of Manuel Díaz), 13, 90, 283
Rodríguez, Isabel (wife of Sebastián de la Peña), 286
Rodríguez, Jerónimo, 174, 199, 361n77, 366n43
Rodríguez, Jorge, 115, 206–7, 214–15, 226, 346n40, 350n32, 368n2
Rodríguez, Juan, 350n33
Rodríguez Ledesma, Francisco, 209, 215, 226, 363n102
Rodríguez, Leonor (wife of Manuel Álvarez), 90, 94–95
Rodríguez, Manuel, 117, 122, 186, 206, 260, 344n12
Rodríguez (*mayordomo* of Tomás de Fonseca), 131
Rodríguez Pardo, Juan, 115
Rodríguez, Pedro (of Las Amilpas), 274, 345n31, 382n126, 386n29
Rodríguez Sánchez, Juan, 144, 358n7
Rodríguez Saz, Pedro, 207–8, 215, 227, 369n16
Rodríguez Silguero, Manuel, 215, 227, 374n110
Rodríguez, Sebastián, 103, 119, 153, 172, 179–80, 214–15, 221–22, 226–27, 260, 264, 275–76, 285–86
Rodríguez, Simón, 74, 94, 173–74, 255, 341n34, 374n2
Rodríguez Tableros, Juan, 62
Rodríguez, Violante, 278, 345n31, 382n140
Rosh Hashana, 352n73. *See also* Judaizing
Rouen, 352n73
Ruiz Agamara, Blas, 137
Ruiz de Alarcón, Pedro, 144
Ruiz de Valderrama, Nicolás and Leonor, 145, 147
Ruiz, Juan, 348n9
Ruiz, Mateo, 135, 163–64, 166, 181, 184, 258, 354n41
Ruiz Ortiz, Juan, 348n16

Saballos, Luis de, 136, 354n50
Sabbath, 28–29, 110, 122, 134, 157, 163, 172, 177, 182, 210, 212–14, 219, 233, 248, 254, 263, 272, 285, 295. *See also* Judaizing
Sabugal (Port. Guar.), 121, 164, 166
Saelices (Spain, Sa.), 138, 142
safe havens, 8, 88–92, 112–13, 121, 290–92
Salamanca (Spain, Sa.), 86, 209
Salceda (Spain, Po.), 220, 341n34, 382n140
Salcedo, Juan de, 126, 331n12
Salinas, Martín de, 136, 139, 340n8, 377n35
Salonica, 92, 143, 245, 287, 344n14, 349n27, 375n11
salvation, ideas about, 2, 79, 155, 169–70, 173, 178, 182, 212, 220, 234, 255, 261, 363n100. *See also* Judaizing

sambenitos, 88, 161, 179–80, 241, 244–46, 253, 255, 272, 283, 371n54
Sampaio, Estêvão, 87, 343n10
San Juan de Ulúa (Mex., Ver.), 21–22, 55, 333n20
San Luis Potosí (Mex., S.L.P.), 47, 74
San Martín de Trevejo (Spain, Các.), 97, 219, 347n73
Sanlúcar de Barrameda (Spain, Cád.), 18, 55, 243, 333n10
Santa Ana, Mateo de, 268
Santa Comba Dão (Port., Vis.), 96, 150
Santalunga (Port., Co.), 135, 181
Santiago Tlatelolco. *See* Tlatelolco
Santiago, Simón de, 101
Santos García, Francisco, 27
São João da Pesqueira (Port., Vis.), 96
São Vicente da Beira (Port., C.B.), 87–88, 93, 95–96, 100, 185, 199, 206, 208, 219, 221, 264, 361n77, 363n109, 365n12, 368n3
Sarabia, Juan, 62
Sarzeda (Port. Vis.), 96
Saucedo, García de, 137
scorn toward Christian matters, 100–101, 103–4, 113, 117, 120–22, 159, 166, 181, 208–10, 212, 221–22, 224, 232, 234, 248. *See also* Judaizing
Sebastião, King, 88
secrecy, need for, 30, 78, 114, 117, 157, 172, 214, 255. *See also* Judaizing
Seia (Port. Guar.), 96, 99, 101
sequestration, 7, 65, 188–89, 193, 196, 202, 246, 250–51, 259, 264, 275, 283, 286
Serna, Juan de la, 199, 219, 266
Serrano, Diego, 341n34
sewing supplies, 195, 197
Sevilla, 97, 143, 186; Calle de la Sierpe, 93–94, 186; entrepôt, 13, 93; gateway to America, 13, 17–18, 22, 93–95. *See also* Casa de Contratación

Shavuoth, 352n72
Ships, 15, 18–20
Sichú (Mex., Gto.), 202–3, 211, 220, 347n73
silver: artefacts made of, 192–93, 195, 238; compounds of, 5, 34–35, 50, 329n7, 330n7; exportation of, 58–59; marketing, 57, 145, 200; *plata de rescate*, 58, 201–2, 367n49,54, 380n102; retail, 81, 185; smithing, 81; taxing, 57–58, 145
singing. *See* music
slaver, 209, 244, 264, 306–7, 365n11
slaves, slavery, 26, 35, 48, 53, 57, 63–64, 92, 108–9, 128, 132, 144–47, 149, 161, 166, 171, 198, 237, 255, 260, 337, 340, 353. *See also* demographics
Soconusco. *See* Guatemala
Solís, Francisco de, 134, 137
Solís, Gaspar de, 64
Sombrerete (Mex., Zac.), 44, 56, 81, 173
Sonsonete (Mex., Son.?), 147
Soto, Pedro de, 133, 137
Sotos, Francisco de, 137
Sukkot (*Cabañas*), 123, 218, 264, 285–86, 295, 352n72. *See also* Judaizing
Sultepec (Mex., Mex.), 35, 44, 81, 116, 213, 227, 330n8, 337n15, 351n35, 373n90
Suster, Adrián, 285, 383n161
Symbol of Faith, 67, 115, 213, 215, 219, 224, 242, 293–94. *See also* Luis de Granada
synagogues, de facto, 112–22, 134, 179, 263, 295. *See also* Judaizing

Tabasco (Mex., Tab.), 355n53
Talavera de la Reina (Spain, To.), 222
Tamaulipas, 117
Tampico (Mex., Tamps.), 59, 89, 108–9, 111, 349n25. *See also* Pánuco
Tapia, Cristobal de, 136–37, 354n49
Tarascan Indians, 34, 62

Tarimeo, Encomienda de, 62
Tavares, Manuel, 99–101, 120–21, 175, 216, 223, 234, 237, 256, 277, 281, 284, 344n14
Tavares, Rodrigo, 100–101, 116, 121, 174
Taxco el Viejo (Mex., Gro.), 127. *See also* Taxco
Taxco (Mex., Gro.), 5, 41, 44, 56, 71, 92, 125–29, 136–37, 162, 225, 293, 339n25
Teba (Spain, Mál.), 97, 361n75
Tecontepec. *See* Tezontepec
Temascaltepec (Mex., Mex.), 35, 44, 81, 339n25
Tenango, Real de (Mex., Gro.), 151. *See also* Taxco
Tepaxco (Mex., Mex.), 74
Tepeaca (Mex., Pue.), 74
Texcoco (Mex., Mex.), 24, 345n24, 369n22, 385n28
Tezontepec (Mex., Pue. or Hgo.), 191, 196, 366n37
Tharsis (Spain, Hue.), 50
Tilcuautla (Mex., Hgo.), 217, 264, 372n71
tin, 35, 125
Tirado Morlite, Rodrigo, 275
Tisha b'Av, 1
Tlalpujahua (Mex., Mich.), 9, 35, 44, 61–71, 129, 139, 211, 229, 279–80, 293, 340n4
Tlapa (Mex., Gue.), 355n51
Tlatelolco (Mex., D.F.), 172, 215, 223, 227, 241–43, 259–60, 264, 280, 294, 376n17
Tlaulilpa. *See* Pachuca
Tlaxcala (Mex., Tlax.), 24, 336n7, 348n16
Toledo, García de, 150
Tolosa, Juan de, 44
tools, household, 196. *See also* tools, mining
Torre de Moncorvo (Port., Bra.), 85, 87
Torres, Diego de, 116

torture. *See* Inquisition
Tovar, María de, 223
Trancoso, Antonio, 202
Trancoso (Port., Guar.), 331n15
Trás-os-Montes (Port.), 10, 87, 95, 346n38
tratantes (merchant investors), 45, 144, 146, 149, 153, 241
Tuesta, Ana de, 268
Tulancingo (Mex., Hgo.), 224
Turkey, 3, 91, 121, 143. *See also* Salonica

UNAM (Universidad Nacional Autónoma de México), 128, 141, 145
Urbina, Josef de, 137, 183
Utrera, 104

vacillating between Judaism and Christianity, 169–70, 172, 271, 276, 361n79
Váez, Ana, 13, 90, 223–24, 227, 286, 368n2
Váez, Antonio, 264, 365n11
Váez, Fernándo, 117
Váez, Francisco, vi, 119, 198–99, 202–3, 216, 219, 221, 226, 264, 366n43, 372n62
Váez, Jorge, 122, 174, 199, 219, 263, 361n77
Váez, Violante, 370n23
Valdés, Gaspar de, 27
Valencia, Feliciano de, 222
Valverde, María de, 272
Vargas, Alonso de, 74
Vasco de Acuña. *See* Acuña, Gascón de
Vázquez, Hernán, 62
Vega, Hernando de, 151
Vega, Juan de, 195
Vega, Lope de, 373n92
Vega, Pedro de, 188–92, 196, 265–67
Velasco, Luis de, 52, 338n8

Venice, 92, 99, 142–43, 168, 338n24, 355n367
Venta del Carpio (Mex., Mex.), 103, 372n62
Vera, Ana de, 342n17
Veracruz (Mex., Ver.), 21–24, 55, 59, 72, 83, 111, 333n21. *See also* San Juan de Ulúa
Verger, Martin, 330n8
Viana da Camiña (Port.,), 354n38
Vilaflor (Port. Bra.), 96, 350n31
Villanueva, Luis de, 137
Villarreal, Marqués de, 137, 357n92
Villegas, Pedro de, 279
Vimoso, Count of, 150
Viseu (Port. Vis.), 11, 78, 87, 96, 125, 331n14

water: canal (ditch, *acequia*), 6, 65, 68; importance of, 38, 49, 63, 67, 70; rights, 64, 67–69, 152, 230, 367n56; seepage, 46–47. *See also* mining
waterboarding. *See* torture

Xichú. *See* Sichú

Yáñez, Pedro, 64
Yom Kippur, 29, 80, 92, 106, 116, 118, 122, 158, 167–68, 177, 180, 182, 206–8, 214–15, 218, 226, 233, 248, 255–56, 263–64, 285, 295, 372n62, 373n94. *See also* Judaizing
Yuntitlán (Mex., Mex.), 74

Zacatecas (Mex., Zac.), 5, 35, 44, 56, 81, 106, 155, 210, 337n13
Zacualpan (Mex., Mex.), 35
Zafra (Spain, Ba.), 354n50
Zamora (Spain, Za.), 9–10, 85–86
Zaragoza, Juan de, 62
Zarfate de Vergas, Francisca, 83, 297
Zarza, Antonia de, 138, 176, 188, 297
Zarza, María de, 138, 176, 188, 297
Zimapán (Mex., Hgo.), 225, 238
Zumárraga, Juan de, 14, 90, 104
Zumpango (Mex., Mex.), 35, 337

www.ingramcontent.com/pod-product-compliance
Lightning Source LLC
Chambersburg PA
CBHW051203300426
44116CB00006B/419